William McKeen is the author of
Highway 61 and editor of *Rock and Roll Is Here to Stay*.
A professor of journalism at University of Florida, Gainesville,
he lives with his family near Wacahoota, Florida.

Rock and Roll Is Here to Stay: An Anthology

Highway 61: A Father-and-Son Journey
through the Middle of America

OUTLAW JOURNALIST

THE
LIFE
AND
TIMES
OF
HUNTER S.
THOMPSON

WILLIAM McKEEN

First published in Great Britain 2008
by Aurum Press Ltd, 7 Greenland Street, London NW1 0ND
www.aurumpress.co.uk

This paperback edition first published in 2009 by Aurum Press.

First published in the United States of America by W. W. Norton & Company, Inc.

A catalogue record for this book is available from the British Library.

ISBN: 978 1 84513 455 6

2010 2012 2013 2011 2009
1 3 5 7 9 10 8 6 4 2

Frontispiece photograph by Tom Corcoran
Book design by Chris Welch
Printed and bound in Great Britain by CPI Bookmarque, Croydon

FOR THE THREE GODFATHERS

MONTGOMERY CHITTY

TOM CORCORAN

BILL DIXON

What a fantastic monument to all the best instincts of the human
race this country might have been. . . .
—*Hunter S. Thompson, 1972*

Q: You said early on that you figured that you'd always been on the margins of
society with a very small percentage of people who are like you.
A: That's where we get the "outlaw." I've never been approved by any majority.
Q: Is that a kind of difficult way to be?
A: If you can make it work, it's not.
Q: Do you make it work? Have you not found it difficult?
A: On occasion. They're still trying to lock me up all the time. The only things
I've been arrested for, it turns out, are the things I didn't do. . . . There's just a
general feeling that I shouldn't be allowed to get away with it. I've been pretty
careful about trying to urge people who cannot live outside the law to kick off
their traces and run amuck. Some people are not made for it. I was a juvenile
delinquent. I was the Billy the Kid of Louisville. It's simple: I believed I was a
writer. I knew I had to be a writer because I was not good at anything else. I
survived by making literature out of what might otherwise be seen as craziness.
—*Hunter S. Thompson, interview with Marianne MacDonald, 1997*

I had gone to interview him at his shack in Colorado during a desperate time
in my life—when my marriage was spinning out of control—and I was acutely
anxious about my future. I always remembered how, as we lurched together
to the airport in his 4×4—he insisted on driving me, drunk, to the soundtrack
of a tape of dying, screaming jackrabbits—he swerved suddenly to a halt. He
shuffled on to the verge to stare at the bright town twinkling on the dark side
of the sky and said: "I come here when I'm feeling out of things, to look at the
lights." I realised then how cut off from things he was feeling.
—*Marianne MacDonald, Times (London), February 22, 2005*

To live outside the law you must be honest. . . .
—*Bob Dylan, "Absolutely Sweet Marie," 1966*

Don't ask me nothin' about nothin', I just might tell you the truth.
—*Bob Dylan, "Outlaw Blues," 1965*

CONTENTS

THE END

> Word of his death was a shock to me, but not particularly
> surprising. . . . More than anything else, it came as a harsh
> confirmation of the ethic that [he] had always lived but
> never talked about . . . the dead-end loneliness of a man who
> makes his own rules. . . .
> I don't even know where he's buried, but what the hell? The
> important thing is where he lived. . . .
> —*Hunter S. Thompson, writing about a friend, 1967*

A fter a certain age, you learn that when the phone rings at midnight on Sunday, it's never good news.

"*Dude!*" It's an old friend. Though we haven't spoken in years, I know his voice instantly. He's a reporter for the *Los Angeles Times*. "Hunter's dead. He killed himself tonight." Pause. "I thought you'd want to hear it from a friend." Then he's all business, asking me about Hunter Thompson and his place in American culture and journalism history. I shake off my grogginess and bark a few words of benediction and semischolarly wisdom into the phone.

I'm supposed to know a lot about Hunter Thompson. I wrote a book on him in 1991 and hosted him when he spoke at my university back in the late seventies. We had drinks together when we were both covering the 1984 Democratic National Convention. When he visited Florida, he'd sometimes call and suggest I drive down to Palm Beach and party with him. Usually, I was relieved to have some other commitment. The thought of partying with Hunter Thompson reminds me that amateurs shouldn't try to play with professionals.

We hadn't spent a lot of time together, so I never felt that I could legitimately call him a friend. But he was good to me. He gave honest, detailed answers to my questions when I was writing my book, and he gave me his unique seal of approval by writing me a note threatening to have my eyes gouged out for writing it: "How fast can you learn Braille?" The letter, with its many vulgarities, is framed in my office. When I put together an anthology a few years ago, while other writers held me up for thousands of dollars to reprint their pieces in our low-budget book, his fax came back with a scrawl over the contract: "This is free for you, Buddy."

Not long after I'd remarried, he sent me an inscribed copy of his book *Kingdom of Fear*, in which he'd named me to his honor roll. He wrote, "Dear Bill: I just got married today, so I'll make this note short. Congratulations on your new one too. Life is humming along smartly out here on the farm. Give me a ring sometime." He doodled on his signature and noted the time: 4:24 a.m.

He was so happy. And now, a year later, this phone call.

So I hang up with the reporter and stand in the middle of the dark bedroom. "What is it?" my wife asks drowsily.

"It's Hunter," I say. Around the house, we call him and Bob Dylan by their first names, in comic presumption of familiarity. "He killed himself." I tell her what I know. Then she says, "Say a prayer for him."

And so I go downstairs, pour myself a couple of fingers of Wild Turkey, and think about Hunter Thompson.

His writing has always been in the shadow of his larger-than-life persona. Even people who didn't read books knew who he was: that crazy dude who took all those drugs and was played in the movies by Johnny Depp and Bill Murray, that wild man who showed up on TV now and then, mumbling so much you couldn't understand a word.

Thompson was his own worst enemy because he fed that caricature. But the fact is he was a marvelous writer. *Fear and Loathing in Las Vegas* is perfect in the same way that *The Great Gatsby* is perfect. Take a pencil and read those books, looking for something that doesn't sound right, something you'd want to change. You'll leave the pages untouched.

He came from Louisville, and his mother tried to raise him to be a Kentucky gentleman, but his father's early death shook Thompson and steered him toward a career as a delinquent. Given a choice of jail or the military, he chose the Air Force and served most of his career at Eglin, the huge base in the Florida Panhandle. After getting chased out of the service, he drifted through the bowels of journalism, once getting fired for destroying a newspaper's vending machine. Perhaps this should be his epitaph: "He had a problem with authority."

He taught himself to write, retyping books by writers he admired: Steinbeck, Hemingway, Faulkner . . . the usual heavyweights. He said he wanted to get inside the rhythm of their language and find his own style.

He drifted through the Caribbean and began sending dispatches to the *National Observer*, a feature newspaper conceived as a Sunday edition of the *Wall Street Journal*. The editors loved his work and his observations about culture south of the equator. After a couple of long-distance years, Thompson came back to the States, but his relationship with the paper soured. Thompson was not the sort of writer to sit in an office and churn out copy with the necktie crowd.

Married and soon to have a son, he settled into the San Francisco Bay area and sold his blood while his wife worked as a motel maid. He was serious about his writing, but it wasn't paying. Then he wrote a piece for the *Nation* about the Hell's Angels motorcycle gang, and book offers stuffed his mailbox. He rode with the Angels for a year, got stomped by them, and had his first national fame, as that lunatic reporter who went on the road with those outlaws.

He had a lot in common with them. He called himself an outlaw journalist because he didn't follow the same rules as everyone else. His journalism was usually about journalism: no matter what he started off writing about, he ended up writing about Hunter Thompson trying to cover a story.

Then came the marriage made in literary heaven: when Thompson began working with *Rolling Stone* editor Jann Wenner in 1970, he'd finally found the perfect partner, someone who understood him and gave him space. Their first major collaboration turned two failed magazine assignments—one for *Sports Illustrated* and one for *Rolling Stone*—into a masterwork.

When it appeared in *Rolling Stone*, the byline read "Raoul Duke." But it was too good for a proud author to ascribe to a pseudonym. When it came out in book form in 1972, *Fear and Loathing in Las Vegas* was credited to Hunter S. Thompson.

My students still carry that book around, tattered paperbacks jutting out of back pockets. To students in my journalism classes, Thompson remains some kind of god. One of my old reporter buddies said, "He did what we all wanted to do, but he actually had the balls to do it."

Thompson told me this in one of our interviews: "As a journalist, I somehow managed to break most of the rules and still succeed. It's a hard thing for most of today's journeymen journalists to understand, but only because they can't do it. . . . I am a journalist, and I've never met, as a group, any tribe I'd rather be part of or that are more fun to be with—in spite of the various punks and sycophants of the press. I'm proud to be part of the tribe."

In my introductory journalism course, I assign the students to pick a book from a list of more than three hundred titles and write a brief report. More than one-third read *Fear and Loathing in Las Vegas*. Hunter Thompson is still a hero to those who want to be journalists.

It has always been that way. When I was a younger, single professor, I knew when the phone rang at midnight it was usually a drunken college student who'd just had some epiphany while reading *Fear and Loathing*, something he or she had to discuss with the professor *right now*. Usually, the student wanted me to come over and talk about Hunter and maybe pick up a twelve-pack on the way. That *Los Angeles Times* reporter had been a frequent midnight caller in school, whenever he had a Hunter Thompson moment to share.

Wenner and *Rolling Stone* gave Thompson license to cover politics and culture, and Thompson settled into his role as American sage from his fortified compound in Woody Creek, Colorado. For most of America, Hunter Thompson was a character, a writer more famous for his personality than for what he wrote. He always blamed Garry Trudeau for ruining his life by modeling the *Doonesbury* character Uncle Duke after him. (He threatened Trudeau's life too, so maybe he was all talk.)

The image was an enhanced version of reality. Thompson spoke in hyperbole but up close was kind to most people who approached him, even when they spurted incoherent drug fantasies: "Hunter, remember that time we had a joint, like eight years ago in the back of a car in L.A.?" He'd politely pretend to remember.

He was a good and decent man.

I'm finishing the Wild Turkey when the phone rings again, at 2:30 a.m. It's a student from my literary journalism class. "Hunter's dead," he says. "Did you hear?"

"Yes, I heard. Are you okay?"

He takes in a long breath. "I'll be all right. I just can't believe it. Hunter's dead."

"Yes, I know."

I may know something about Hunter Thompson, but I don't know why he did this.

Say a prayer for him.

Chapter 1

GETTING AWAY WITH IT

Peggy Maley: "What're you rebelling against, Johnny?"
Marlon Brando: "Whaddya got?"
—From The Wild One, *1953*

H e was wired different. Look at his brother: same basic genetic material, same schools, even the same bedroom. Just two years apart, yet they were opposites, like Elvis Presley and Shirley Temple.

Davison Thompson became a respectable businessman, a civic leader, a dignified gentleman in suburban Cleveland. And his brother became Hunter Thompson, outlaw journalist and celebrated literary bomb thrower. They shared a home, but it's not hard to guess which one painted the "gates to hell" on their bedroom floor during high school.

Hunter was an enigma all his life. He puzzled his mother, who often wondered why he did the things he did. But she understood that her eldest son had magnetism. After he'd become famous, she was fond of saying that his charisma was there all along, although he was difficult from the moment of his birth. Life as Hunter Thompson's mother was no weenie roast.

He was a pain in the ass. He was fearless. He was cruel, but also capable of great kindness. He was a loyal friend. Near the end, he was frequently sentimental. Sometimes brusque and rude, he could also be a courtly Southern gentleman. Virginia Thompson had worked overtime to raise sons with good manners.

"Hunter came out of the womb different, and somewhat angry," said Sandra Conklin, who became his first wife. "From talking to his mother, he was always different. He always had that charisma. Kids would come in front of his house and wait for him to come out."

Hunter was a lightning rod for trouble. He was the scourge of the block, the kid the neighborhood parents feared, the criminal in training. Many forbade their sons from associating with him, and most would have disowned their daughters for the petty crime of smiling at him. Even as a child, he worked a room. When Hunter was around, the chemistry changed; you felt his presence before you saw him. In that seen-and-not-heard generation, Hunter struck even grown-ups mute with his powerful personality. His childhood friend Gerald Tyrrell said there was never any doubt where the neighborhood boys would gather to hatch their daily plans. It was always Hunter's house—and not because Jack Thompson, oldest father in the neighborhood, was a mostly mute presence in the porch chair, shrouded in cigarette smoke and the murmur of baseball radio. And it wasn't because Virginia Thompson was unconventional and sometimes drank too much and was more lenient than other mothers. It was simply because of the force of Hunter's personality. "He was the most charismatic leader I've ever known," Tyrrell said.

Hunter Thompson followed the great flood of 1937 into Louisville. In January, persistent rain swelled the Ohio River, and it rose thirty feet above flood level, leaving 70 percent of the city underwater. Ninety people died, 175,000 were evacuated, and the city was devastated. Six months later, the city was still in recovery when Hunter Stockton Thompson was born on July 18, 1937. Jack and Virginia's friends dubbed him "fat baby" (he was eleven pounds), but Virginia marveled over her first child. Her husband was not as easily impressed.

Jack Thompson was already on his second life. He'd been married, fathered a son (Jack Jr.) and widowed, all before meeting Virginia Ray. Jack had spent thin years in the mountains of eastern Kentucky, trying to sell life insurance to coal miners and Appalachian farmers—poor prospects for major-medical policies. After his first wife's death, he deposited his little boy with relatives and moved to Louisville to work for First Kentucky Fire Insurance. More than a decade after the death of his first wife, he met Virginia Ray.

Virginia was the daughter of a Louisville businessman and from a background of small-scale prosperity. The Rays manufactured carriages until cars drove them out of business and Virginia's father, Presley Ray, went into insurance. The family did well enough to send Virginia to the University of Michigan for two years, but not well enough to support her through graduation. When Virginia Ray met Jack Thompson in 1934, the nation was crawling out of the Great Depression. Jack courted Virginia for a year, and then they married; Virginia was twenty-seven and Jack forty-two.

Within two years, they had a son: Hunter Stockton Thompson (named for Virginia's parents, Lucille Cochran Hunter and Presley Stockton Ray). Parenthood was a new and mystical experience for Virginia, but Jack had been there before. Being older, he was less patient with a crying infant at three in the morning. Virginia was a single parent from the start.

Some children are a challenge; these are often the ones parents love the most: sons incapable of avoiding trouble, who torment their little brothers, who never stop moving and cannot keep quiet, who rarely sleep, but when they do, sleep the sleep of angels. Hunter was a difficult child. He was also charming, extraordinarily handsome, and self-assured. His three-year-old studio portrait shows a cocky kid, mustering as much swagger as he could from a sitting position. He was confident and betrayed no jealousy when brother Davison was born when Hunter was two.

By the mid-1940s, if Jack Thompson wasn't living the American Dream, at least he was in the neighborhood. He and Virginia shuffled their sons through rental homes until the winter of 1943, when Jack finally had a down payment for the two-story stucco bungalow at 2437 Ransdell Avenue. It cost $4,100 and was in the heart of the Highlands, Louisville's first suburb.

The Highlands was part of the Cherokee Triangle, a collection of wooded streets bound by Cave Hill Cemetery at the north, Cherokee Park to the east, and Bardstown Road on the west, the main thoroughfare in those pre-Interstate days for country folk going into the city.

There was no television, so mothers and fathers sat on porches in the evening, smoking, reading the *Louisville Times*, watching children play, and gossiping with neighbors. People said hello to strangers. In season, street vendors went door-to-door, selling strawberries. Mothers read to children on porch swings. Fathers played catch with sons in front yards. In the morning, fathers rode to downtown jobs on city buses, and nearly all of them wore hats.

Cherokee Park was the designated municipal wilderness for children of the Highlands. Hunter called it "beautifully wild and uncivilized: no buildings, no taxis, no traffic lights—just a sprawling and lonely woods." The park was designed in the 1890s by Frederick Law Olmsted, creator of New York's Central Park, and was one of the last projects Olmsted completed before being confined to a mental institution.

Louisville was rich with history and tradition, including athletic clubs, literary societies, and a whirl of debutante balls and cotillions. Though just across the Ohio River from Yankeeland, Louisville's feet were deeply rooted in the South, with a veneer of gentility laid upon a foundation of vice. The primary industries were tobacco and liquor, and gin-guzzling gamblers lined up at Churchill Downs betting windows every May to wager on the fastest two minutes in sports. Half of the world's bourbon came from Louisville. Some said that's where most of it was consumed. Local distilleries produced Jim Beam, Maker's Mark, Old Crow, and Wild Turkey.

The cultural emphasis on smoking and drinking complicated growing up in Louisville. So did new wealth. As more business came to the city, executives from General Electric and Reynolds Aluminum brought their families and built lush homes out beyond the Cherokee Triangle. Those fine houses in the Highlands that men like Jack Thompson had struggled to buy became less desirable. Jack Thompson's American Dream had simply been the safety and security of a good neighborhood for his wife and sons. But now the pursuit-of-happiness bar was raised. Suddenly, Louisville had conspicuous affluence. The city grew to the east and redrew class lines to match the geography.

"It was very much a closed community," said Porter Bibb, a childhood friend of Hunter's. "There were houses on the hills, and the people who lived in the east end were the people who ran the city and the people who lived in the west end were the people who did the heavy lifting. Hunter lived in the middle." Bibb certainly didn't do any heavy lifting. He was old money and the only friend Hunter had with a variety of lettuce named for his family. Bibb said the Thompsons were part of the city's modest middle class. "They lived in a kind of limbo area called the Highlands," Bibb said. "It was not affluent, but not poor."

A few months after Jack Thompson bought the house in the Highlands, Hunter started first grade at I. N. Bloom Elementary School. It was a little white clapboard school, built in 1865, with a wood stove heating two classrooms. Pupils sat at long tables, facing a portrait of President Roosevelt smiling down benevolently from above the chalkboard.

School started after Labor Day, but it wasn't until November that Walter Kaegi arrived at I. N. Bloom. Although his father worked in Louisville, the family had lived across the river in New Albany, Indiana, until they found a home in the city. On his first day, Walter stood nervously at the front of the class as Miss Rudell introduced him to his fellow students. First grade was hard enough, he thought, but to be a *new* first-grader, two months after alliances had been formed—*that* would be painful.

Miss Rudell told Walter to sit at the long table, in the seat next to Hunter Thompson, and then she began the day's first lesson. After a few minutes, Hunter nodded at Kaegi and muttered an introduction. Keeping their voices low, they whispered their six-year-old résumés: what their fathers did, where they lived, what their parents were like. It didn't take long to find common ground. Both fathers, they discovered, whipped their sons with razor straps.

"My dad likes to whip me in the *snoshole*," drawled Hunter. The way he said it, and that he even *said* such a thing, made Walter explode. "We roared, and so we were disciplined," Kaegi recalled. Here he was, the model of the good boy, and twenty minutes after meeting Hunter, Walter Kaegi was doing time in the cloakroom.

In addition to Walter Kaegi, Hunter made another lifelong friend in first grade: Clifford "Duke" Rice. Their first-grade year was America's first full year at war, and Rice remembered Hunter's fervor as he pulled weeds in the class victory garden. The motive for Hunter's amped-up work ethic was escape from the classroom. "It got us outdoors," Rice remembered. "Inside, it was old and dark and all of the teachers were women." Kids also picked up on the grim tone from the adult world and were determined to help the war effort in Louisville. Hunter pulled a wagon house to house, collecting tin cans for a scrap-metal drive.

At school, the war was a fact of daily life. The windows at I. N. Bloom were fitted with black curtains for protection during air raids. Louisville's airport turned into a training ground for pilots and an assembly point for cargo planes. Up and down the Highlands' wooded streets, front windows displayed star banners indicating sons or husbands fighting in Europe or the Pacific.

But beyond the victory gardens and tin-can drives, the greatest disruption the war brought to the lives of six-year-old boys was the ransacking of Major League Baseball rosters. Despite not having a big-league team, Louisville was a baseball-crazy city. (It had been one of the original franchises when the National League was formed in 1876.) Most of baseball's biggest stars were serving their country, so teams were filled with third-raters. The drop-off in quality was an outrage to Hunter and Duke, who believed that Hitler and Mussolini were evil men, primarily for ruining America's great national pastime. Baseball loomed large in Hunter's life; it was a rare bond he shared with his father.

Jack Thompson was older than most fathers of small boys. He didn't have the stamina to be an active father to Hunter and Davison. Up and down Ransdell, fathers played catch with sons in front yards. Jack Thompson watched from the porch, smoking Chesterfields, and listening to the St. Louis Cardinals on KMOX. "He was passive," Tyrrell recalled. "He just sort of sat there on the porch and watched us."

Inside the house, alone with his family, Jack was more animated, listening intently to the news and sports. He'd hear the war news, then curse "those sneaky Japs," take a slug from his jigger of whiskey, and slap the arm of his chair. Hunter remembered those moments all of his life: sitting with his father, occasionally taking a sip from his dad's glass. "I soon became addicted to those moments," he recalled. "There was a certain wildness to it, a queer adrenaline rush of guilt and mystery and vaguely secret joy."

The city was their playground. "Louisville was our town," Gerald Tyrrell recalled. "We went anywhere. We were pretty fearless. It was a great way to grow up."

"We went all over," said Debby Kasdan, who shared classes with Hunter from first grade through freshman year in high school. "We'd get on the bus and go to movies downtown. We'd see a double feature, then cross the street to another theater and watch another double feature."

Hunter and his friends rode the bus over to Parkway Field to see a doubleheader with the Louisville Colonels, the minor-league farm team for the Boston Red Sox. Hunter and the boys would be gone all day, but parents didn't worry.

Hunter, Walter Kaegi, Duke Rice, and Debby Kasdan went through I. N. Bloom Elementary School together, and Gerald Tyrrell and Neville Blakemore were one grade behind. Hunter was chairman of the board for the neighborhood boys, and the Thompsons' front yard was the executive suite. "We'd go to his house and figure out whether we were going to play in Cherokee Park or if we were going to play basketball or whether we were going to play baseball or some football," Tyrrell said. "Sometimes we'd walk over to Bardstown Road and get downtown on the bus. Hunter had the imagination to make the suggestions of what we were going to do."

Hunter provided consistency for his friends. When Tyrrell's diplomat father was assigned to China for a year, he took his family along. The next year, the day after returning to Louisville, Tyrrell got up early, dressed in his jeans and T-shirt, and showed up at Hunter's house. It was as if he'd never been gone. The most he got was a *where-you-been* from a couple of the kids and a new Hunter-bestowed nickname to mark his year in China: Ching.

The Civil War was still being fought. Hunter wore a Confederate cavalry cap and challenged new kids in the neighborhood with their affiliation: *Are you a Yank or a Reb?* Hunter started fistfights if he got the wrong answer. The neighborhood boys were well-versed in the Second World War, but Hunter's interests went well beyond recent history. While still in elementary school, he read Thucydides' accounts of the Peloponnesian wars. This impressed Walter Kaegi, who had the same interest. He grew up to earn a degree at Harvard and become professor of Byzantine history at the University of Chicago.

Playing war took all day, and some of the battles raged long past dusk. Sometimes the war games were life-size. Hunter and his friends wore Army surplus helmet liners and staged bare-chested battles in the woods around their neighborhood, throwing rocks, bloodying foreheads, and irritating parents. As provocateur, Hunter was the flash point for anger; parents warned their sons to stay away from him. He was dangerous.

"Hunter was a sweat to be around," Neville Blakemore recalled. "I got increasingly uneasy with being around him because I knew he would eventually think of something to do to me."

Even in elementary school, Hunter had issues with authority, but what made him the bane of his teachers made him a folk hero to classmates. The other kids grew to like him, even if he scared them. He was funny without telling jokes, popular without being arrogant, smart without barking out correct answers like a trained seal.

Hunter's mischief began to reach beyond his circle of friends. He began to think in a larger scale, in pranks that might alarm or amuse the neighborhood. He became a meticulous planner of creative vandalism.

Each fall, home owners raked leaves into gutters to be burned. Hunter decided to accelerate the process, making clothespins into small spring-loaded bombs. Using a match, he rode his bike between the piles, snaking from one side of the street to the other, flicking his match-stick bombs into the piles as he coasted by. The leaves caught and slowly smoldered until twenty minutes after Hunter left, they burst into flame. Fire trucks were called and the police went door to door, trying to find the clothespin arsonist.

But even as a child, Hunter was fairly complex. He wasn't just a juvenile delinquent; he was also a budding scholar. Gerald Tyrrell said leaving aside the year living in China, his childhood was fairly typical for a Depression-era baby, except for one of the Hunter-inspired group activities.

"We'd pack up and get our bikes and ride to the Highland branch library," Tyrrell said. "There'd be a lot of camaraderie and loud talk, until we'd get to the steps of the library. Then we'd get quiet, go in, and get a book, and sit down and read. We'd leave in about two hours and get noisy again. It wasn't until much later that I realized it wasn't the normal stuff for a gang of boys to do." They graduated from conventional boys fare to more sophisticated material. "In the earlier days we read sports books and war books," Tyrrell recalled. "Later on, we matriculated to history and people like Napoleon and Churchill."

Boys don't generally start newspapers, either. In fourth grade, Walter Kaegi got hold of a mimeograph machine and started a neighborhood newspaper called the *Southern Star*. Kaegi was editor, and the staff included Hunter, Duke Rice, Debby Kasdan, and another Bloom classmate, John Bruton. Kaegi was the driving force behind the newspaper, but Hunter wrote much of the largely incestuous copy. The lead story in the first issue, from Columbus Day 1947, was about a fight Hunter and Duke Rice provoked with new neighbors who gave the wrong answer to the Civil War question. Another story offered a detailed account of Kaegi's dog vomiting. The dog, Robert E. Lee, also appeared in the second issue, when his foot was run over by a neighbor's car. Recognizing a trend, Kaegi had the standing head "Dog News" in the third issue of the *Star*.

Visiting relatives, dead snakes, and neighborhood baseball games provided the *Southern Star* with its news, allowing it to live up to its cumbersome motto, "Amazing Neighborhood Activities Come to Light on the Front Page of the Star." But the *Star* reached beyond its circulation area for news. Whatever interested the staff made the paper. When a trained gorilla died in the Cincinnati Zoo, Kaegi put it on the front page, because he liked gorillas.

The paper earned a small spotlight feature in the *Courier-Journal*, which was impressed that Kaegi paid his staff between one and three cents a story. Hunter earned his first byline at age eleven, in a sports story featuring himself and his heroics as forward on his basketball team.

Even though the *Southern Star* was Walter Kaegi's project, staff meetings were held at Hunter's house. Debby Kasdan, the only girl on the staff, dreaded those meetings. "He scared me," she said. "Even then, as a child, he had this deep, rumbling voice, almost like a growl. I remember his mother as very genteel. She was such a Southern lady. She always served us lemonade, which seemed to annoy Hunter. The two of them seemed incongruous to me. I remember he'd say something and she'd say, 'Oh, *Hunter*! Oh, *Hunter*!' It was this shrill, teasing kind of voice. She was the sort of woman who wouldn't go out of the house without a hat and gloves. And her son was the opposite."

Kaegi agreed. Virginia Thompson was "a very caring mother."

Hunter was a planner and invested years in plotting his move into Louisville's adolescent social strata. Of the clubs and social organizations in Louisville, Hunter had his eyes set on the most prestigious: the Castlewood Athletic Club and the century-old Athenaeum Literary Association. He couldn't join either until he was a teenager and was invited. Hunter wanted in both; Castlewood was a feeder for the Athenaeum, and so he decided he must first get the attention of the Castlewood brain trust and make himself into an attractive prospect. He led a push to start an athletic club for I. N. Bloom Elementary students. Along with Duke Rice and Gerald Tyrrell, Hunter founded the Hawks Athletic Club and began organizing competitions with other clubs and neighborhood teams. Eventually, it did earn him an invitation to Castlewood.

"Hunter was the first one of our immediate age group to get into Castlewood," Gerald Tyrrell said. "I don't think he was in the sixth grade yet when he got in. It wasn't until the end of football season in the eighth grade that I got in."

Hunter played baseball in a church-sponsored league, like many of his friends. Hunter met Porter Bibb when they were eight. "Hunter was an extremely good athlete," he remembered. "He was one of the best baseball players of that age I'd ever seen." Bibb was never on a team with Hunter but often played against him. When Hunter was in the on-deck circle, Bibb said the word would spread up and down the bench: "Uh-oh—here comes Thompson up to bat." As he grew older, however, a physical anomaly—one leg was longer than the other—was exacerbated, and Hunter was not as fast as his friends on the bases. Dreams of Major League Baseball died on the vine. The shorter leg gave him a distinctive walk—more of a lope, actually—that afforded him a lifetime of memorable and dramatic entrances.

With his prematurely deep voice and his furrowed brow, Hunter often sounded and looked angry, even when he wasn't. When he was impatient or questioned a teacher's authority, the voice-and-brow combo made him appear menacing. Teachers recoiled when he barked questions in class. When Hunter was elected to head the student safety patrol in elementary school, the principal protested, calling him "Little Hitler." "I wasn't sure what that meant," Hunter recalled, "but I think it meant that I had a natural sway over many students and that I should probably be lobotomized for the good of society." Walter Kaegi remembered Hunter getting antsy in the school cafeteria line, annoyed at being bumped by the students behind him. "You sweaty swine," he snarled, and the students flinched. When Hunter yelled, classmates jumped.

John Bruton said Hunter was "the pole around which trouble would occur." Kaegi said classmates wanted to be friends with Hunter, mostly because they feared him and saw friendship as insulation from a possible beating. "Some had an apprehension that he could get them in trouble," Kaegi said, "and he *did* get people in trouble."

Tyrrell and Hunter lived a block apart. Neville Blakemore, who had moved in and out of the neighborhood (and even lived in Washington during the war), stayed at his grandmother's house, one block from Hunter. It was a short bike ride to the Castlewood neighborhood, where Walter Kaegi and Debby Kasdan lived.

Walter Kaegi's house backed up to Beargrass Creek. "It was just a drainage area," Debby Kasdan said. "You could watch the frogs or gather watercress. We called it the Swamp. It wasn't a true swamp, but to us, at that age, it was mysterious and dark."

The creek wasn't just a geographic boundary. When Hunter led the boys down to the creek to throw stones, they found black boys on the other bank. Hunter sometimes took his BB gun down to the creek and urged his friends to provoke the black kids. And so they would do that—even though they sometimes were chased back across the creek and had to hide in Kaegi's house until the black kids went away. But when Hunter suggested it, they would do it again.

"He had not just charisma," Kaegi said. "He almost had demonic power—in a positive sense, not a negative. It was also in his eyes and the expression on his face. His eyes were very, very captivating. When you've seen them, you'll always remember them."

In seventh grade, Hunter decided he wanted to ride his bike out into the country. He ended up leading a dozen friends on a twenty-mile ride; pretty heavy duty for eleven- and twelve-year-old boys. When Hunter fell in love with bullwhips after watching too many Lash La Rue movies, he insisted his friends share that love. He even acted out street theater with his gang, pretending to whip a boy on the sidewalk and have his friend burst into a store, feigning agony. It scared the customers, and Hunter liked that.

Hunter read about epilepsy during one of his afternoons at the Highland branch library and taught his friend Henry Eichelberger to mimic a grand-mal seizure. Hunter watched from the sidewalk as his protégé writhed on the floor of Nopper's Pharmacy and customers screamed. He began to use the fake seizures and other sidewalk dramas as hazing rituals for the Hawks and later for Castlewood. He also would shoplift while the store's manager was distracted by the seizing confederate.

As Hunter exercised power over his friends, his parents had a new distraction. Jack and Virginia were surprised with a third son in 1949, when James Garnett Thompson was born. Virginia was forty-one and Jack was an ancient fifty-three. Hunter was twelve and to him, this little brother was a generation removed.

Hunter's pranks had gone mostly unnoticed and largely unpunished until he was nine and the FBI came knocking.

The summer after his third-grade year, two federal agents stood in the foyer of the home on Ransdell and told Virginia Thompson that Hunter was the prime suspect in the destruction of a mailbox, a federal crime that came with a five-year prison term.

"Not prison!" Virginia Thompson screamed at the agents. "That's insane. He's only a child. How could he have known?"

One of the agents pointed out that Hunter was old enough to read the warning on the mailbox about the penalty for vandalism. Before anyone else could speak, Jack Thompson chimed in: "How do you know he's not blind, or a moron?"

Hunter picked up the moron argument, despite the fact that the agents' surprise visit had caught him reading the sports section of the *Courier-Journal*. Of course, Hunter *had* destroyed the mailbox, using an elaborate set of pulleys and ropes that turned it over and pulled it into the path of a bus driven by one of Hunter's adult enemies.

The agents told him that his accomplices had confessed, but Hunter knew that his pals were loyal and would never rat on him. He remained silent, playing the moron. The agents continued presenting their evidence in the Thompson living room. "A nice kid like you shouldn't have to go to federal prison," one of the agents said. All they wanted, they said, was a confession.

His father looked to him, resigned: "Don't lie to these men. They have witnesses."

Hunter turned to the agents. "What witnesses?" he asked.

There was a long silence. Jack Thompson looked at his son a moment, and then turned to the agents. "I think my son has a point," he said. "Just exactly who have you talked to?"

Hunter ticked off the names of friends who could be the finks who ratted on him, but who had firm alibis. His father cut him off. "Shut up," he said, through gritted teeth. "Be quiet and let *me* handle this, you fool."

And that was all it took to end Hunter's first major run-in with the law. The FBI agents could not bully him into a confession, and Jack stood up for him. Most children would have been frightened or scared straight. For Hunter Thompson, the experience empowered him and gave him an operating principle that served him well the rest of his life. It made him think: *Maybe I can get away with it.*

"The mailbox incident was a confidence-builder," Hunter said late in life.

It came on slowly. Jack Thompson was often tired and his muscles ached. It got harder to see and his eyelids drooped slightly. Chewing was painful and swallowing was torture. Jack was a quiet man, not fond of long conversation. It wasn't like him to complain and draw attention. He was used to being in the background, and so Jack Thompson suffered in silence.

Finally, the pain was too much. Jack was admitted to Louisville Veterans Hospital for treatment. Three months later, he died at fifty-seven, just before the Fourth of July holiday in 1952. He had been suffering from myasthenia gravis, a rare disease that attacked the immune system.

Jack Thompson's death overwhelmed the family. Virginia had to go to work—she got a job at the public library—and her widowed mother moved in to manage day-to-day family life and the three boys, aged fourteen, twelve, and four. Lucille Cochran Ray was Memo (*Mee*-Mo) to her grandsons. Hunter adored her. Aunt Elizabeth and Aunt Lee also helped with the Thompson boys. But Hunter resented his mother for going to work and knew that his unvarnished love for Memo and his aunts had the added attraction of irritating Virginia.

Hunter's friends didn't remember Jack Thompson speaking much, but inside the house, he exerted authority over his eldest son. "His dad was a nice and quiet man who kept him on the straight and narrow as best he could," Duke Rice said. "When he died, there was no one to do that. His life got turned upside down from that point on." Hunter was already wild, but now he'd lose even this tempering influence. He was off to a good start on being bad.

Life changed in the Thompson home. Left alone to support her family, Virginia Thompson came home from work and uncorked a bottle. Some nights were worse than others, and Memo kept her apart from the boys. "Your mother's sick again," she told them, and then she'd escort her daughter to bed.

Hunter grew to hate his mother's behavior. He once screamed at her, and she ran for the phone on the landing to call for help. He got there first and ripped it out of the wall. Jim, who was four then, remembered that and other epic battles, with Memo serving as referee. "Hunter had a real short fuse with all of this stuff," he said. "He was intolerant and mean."

Hunter no longer invited friends over when Virginia was home. He had gone to Sunday school regularly at the insistence of his mother, but with her drinking and without his father standing behind her, she lost authority and Hunter refused to go. (He had been active enough in his church to be selected as representative for a Presbyterian youth camp in North Carolina.)

Hunter dated several girls, including Judy Stellings, who went to the Louisville Collegiate Girls School, near the Thompson house. She met him at a party when they were both fourteen, and they dated through high school. She had the honor of being the first girl he drove on a date.

"He was a cute, jolly, fun kid and he made me laugh," she said. "I had a crush on him. Hunter was hard to dislike. I was fourteen and not as precocious as a fourteen-year-old is today. I was somewhat sheltered and naïve. He'd had his sixteenth birthday and came out [to the Stellings home in Anchorage] to pick me up in his mother's car. It was a total surprise. We went out and played mini-golf."

Hunter had his charms and could win over parents, but not when thievery was involved.

"My mother was going to have a bridge party," Stellings recalled. "In our house, you walked in on the second floor. Hunter came through the house, walked downstairs and Mother had bourbon and what-all set out in the bar for her party the next day, and he picked up the bourbon and walked out the back door. When my father discovered the missing liquor, he called the house and his mother answered the phone and she said, 'He's still asleep. I can't wake him up.' But she got him up, and Dad told Hunter in no uncertain terms that the bourbon must be on the counter by noon."

Her father forgave Hunter and allowed him to continue seeing his daughter. "In high school, everybody dated," she said. "Of course, 'dating' had a different meaning then than it does now. We would go to parties, we would go to Athenaeum Hill, we would go to dances. On Sunday afternoons, Hunter would come out to visit. He loved Bing Crosby. He'd come out, and we'd sit by the fire and listen to Bing Crosby. 'Galway Bay' was one of his favorite songs. Later, when he was in the Air Force, he wrote me letters about those lazy Sunday afternoons and how much they meant to him."

Not all parents were as forgiving as Judy Stellings's folks. Hunter met Susan Haselden in junior high, but once her parents got a few whiffs of Hunter's personality and dangerous habits, they forbade their daughter to see him. Hunter and Susan kept their relationship secret for years, and she remained one of his steady correspondents well into adulthood. She was a country club girl—her parents were members at Owl Creek—and Haselden was clandestinely escorted to club dances by the reprobate.

He became a night crawler. As soon as he got his driver's license, he was gone. He'd made a contraption with four wheels and a washing-machine motor on it, more motorbike than car, and "dangerous as hell," as Tyrrell remembered. Virginia couldn't let her son ride around in that thing, so she gave Hunter the car keys. She'd wait up until dawn for his return.

He found trouble, beer, and friends like Sam Stallings. Hunter learned how to get alcohol. He walked into liquor stores and frightened clerks into giving him a bottle to get rid of him. He bribed black waiters at debutante balls. Sometimes he stole it. Whiskey became his partner.

"The first time I got high," Gerald Tyrrell remembered, "there were four of us. We were thirteen. We bought a half pint of gin from a waiter down at the Kentucky Hotel who bootlegged it. We bought a bottle of ginger ale and just had a great time, giggling and carrying on. And I got into trouble then with Hunter. All the trouble I got into in my life, it was always with him."

Hunter started at Atherton High School but transferred to Male High after the football team beat up Hunter when he criticized the players' performance. That was the excuse Hunter needed. He wanted to be at Male anyway. Male sent its graduates off to the Ivy League, and some of its faculty members chose jobs at Male over positions at the Ivies. Male was also where the Athenaeum Literary Association was started in 1824 and where most of the members still came from. The Athenaeum had a grand history in Louisville; Robert Penn Warren was just one of the literary figures who had been a member of the high school club. Some of Hunter's old friends were already in the society—Jimmy Noonan, Porter Bibb, and Ralston Steenrod. He met Paul Semonin, son of Louisville's leading realtor, at the Athenaeum's Saturday night meetings, and they became close friends. Like most of the members, Semonin came from wealth. Hunter didn't have that, but the bad-boy background made him popular as a club mascot.

"The Athenaeum was kind of a combination of cultural interests and social status," Semonin said. "It was a product of Louisville society. It was a way of plugging into something traditional. Of course, it was a tradition that was not 'working class' or anything like that. It was something that had to do with being a part of the upper class. And it had to do with having an interest in literary things—although I have to say that was mixed heavily with socializing and partying and things like that. Being in the Athenaeum was sort of like an initiation into the world of drinking under age. I once saw it described as sort of a purely cultural society, as if it were people who were just interested in literature and writing, kind of highfalutin stuff. Of course, that wasn't it at all. I think the type of camaraderie that developed had much to do with going out to Cherokee Park and drinking on the hill or partying together as it did with the actual literature we were interested in or produced."

The Athenaeum was at the top of "a very unusual social structure," according to Porter Bibb. "It was the most amazing contradiction to being a teen in that it required its members to elect people, like a secret society—like Skull and Bones at Yale," Bibb remembered. "From all over the city, there were about fifteen people each year brought into the Athenaeum and it was for three years—sophomore, junior, and senior year of high school. Every Saturday night you had to put a suit on, a white shirt, and a dark tie. We would sit there for two or three hours, and each Saturday evening, selected members were required to produce something of 'literary quality,' and read their work in front of the whole group and be critiqued. And then we would break and go out and raise hell. We would go to parties, and take the suits off, and be normal teenagers. It was a rather extraordinary thing, for forty-five testosterone-packed teenagers to sit there for three hours or more every Saturday night, reading the poems, the short stories, and the essays that they had written, and being critiqued by their peers. The result of all this every year was a literary magazine. That was where Hunter first was published."

The *Spectator*, the Athenaeum yearbook, featured poems, drawings, stories, and essays. Hunter's first member photograph shows him still with candy-cheek chubbiness, and his pieces are sometimes heavy-handed, but still impressive considering they were the work of a fourteen-year-old.

His *Spectator* essay titled "Security" even laid out a coherent Hunter Thompson philosophy. After an attack on conformity, Hunter concluded, "Who is the happier man, he who has braved the storm of life and lived or he who has stayed securely on shore and merely existed?" Hunter's models for rebellion included Marlon Brando, James Dean, and Montgomery Clift, whose contempt for society oozed from theater screens. He assimilated their simmering resentment. (In the *Spectator*'s list of members, Hunter was listed under the alias Marlon and was wanted for "you name it.") Other elements of the Hunter ethos were already in place. "Even back then, he was always kind of a champion of the underdog," Judy Stellings said.

Semonin recalled reading and discussing Ayn Rand, George Bernard Shaw, and H. L. Mencken with Hunter, whose early attempts at satire in the *Spectator* ("An Open Letter to the Youth of Our Nation" by John J. Righteous-Hypocrite) showed him trying too hard. But the literary dialogue with Semonin and Bibb and the others continued, usually with the accompaniment of cold beer or locally distilled whiskey.

The weekly association with the Athenaeum and stepping inside that grander social circle meant that Hunter's games and pranks took on more scope. "We shared an interest in shock value," Semonin said. "We liked the playfulness, the humor, and the wildness. It was all street theater, acts of defiance."

Hunter's most successful street theater was a staged kidnapping in front of patrons waiting in line to get into the Bard Theater in downtown Louisville. While moviegoers watched, a Hunter confederate was dragged from the line and into a car, which sped away. That prank made the newspapers, and Hunter reveled in the anonymous publicity.

Hunter ended up in jail, not for the fake kidnapping, but for other minor pranks. After he trashed a filling station on Bardstown Road, police came to Male High and led him from the classroom in handcuffs. Hunter, Tyrrell, and a couple of other friends were busted for buying underage booze at Abe's Liquor Store. All the boys were let go, except for Hunter. Because of his petty criminal record, he was made into an example. When schools, gas stations, or pool halls were trashed, the cops knocked on his door first. Once, he even robbed a collection box at a neighborhood church.

Jim Thompson, twelve years younger, remembered his older brother as a wild man who terrorized them. Playing with a gun up in his room, Hunter fired a shot through the floor and into the family china cabinet. He also painted an elaborate tableau of the gates of hell on his bedroom floor. He kept a rug over it, but required little prompting to reveal it to visitors.

Virginia Thompson gave Hunter her car keys and all the freedom he wanted, but she didn't abdicate the parental right to worry. Jim, then just six years old, would tiptoe downstairs in the middle of the night and find his mother sitting in a chair by the window, smoking, drinking, waiting for Hunter to come home. Despite his petty-but-growing record, Virginia Thompson always defended her son. He wasn't really doing anything evil, she rationalized, he was just playing pranks.

Some of Hunter's Friday night parties stretched through Monday mornings. He and Sam Stallings, his partner in nocturnal crime, spent occasional nights in jail for drunk driving. Hunter grew wilder. He, Tyrrell, and two other friends were busted when a liquor store got wise to their scam to buy alcohol underage and cops staked out the store. The other parents were furious that Hunter got their sons arrested. Tyrrell was ordered by his parents to stay away from Hunter. He rebelled by getting drunk with his friend for twenty-six nights in a row. No one could stop Hunter, bent on being Louisville's number-one rebel.

"We stole cars and drank gin and did a lot of fast driving at night," Hunter wrote of his adolescence. "We needed music on those nights, and it usually came on the radio—on the 50,000-watt clear-channel stations like WWL in New Orleans and WLAC in Nashville. . . . Music has always been a matter of Energy to me, a question of Fuel. Sentimental people call it Inspiration, but what they really mean is Fuel."

Delinquent, yes. Heavy drinker, yes, but also a heavy reader. Ralston Steenrod, fellow partier, went on to major in English at Princeton and later become a Louisville attorney. Off in the hallowed halls of the Ivy League and surrounded by sons of wealth and privilege, he realized that none of them could hold Hunter's jock when it came to knowledge of literature and possession of original thought. Back in high school, after a night out, Steenrod recalled often taking Hunter home. "His bedroom was lined with books," he said. "Where I would go home and go to sleep, Hunter would go home and read."

Yet in the halls of Male High, Hunter could be easily tormented. As graduation neared, students announced their college plans. One Ivy League–bound snot backed up Hunter in the hallway and asked, "Where are *you* going next year?" "I don't know," Hunter said, "but I'm going *somewhere*."

Ralston Steenrod and Sam Stallings were driving around in Steenrod's car with Hunter the night they encountered two couples necking in a parked car in Cherokee Park. It was June 1955, less than two weeks before high school graduation. Steenrod parked and the three boys approached the passionate couples. Stallings leaned in the window, demanding money, but the couples refused. Then Hunter said if they didn't give them any money, he would rape one of the girls. Terrified, the young lovers handed over cigarettes and wallets, and the three bandits drove away, later dividing the booty: eight dollars filched from the kids. Joseph Monin, driver of the other car, later said that Stallings threatened him with a gun. Steenrod subsequently dropped off Stallings and Hunter, and was picked up by police before he could get home. Monin had copied down the license number.

Cops tracked down Hunter and Stallings. Steenrod and Stallings were both sons of prominent attorneys. Steenrod got probation and Stallings got a fifty-dollar fine. Because he had threatened rape, and because of his lack of connections, Hunter was sentenced to sixty days in jail.

When Judge Joseph Jull announced Hunter's sentence in court, a young woman in the gallery stood up to protest. She was one-fourth of the necking couples that had been robbed. In the time between the robbery and the sentencing, she and her friends had gotten to know Hunter during jail visiting hours and appeared in court to testify on his behalf, more evidence of his charismatic personality.

Virginia Thompson was there, too, pleading for her son's future. "Please don't send him to jail," she begged Judge Jull.

Judge Jull was snide. "What do you want me to do? Give him a medal?"

Hunter was in tears. The judge, unmoved, recited Hunter's record—a litany of petty offenses. "I feel I've done you an injustice by waiting so long to take a positive step," Jull said.

Steenrod's father asked the judge to release Hunter and require him to enlist in the service, "which would make a man out of him."

Judge Jull would have none of it.

Sixty days. The judge pounded his gavel.

Judy Stellings didn't abandon Hunter. She was one of the few people outside of his family to visit him in jail. "He got a raw deal," she said. "Nothing happened to the people he was with. Sam was the true rotten egg, continually in trouble. He was a really unpleasant person. Ralston got off and went off to his life in Princeton. Everybody got off but Hunter. His mother did not have the influence, the money, or anything else that the others had. She didn't know how to go about protecting him.

"I insisted on going to the jail. I shouldn't have. It was embarrassing to him. He wrote me later that he wished I hadn't seen him there. His mother was there and she didn't have any money, so I gave her money to pay for her parking. She wrote me a nice note and sent me a dollar back."

Hunter missed his high school graduation ceremony. He would soon be voted out of the Athenaeum Literary Association. As he sat in Jefferson County Jail, beginning his sentence, he knew that he would not return to the life he had known. He had proclaimed his innocence and had become a sacrifice. There would be no college; he probably *would* go into the service. Every day in jail, he wrote his mother letters of sadness, repentance, and anger. The whole event embarrassed him, particularly the threatened-rape charge, and he begged his mother to forgive him. He also angrily swore at the authorities. "The police lie," he wrote his mother. "Injustice is rampant."

"I look back on my youth with great fondness," Hunter Thompson wrote near the end of his life, "but I would not recommend it as a working model for others."

Chapter 2

SQUARE PEG, ROUND HOLE

*It is also requested that Airman Thompson be officially
advised that he is to do no writing for any kind for internal
or external publication. . . .*
—*Air Force memo, August 23, 1957*

*H*e was afraid of electricity, and they wanted to turn him into an
electrician.

To Hunter, it symbolized his problem with military service . . .
or of any confrontation with authority. Whatever *they* wanted, he opposed.
Considering the confines of indentured servitude in the armed forces,
Hunter might have wondered whether it was a better choice than jail.

But he had had few options in Jefferson County Jail. He got a month
knocked off of his sentence for good behavior, but this good news was
delivered by Judge Jull with an ominous warning: "We'll be watching
you." He served notice that until Hunter was twenty-one, he would be
allowed to breathe but not do much else in Louisville, Kentucky. Hunter
got a job driving a truck for a furniture store and almost immediately
backed the truck through a showroom window. The cops showed up and
Hunter decided it was time to begin his military career. It was either that
or jail, he figured. He walked to the Army recruiting office, but was told
he'd have to wait. At the Air Force recruiting office down the street, there

was no cooling-off period and he could enlist immediately. Finally, he was leaving home. "Louisville is a good place to grow up and a good place to get away from," he said.

Hunter first put on the crisp khakis of the U.S. Air Force in the late summer of 1955 and arrived drunk at Randolph Air Force Base, in San Antonio, impressing his drill sergeant by vomiting during his first roll call. During basic training, he rose early, ate bad food, answered to his supposed superiors, and quickly mastered the art of simmering resentment.

The Air Force decided he would make an excellent electronics technician.

But I want to be a pilot, Hunter told them. *Why else would I be in the goddamn Air Force?*

You will make an excellent electrician, the Air Force decreed.

And so after basic training he was sent to Scott Air Force Base, near Belleville, Illinois, across the Mississippi River from St. Louis. He spent a miserable six months at Scott, but squandered many of his off hours in the Pine Room Tavern in Mascoutah, a village just south of the base. He'd drink a pitcher of frigid beer and dine on fifteen-cent hamburgers supplied by a laissez-faire bartender who kept the bar open, even with Hunter as the only customer. Hunter spread his supplies over the counter—books, papers, pens, cigarettes—and wrote letters to his friends and family. Some friends were still back in Louisville, and some off at Ivy League colleges. He'd made friends in the Air Force, but he was still lonely, missing his old running buddies and their adventures. He sat at the counter of the miserable bar in the middle of Bumfuck, Illinois, and wrote sentimental letters to his lost friends, angry diatribes at the mongrel dogs who controlled his life, and pleas for forgiveness to his mother. Back in jail, filling pages of notepaper, he'd discovered the therapeutic effect of writing. In jail, he wrote his mother daily, admitting that he had gone too far and brought her shame. He also wrote to his friends and composed assignments for a correspondence course.

There was volume and desperation in his writing. He wanted to keep his friends, and he worked hard at it, writing several long letters a week. "I find that by putting things in writing I can understand them and see them a little more objectively," he later wrote. "I guess that's one of the real objectives to writing, to show things (or life) as they are, and thereby discover truth out of chaos."

He maintained the letter-writing habit his whole life and, sitting at the

Pine Room's bar, wrote his mother newsy letters, full of optimism. If he resented his friends going off to college, he didn't write it down. Hunter could not be described as being content with his life, but he was ripe with ambition and fully prepared to deal with the obstacles a military stretch threw at him. He faced problems by drinking. He later told a friend he was intoxicated for much of his six months in the Land of Lincoln. It didn't help matters that he was fairly close to Louisville and could go home to drink with his friends who had stayed in town and to entertain those same friends when they drove to Illinois.

Hunter was picked as a promising electronics technician because he aced the Air Force radio-tech exam. Hunter shrugged off the triumph. Tests were easy. You didn't need to know about radios and electronics; you just needed to be savvy in answering multiple-choice questions. He scored so high, the military thought he was the second coming of Marconi. But Hunter hated working with any kind of electronic or electrical component because he feared electrocution. In all-night classes in intelligence electronics, Hunter tried to deal with his fear by giving surreptitious electronic shocks to his classmates—and himself. The minor pain he felt was offset by watching his fellow airmen jump. This warped joy was his introduction to his new friend, electricity.

"Electricity is neutral," he wrote years later. "It doesn't want to kill you, but it will if you give it a chance. Electricity wants to go home, and to find a quick way to get there—and it will. Electricity is always homesick. It is always lonely. But it is also lazy. It is like a hillbilly with a shotgun and a jug of whiskey gone mad for revenge on some enemy. . . ."

Squadron commander Ted Stephens battled with Hunter over his pranks, his work ethic, his attitude, and his drinking. Although he could have busted Hunter, he chose to give the eighteen-year-old airman a second chance . . . *and a third* . . . and they lost count after five. Hunter was stunned. If Stephens had followed the manual, the insubordinate airman would have been in the stockade. But Stephens kept giving Hunter more chances, which he eventually screwed up. Still, Stephens didn't throw the book at him.

Stephens was a rarity. Hunter quickly earned a reputation as an attitude case around the base. He didn't fit into the military mold, and since he was popular with fellow airmen, officers began to worry that he might spread his malcontent ways.

Hunter also went through military-intelligence training at Scott but refused to accept a security clearance from the Air Force. "I didn't honestly consider myself a good security risk, because I disagreed so strongly with the slogan 'My Country, Right or Wrong.'" Nevertheless, he graduated from that program and somehow managed to pull the seemingly plum posting at Eglin Air Force Base, the huge installation in the Florida Panhandle between Tallahassee and Pensacola. Eglin was almost the size of a New England state. The nearest civilian outpost of any size was Fort Walton Beach. The beach near Eglin was desolate and beautiful. The base was just south of Alabama and closer to the Deep South than other parts of Florida, which was still more than a decade away from becoming the theme park capital of the world. Much of the Panhandle was wild and the beaches were dangerous; airmen who went swimming were sometimes pulled into the Gulf by the riptide.

Hunter was posted to Eglin in July 1956. He had feared ending up a fail-safe toggle-switch jockey in the Arctic Circle, controlling mankind's destiny, like his friend from Scott Air Force Base, Ted Peterson. Peterson had outscored Hunter on all of his tests and yet ended up in Anchorage. How did Hunter pull the Eglin gig on the glorious and balmy Gulf Coast? He'd rolled in shit and landed in a field of yellow daisies. Hunter couldn't help rubbing it in. He wrote Peterson, pretending to beat himself up for not requesting an assignment to Alaska; then he interrupted himself: "That raucous noise you just hear was probably my screech of laughter, floating through the northern pines and across the northern wastelands, and into the smelly confines of your shack."

That isolated stretch of the Gulf Coast had played a strategic role in the Second World War. The Army and Navy rehearsed for the D-Day landing at Carabelle Beach and the Army Air Corps (it would not become the Air Force until 1947) practiced for General Jimmy Doolittle's raid on Tokyo by bombing the hell out of the 384,000 acres of Florida woods that made up Eglin. After the war, Eglin's remote locale made it attractive for weapons and aircraft testing. Locals said it was the East Coast version of Area 51. That sparse region of the Panhandle led the nation in UFO sightings. It was one of America's largest military bases in terms of pure acreage, and there was a feeling that it was a good place to hide things.

But the plum assignment did not improve Hunter's mood. He was still surly, resentful of military wheel-spinning. Driving his beat-up clunker back to base one night with a bottle of booze for company, he grew angrier as he neared Eglin. When he reached the front gate, instead of stopping, showing his badge, and saluting the geek drawing night duty, he slowed only enough to give himself a good shot with the bottle of gin. It went sailing past the checkpoint airman and shattered in the guardhouse. The bottle-throwing soon became part of the lore that followed Hunter. Colonel Frank Mears, the base commander, was furious and wrote a stinging reprimand. But Hunter figured, *What's the worst that could happen? They kick me out of the service?*

Eglin had an education office, and Hunter thought it might help him crawl out of the hole the Air Force had thrown him in. He signed up for night classes at Florida State University, then still a sleepy college up the road that had recently begun admitting male students. He thought a literature course might be fun, and maybe a psychology course. The director of the education office thought it was interesting that Hunter wanted to take the literature course. They started talking, and Hunter said he hated everything he was doing at Eglin.

"Know anything about sports?" the officer asked abruptly.

"Sure," Hunter said. "I was editor of my high school newspaper." He also ad libbed that he'd covered high school sports for the *Courier-Journal*. It was a lie, of course.

"Well, we might be in luck."

An Air Force base was a closed society with its own rules and customs. Huge billboards out on the civilian highways surrounding Eglin were decorated with pictures of looming B-52's and the slogan "Peace Is Our Profession." But why advertise or tantalize civilians with messages of welcome? In that paranoid Cold War era, Air Force bases were locked tight.

At five o'clock every afternoon, life stopped on the base as loudspeakers in palm trees blared the national anthem. Drivers pulled over, got out of their cars, and stood at attention. In the base movie theater, where admission was thirty-five cents, the whole audience stood before the main feature, while the anthem played as a black-and-white flag rippled on the screen. After the previews but before the main film started, a short film was shown of an F-105 in flight as a stentorian voice read "High Flight," a poem written by Gillespie Magee, a pilot killed four days after the Pearl Harbor attack. The poem reveled in flight (*I have slipped the surly bonds of Earth*) and concluded, "I've touched the face of God." Sometimes the theater was quiet enough to hear young airmen sniffle.

Most of the officers and many of the enlisted men had families, so the Air Force base provided them with shopping, schools, playgrounds, swimming pools, and all the usual accessories of home life. The housing was often wretched, but it was free—part of the package deal of military family life. Mosquitoes swarmed in the Panhandle, but the base helped by sending around a pesticide truck on Friday afternoons, blanketing the neighborhoods in thick clouds of DDT. Children rode their bikes into the fog and imagined they were at war.

And then there was the newspaper. The weekly delivery of the base paper was an event. Children were plucked from school to ride in the back of a pickup truck, roll up copies of the paper, and fling them into the yards as they passed.

After the education officer told Hunter about the sports-writing job, it was a matter of days before he was on the *Command Courier* staff. He hadn't been in Florida a full month when Hunter S. Thompson's first byline appeared in the *Command Courier*, on August 30, 1956. The transfer to information services changed his life.

For Hunter, working for the newspaper meant freedom. He no longer had to wake to reveille and jump when his squadron commander barked. He had the most valuable commodity an American enlisted man could have: some measure of personal freedom. He set his own schedule. Being a journalist for the base paper was as close as he could come to being a civilian.

"I now have the best deal I could possibly have in the Air Force," he wrote to Gerald Tyrrell, who was starting at Princeton that month. "Acting the part of the experienced, competent journalist day after day has been quite a strain on my nervous system."

He had been raised on a diet of old newspaper movies—Cary Grant and Rosalind Russell in *His Girl Friday*, Jimmy Stewart in *Call Northside 777*, Edward G. Robinson as the crusty editor in *Five Star Final*. Too young for legitimate crust, Hunter did his best to act the part: cynical on the outside, idealistic on the inside. *I can fake that*, Hunter thought.

He flipped through a journalism textbook he found in the base library and learned a few key phrases to help him pass: *lede, nut graf, 30*. . . . His bosses fell for it. No one checked out his claims of having edited his high school paper or covering sports for the *Courier-Journal* back in Louisville.

Hunter learned on the job. The writing was easy for him. He loved all the strong verbs, the language of the sports writer, and his stock phrases, his "sportugese." Hunter wallowed in the terms of the genre. Bowlers were *keglers*, basketball players were *cagers*, and football players were *gridders*. A quarterback was a *field general*, and a demanding coach was a *fiery mentor*. He slung his clichés well:

ARMY CAGERS COP 7 OF 10 SPOTS ON TALENT
LADEN ARMED FORCES ALL-STAR HOOP QUINTET

He did a great job of fooling his superiors. In his first few weeks with the *Command Courier*, Hunter broke most rules of American journalism and the English language. He seemed unaware of Associated Press Style, his spelling was atrocious, and when in doubt, he tossed in random bits of punctuation. His stories were fecund with clichés and sports jargon, and he was innocent of the simple verities of publication design. He edited the sports page as if he were a human shovel, squeezing as many stories as he could into his allotted space. He wrote about golf, motorboating, tennis, boxing, and the base Little League teams. He was egalitarian—officers' wives and children shared space with airmen's exploits. The women's softball team, the Eglinettes, were spotlighted when its "ace hurler" stomped Fort Benning's WACS, 11–1.

Hunter said writing sports had a huge effect on his development as a writer. "Look at the action verbs and the freedom to make up words," he said. "As a sports editor, you'll have twenty-two headlines and not that many appropriate words." After a while, it grew tiresome to say "Team A beat Team B." Hunter loved coming up with euphemisms. "At the Air Force base, I'd have my section: *flogs, bashes, edges, nips, whips*—after a while, you run out of available words. You really get those action verbs flowing."

The centerpiece of the sports page was Hunter's column, "The Spectator." In it, he could write about whatever pleased him: the Kentucky Derby, the last season of the Brooklyn Dodgers, and even the injustice of preventing the best team in college football, the University of Oklahoma Sooners, from playing in the Orange Bowl because of a prohibition of back-to-back appearances. That piece even had a title that would sound at home in Hunter's writing twenty years later: "Voodoo in the Orange Bowl." He debuted in "The Spectator" a technique he later used in *Fear and Loathing in Las Vegas*—the fake editor's note. To buy himself a three-day leave, he wrote a column as if it had been pieced together in his absence. "The Spectator is on a well-deserved three-day pass. During his absence, flotsam and jetsam of the sports world found its way to the Spectator's desk. *The Courier* staff put it together for your perusal. Peruse—on us.") In *Fear and Loathing*, he would insert notes in the narrative: "At this point in the chronology, Dr. Duke appears to have broken down completely. . . . We were forced to seek out the original tape recording and translate it verbatim." The fake editor's note provided anonymity and allowed Thompson to work an attitude into "The Spectator" that he couldn't with his regular byline, such as some thoughts on international sports and sharing a golf joke.

"The Spectator" also allowed Hunter to develop another trademark: turning a minor subplot involving himself into an epic. Missing his first Kentucky Derby in years was worth historical comment, and Hunter cast himself in the self-deprecating role he wore so well in his later work:

> For the first time in eight years, peace will reign in Box 152 at Churchill Downs on Derby Day. No cries of disappointment, no overturned chairs, no crowd of garrulous fops will trouble that spot. A pair of red-rimmed eyes, throbbing after the inevitable revelry of Derby "gatherings"; a rumpled tan cord suit, misshapen from overwork; a pair of nicotine-stained hands, gripping the rail for support; an enormous collection of mint-julep glasses cluttering the floor— these familiar trademarks will be absent when the crowd of 100,000 stands to sing "My Old Kentucky Home" as the horses parade to the post.
>
> But the historic event will go on, even in the absence of the Spectator, whose previous commitments make it impossible for him to join in the annual ceremonial by the banks of the Ohio. . . .

Home still had a strong gravitational pull. In letters to family and friends, he described the detail of his daily life, writing with Southern-gentleman graciousness to his aunt Lee, and with a more conversational, yet still formal, style to friends. He could be a chameleon. He bulletined a letter to Tyrrell as if his life at Eglin were a lost passage from Dos Passos's *U.S.A.* With Menckenesque flourish, he wrote his mother about his job and his classes at Florida State. He wanted her to know he was too busy to get into trouble. He wrote Judy Stellings to ask whether she had his Male High School ring and that if she would send it back, he would steal a model airplane for her. He also asked for her picture.

Aunt Elizabeth worried about him, but he tried to put her at ease. "I have found something which will keep me busy and which is also enjoyable," he assured her in a letter. "I have been able to keep out of mischief and finally settle myself on an even keel for once." He even confessed nostalgia. "I'm beginning to feel like my wilder days are behind me."

He controlled his schedule and made sure it was grueling. No one stood over him to demand that work be done. The freedom made him work harder. During his first two months on the job, he lost twenty pounds and much sleep. He estimated that each day he drank twenty cups of coffee and smoked more than three packs of cigarettes. His pay was $130 a month, which allowed him to announce his presence with authority at the Seagull Bar on the narrow spit of Okaloosa Island, the barrier between the Gulf of Mexico and the mainland. There he drank, smoked, and made off-the-wall bets with the sun-burned regulars.

For the year he worked on the *Courier*, Hunter was on his own to figure out how to run the sports page. He read the major newspapers' sports sections that came into the office and soon pared back on hyperbole. Rather than go over the top, he erred on the side of subtlety. He gathered information from several national newspapers, and "The Spectator" column showed no allegiance to Eglin-only sports.

Hunter wasn't above bragging about his home-state sports heroes (he loved to celebrate Adolph Rupp's run as head basketball coach at the University of Kentucky) or even bringing his friends into the column. He cadged a trip home to Louisville from the brass in order to cover the Bluegrass Festival, which inaugurated the city's new coliseum with a basketball tournament. The University of Louisville beat fifth-ranked St. Louis University in a piece Hunter titled "Appointment in Waterloo." He included an interview with another veteran sports sage—Porter Bibb, sports director of New Haven's WYBC. He used the worldly-sounding Bibb to heap lavish praise on the Louisville Cardinals.

The weekly grind lubricated Hunter's prose, and soon he began hacking through the thick sentences and awkward structures. Clichés were trimmed, and he rarely hesitated to unfurl his opinions in his column.

He did more than write. He also had to lay out pages, fit headlines, and take pictures. He became so interested in layout and the need to fight the genetic vertical design of the page—a newsprint page being taller than it was wide—that he designed photographs and stories in horizontal units. He began to take feature pictures to match the spaces he needed filled in on the page, not because they had any real news value.

Hunter was popular with most, but not all, of the staff. "He was a wise guy," said Joe Gonzalez, who worked alongside him. "He smoked a cigarette in a cigarette holder. And he was quite good at making up stories about things that would happen—that didn't exactly ring true, of course. I didn't like him. He was an egotist. He was always one for telling you, 'In twenty years, you'll still be writing for a base newspaper, and I'll be writing best-selling novels.' That was the type of person he was. He was also kind of a leech. He was always borrowing money from other people and taking trips on their money, and he never paid anybody back."

Hunter also irritated Colonel William Evans, chief of the information services office, with his rebellious attitude. But that attitude made him a hero to many of his fellow airmen. Instead of the malicious mischief from his Louisville days, his pranks and practical jokes now took the form of fake news releases. In one, Hunter presented fellow airman Gene Espeland as the hot new prospect for the Boston Celtics. In a farewell tribute, as Espeland left the service to return home to Montana, Hunter went over the top:

> One of the most colorful athletes to ever wear an Eglin uniform, Gene was what they would call in France "un type." Here, we call them "characters," but they tend to be the same the world over, and without them, life would be intolerably dull.
>
> And so, as "The Ace" heads out to Montana, where the dog tracks will undoubtedly welcome him, the list of athletes departing the base gains another name.

Espeland was embarrassed by the attention Hunter foisted on him. "He made up the craziest stories," Espeland recalled. "A little something would happen in the gym and he'd make a great big story. He had one story where I hit nine forty-foot jumpers, and then he took a picture of me reenacting a ninety-foot jumper that I threw the length of the floor."

Being a sports writer meant travel and getting off base on someone else's tab, a godsend gig. He covered practically anything, even sports he knew nothing about. Back then, large military bases fielded football teams, and they traveled to away games in style, and Hunter got to go along. The Eglin team was especially good in 1956, since it featured three future stars of the Green Bay Packers: quarterbacks Bart Starr and Zeke Bartkowski and receiver Max McGee, all of whom had been called up for duty for the Suez Crisis. That year, Eglin beat the Scarlet Knights of Rutgers.

There was enough freedom in the job that Hunter and some of the other *Command Courier* staff moonlighted for the *Playground News*, the weekly newspaper in Fort Walton Beach. Later, Hunter liked to amplify his legend, saying he'd pissed off superior officers by breaking a no-moonlighting rule. Not true, said Joe Gonzalez and Bill White, two other airmen on the *Courier* staff who moonlighted at the civilian weekly. "We both got onto the newspaper exactly the same way," Gonzalez said. "We both worked on the base newspaper at Eglin and took part-time jobs on the *Playground News*. You had to get permission from the brass, but moonlighting was okay."

When Hunter had tired of covering the area's Class-D baseball team, his *Courier* colleague Bill White said he wanted the job. "It's yours," Hunter pronounced. But White needed something more official in order to get press credentials. With a flourish, Hunter pulled out a piece of *Playground News* stationery and rolled it into his typewriter. " 'To Whom it May Concern,'" it started, " 'Please admit Bill White' . . . and so on and so forth, and he signed it 'Hunter S. Thompson.' That was my press pass. I carried it in my wallet for years, and I've still got it. I never had any idea that Hunter would become as well-known as he did."

Life was busy. Hunter made weekly trips to Tallahassee to attend classes at Florida State and to romance Ann Frick, a fellow student. He was smitten, and they maintained their long-distance relationship even after his Florida tour of duty ended.

Hunter chipped away at a college degree, two classes each semester, knowing he would never catch up with the Ivy Leaguers he'd gone to high school with back in Louisville. But in his letters there was no resentment of well-heeled friends, and he freely gloated about the life he'd cobbled together as sports journalist in sunny Florida.

However, his superior officers thought he abused his freedom. Statement of the obvious: Hunter S. Thompson and the U.S. Air Force did not get along. Tossing bottles at the guardhouse had irritated the electronics squadron leaders. The fake press releases and news stories infuriated Colonel Evans, chief of the information services office. After several months of Hunter's horseplay, Colonel Evans began to clamp down.

Hunter embellished his antics for Judy Stellings. He wrote to her in March 1957 that nine sergeants had cited him for insubordination, that he had been arrested for driving a scooter recklessly, and that he had been found drunk on duty. After an "all-night orgy," he wrote he'd fallen asleep on Colonel Evans's office couch and was surprised by his commanding officer on arrival the next morning.

There was probably some truth in the story; more likely, though, he was trying to entertain his old girlfriend with an elaborate tale. But his acting-out indicated that he was tired of the military. He told a friend he was weary of service-life hassles. He did not fit into a rigidly structured organization.

But he did well enough on the *Command Courier* and with most of his Air Force buddies to contemplate trying to advance himself in the military. If he did well on the *Courier,* he figured, no reason he wouldn't be a good candidate for the Armed Forces Press Service. That would mean a posting to New York with its bars, bohemians, and women. His first six months as *Courier* sports editor were productive. But thereafter he started getting into trouble again: drinking, carousing, insubordination born of the freedom that came with the job. He began alienating some of his Eglin friends. Isolated and restless, Hunter fell into a funk.

Good news arrived in the mail. The Athenaeum Literary Association informed him that he had been reinstated as a member of the class of 1955. The news boosted Hunter's spirits. He gushed his gratitude in a letter addressed to all Athenaeum members:

> Of all the things for which I am grateful to the Athenaeum, I think the most important thing I learned was the importance of thinking. Had I gained nothing else, the acquisition of this quality would have made those three hectic years worthwhile. A man who lacks the ability to think for himself is as useless as a dead toad, while the thinking man has all the powers of the universe at his command.

As his relationship with the Air Force spiraled downward, he wrote to a friend, "I don't feel that it's all necessary to tell you how I feel about the principle of individuality. I know that I'm going to have to spend the rest of my life expressing it one way or another, and I think that I'll accomplish more by expressing it on the keys of a typewriter."

Hunter could say a lot without opening his mouth. He had a smirk, thick with condescension. Elvis would have envied his sneer. His eyebrows rose like arching leeches as each new idea crossed his face. He could maintain the façade of saluting-and-obedient Airman Thompson, but his superior officers were not stupid men, blind to Hunter's insolence. Hunter thought it best to add some space between them.

Hunter found an abandoned beach house on the Gulf and moved in, dubbing his new pad "Xanadu," both after the empty and tragic *Citizen Kane* castle and the stately pleasure dome of Coleridge's *Kubla Khan*. (He also adopted "Cuubly Cohn" as one of his pseudonyms for the *Playground News*, making it appear from the variety of bylines that the *News* had a large staff.) When Hunter invited friends over for rivers of booze, he did his best to make the rickety house live up to the second meaning.

Despite his crush on Ann Frick at college, he was keeping up other relationships as well. While at a Gulf Coast bar, he'd met and begun a scorching romance with a former Illinois beauty queen named Kraig Juenger. She was married (though separated when she met Hunter) and a worldly woman of thirty-four. Hunter was eighteen. They spent two weeks together at the beach and along the banks of the huge Choctawhatchee Bay, separated from the Gulf of Mexico by the narrow spit of Santa Rosa Island and Destin. The bay, ringed with decaying Southern mansions, was a good place for a couple to lose itself. After her return to Illinois, Hunter pointed his car due north, to visit her home in Collinsville, not far from Scott Air Force Base. But much of the affair was played out in the passionate letters they exchanged, and their obsession endured long after they stopped seeing each other.

Back in Illinois, Juenger was pestered with doubts about her relationship with Hunter and all of its baggage. *Was she foolish to think he might be serious about her? Did Hunter care about her at all?* In his letters, he opened up to Juenger and tried to shatter any misconceptions she might have: "I don't think you have any idea who Hunter S. Thompson is when he drops the role of court jester," he wrote. "First, I do not live from orgy to orgy, as I might have made you believe. I drink much less than most people think, and I think much more than most people believe. . . . I am basically antisocial."

All the while, Hunter continued his affair with Ann Frick in Tallahassee.

After a year of wrestling with Hunter, Colonel Evans, who supervised Eglin's information services and faced the Thompson Problem daily, finally wrote to the base personnel office. "This Airman, although talented, will not be guided by policy or personal advice and guidance. Sometimes his rebel and superior attitude seems to rub off on other airman staff members. He has little consideration for military bearing or dress and seems to dislike the service and want out as soon as possible."

Colonel Evans was right. Hunter certainly wanted out, but he didn't want a dishonorable discharge. In his own way, he was proud of his military service and believed his experience was good—in theory at least. "I'm for the draft," Hunter said late in his life. "I think everybody should be in the military. It civilizes the military."

In mid-October 1957, as he careened toward a discharge—not fast enough for Colonel Evans—he met with an officer to discuss his situation. Hunter used the opportunity to talk about his religious beliefs and his political philosophy. By his account, the officer listened to this soliloquy and then said, "I don't know exactly what it is about you, Thompson, and I didn't understand much of what you said; but I can see at a glance that there's not much sense in trying to make you either act or think like an airman should. I'll let you know within two days—twenty-four hours, if possible—how soon you can be discharged."

By early November, he was on his way out. As he wrote Juenger, "The case of THOMPSON V. THE USAF had come to boiling, bubbling climax. The mule train of military bureaucracy, with the help of a few expertly placed jolts of high-detergent oil, has been rolling in high gear for the last two weeks and, believe it or not, has finally come to a logical conclusion: that being that 'a square peg cannot exist in a round hole.'"

The honorable discharge became official on November 8, 1957, but Hunter couldn't leave without a parting shot. On purloined Eglin stationery used for official press releases, Hunter wrote, "An apparently uncontrollable iconoclast, Thompson was discharged today after one of the most hectic and unusual Air Force careers in recent history. According to Captain Munnington Thurd. . . . 'I almost had a stroke yesterday

when I heard he was being given an honorable discharge. It's terrifying—
simply terrifying.'"

Hunter sent the mock press release to friends to announce his separation from the Air Force. The release was also printed in the *Command
Courier*.

As Hunter drove through the scrubland of the Panhandle and away
from his military career, he was starting his second beginning. His childhood ended in jail. His new beginning came in the military, where he discovered journalism. Now he was out of the service, ready to start again.
He could point the car toward St. Louis and Kraig Juenger. But he was
wise enough to know that a year on a base paper wouldn't get him a job
at the *St. Louis Post-Dispatch*. What he wanted was New York, but that
was probably even more out of reach than St. Louis. There was always
college, but after the freedom he'd discovered as a journalist—even one
attached to a branch of the armed forces—the life of a college student
wouldn't be satisfying, even if he could find a college that would accept
him.

For now, the pull of home was strong. He headed to Louisville—to his
family and to Thanksgiving. Everything would follow from there.

Chapter 3

THE DARK THUMB OF FATE

I'm very much into rhythm—writing in a musical sense.
I like gibberish, if it sings.
—*HST to author, 1990*

nemployment did not last long. After a brief visit to Louisville, Hunter placed a *my-services-available* ad in *Editor and Publisher* magazine and found himself the subject of a small bidding war. The *Tribune*, an hour due north from Louisville in Seymour, Indiana, quickly came to an agreement with Hunter. He would get $260 a month as the *Tribune's* wire editor. But after striking the deal, Hunter got a call from the *Jersey Shore Herald* in Pennsylvania, offering more money ($325 a month) and a better job: sports editor. He packed his bags after Thanksgiving and headed off in his 1949 Chevy to start his first full-time civilian job on December 9, 1957.

He didn't last the month in Jersey Shore.

Innocently, Hunter had believed that the name of the town implied that New Jersey was nearby . . . and that the town was near water. A branch of the Susquehanna did wrap itself around Jersey Shore, and there was something nearby called Rosencrans Bog, but who would want a shore by *that*? It was sort of like the frozen tundra packaging itself as "Greenland," when the closest green was across the ocean in Iceland.

Jersey Shore was a miserable little town in the middle of Pennsylvania, bowled out of the Endless Mountains. Almost immediately on arrival, Hunter regretted having taken the job. The newspaper was lousy and the town was worse. "If a man really wanted to bury himself," he wrote his mother, "I can think of no better place to do it than Jersey Shore."

His apartment was above Regan's Grill, a greasy diner, and the rear view from Hunter's apartment was rural; he shaved while viewing a dilapidated barn. What social life there was also was stifling. The *Herald* was an afternoon paper, so he was at work by seven in the morning and done for the day by two. He joined the Elks Club so he could drink in the evenings, yet the Elks Club was not a good place to meet women. "The only women under forty in Jersey Shore go to high school," he carped to a friend. He was caught in a trap—the bad job made his life in Jersey Shore impossible; the life in Jersey Shore made his bad job even worse. He wrote a letter berating the travel adviser for the American Automobile Association for creating the road map that had guided him to the town. "It was nice of you to get me routed," he wrote, "but it would have been nice if all the roads had been out." Jersey Shore was, he said, "totally inadequate for my every need."

There was one tolerable *Herald* employee, an older gent with the soul of a poet, who taught occasionally at a nearby teachers college and wrote features for the paper. As capital *W* Writers (as they saw themselves), Hunter and his friend gravitated toward each other and commiserated about the sorry state of Jersey Shore. They hatched a mutually beneficial plan.

The Poet had a daughter, recently graduated from college and working in Chicago for the *Encyclopaedia Britannica*. She planned a visit for the Christmas holidays. *Want to meet her?* Hunter lunged at the opportunity. The Daughter arrived by train, and the trio retreated to the Poet's home, a modest farm outside town. A torrential rainstorm hit during dinner, and when Hunter suggested he take the Daughter for a ride, the Poet, contemplating the less-than-impressive Huntermobile, gave him the keys to his car. *It'll be better in the mud*, the Poet said.

Strange time to go for a drive, but Hunter was desperate for conversation. He exploded with talk, rambling on like a lonely fool. "I hadn't seen a human being in about five weeks," he said. He was "very pleased, like some guy who'd been given a great present" to have this beautiful young woman all to himself. It was a monsoon, and they were raving drunk on a Pennsylvania brew called Ram's Head. Then the car got stuck in the mud. While the girl stayed in the car, Hunter foot-slogged it up the road and woke a pissed-off Pennsylvania Dutch farmer at two in the morning. The farmer helped free the car, but the bumper and door were ripped off in the process. Hunter limped the water-logged car back to the Poet's house and got back into his '49 Chevy and retreated to his loathsome apartment.

Next morning, Hunter was going through wire dispatches at his desk when he heard a horrible sound outside. Other staff members rushed to the windows to find the source of the metallic grinding. It was the Poet, driving the defiled car up the street, door and bumper dragging. Hunter caught a glimpse of his face, a mask of ferocious anger.

Seemed like the whole staff headed to the parking lot at the back of the building to see the enraged Poet park the car. As the newsroom emptied, Hunter walked out the office's front door, quickly packed his meager belongings, and pointed his car east. He never returned to the *Herald* office and didn't pick up his last paycheck. As he wrote a friend, "This romp with the young woman would have been all the excuse the Quaker bastards needed to emasculate me," so he felt the urgent need for an exit.

The road wound through Pennsylvania farmland and, two hundred miles later, over the New Jersey flats. Manhattan had a magnetic pull on the Huntermobile. The Bohemian romance of the city beckoned him, and he was stunned by his first sight of the skyscrapers. *Finally*: New York City.

"All of a sudden, it was looming up in front of me," he recalled, "and I almost lost control of the car. I thought it was a vision."

His first stay in New York was brief and primarily for strategizing. He hooked up with Jerry Hawke, an Air Force buddy attending Columbia Law School. Hawke said Hunter could crash at his Morningside Drive apartment until he could make permanent living arrangements. Hawke had two roommates, but the apartment wouldn't be too crowded during the holidays.

Hunter was full of half-formed plans, including the idea that he could join Hawke as a Columbia student. After a quick trip back to Jersey Shore to surreptitiously pack his remaining belongings, he returned to New York on Christmas Eve to plot his next move.

He gave himself a January 11 deadline—the date of the College Boards at Columbia—to decide what direction to go: either back to newspapers or on to college. He also had a slim shot at Vanderbilt and had gotten some of his friendly commanding officers from the Air Force (and there were one or two of them) to send letters to Nashville on Hunter's behalf.

There was always the pull of home—and, beyond that, the pull of St. Louis. Maybe the *Post-Dispatch* wasn't an unreasonable goal, after all, and Kraig Juenger was there. He wrote to suggest that if school or job didn't pan out, he might show up at her door.

In the meantime, it didn't hurt to put in applications, starting at the top—the *New York Times*—and moving through the rest of the city's newspaper food chain: the *Herald Tribune*, the *Telegram*, the *Journal*, the *Daily News*, the *Mirror*, and on down. "If there is a Jesus," he wrote Susan Haselden, back in Louisville, "he will then have one of his finest chances to gain a convert. I now have the sum total of $100. When that runs out, there will have to be a Jesus—or a job."

It would require deep faith to be rewarded with a job on the *Times*, so Hunter spent the holidays not just drinking but also working on his craft. He picked up a raft of papers each day, picked out sports stories in each that he liked, then methodically rewrote them to see whether he could improve them . . . *Hunterize* them. Immediately, it became apparent that getting a job in this city would be tough.

Hawke's roommates welcomed Hunter into the Columbia University social circle, and one of them, John Clancy, took Hunter along to hear Thurgood Marshall, then the chief counsel of the NAACP, speak at the law school. Hunter wasn't used to seeing a black man hurling such authority, especially in front of an all-white all-privileged audience of Ivy Leaguers. Marshall's basso profundo, bold confidence, and powerful personality impressed Hunter.

Unemployment meant lots of time to read and write. He began writing short stories, using the pseudonym Aldous Miller-Mencken, after three of his heroes: Aldous Huxley, Henry Miller, and H. L. Mencken. By January 15, Hunter was down to $4.46 and still unemployed. Highlife with friends continued. His Athenaeum friend, Paul Semonin, was studying at the Art Students League. Another Louisville buddy, Floyd Smith, was also at Columbia. Gerald Tyrrell was at Yale and Ralston Steenrod at Princeton. *There were drinks to be drunk.* He developed a new motto: *To hell with the rent . . . I'll drink instead.*

After a month of looking, a job fell from the sky: He was hired as a copyboy for *Time* magazine, earning $200 a month, far below his Jersey Shore salary and in a much more expensive place. Still, it was *Time* magazine, a great foot in the door, and even though it seemed like a bottom-dweller job, it required a three-hour interview and had heady competition. His fellow copyboys had degrees from Harvard and Yale and were multilingual.

He did not start the job until February 1, so he still had to coast to the end of January on the fumes in his wallet. He wrote his mother, fishing around to see if his grandmother had any money to throw his way; he was desperate, but too embarrassed to call and ask Memo himself. He had also written to Eglin Air Force Base to beg the financial affairs office to send an overdue $70 check owed as part of his separation agreement.

As if he needed to sell the *Time* magazine job to his mother, he pointed out that the magazine would help with tuition at Columbia. He was able to register for courses in literary style and short-story writing.

Once again, he managed to fall into yellow daisies. Hawke and Clancy had been benevolent landlords, but Hunter felt he had overstayed his welcome. He was offered a new residence as an apartment sitter nearby, on West 113th Street, the West Side Highway providing the steady drone of background music for his writing. He was on his own, but not overly satisfied with his new lodgings ("a cramped dungheap"), and not admired by neighbors. He threw garbage cans down the marble hallways to amuse himself with the racket. He pounded on the doors of the attractive women and terrorized the next-door Chinese tenant with his tirades. But he was able to stay at the apartment through April, when he finally found another, in Greenwich Village.

The "weekend" for *Time* employees was Monday and Tuesday. Hunter worked half days on Wednesday and Thursday and cranked up for twelve-hour workdays on Saturdays and Sundays. *Time* provided well for employees on deadline, serving a buffet and full bar in the newsroom. *Bad idea.* Someone on the staff usually got blind drunk and made a fool of himself. Hunter could hold his liquor, but it fueled his belligerence. Even though he was the new guy, he used the weekly buffets to insult staff members who outranked him and, since he was a copyboy, everyone outranked him. He was on thin ice from the beginning of his career. None of this kept him from feeling—and occasionally showing—contempt for the writers and editors he despised as hacks.

The magazine work schedule blended generously with the class schedule at Columbia, so he could devote two full and two half days to classes. Still, he was restless, and mused to friends about escaping New York ("a huge tomb, full of writhing, hungry death"), which quickly had lost its novelty. He dreamed of San Francisco, where he'd never been, and, beyond that, to other far-flung locales: Italy, Tahiti . . . somewhere in the sun.

But New York was the heartbeat of the world, and Hunter wanted to be close to the action. He continued to read and educate himself. He was still infatuated with Sherwood Anderson's *Winesburg, Ohio* and, like many young writers, sought to also unmask the hypocrisies of middle-class America. He admired Jack Kerouac's *On the Road*, which had been published the preceding year, but he did not embrace the beat-generation writers en masse. Kerouac's other work did not impress him, but he considered him important "in the political sense." Columbia University's library was a hop-skip from his apartment, so he continued his studies with works by Norman Mailer, Isak Dinesen, Jean-Paul Sartre, Edmund Wilson, and Thomas Jefferson. He deeply admired Henry Miller and Aldous Huxley and also had the requisite infatuation with Hemingway, Faulkner, and Fitzgerald. He did all of the required reading of his generation: J. P. Donleavy's *Ginger Man*, Miller's *Tropic of Cancer*, William Burroughs's *Naked Lunch*. Friends thought Hunter was trying to live the life of Sebastian Dangerfield, the repellent yet fascinating protagonist of Donleavy's book.

Louisville friend Floyd Smith started at Yale, but then transferred to Columbia and fell back into the Hunter Thompson orbit in New York. Hunter "was probably better read than any of us," Smith said. "Philosophically, I always felt that he was firmly based in the stoicism of Hemingway and the hedonism of Fitzgerald."

During his downtime at the magazine, Hunter squirreled himself away in his cubicle and deliberatively retyped *The Great Gatsby* and *A Farewell to Arms*. Years later he said, "I'm very much into rhythm—writing in a musical sense. I like gibberish, if it sings. Every author is different—short sentences, long, no comma, many commas. It helps a lot to understand what you're doing. You're writing, and so were they. It won't fit often—that is, *your* hands don't want to do *their* words—but you're learning."

Friends thought this was a nutty exercise, but Hunter defended it. "I just want to feel what it feels like to write that well," he told Porter Bibb. It also alerted him to the importance of cadence in writing. "Basically, it's music," he said. "I wanted to learn from the best."

The ebb and flow of Hunter's mental stability was tied to his financial fortunes. Always on the verge of fiscal collapse, he spent much of early 1958 vacillating between the intense life of being a young writer in the center of the universe and the depressing reality of having no money and feeling outplayed by people with much more experience. To be a copyboy, laboring under the thumb of hacks, was galling. Yet what was he? He tortured himself in his self-analytical letters to the friends in this network he struggled to keep alive.

Gerald Tyrrell was lining up a shot at the pool table of his fraternity house at Yale when he looked up to see Hunter nonchalantly walk into the room, puffing on his pipe. They had been in touch by mail and seen each other in Louisville during holidays, but Hunter's appearance in New Haven startled Tyrrell. Hunter invited himself along on Tyrrell's date with a student nurse. "It was the last time I ever saw her," he said. "She thought Hunter was acting weird." Tyrrell returned the favor by visiting the city and found Hunter's refrigerator bare but for a jar of peanut butter. "I think he was enjoying New York, from an impoverished point of view," Tyrrell recalled. "He drove this old car and parked it with impunity, wherever he wished. And wherever he parked the car, he'd get a ticket. And he'd just slide that ticket into the glove compartment. At one point, I think he had 122 tickets."

By April, Hunter had moved into a black-walled basement dive on Perry Street in Greenwich Village, accessible by a catwalk that led by an ancient furnace. He thought it was an artist's conception of hell. He sublet the cave from a failed songwriter who'd nearly been driven insane by the subterranean darkness. The name on the lease belonged to a drug addict who was in Europe and who might return at any moment. It was a depressing home with walls and hand-me-down furniture all painted black. From the moment he moved in, Hunter wondered what sort of weird psychological effect the relentless darkness would have on his already disturbed psyche. To Susan Haselden, he wondered how long he could stand to live in the dump and said he longed for Owl Creek, the country club back in Louisville. He pictured himself floating in the club pool. Instead, he was in the middle of what he called a "virtual cave of howling drunken insanity," playing host to a gaggle of charmed and enthusiastic friends who visited the city and crashed in his tomblike apartment. He described his situation to an Air Force buddy: "There are people sleeping everywhere—on my bed, on the couch, on the cot, and even on sleeping bags on the floor. Everything in the place is covered with stale beer, most of my records are ruined, every piece of linen, towel or clothing in the place is filthy, the dishes haven't been washed in weeks, the neighbors have petitioned the landlord to have me evicted, my sex life has been absolutely smashed, I have no money, no food, no privacy and certainly no peace of mind."

He worked his way through the coffeehouses and bars in the Village and found that he could still be surprised by life in the city. There were people who lived in bars, who received their mail there, and he even found people "so lonely" that he couldn't "stand to talk to them." After only six months in the city, he felt that he had sized it up pretty well: "Mid-town Manhattan is an unbelievable circus, Harlem is hell on earth, the Bronx, Queens and Brooklyn are all tombs, and this goddamned Village is enough to frighten any honest beachcomber to death."

But intensity-of-life moments still overwhelmed him on occasion. "I rode down Fifth Avenue with the bus window wide open and a blasting wind in my face," he wrote. "I can't remember when I've felt more alive. With the searchlights from the Empire State Building sweeping the black night over Central Park, a full moon glimmering on the lake and the towers of Central Park West rising over the trees, I felt like I was gliding through a dream."

Porter Bibb worked for *Newsweek* that summer, and Hunter invited him across the street to the weekend party nights for *Time* magazine's deadlines. Hunter had no stature within the magazine, but nonetheless felt entitled to have friends eat at Henry Luce's lavish trough of roast beef and salmon, and get shit-faced on the old man's free booze.

Bibb repaid the favor by taking Hunter and Paul Semonin to the Yale Club Bar. Semonin brought a girlfriend who was a beatnik pinup girl. She gave them marijuana. Bibb remembered Hunter introducing him to black jazz musicians who were snorting cocaine, long before it became the fashionable drug of choice (and long before Hunter ever tried it). Bibb had never even heard of cocaine, but Hunter's social sonar pulled him into new and bolder orbits.

In sober (and other) moments, Hunter continued to write short fiction that was routinely rejected. Along with that disappointment, he was imprisoned by his guests and his compulsion to socialize and began to resent his self-imposed party lifestyle. A great writer must be lonely, he thought, and what he missed, in an odd way, was loneliness. He went from the bottom-of-the-pot Jersey Shore to the nonstop Greenwich Village social whirl.

At *Time*, he'd met fellow copyboy Gene McGarr, who lived a few blocks away, but in an opposite world: McGarr's apartment was at the top of a six-story building and accessible only by a ladder. They were drinking buddies, prank players, and both passing time until their genius was recognized.

Hunter and McGarr were artists at getting into trouble. One Saturday night, they visited the Riviera, a West Village bar that was packed on weekends. Hunter had discovered a bag of lime, the ground stone used to mark football fields, by the furnace outside his dank apartment. Hunter took the fifty-pound bag along on their bar-hopping. A slow leak in the bag ignited Hunter's appetite for street theater. Hunter and McGarr and the leaking bag went into the bar. "Hunter takes the bag off his shoulder, slams it on the bar, and this kind of mushroom cloud of cement rises from the top of the bag," McGarr said. Almost immediately, the well-dressed Saturday night crowd began yelling, " 'What the shit? Get the hell out of here!' The bartenders start coming for us, and the bag spills." As Hunter and McGarr backed out through the narrow entrance, Hunter grabbed the bag by its two corners and swung it, sending sheets of lime over the crowd, dusting them with a huge wall of powder. "My fucking suit, you son of a bitch!" one patron screamed. The beating they got from the bartenders was worth it, Hunter said.

Most of their after-hours journeys were not so extreme. They had the usual run-ins with drunks begging for a pull from the rum bottle they carried or got into shouting matches with obnoxious twits they prided in heckling.

Hunter took time in the late summer for a hitchhiking trip. He headed to Tallahassee to gauge how he felt about Ann Frick, expecting his feelings for her purged. Instead, he realized she was the woman with the strongest hold on him. Despite figuring she would remain only "a pretty picture in my wallet," he found his feelings reawakened, and he told her, when he returned to his New York life, he had to dismiss a girl he'd been dating for several months because she didn't meet his high standards after seeing her. He'd also begun early work on a novel, drawing on memories of debutantes and country-club dances in Louisville and how a Kentucky hillbilly fared in the big city. *Not much of a stretch*.

Impatient with *Time*, Hunter also began looking for other jobs, using unusual job-application tactics. *Time* had run a flattering piece on the *Vancouver Sun*. Hunter promptly sent the editor an application on the condition that the magazine piece wasn't a tissue of lies. Hunter outlined his regard for his profession: "As far as I'm concerned, it's a damned shame that a field as potentially dynamic and vital as journalism should be overrun with dullards, bums and hacks, hagridden with myopia, apathy, and complacence, and generally stuck in a bog of stagnant mediocrity." In a letter of complaint to *Editor and Publisher*, the bible of the newspaper industry, Hunter let loose another tornado of blasphemy: "How many newspapers are there in the country today that actually command the respect of anyone who knows a damned thing about journalism? I'd have a hard time counting ten. And there's where we come to the pith and substance of the whole problem: since journalism has lost its ability to command respect as a profession, it has sunk to the level of 'just another job.'" At the conclusion of his diatribe, Hunter asked for a job with the magazine.

He needed one. To friends, he said that he "gave up on *Time*" just before Christmas 1958. Later, perhaps to enhance his reputation as a rebel, he said that he was fired for insubordination and that he had destroyed an office vending machine. The truth is probably somewhere in between. One certainty is that Hunter and vending machines never got along.

As a writer, Hunter often mixed fiction with fact, but rarely did it more skillfully than on his job application at the *Middletown Daily Record* in upstate New York. Nestled in the Catskills, sixty miles north of New York for the crows and a two-hour meandering drive for humans, Middletown was an attractive place to land: close to Manhattan civilization, yet wide open to possibilities as a proving ground for a young journalist working in a small town, stacking up clippings to fatten a résumé wanting to attract a better job.

The *Daily Record* was in its infancy, a three-year-old newspaper when Hunter joined, already turning heads for its typography and design. It was the first newspaper of its kind in America, a product of the new, offset printing method that was to become the norm in newspapers. As opposed to the noisy production of the cumbersome hot-type method (each letter being forged in lead that was cooled, then set into a form on a page), the *Record* was done by a photographic process. The stories and pictures were produced on paper, cut apart, and pasted onto a page to be photographed and burned onto a printing plate. Within fifteen years, most American newspapers were printed this way.

Hunter tacked two years onto his age and claimed he had graduated from college. He exaggerated his journalism experience and, to his delight and horror, was hired for the *Record*'s young city staff. Though he feared being unmasked as an unschooled imposter, he was pleased to be part of this new experiment in printing that had already earned comment from *Time* and *Editor and Publisher* magazines. He'd long since gotten rid of the Huntermobile, unnecessary in Manhattan, and so appealed to his mother to borrow $550 to buy a 1951 black Jaguar, a car befitting a serious young writer.

Almost immediately, Hunter was in trouble. When he dined at a restaurant across the street from the *Record*'s offices, he offended the owner by repeatedly sending back his order of lasagna. Finally, the owner confronted the tough-to-please customer and asked what was wrong with it. *It's rotten*, Hunter announced. The owner attacked him with a wooden kitchen fork, and Hunter retaliated with his fists.

The next day, Hunter was summoned to the publisher's office and found the fuming restaurant owner there, clad in his chef's apron. Hunter was shocked when the publisher threatened to fire him over the lasagna incident. He'd been doing good work—better work than the *Record* deserved, in his mind—and all he'd done was send some rotten lasagna back to the kitchen, where it belonged. He mumbled the minimum required apology and choked on his anger.

Still, making friends was never difficult for Hunter. He met photographer Bob Bone at the *Record* and through him made several other friends from Middletown's small supply of the young and hip. The social life centered on drinking and discussions of literature.

Hunter was doing all the usual small-town stories: town council, Lion's Club, ambulance runs. Editor Al Romm thought Hunter had promise, but apparently not as much promise as Hunter felt he had. "He was already skating on thin ice since he refused to wear shoes while in the newsroom," Bone recalled.

The last straw came when Hunter killed a vending machine. He'd gone to get a candy bar from the machine behind the composing room. *One nickel, no action. Two nickels, no action.* So he kicked it. The bottom tray fell out, spilling candy bars everywhere. Hunter took what was due him and shoved the other candy back into the storage tray under the machine. Later in the day, the composing room staff figured out how to get to all of the candy bars and snacked for free.

The next day, Hunter had to pay for all of the stolen candy bars and was fired. Romm told him, "At this point in your career, your idiosyncrasies outweigh your talents."

He had lasted six weeks.

As he described himself in a letter of application for a new job, Hunter admitted he was no day at the beach. "Some people find it exceedingly difficult to get along with me and I have to choose my jobs very carefully," he wrote. "I have no patience with phonies, dolts, or obnoxious incompetents and I take some pride in the fact that these people invariably dislike me. I admire perfection or any effort toward it and I would not work with anyone who disagreed with me on this score."

He received no response to his application. Unemployment was becoming a way of life. He had been living in Middletown in an apartment on Mulberry Street, but the income crash led him to find different accommodations. He found a cheap cabin in nearby Cuddebackville, a few feet from the banks of the Neversink River. It had unreliable heat and no electricity. Calling it a cabin dresses it up some. It was a two-room shack with one room a combination bedroom and kitchen.

The latest firing had put him at a crossroads: he could continue with the fantasy of being a writer, or he could actually make the commitment. He could turn the autobiographical sketches into a novel and become a real writer. He came to regard the firing in Middletown as a key event in his life, because it forced him to put up or shut up. This was the time and the cabin was the place to become a writer.

He had always saved copies of his letters and made self-portraits by setting the timer on his camera. He became even more compulsive during his stay in the cabin: he photographed his empty rooms, his manly stance on the porch of his cabin, his solitude over his typewriter. He not only filled crates with carbon copies of his letters; he also kept files of his self-portraits. He had an enormous need for self-preservation and decided that he would document every stage of his life.

He started off by trying to look the part of a writer. He grew a beard, which some friends considered a Hemingway affectation, and played out the role by working endlessly in a hermetic existence, fed by newspapers, liquor, coffee, and the occasional can of tuna or soup. Few people intruded. Judy Booth, former girlfriend of his brother Davison, was a student at Smith College and came for a weekend. She and Hunter had an off-and-on romance that eventually stilled from Hunter's unwillingness to develop a serious relationship.

Isolation from the city bred melancholy in Hunter, who had begun to feel ancient at twenty-one. "A thousand years from now our lives will be, at best, a few sentences in someone's history book," he wrote Ann Frick. "Time seems to be going much faster," he lamented. "I'm beginning to get the idea that life is short. It makes me feel that whatever I do in the next few years will be very important."

There were other artists in those woods. Composer David Amram, already well known for his collaboration with Jack Kerouac, "Pull My Daisy," had a country place near Hunter's rented cabin. "There was a tiny road side store called the Huguenot Superette," Amram recalled. "It was almost always empty, and the owner, after months of stony silence, finally spoke to me confidentially one afternoon about seeing flying saucers and saucer people in the field across the road, and how he had never dared to tell anyone, except for two people. Those two people were myself and someone else he described as 'that crazy writer upon the hill in the cabin.'"

It wasn't long before Hunter and Amram sought out each other. "He was very lean," Amram remembered, "and he had real intense eyes. He was a very good-looking guy, very slim and kind of dynamic and healthy-looking. I visited him at his cabin once or twice. It was a nice little place up on the hill. It was very unspoiled country."

Hunter had outgrown his Kerouac fixation; in fact, he disliked everything that had been published since the success of *On the Road* and thought the writer might be a one-trick pony. He wasn't starstruck around Amram, but admired him as a successful artist who did not compromise talent to match public taste. Amram remembered him as a young man hungering for other people who read. What Hunter missed about daily life in Greenwich Village was talking to people who took literature seriously. He was lucky to find a gifted musician picking through the loaves of week-old bread at the Superette.

He once said that he truly became a writer in the cabin on Highway 209, aligning himself with Ernest Hemingway and Scott Fitzgerald, even keeping tallies of rejection slips relative to their various ages. Hemingway suffered eight years of rejections before publishing his first story in the *Atlantic Monthly*, and Fitzgerald papered his walls in the 122 rejection letters he got before his first sale. Hunter calculated that at the three-rejections-a-week pace he'd established by the summer, he would catch up with Fitzgerald a few months into the 1960s. He pinned his greatest hopes on his novel in progress, and figured he might actually find success ahead of the Hemingway-Fitzgerald pace.

Hunter would escape to New York in his black Jag and spend drunken weekends seeing his friends. He'd seek out Amram at his city apartment when he got to the Village. "We'd go to the Lion's Head Bar and the White Horse and different places people would go to hang out," Amram recalled. "The writers that went to these places were also equal in numbers with the everyday people like carpenters. The writers didn't get special treatment. Hunter was very comfortable with the nitty-gritty. He understood the Southern concept of 'down home,' of the very important link to being a human being."

Back in the Catskill cabin, Hunter diligently worked on his novel. By the end of June, he'd finished three chapters of *Prince Jellyfish* and planned to ship off the work in progress to Robert Ballou at the Viking Press. He'd sent a query letter to Viking and gotten the standard response from the publisher, but Hunter hadn't been rejected enough to recognize a form letter. All he knew is that he had a name—Ballou's—and that gave him a glimmer of hope that a real person, an editor at a major publishing house, would read his book. He immediately wrote back to Ballou that his note made him feel more like a writer.

He suddenly developed a deep kinship with all who'd worked the lonely trade, and even reached out to some. To William Faulkner, he wrote about the place of the writer in the modern world. "As far as I can see, the role, the duty, the obligation, and indeed the only choice of the writer in today's 'outer' world is to starve to death as honorably and defiantly as possible. This I intend to do, but the chicken crop in this area is going to be considerably depleted before I go."

No response from Faulkner, but Hunter's spirits remained high. He felt part of the tribe. Euphoric despite his poverty, he wrote Ann Frick to have faith: "They ain't throwin' dirt on my coffin yet."

Prince Jellyfish wasn't just close to the bone; it was in the marrow. He wove friends' names and places from his past into the narrative. The hero, Wellburn Kemp (named after two admired—and dead—Louisville friends), was a transplanted wastrel in New York, adrift and floating above the struggles of other mere mortals, as a jellyfish. The strongest literary influence was J. P. Donleavy's *Ginger Man*. Like that novel's Sebastian Dangerfield, Kemp is selfish and arrogant and yet too charming to be firmly repellent. Much like his life, Hunter's novel was episodic and included insight into what it was like to be inside Hunter Thompson's head during a job interview. As an editor asked Wellburn Kemp lame questions, acid responses welled up inside until Kemp was able to spit out a more acceptable answer. Hunter wanted to make things come out better in fiction that they had in his life, and so when Kemp was offered a copyboy's job, not the job he expected to be offered, he indignantly walked out. In another section, Kemp returned home for a vacation and took a nostalgic turn through Cherokee Park. Kemp, the idealized Hunter, had of course done no jail time and has finished college. Even in those years when he sat in his drafty cabin, trying to write the great American novel, it seemed that whatever Hunter started out writing about, he ended up writing about himself.

"As things stand now," a twenty-one-year-old Hunter S. Thompson wrote in June 1959, "I am going to be a writer. I'm not sure that I'm going to be a good one or even a self-supporting one, but until the dark thumb of fate presses me to the dust and says, 'You are nothing,' I will be a writer."

Hunter's idyll at Cuddebackville ended in early August. He spent the summer living hand to mouth, working on *Prince Jellyfish* and his always rejected short stories, with no success or even a glimmer of interest from the outside world. He lost his thirty-dollars-per-week unemployment insurance and fell behind on his rent. To try to extort blood from this stone, his landlord ("a down-to-earth bastard," Hunter called him) removed a wheel from Hunter's incapacitated Jaguar (the steering was giving out) and held it hostage. Hunter's car insurance also was cut off for lack of payment. While hectoring Rust Hills at *Esquire* to accept one of his short stories, "The Almost Working Artist," Hunter said he would accept $900 or best offer for the Jag. "If you know of anyone who wants to hire a neo-literary mountain hermit, please let me know."

There was only one thing to do: escape. He ran away to the home of friends, towing the falling-apart black Jag down Highway 209 in the dead of night to the nearby town of Otisville. There, he moved into the house of a couple he'd gotten to know through friends at the *Record*. Ann and Fred Schoelkopf gave him sanctuary and a level of stability he hadn't had since leaving Louisville.

"He stayed in and out of our place," Fred Schoelkopf remembered. "He had a room in our house. There were four rooms on the second floor, and we said he could use one as long as he needed. He'd go off on one of his adventures and leave his stuff here. We didn't pay too much attention to his comings and goings. Sometimes, he was there every day for weeks and months, working on his writing. We kept a free and easy place, and the doors were open for Hunter."

With this stability, Hunter had his refuge with the Schoelkopfs in Otisville, where the isolation fed his writing. He was also not far from the bacchanalian pleasures of his life in the city and his network of friends there, his collection of women, and several couches open for Hunter in those odd moments when he needed sleep.

"He rarely slept when most people would sleep," Schoelkopf recalled. "He worked into the night. If there was something to drink available, he drank it. When we talked, he always wanted to talk about writing. He was really a writer. He was on our phone constantly, trying to get something published."

He became close to the couple and was spoiled by Ann's home-cooked meals and by the cash they gave him every now and again for writing supplies—and for cigarettes and booze. "If it hadn't been for Ann and Fred Schoelkopf," Hunter wrote, "God knows what sort of dire fate I'd have come to."

Still, Hunter hated the feeling of imposition, so he decided he needed a change of scenery to make the final push to finish his novel. That meant home. But before heading west, he decided to visit friends in New York. He and Gene McGarr were back in a hell-raising mood, so they climbed the fence at James J. Walker Park, on Leroy Street in the Village, and skinny-dipped in the park pool with their dates. Four young thugs showed up and announced that the pool was their territory. They kicked the clothes into the water, but Hunter and McGarr leaped out and began beating the kids, tossing them into the pool. Hunter was pummeled with sticks and eventually lost consciousness. He awoke in an emergency room, on a tile floor next to McGarr, being hosed down, their blood swirling down the drain in the floor. After that, Hunter claimed, he rarely visited the city without a lead pipe.

His driver's license had expired, so he hitchhiked to Louisville. Since many of his friends were gone and he was older, the city had lost many of its mysteries, but home was home. "You may not appreciate this," he wrote to his mother by way of warning, "but what I'm going to do now is . . . shut myself in the back bedroom and finish this novel."

By early September, he was laboring on the book. On his return to Louisville, he sent three chapters and an outline to Viking Press to get the fabled advance. He got the standard "we would not care to publish" form rejection letter. He immediately fired back a letter to the rejecting editor, Jack Benson, vowing to make him regret the day he turned down the opportunity to publish a book by Hunter S. Thompson. Since the letter offered no suggestions for improvement or made any comment on the novel's worth, Hunter told Benson he was incompetent.

Correspondence distracted him from the book. Before leaving New York, he had applied for a job on the *San Juan Star* in Puerto Rico, leaving his mother's address on his application. In his insufferably high-minded letter to the *Star*'s editor, he spoke with disdain of the American press and offered as his ideal the philosophy of Joseph Pulitzer reproduced on a bronze plaque, which claimed that a newspaper's loyalty was to truth and the public welfare and not to government or profits. Hunter also bragged of his prodigious writing talent and his manuscript under consideration by Viking. He was rejected with a smart-ass letter that infuriated him. He had included his killing of the candy machine on his résumé (he had to explain why he'd been at the *Record* so short a time), and William Kennedy, managing editor of the *Star*, said that if they ever got a candy machine and decided that it needed to be kicked in, they would be sure to call him.

Hunter immediately wrote back and offered to kick in Kennedy's teeth and shove Pulitzer's bronze plaque up his ass. It was, of course, the beginning of a beautiful friendship.

Finishing the novel was hell. The rejection from Viking was depressing, but Hunter tried not to get discouraged. He wrote William Styron, whom he admired, to ask the name of a literary agent who might help sell

Prince Jellyfish. Styron, unlike Faulkner, wrote back and offered the name of his agent, Elizabeth McKee.

By November, he was back in his bedroom at the Schoelkopfs' house in Otisville with portions of his novel in the hands of an agent, which subsequently was rejected by some of America's finest publishers. He also stayed with Paul Semonin at his cabin in the New Jersey woods and with Eugene and Eleanor McGarr in the city. He was dependent on the kindness of friends and always tried to repay hospitality as best he could.

Hunter was restless. Bob Bone, his friend from the *Middletown Record*, had surfaced at the *San Juan Star*, and Hunter wrote to ask what it was like to work there. Puerto Rico had to be preferable to another winter in some dim, bone-chilling outpost like the Cuddebackville cabin. Hunter's correspondence with Kennedy had quickly gotten through the threatening stage of getting-to-know-you formalities and become a creative outlet for both of them. Hunter further delayed finishing his novel by writing a one-act play for Kennedy (about the decline and fall of American journalism) and indulging in hipster-speak. Kennedy encouraged Hunter to come to Puerto Rico, so they could exchange insults in person over drinks.

Hunter read the *Editor and Publisher* want ads and applied for anything that looked interesting. His application letters were confident, even arrogant, and challenged employers to write back. Eventually one did. Amazingly, it was an editor named Philip Kramer who was starting a new magazine in Puerto Rico that he said would be "the *Sports Illustrated* of the Caribbean." It was exactly what Hunter was looking for.

Chapter 4

A NATURAL INGRATE

I had the misfortune of being nourished by the visions and
dreams of great Americans—the poets and seers.
Some other breed of man has won out.
—Henry Miller, 1945

They had met in a bar on Christopher Street in the Village in 1958. Sandra Dawn Conklin was in the city, visiting her Goucher College roommate, Eleanor McGarr, Gene's bride. Eleanor had graduated from the all-girls school, and Sandy, still finishing her degree, had come up for Thanksgiving break in New York. Eleanor and Gene introduced Sandy to Hunter at a bar.

"I had a fiancé at the time," Sandy recalled. Hunter bird-dogged her. "I was flattered but not yet smitten and after all I had a fiancé."

The next time they met, in 1959, Sandy was on a date with Hunter's old friend from Louisville Paul Semonin, who was studying in New York and spending a lot of his time living in Hunter Thompson–like isolation in the New Jersey woods. At some point during the evening at the bar, Semonin climbed onto a table and began dancing.

That gave Hunter the opening he needed. He slid onto the seat next to Sandy. She was beautiful: with an open face, blond hair, and tight sweaters and short skirts that flaunted her figure. When speaking to women, Hunter could make them feel as if they were the center of his universe. His eyes bore into theirs, and while they spoke, he drew thoughtfully on his pipe, often nodding in agreement with what they said. It was an act, his friends said, and it often worked.

It had not worked immediately with Sandy. Friends didn't think calm-and-quiet Sandy could be interested in Hunter. Moreover, there was the fiancé thing. And here she was, on an innocent date with Semonin. She had earlier been set up on a blind date with another Louisville transplant, Ralston Steenrod, studying at Princeton. She joked that everyone she met in New York seemed in some way to be orbiting Hunter Thompson. As a stable young woman, she seemed ill matched with noisy prankster Hunter. After she moved to the city, she was drawn into Hunter's world. The fiancé was forgotten. That Sandy was quiet and nurturing was in her favor.

Virginia Thompson fronted her son his plane fare, and he arrived in Puerto Rico the first week of 1960, ready once again to start over. It didn't seem that the job would be that hard, and Hunter thought he might have stumbled into the best situation he could expect, considering his checkered employment history. The Puerto Rican life was good. He rented a beach shack (a pillbox, he called it) and began each day with a bracing swim in the ocean and a stroll down the beach. Unfortunately, he eventually had to go to work.

Kramer had talked a good game during Hunter's New York interview, but *Sportivo* didn't have a chance of being the *Sports Illustrated* of the Caribbean. It probably couldn't even be the *Sports Illustrated* of East McKeesport, Pennsylvania. Bowling was the new fad in Puerto Rico, and Hunter's assignment was to hang out at bowling alleys and write pieces filled with names of the local bowlers. He was a stenographer, not a journalist. And he was a stenographer for a bunch of *bowlers*, for God's sake. It was humiliating for someone with Hunter's ego and ambition.

After the job, Hunter's primary concern was clothing. "If I were anything but a writer," he wrote Sandy, "I couldn't get away with the way I've been dressing down here in this very formal, over-priced Valhalla." He wrote his mother, begging her to send him his brother Davison's hand-me-downs or to find any bargains she could scrounge up: shirt size, 15-35, pants, 34 waist.

He wasn't prepared for the insane cost of living on the island, and the familiar financial panic set in. It was like Cuddebackville all over again, with a warmer climate and the distraction of a tedious job. It took only a few weeks for Hunter to conclude that he had made a monstrous mistake. His initial good impression of Kramer evaporated, and he claimed he was working for "a liar, a cheat, a passer of bad checks, a welshing shyster."

He got in touch with his friend at the *Star*, Bob Bone, and showed up at the newspaper office to meet pen pal William Kennedy face-to-face. He also met business editor Fred Harmon, who informed Hunter that there was no candy machine in the office, but he was welcome to kick in the cigarette machine.

In the meantime, Hunter managed to interest Mark Etheridge, editor of his hometown paper, the *Courier-Journal*, to list him as a Caribbean correspondent. He also sold a couple of pieces to the *New York Herald-Tribune*, and single pieces to the *Milwaukee Journal* and *Baltimore Sun*. He sold and resold essentially the same tourist story to editors of travel sections in mediocre newspapers across America. He even earned a few bucks here and there as a male model.

Still, despite the work and Kennedy, Bone, and his other new friends, Hunter was lonely, so he reached out to Paul Semonin and encouraged him to make the jump to the Caribbean. Semonin landed a job as a proof-reader on the *San Juan Star*, and he and Hunter rented a concrete-block beach house for fifty dollars a month, in the remote village of Loiza Aldea, seventeen miles from San Juan. The roads were so bad and the swamps so fetid that it took an hour to get into San Juan. Hunter and Semonin were the only gringos in the village, and the place had lots of drawbacks. But the little shack had a great selling point: it was in a paradise, right on the beach.

Semonin's company was not enough to assuage Hunter, and he peppered Sandy with letters, urging her to join them. She had steady, if unglamorous, work as a secretary, but she liked adventure. Hunter found that the distance was eating at him. He was used to women throwing themselves at him and offering testaments of devotion. By this time, Sandy had learned to adore Hunter, but she didn't want to limit herself. He wrote to her, making it clear that although he had no problems telling her about the many women in his universe, he expected different behavior from her. If she had these adventures, he wrote, "have the simple goddamned decency not to write me about it." When there was a lapse in correspondence, or when he couldn't reach her by phone at four in the morning, he flew into a rage. She had grown into him, and he shook with jealousy. At first, he'd had a *do-what-you-want* attitude about her coming to Puerto Rico. That soon turned into a demand. "I want you to come down here and, if you do nothing else, merely lie naked with me on this living room bed and stare at the sea until I get carted off for jail."

By May, Sandy was living with Hunter and Semonin in the Loiza Aldea shack. Hunter introduced Sandy as his common-law wife. They were comfortable with that for now. Clothing was optional in their beach shack, and they drank rainwater, ate rice and spaghetti, and downed as much rum as they could manage.

The quarters were so tight and Hunter and Sandy were so relentlessly sexual that Semonin was uneasy. After all, he had dated Sandy first. Considering the circumstances, Hunter and Sandy could have used an infusion of couth, he thought. He was grateful that his job on the *Star* allowed him to escape five nights a week to San Juan on his motorscooter.

Disenchanted with *Sportivo*, Hunter worked the freelance market and sold the *Courier-Journal* a story on Paul Semonin, favorite son of Louisville, working in an island paradise to perfect his craft as a painter. He did this without Semonin's knowledge or cooperation. When Semonin learned of the piece, he was furious. There had been no formal agreement between them to write an article, particularly something that would be read by friends and family back home. The quotes were only distant ancestors of things Semonin had said in casual conversation at the shack, and some were entirely fabricated. When he confronted Hunter with both the invasion of privacy and the faked quotes, Hunter merely shrugged. To him, it was no big deal.

Stiffing a restaurant on a tab and spending a night in jail also was no big deal to Hunter, but it was to Semonin. "He had a need for histrionics and embarrassment," Semonin said. "I went to jail with him in Puerto Rico because we jumped a check in a restaurant. Hunter took me out to dinner. We went to this restaurant and ate. He didn't have any money to pay for it. I didn't have any money at the time. So we left the restaurant, and finally the owner called police and they found us walking back to our beach hut and arrested us. They put us in the jail in San Juan. And the thing I remember about this is Hunter, at three o'clock in the morning, standing before the judge and answering the judge's request about whether we had something to say. And Hunter was talking about how the police were Nazis and that it was an outrage that we were treated this way. He immediately projected it into an extreme, fascistic act. Looking back, that was the model for what I'd call his paranoia. But it's much more active than paranoia, because he creates the drama and escalates everything to a point that's far beyond the realm of reality. It goes back into that impulse he had for street theater."

Luckily Hunter had Bill Kennedy as a friend. "I got a call and got some money to the people in authority and bailed those guys out in the middle of the night," Kennedy said. But the incident infuriated Semonin, and he began to fight Hunter's gravitational pull.

Hunter started to shape a story around his life in the shack and the three roommates, the sleazy world of cheap journalism on the island, the night life at bars, and the inherent racial conflicts. He made notes and, even though he had no success with his first novel, was beginning to plot his second

Semonin fled to the Virgin Islands to hook up with another Louisville friend, Harvey Sloane. Tired of Puerto Rico and looking for another adventure, on a whim Hunter and Sandy joined them. Hunter and Semonin then hatched a plan in St. Thomas to travel by freighter to Europe. They were mulling this plan over drinks when they met charter boat captain Donald Street. He had a 55-foot sailboat and asked Hunter, Sandy, and Semonin whether they wanted to crew with him as far as Bermuda.

It sounded like a good idea at the time. Sandy and Semonin jumped in, doing whatever Street asked them to do. Hunter, on the other hand, did not cooperate. He'd had enough orders in the Air Force to last him a lifetime and didn't need Street barking at him. They were at odds from the moment they set sail. The *Isle Aire* was a 55-foot schooner, and the presence of two sulking men trying to avoid each other made it the most uncomfortable 55 feet in the hemisphere.

By the time the voyage ended in Bermuda, Sandy had had enough, and returned to New York. Hunter and Semonin stayed, trying to get on a freighter for Europe, but no captain considered them seaworthy.

Marooned in Bermuda with no money to escape, Hunter passed his twenty-third birthday, feeling older than most of the people he knew. "If I could think of a way to do it right now," he wrote his mother, "I'd head back to Louisville, sit on the porch drinking beer, and drive around Cherokee Park for a few nights, and sink back as far as I could into the world that did its best to make me. . . . [T]hanks very much for giving me a good home and a happy, hectic childhood that I never tire of remembering."

Hunter was able to turn his plight into a piece for the *Royal Gazette Weekly* ("They Hoped to Reach Spain but are Stranded in Bermuda"). Desperate after three weeks—and by that time living in a cave on the outer reaches of Hamilton—Hunter wrote to the McGarrs, who were in Spain. Gene was on a Fulbright grant, studying Spanish culture. He wasn't rolling in dough, but still managed to send $200, asking that Hunter pay him back in a year, when he needed to come home.

Hunter, Sandy, and Semonin reunited in New York. Sandy got a job with United Airlines, Semonin resumed his art studies, and Hunter drew a couple of freelance assignments from the *Herald-Tribune*. On August 1, Hunter appeared as a contestant on Johnny Carson's game show *Who Do You Trust?* winning $50, though losing the big ($300) money by being unable to identify the inventor of penicillin.

He began writing a novel drawn from his months in Puerto Rico. *The Rum Diary* also paralleled his experiences, but strayed more from the strict autobiographical territory of *Prince Jellyfish*. It gave him a chance to write about the sleaziness he'd found in the bowels of journalism and to set the story in an exotic, though not idealized, island locale.

Once again, though, no one was paying him to be a novelist. He hadn't given up on *Prince Jellyfish*, which he sent to Grove Press with a note calling his book "at best, a minor novel." Again rejected with a form letter, Hunter was furious, not just that his manuscript was rejected but that his solitary nocturnal hours didn't merit a personalized reply. Though each rejection stung, Hunter felt greater pain when William Kennedy was blown off by a publisher. While putting himself through the daily grind on the *San Juan Star*, Kennedy, like many journalists of his generation, took a day job in journalism to pay the bills until he would be able to live off the income of his real writing. Hunter admired Kennedy's work, and when Kennedy's *The Angels and the Sparrows* was rejected, Hunter became cheerleader. He was a treasure trove of rejected-writing statistics and told Kennedy not to despair; Patrick Dennis's *Auntie Mame* had bounced around like a ping-pong ball before finally finding a publisher.

Perhaps because Kennedy was already over thirty, Hunter felt more desperation for his friend than for himself. Hunter saw himself as not quite ready for the big leagues; Kennedy, on the other hand, was. Kennedy was an artist, and each of his rejections hurt Hunter as much as—if not more than—one of his own. "I've compromised myself so often that I can't honestly see myself as a martyr anymore," he wrote Kennedy. "You approach your writing more honestly than I do mine."

By the end of summer, Hunter was ready to blow the city and had enlisted Semonin as partner in a plan to go cross-country for a Kerouac *On the Road* experience. Semonin arranged the job: driving a Ford Fairlane to Seattle for its new owner, picking up hitchhikers along the way. Hunter saw the trip as being rich with story potential. Sandy, for her part, decided to head to Florida in the fall to work in her mother's travel agency and join Hunter, once he'd found refuge on the West Coast.

By the end of September, Hunter and Semonin were on the road, taking the Fairlane through Louisville on their way through the Great Plains and the mountains, before finally reaching the Pacific Northwest. The country was in the middle of the Kennedy-Nixon presidential campaign, and Hunter witnessed a Kennedy campaign speech during a stop in Salt Lake City. Later, he took a freeway exit to watch the first Kennedy-Nixon debate on TV in a tiny village near Salem, Oregon. It proved to be a watershed moment. "That was when I first understood that the world of Ike and Nixon was vulnerable . . . and that Nixon, along with all the rotting bullshit he stood for, might conceivably be beaten." Until that moment, Hunter later recalled, it had never occurred to him that politics in America had anything to do with real human beings.

After delivering the car, Semonin and Hunter hitchhiked south to San Francisco, where they stayed in John Clancy's apartment. Clancy had finished up at Columbia Law School, where he had served as a temporary landlord/roommate for Hunter, and worked in the Bay Area. He had moved to Berkeley, preparing for marriage and military service. He was happy to let Hunter and Semonin use up the last few days of the lease on his San Francisco apartment. Hunter inhaled the remaining seeds and stems of the beatnik movement, going to City Lights Bookstore, North Beach, and other ports made famous by Kerouac, Ginsberg, Corso, and the gang.

"I have still not decided if San Francisco is good or bad," he wrote Sandy. "Whether it is or not, I'm hitting the streets Monday in search of a job. My fortune now rests at $9. If you have any extra money, please send it along."

He was across the continent from Sandy and felt that he had merely exchanged poverty in New York for poverty in San Francisco. It was a fool-ish move, he thought, but then most of his moves had been ill advised. "I wake up each morning without more than a vague idea of where I'll sleep that night," he wrote Gene McGarr, while begging an extension on repaying the $200 he borrowed to flee Bermuda. "I am continually hungry, I have been arrested for shoplifting (a package of cheese—my only attempt at theft, so far), and, as far as I can see, I still have no prospects for a job."

Hunter spent a month trying to find a writing job, but San Francisco was as talent rich as New York, and he didn't see many alternatives besides killing himself (spectacularly, of course, in a planned dive off the Golden Gate Bridge) or a midwinter hitchhike across the continent that would throw him into an irretrievably foul mood.

Semonin was worn out from nearly a full year with him, so Semonin vowed to stay in San Francisco and scrounge. "Whatever happens will be all right," Hunter assured Sandy. "I do not care and I have no plans. I'll go as far as the rides take me, sleep on the beach and beg, if necessary, for food." But Hunter had been reading Henry Miller and was full of the romance of what he saw as the ideal writers' colony of Big Sur, 150 miles south of San Francisco, pushed up against the Pacific by a narrow band of mountains.

Hunter was the product of all of his influences: the big guns, like Hemingway and Fitzgerald, were fairly obvious as major shadows over his writing. The stark Hemingway style ("He walked back to the hotel in the rain") echoed through Hunter's writing all of his life. As a social critic, Hunter learned from Henry Miller's writing. A generation earlier, Miller had documented his love-hate relationship with America, much as Hunter would at the end of the twentieth century. Throughout his expatriate years in Paris—during the Great Depression, not during the glamorous twenties of Scott, Zelda, and Ernie—Miller wrote *Tropic of Cancer*, the book that was banned in his home country until 1961. (It was published by Obelisk Press in Paris in 1934.) The deep eroticism of the novel made it notorious, but stylistically it was a combination of fiction and fact that Hunter would adopt in his own writing.

Yet the frank sexual language and images in the book overshadowed Miller's statements of philosophy, his manifesto as an American writer. If we didn't know this was Henry Miller writing, we might think this was a job description for being the young Hunter Thompson:

I am a free man—and I need my freedom. I need to be alone. I need to ponder my shame and my despair in seclusion; I need the sunshine and the paving stones of the streets, without companions, without conversation, face to face with myself, with only the music of my heart for company.

Miller returned to America just as the Second World War was beginning in Europe. In a cross-country trip, he examined the remnants of the country he'd left a decade before and wrote *The Air-Conditioned Nightmare*, a book explicit not about sex but about the faults he found in his fractured homeland. Hunter would come to share Miller's belief in America's potential in the face of the disappointing reality. As Miller wrote,

I had the misfortune to be nourished by the dreams and visions of great Americans—the poets and seers. Some other breed of man has won out. This world which is in the making fills me with dread. . . .
    The most terrible thing about America is that there is no escape from the treadmill which we have created. There isn't one fearless champion of truth in the publishing world, not one film company devoted to art instead of profits. We have no theater worth the name, and what we have of theater is practically concentrated in one city; we have no music worth talking about except what the Negro has given us, and scarcely a handful of writers who might be called creative.

At the end of his cross-country trip in 1940, Miller found Big Sur, which he called his "first real home in America," even though he was born and had grown up in Brooklyn.

Although Hunter admired Miller's writing and was his neighbor across the steep cliffs on the coast, they never met.

A tapered wilderness strung along State Highway 1, the Big Sur peninsula had a history of attracting writers and rebels, from Robert Louis Stevenson and Jack London, up through Miller and John Steinbeck.

It was rough country, and not just the land could be inhospitable. Some of the residents were cranky. There were wild boar in the woods. People like Henry Miller came to Big Sur mostly to hide out. Strangers usually remained that way. Hunter had moved to Big Sur because of Henry Miller, but despite waiting by Miller's mailbox daily, hoping for a casual encounter, he never met the writer.

Hunter found a cabin for rent and then, as 1961 was beginning, fell into an opportunity as caretaker for property owned by the Murphy family. The land included an assortment of hot sulfur springs offering Pacific vistas and several shacks tossed into the woods. There was the big family house and the caretaker's cabin, where Hunter would live and fulfill his duties as guard for the wilderness estate.

Having a Big Sur return address raised his literary profile. Though he had no real success, he had the isolated lifestyle of the working artist and he was among them—not just Miller, who lived nearby, but also Dennis Murphy, whose novel *The Sergeant* had been a raging success and quickly sold to Hollywood. Murphy was pals with Jack Kerouac, and Big Sur was the weekend refuge of the Beats. Hunter felt he had currency from the address to write a *how's-it-going* note to J. P. Donleavy and ask what he was up to. There was no answer.

Finally, after a year on the road with ever-changing addresses, Hunter had found a home. He sent for Sandy.

"It was one room on top of the other and with a big window that looked out onto the ocean, out and down, just right on the edge of a cliff," Sandy recalled. "Fifteen dollars a month. It was paradise. And he worked and he worked and he worked. He absolutely worked every night and every day. He was very serious . . . *very* serious."

Hunter also took his caretaker duties seriously. The open-air baths on the Murphys' land had drawn homosexuals from San Francisco for years, and Hunter took it upon himself to roust them from the baths—just as the night was settling down and the couples felt themselves at peace with nature. Suddenly, a howling, jibbering, gun-toting madman would emerge from the woods and frighten them off.

As caretaker, Hunter also felt he needed to be armed. Through Jo Hudson, a local sculptor, he'd developed an interest in weapons. Like most boys growing up in Louisville, Hunter had a small rifle. But he never hunted until he met Hudson. The artist knew where to find game. Guns seemed a natural accoutrement of a gentleman-crazy in Big Sur. So did dogs—the larger the better. He and Sandy got a Doberman pinscher named Agar and beheld the sunsets from their vistas in the Santa Lucia Mountains over the Pacific, where occasionally they could watch whales migrating south. Clothes were largely optional in Big Sur, a policy Hunter and Sandy embraced.

There were other friends as well. Singer Joan Baez was also a new arrival in Big Sur, where bargains could be had. "For thirty-five dollars a month, we rented a cabin consisting of one bedroom (doubling as a living room), a tiny bathroom, no closets, and a kitchen," she wrote in her autobiography. "We had four dogs and many cats." Primitive life meant no telephone—and that made booking concert dates difficult.

Baez and Hunter were not friendly neighbors at first. Ever the pacifist, she was put off by his guns and boisterous behavior, and the more he realized that his behavior irritated people, the more he ratcheted up his antics. Eventually they developed a fondness for each other, but it took a long time.

Hunter also befriended Lionel Olay, a middle-aged freelancer eking out a hand-to-mouth existence on Big Sur. He had written the thirty-five-cent paperback pulp fiction classic *The Dark Corners of the Night*. Olay's life-given-over-to-writing inspired Hunter deeply. Olay never seemed to worry about money. The work came first. Olay also gave Hunter the model of a *don't-give-a-shit* writer who didn't worry about offending sources or stepping on editors' toes.

For the first half of 1961, Hunter and Sandy shared their cottage on the edge of a cliff overlooking the ocean. The Murphy property was being reinvented that spring as the Esalen Institute, which was to be a non-profit think tank where out-of-the-mainstream writers, artists, and philosophers could come together, hang out in the hot baths, and solve all of the world's problems. Esalen would end up drawing Aldous Huxley, Joseph Campbell, Kerouac, Ginsberg, Baez, and others who gathered there to "explore human potential." That's what Michael Murphy—member of the property-owning family—and his friend Dick Price had in mind. Esalen took its name from the Esselen tribe that used to live on the point. As the touchy-feely think-tank idea was being developed and renovations made to some of the structures on the property, Hunter and Sandy looked after the day-to-day maintenance.

"We were living in the servants' quarters of the big house at the Esalen property," Sandy remembered. "On the Pacific. It was wonderful."

It was wonderful, of course, as long as she maintained her role of being subservient to Hunter. Their relationship had fallen into a pattern in which all aspects of their lives were directed toward Hunter's work. He saw the job as caretaker as an entitlement to live on the spectacular California coast. Hunter wrote all night, slept much of the day, and when he woke, Sandy's job was to take care of him. So any true caretaker duties also fell to her.

For the first several months, his writing contributed nothing to the family income, so Sandy spent those hours when Hunter slumbered working as a maid. She also made the three-hour drive to San Francisco twice a week to do temp work. Some neighbors found her role as Hunter's slave offensive. He acted like a man who expected servitude. They fought, and sometimes Hunter slapped Sandy. Since he slept through much of the day, her job was to keep the world away. When he awoke, usually after noon, she'd make breakfast and he would sit overlooking the ocean, smoking, drinking coffee, reading newspapers, and often reading what he'd written during the night. He sometimes asked Sandy to read aloud what he had written, but did not expect criticism, only vindication.

He'd begun referring to *The Rum Diary* as "the Great Puerto Rican Novel," believing he was into semivirgin terrain, since the only Western writer mining Latin America was Catholic-obsessed Graham Greene. Hunter believed he could look at that part of the world with his new sensibilities and unflinching eye, avoiding the sort of religious moralizing that marked Greene's books.

But the publishing world took no notice of his work. He had written off *Prince Jellyfish* after it bounced all over Manhattan, but he felt that by going to somewhere foreign, *The Rum Diary* had more chance of success. He constructed a story with more scope and ventured outside the raging and superior interior monologues of Wellburn Kemp, the "Jellyfish" protagonist.

"The big money is just around the corner," he wrote to Ann Schoelkopf, "and it won't be long until I get my hands on it." Given his faith in himself and now with the luxury of time and reliable, spectacular shelter and a nurturing environment, Hunter felt poised for success and recognition.

Semonin had given up on California and landed in Aspen, Colorado, just before Christmas 1960. He wrote Hunter, beckoning him to the mountains, where he would find the beauty and isolation he needed to write. Hunter made a brief visit, having cadged a small assignment that paid his way: delivering material to a decorator. He showed up at the home of local writer Peggy Clifford, with whom he began a friendship. "It was snowing, and I showed up on Peggy's doorstep," Hunter said, "a freak from Kentucky with a pile of trash on top of a car that had to be delivered to some decorator in Aspen. I thought Peggy would be horrified. . . . Peggy fed me, gave me a place to sleep, money for the train when the decorator quibbled, and a ride to the train in Glenwood Springs. Here came a vagrant through town, a Neal Cassady kind of freak, traveling with a giant Doberman and a monster crate that was heavy and made to be a home for the dog on the train, if we ever got on the train, and she took care of everything."

Hunter filed it away; Aspen was good, but he and Sandy were on a roll in Big Sur—living in the servants' quarters, raising a Doberman, writing, seeing the sunset over the Pacific . . . it was all too good—for Hunter, at least.

"When we were in Big Sur, I got pregnant," Sandy recalled. "I had two abortions. In Mexico. There was never any question in my mind, both times. We were very poor. We were not at all ready. Had I had either of those children, Hunter would have had to have left me."

While Sandy tiptoed around Hunter, waited on him, made sure he had a quiet, child-free home in which to work, rejections piled up. Unhappy that he wasn't getting any publications, he decided the problem was with his agent. On Olay's recommendation, he wrote Sterling Lord, agent for both Kerouac and Mailer, sending him a sampling of his writing, offering details of his lack of success, and bemoaning that he was sinking into a bog of poverty.

For a quick paycheck, Hunter retreated to journalism. If the publishing world was ignoring his fiction, he thought he could build a track record in magazines and work from there. He realized he was in the middle of a world about which the rest of America might be curious, so he began pitching an article on Big Sur to *Playboy*. Infuriated when his article was rejected, Hunter pitched the piece to a rival men's magazine, one that was a whole lot sleazier, and was shocked when it was accepted.

Hunter had his first publication in a national magazine and $350 to show for it. When Sterling Lord rejected him, Hunter fired back a brutal letter (he called him pompous and moronic) and crowed that he was finally on his way.

"Big Sur: The Garden of Agony," appeared in *Rogue* in the summer of 1961. Although it didn't have gratuitous first-person references, it was clearly Hunter's voice and attitude. Mostly, he dealt with myths and realities of Big Sur: the free love, the wild sex, the baths, the orgies, the general wildness of the continent that had been shaken down at this ragged edge by the sea. He used his friends as sources and put his observations into the mouth of a character he called "the writer."

The piece also dealt frankly with Henry Miller and the shadow he cast over the area. Several of Miller's books, including *The World of Sex*, had yet to be published in America. But *Tropic of Cancer* was available overseas and was carried in haversacks back into the states. It was enough to encourage literary groupies and sex nuts to trek cross-country to knock on the writer's door in the middle of the night. Miller was a prisoner of his audience, many of whom came to him as the one who lived out their fantasies.

The Big Sur article pissed off the community, as if Hunter had disclosed family secrets—and, in a way, he had. He'd referred to the community as "a Pandora's Box of human oddities." There were also those who felt the article would increase the influx of sex-crazed morons into the area (*Rogue*, after all, didn't have the literary credibility of *Playboy*). There was the stuff about the popularity with homosexuals, which was not considered a good selling point in 1960. "He wrote about some baths which were on the property, which was a haunt for gay people," Sandy said. "And in those days it was hard—it was hard for the landlady to hear." And by painting the area as a sex-and-deviance theme park, Hunter had deeply offended the dominant family and added more fuel to the fire.

The Murphys' grandmother, Vinnie, owned the estate and was not pleased. The *Rogue* article was a mixed blessing: it was Hunter's first national publication, and it was also the reason used to evict him.

It had been nearly a year of peace and solitude, longer than he had any right to hope for, considering his track record. Unable to find another cabin to rent, he decided to return home, to his mother, to the peace and sanctuary that he needed to finish *The Rum Diary*. Sandy went ahead to New York. She planned to stay with friends and work as a secretary to contribute to the Hunter Thompson Survival Fund.

Back home on Ransdell Avenue, Hunter labored to finish his book. He'd sold a short story ("Burial at Sea") to *Rogue*, his first published fiction, but he was angered when the editors chopped hundreds of his words. He'd accepted their suggestions with the Big Sur article, but he was fiercely protective of his fiction. Louisville was "grey and wet and full of so many ghosts and memories that I get the Fear whenever I go outside." He secluded himself with his novel and pitched articles on conservative politics and bluegrass music to various national magazines, most of which declined the honor of publishing them. He made a brief trip to eastern Kentucky for a winter music festival and sold a piece to the travel section of the *Chicago Tribune*, another major-newspaper publication to add to his résumé.

He stayed home through the holidays but by January was back in New York with Sandy, plotting his next move. He felt that Latin America was underreported (or ineptly reported) in the North American press, and he likewise felt that he was the man to rectify the situation. And he had the means to do so. His grandmother, Memo, had died, leaving Hunter $15,000. He immediately bought a camera and booked passage to South America, prepared to unleash himself on the world as a foreign correspondent.

Before setting up to leave, Hunter spent the winter and early spring of the year finishing *The Rum Diary* (he called it "a book of flogging and fighting and fucking") and handed the manuscript over to his new agent, Candida Donadio. By the time he was finished, he had come to think of the book as a waste of time, especially after reading Isak Dinesen's *Out of Africa*, which he considered a masterwork. He and Sandy had farmed out most of their possessions and were sleeping on a mattress on the floor of a shabby apartment.

He wondered why he chose to put himself through such a life. "I'm damned if I can figure out why people keep at it," he wrote Lionel Olay. "Like most young writers, I am a natural ingrate and will always think that my work and my views are above and beyond advice—at least until I finish one thing and can get far enough away from it to see it clear and mean like a girl who drives you mad when you're drunk and then looks like hell in the morning."

He had Sandy, but he was addicted to womanizing. Time, as he saw it, was the enemy. "I am plagued with a mounting suspicion that time is going to force me to leave a lot of women undone," he told Olay. "There is just too goddam much to do and too many places to be all at once. There are nights when I want to be in San Francisco and New York and Rio and Madrid at the same time, and it seems unjust that I can't. If I had my way, I'd be in love all the time all over the world with a rifle in one hand and a typewriter in the other and a bellyful of good whiskey." To Bill Kennedy, he wrote, "A beautiful woman is such a wonderful creation as to make all novels seem like scum. It is enough to make a man believe in god."

Hunter had accumulated another trunkful of letters and manuscripts, which he sent home to Louisville. He asked a fellow Doberman lover to take care of Agar ("When a person spends as much time on the move, as I do," he wrote, explaining his concern for the dog, "he becomes more than normally attached to the few tangible things he can call his own.") Boarding Agar became local news, and the *Courier-Journal* ran a story about Hunter's concern that the dog's separation from his master could be emotionally detrimental. "It can be tough to have a globetrotter for a master," the newspaper reported, calling Hunter "a writer whose wanderlust sometimes takes him . . . on short notice." Sandy was staying in the city, providing some stability for his life thanks to her secretarial job with Nuclear Research Associates, a firm based in Queens. Scientists there manufactured amphetamine on the side. Considering what Hunter had in mind for Sandy's role in their partnership, it would come in handy. Hunter's plan was to write travel stories that he could send off to a variety of American newspapers, where travel editors lived on freelance copy. Hunter intended to send his stories to Sandy, have her type several copies of each, and serve as his freelance manager. With all that typing, the speed would be vital.

Finally, on the evening of April 24, Hunter set off for South America. It would be from that far-flung locale that Hunter's voice was finally heard in American journalism.

Chapter 5

OBSERVER

There's another side to reporting that seldom shows up in
formal dispatches—the personal experience of the
digging, inquisitive newsman. Witness these excerpts from
Mr. Thompson's personal letters to his editor in Washington.
—National Observer, *December 31, 1962*

The *Wall Street Journal* was always much more than its name implied. On most days, the left-hand column on the front page contained the best newspaper feature in America. Usually an expertly crafted article devoted to a social issue, the column-one stories pioneered the little-person/big-picture approach to explanatory journalism, using the traditional narrative techniques of storytelling to draw readers into a larger issue. By focusing on an individual, the writer opened a window to reporting larger, social issues. Newspapers en masse began using this technique in the sixties, and if the *Journal* could have copyrighted this approach, every publication in America would be in its debt. Editor Barney Kilgore decided in the early sixties that the *Journal* needed to better exploit that talent.

Kilgore conceived the *National Observer* as a Sunday edition of the *Wall Street Journal*. Indeed, it was published on Sundays for the first several months until circulation and distribution problems convinced the parent company, Dow Jones, that it was more feasible to make it a Monday-delivery newspaper.

Kilgore set his sights on doing something different, and his target audience was young people who hadn't yet developed strong reading habits. It was not an entirely smooth start-up. The company wasn't willing to commit much money to the project, which, in the beginning, was produced by a skeletal staff.

Kilgore wanted to experiment, and the *Observer* was his playpen. At first, he proclaimed the newspaper would not need reporters. "We don't need more people telling us what has happened as much as we need people who can put together events and explain them," Kilgore told the investors. The idea owed a lot to *Time* magazine, which, when founded by Henry Luce and Briton Hadden in 1923, said that it would sound as if it was "written by one person, for one person."

"In the beginning there was a lot of reprinted stuff," said Jerry Footlick, one of the charter staff members. "Eventually it evolved, and we started sending reporters to go out and really cover some stories. The more that happened, the more people thought that was the right thing to do. The *Observer* was fun, it was interesting. It was all written in the newsroom for the first year or two, with a lot of reprints."

After a few months, Kilgore's gamble began to pay off. The *Observer* was just beginning to make a splash when Hunter was in New York, preparing for passage to South America. Thinking it might be a good market, he sent a note to Clifford Ridley, who handled the *Observer's* feature section, telling him where he was going and offering his services. Hunter's portfolio was not all that impressive, but Ridley liked the braggadocio of Hunter's letter. Before Ridley had a chance to respond, Hunter had sent his first story.

It was to be a good collaboration. Ridley showed the piece to the *Observer's* top editor, Bill Giles, and he became Hunter's biggest supporter. "Bill gave Hunter a contract for six pieces at $1,000 a piece," Footlick recalled. "That was a lot of money in the sixties. There were some other staffers, old *Wall Street Journal* types, who were Bill's top editors beside him, who thought Thompson was a total kook. Yes, a good writer, they said, but you couldn't trust him. But Bill had great faith in Hunter from the start."

Hunter was lucky to be working for the *Observer*, which was struggling to establish its voice and did not have a clearly defined style. "One complaint we heard about the *Observer* was that it was too dull," Footlick said. "Well, Hunter was not dull."

Although he'd sold articles to some major newspapers, including the *New York Herald Tribune*, the *Baltimore Sun*, and the *Chicago Tribune*, Hunter's writing was too loose and ragged for most mainstream newspapers and not slick enough for America's major consumer magazines.

The *Observer* allowed him to be methodical in his writing and build leisurely to a point, much like the *Journal's* column-one features. Hunter was able to write stories that fit within the *Journal's* corporate style, and yet was given enough license to stretch out and do something unusual.

First stop was Puerto Rico, where he stayed for ten days with William Kennedy and his family. Kennedy continued to be frustrated by his inability to get anywhere in the publishing world, a frustration he and Hunter shared. After rum and commiseration in Puerto Rico, Hunter began his journey, managing a ride on a boat to Colombia, paying smugglers forty dollars for passage. In Aruba, he did a conventional piece on tourism, illustrated with a self-portrait (identified as "an American tourist") lounging on the beach, smoking, and taking notes in the sun. Neither Ridley nor any of the other *Observer* editors had set eyes on Hunter; they didn't know he was modeling for his own photographs.

The trip with the smugglers helped Hunter find the meat of his first major *Observer* piece, "A Footloose American in a Smuggler's Den." Like most of his writing, the story featured Hunter Thompson as its central character. After three paragraphs of Hemingwayesque introduction, the story turned into a comic misadventure. Upon arriving in a tiny village as "the first tourist in history," he is greeted by the entire population "staring grimly and without much obvious hospitality." In this village, he learned, men of the village wore neckties knotted just below the navel—and nothing else. "That sort of information can make a man feel uneasy," he wrote, "and as I climbed the steep path, staggering under the weight of my luggage, I decided that at the first sign of unpleasantness, I would begin handing out neckties like Santa Claus—three fine paisleys to the most menacing of the bunch, then start ripping up shirts."

Throughout the summer and fall of 1962, Hunter traveled through Aruba, Colombia, Peru, Ecuador, Bolivia, Uruguay, and, finally, Brazil, where he would stay until May 1963. Bob Bone, Hunter's friend from the *Middletown Record* and Puerto Rico, was working for a financial magazine in Rio and that became Hunter's home base.

"Hunter showed up on Copacabana Beach," Bone recalled. "I spotted him while riding in a convertible with a friend, and we stopped to let him in the car. He had a drunk monkey in his jacket pocket. His explanation was that he met someone in a bar who would buy him a drink only if he could buy the monkey a drink at the same time. The monkey eventually committed suicide, leaping into the air from the balcony of my tenth-floor apartment—we presumed a victim of the DTs."

For the year that he traveled through South America, Hunter continued to dwell in the uncertain world of the freelance writer. He had a steady market with the *Observer*, but he lived paycheck to paycheck and constantly battled over expenses. The cost of living was lower in South America, but all of the travel quickly ate through the Memo inheritance. His dreams of churning out variations on the same theme, feature articles slightly modified for different newspaper travel sections, did not come through on the scale he had imagined. But once he had the *Observer* platform, the multiple placement of articles wasn't that important anymore. He did occasionally publish a few pieces, such as "Beer Boat Blues" in his hometown *Courier-Journal*.

The difference between his new world and the old hand-to-mouth features existence was that the *Observer* editors loved his work and that he was building an audience with the newspaper's readers. Each dispatch sent to Ridley came with a typically wild and profane Hunter letter. The stories were for the mass audience; the letters to Ridley were adults-only. Ridley recognized the wonderfully incisive and insane quality of the letters, and eventually he stitched together several excerpts from the correspondence and turned it into a feature called "Chatty Letters During a Journey from Aruba to Rio."

In these letters to Ridley, Hunter's Gonzo style began to rear its head. One of the characteristics of the style Hunter developed was his preoccupation with *getting the story*. In fact, *getting the story* became the story. His writing could be classified as metajournalism, journalism about the process of journalism.

In one of the letters from the Hunter-Ridley correspondence printed in the *Observer*, he adopted the conspiratorial *just-between-the-two-of-us* tone he came to use so often. Writing about Ecuador, he said, "I could toss in a few hair-raising stories about what happens to poor Yanquis who eat cheap food, or the fact that I caught a bad cold in Bogota, because my hotel didn't have hot water, but that would only depress us both. As it is, I am traveling half on gall." (In his political reporting in 1972, he used that sort of technique—"I could run that story out right here, but the nuts-and-bolts people are screaming for my copy"—another attempt to bring the audience into the process of journalism on deadline.)

The casual tone of his correspondence worked well in the *Observer* and empowered him to adopt that voice in his journalism. From a note written in Guayaquil, Ecuador: "Things are not going well here, my man." Later, in a letter from Lima, he sounded as if he were on the verge of a Gonzo-journalism breakthrough: "Some **** has been throwing rocks at my window all night and if I hadn't sold my pistol I'd whip up the blinds and crank off a few rounds at his feet."

The comfortable tone of the "Chatty Letters" anticipated the writer-reader bond he worked into his Gonzo journalism. He was much more himself in the letters than in his articles, in which he was still trying to write something "professional," something that could conceivably be published in the *New York Times*. "During the Rio days," Bob Bone recalled, "Hunter talked a wild game, but he was writing pretty straight copy. He had to get published by *The National Observer* to pay the rent. But he discovered his success later, when he began to write just like he talked."

His *Observer* story about a Rio nightclub shooting was reminiscent of Ernest Hemingway's dispatches from the Spanish civil war. Like Hemingway, Hunter referred to himself in the third person and also emphasized his closeness to the action.

Here is part of a Hemingway account:

> They say you never hear the one that hits you. That's true of bullets, because if you hear them, they are already past. But your correspondent heard the last shell that hit this hotel. He heard it start from the battery, then come with a whistling incoming roar like a subway train to crash against the cornice and shower the room with broken glass and plaster.

Here is another Hemingway dispatch from Spain that presented his cavalier attitude toward violence:

> In the morning, before your call comes from the desk, the roaring burst of a high explosive shell wakes you and you go to the window and look out to see a man, his head down, his coat collar up,

sprinting desperately across the paved square. There is the acrid smell of high explosive you hoped you'd never smell again, and, in a bathrobe and bedroom slippers, you hurry down the marble stairs and almost into a middle-aged woman, wounded in the abdomen, who is being helped into the hotel entrance by two men in blue workmen's smocks. She has her two hands crossed below her big, old-style Spanish bosom, and from between her fingers, her blood spurting in a thin stream. . . .

A policeman covers the top of the trunk from which the head is missing; they send for someone to repair the gas main and you go into breakfast. A charwoman, her eyes red, is scrubbing the blood off the marble floor of the corridor. The dead man wasn't you nor anyone you know and everyone is very hungry in the morning after a cold night and a long day the day before up at the Guadalajara front.

Hunter was not writing about war in Rio, yet his dispassionate description of the aftermath of violence at the Domino Club strongly evoked Hemingway's reporting from a quarter century before. He referred to himself as an "American journalist" awakened by a 4:30 a.m. call from a friend, telling of the Brazilian army going wild in the streets in the city's nightclub district:

Ten minutes later, the half-dressed journalist jumped out of a cab a block away from the action. He walked quickly, but very casually, toward the Domino Club, with his camera and flashgun cradled in one arm like a football. In a Latin American country nervous with talk of revolution, a man with good sense runs headlong into a shooting party, because he is likely to get stitched across the chest with Czech machine gun slugs.

But at 4:45 the Domino Club was quiet. It is—or was—a well-known clip joint, catering mainly to American tourists and wealthy Brazilians. The lure was girls—some young and pretty, others slightly piggy and painted after long years of service.

Now the Domino is a shell, a dark room full of broken glass and bullet holes. The doorman is dead; he was cut down by gunfire as he fled toward a nearby corner. The bartender is in the hospital with a bullet creased down the side of his skull, and several patrons are wounded. Most observers say another man is dead, but the bodies were taken away so quickly that nobody can be sure.

The raid by the soldiers in retaliation for the beating of one of their colleagues in the Domino a few weeks before was described in graphic detail by Hunter, with barely concealed outrage. At one point he even quoted himself, wondering what the reaction would be to a similar incident back home, were soldiers from Fort Knox to open fire in a Louisville nightclub.

Thompson's next pieces covered Brazil's post-election trauma, and Bolivia's economic conditions. He also ventured into the history of the Inca, observing that wealth now was measured not in gold but in the sleeping politics of the Indians. It was a traditional piece, one that would have been at home on the opinion page of the *New York Times*, and marked his first major venture into political analysis.

The Inca political piece, along with the story of the nightclub shooting and the chatty letters, showed Hunter's versatility. He was building a strong portfolio, but the *Observer*'s inability to find a large audience kept his distinctive articles from reaching legions of readers. Within the world of Dow Jones and the serious news junkies, however, the *Observer*'s "roving South American correspondent" had made an impression.

Hunter's tenure in South America coincided with the era of the "Ugly American" from Eugene Burdick's novel of that name, which portrayed the negative American image in the Third World. Hunter saw much ugliness, though not just confined to his compatriots. He found his paradigm in the image of an unfeeling Briton firing golf balls from a rooftop apartment into the slums of the Colombian city below. In "Why Anti-Gringo Winds Often Blow South of the Border," a piece published at the end of his tenure below the equator, he began and ended his essay with that appalling image.

One of my most vivid memories of South America is that of a man with a golf club—a five iron, if memory serves—driving golf balls off a penthouse terrace in Cali, Colombia. He was a tall Britisher, and had what the British call "a stylish pot" instead of a waistline. Beside him on a small patio table was a long gin-and-tonic, which he refilled from time to time at the nearby bar.

He had a good swing, and each of his shots carried low and long out over the city. Where they fell, neither he nor I nor anyone else on the terrace that day had the vaguest idea. The penthouse, however, was in a residential section of Rio Cali, which runs through the middle of town. Somewhere below us, in the narrow streets that are lined by the white adobe blockhouses of urban peasantry, a strange hail was rattling on the roofs—golf balls, "old practice duds," so the Britisher told me, that were "hardly worth driving away."

Hunter's essay had some of the flavor of Graham Greene's novels of the era, such as *Our Man in Havana* or *A Burnt-out Case*. The piece powerfully showed the displaced American or Briton in conflict with another culture.

Down in South America, Hunter was largely unaware that he was part of a movement soon to be called New Journalism. Of all the major players in this loose-limbed movement, Hunter was the farthest removed. Most of the action was taking place in New York. "Hunter's stories were just different," Footlick said, "and this was the time when the so-called New Journalism was just beginning to happen. This was early, and it was just different. People just weren't used to it."

While Hunter chronicled the lives of drug smugglers in South America, Tom Wolfe, Gay Talese, and others were stretching the definitions of daily journalism in New York's major newspapers. They were all in competition, Wolfe said, to be the "best feature writer in town." Talese, a reporter for the *New York Times*, began writing features for *Esquire* that redefined the celebrity interview. Reading Talese's story about former heavyweight boxing champion Joe Louis, Wolfe was awakened to the possibilities of what could happen when journalism used the techniques of the fiction writer. Talese's account of a weekend with Joe Louis was undoubtedly true, yet it read like a short story. There was little exposition, but mostly a presentation of scene and sequel.

Wolfe was a reporter for the *New York Herald Tribune*. Having earned a doctorate in American studies from Yale and reported for the *Washington Post*, he had landed in the *Herald Tribune* newsroom in 1962 in the middle of the great feature-writing competition in New York. All the writers were out to prove that they were the best one in town. Most of them moonlighted and tried to pitch their articles to *Esquire*, which was publishing some of the most innovative nonfiction writing in the country. Wolfe wangled an assignment from the *Herald Tribune* to do a story on a car rally in California. He sold *Esquire*'s editors on the idea, giving them the assignment without the expense of funding the trip. Wolfe returned to California, wrote the piece for the *Herald Tribune*, but had a terrible time trying to write the *Esquire* piece:

> At first, I couldn't even write the story. I came back to New York and just sat around worrying over the thing. I had a lot of trouble analyzing what I had on my hands. By this time, *Esquire* practically had a gun at my head because they had a two-page color picture for the story locked into the printing presses and no story. Finally, I told Byron Dobell, the managing editor at *Esquire*, that I couldn't pull things together. O.K., he tells me, just type out my notes and send them over and he will get someone else to write it. So, about 8 o'clock that night I started typing notes out in the form of a memo that began, "Dear Byron." I started typing away, starting right with the first time I saw any custom cars in California. I just started recording it all, and inside of a couple of hours, typing along like a mad man, I could tell something was beginning to happen. By midnight, this memo to Byron was 20 pages long and I was still typing like a maniac. About 2 a.m. or something like that, I turned on WABC, a radio station that plays rock and roll music all night long, and I got a little more manic. I wrapped up the memo about 6:15 a.m., and by this time it was 49 pages long. I took it over to *Esquire* as soon as they opened up, about 9:30. About 4 p.m., I got a call from Byron Dobell. He told me they were striking out the "Dear Byron" at the top and running the rest of it in the magazine.

Thus Tom Wolfe found his style, in an article titled "There Goes (Varoom! Varoom!) That Kandy-Kolored (Thphhhhhh!) Tangerine-Flake Streamline Baby (Rahghhh!) Around the Bend (Bruuuuuuummmmmmm-mmmm)." Wolfe's entry into the competition signaled the beginning of the revolution in journalistic writing that would take place in the sixties. Wolfe became movement historian, citing Fielding and Dickens as major influences on the "New Journalism" (he hated the term) and making his claim that journalism would become the new art form of the era. As evidence, he noted John Hersey's *Hiroshima*, which documented the lives of six bomb survivors in the days after the blast, and Truman Capote's *The Muses Are Heard*, an account of an American troupe of *Porgy and Bess* on tour in the Soviet Union in the Cold War fifties.

Yet the New Journalism as a form can be best dated from the early sixties—with Talese, Wolfe, Jimmy Breslin, Terry Southern, Joan Didion, John Sack, Barbara Goldsmith, and George Plimpton in the forefront, and most of the major writers orbiting the *New York Herald Tribune* or the *New Yorker*. Eventually, Capote and Norman Mailer, both of whom were largely critical of journalists, ended up writing the nonfiction classics *In Cold Blood* and *The Armies of the Night*. There was no conspiracy . . . no club meetings . . . but everybody seemed to be up to something. Terry Southern, writing in *Esquire*, produced a wickedly funny piece about a baton-twirling competition at the University of Mississippi that—were the byline removed—someone could easily assume was written by the Hunter Thompson of a decade later. Like Hunter's writing, Southern's used the technique of making the process of getting the story into the meat of the story.

Hunter Thompson, who would become one of the major figures of New Journalism, was at a far distance from and to a large extent unaware of this new kind of nonfiction writing he was supposedly helping to define. While Wolfe, Talese, and the other big guns were flexing their muscles in *Esquire*, Hunter was thousands of miles away, on the front lines in South America for the *National Observer*.

The *Observer* wanted color, and it wanted dispatches from all over the world. Hunter's far-flung stories got elegant display, often on the front page, with their exotic tales of the strange and still-wild world of South America. Readers loved his stories of tin miners, drug smugglers, and jungle bandits. Hunter was making relatively good money and having a hell of a time, but even the good times got old.

Paul Semonin was studying in Ghana and contemplated coming to South America for a visit. Hunter warned him off. Most of the places he'd seen were "a pure dull hell and full of so many nagging discomforts that [he was] tempted at times to write this continent off as a lost cause." Semonin was a regular correspondent, and Hunter mocked him for his interest in the African people and culture, and his altruistic concern for minorities. He addressed Semonin in letters as "Nigger Boy" or "Spic."

"I never felt in some ways he got beyond his racial prejudice," Semonin said. "It was a gut thing with all of us, growing up in the South. We had that in our bones. He wrote me a letter when I was coming out of Africa and addressed it to me, 'Dear Nigger Boy.' He always chose those sorts of provocative leads on his letters. I had written him something about having met Malcolm X in Ghana and was very much interested in black national politics. But that ['Nigger Boy'] was just something that came out in a burst, but looking back I can see, underneath it, some kind of insensitivity."

He was moving with a faster crowd than he had in Middletown, or as a copyboy at *Time*. In Quito, Rio, and the other major cities, he was drawn to the visiting heavyweight correspondents from the major American and European newspapers and television networks. He drank with them and, on occasion, raised hell. While in Rio, Hunter became friends with Charles Kuralt, Latin American bureau chief for CBS News. Kuralt started out in newspapers in North Carolina and latched onto the network first as a writer and later, during the 1960 presidential campaign, as an on-air correspondent. He and Hunter remained friends and regular correspondents for the rest of their lives. "My greatest talent is in my ability to choose good friends," Hunter said of Kuralt years later. "It's about as important as things get."

During Hunter's stay in Rio, Hunter was arrested for shooting rats at the city dump with a .357 Magnum. In jail, he charmed the cops, who soon dropped the charges since Hunter had ditched the gun and there was no proof he had actually shot the rats. On the verge of release, Hunter leaned back in his chair and the bullets from the Magnum slipped from his pocket and clattered to the floor. It took intervention by the U.S. embassy to spring him from jail.

Empowered by Dow Jones, now that he was sitting at the grown-up correspondents table, he began parrying by mail with *Washington Post* publisher Philip Graham. He first ridiculed Graham for his comments on the *National Observer* in an article in *Newsweek* (which Graham also owned). Graham mocked the *Observer* for being a newspaper without reporters, but Hunter was quick to point out that he was the registered correspondent for the *Observer* in Rio and that neither the *Post* nor *Newsweek* had a correspondent there. "I'm beginning to think you're a phony, Graham," Hunter ended the letter. Graham took the bait, telling Hunter that he was late in coming to that "phony" conclusion, that many prominent Americans had held that belief for years. Graham asked Hunter to write and tell him about himself. Hunter rose to the occasion, and he and Graham began getting to know each other through the mail. (They never met. Graham invited Hunter to Washington when he returned to the states, but Graham was being treated in a mental hospital when Hunter finally returned. Hunter invited him to Florida, where they could meet at Sandy's mother's home. It remained a short, doomed correspondence. Graham killed himself in August 1963.)

Hunter settled—as much as he ever settled—in Rio, and Sandy flew down to surprise him. No woman, not even the maddeningly memorable Ann Frick, had ever had such a hold on him. He might have confronted another woman who had done something so audacious—*Who invited you to this party?*—but he took in Sandy, and they enjoyed the life on Copacabana Beach and now and then could delude themselves that they were merely another beautiful young American couple on vacation. She was the sort of woman his ego and single-mindedness demanded, and she was also much better than he deserved. But not long after she arrived, Hunter decided that it was time to leave.

"Rio was the end of the foreign correspondent's road," he said. "I found myself 25 years old, wearing a white suit, and rolling dice at the Domino Club—the foreign correspondent's club. And here I thought, 'Jesus Christ, what am I gonna do now?' Then, I would roll dice more and write less and worry about it until I'd have a nervous breakdown. It makes you change whatever you're doing."

Feeling what he called "a frenzy of patriotism," owing to President Kennedy, the Peace Corps, and a feeling of optimism about the country he loved, Hunter decided it was time to go home. Sandy flew to New York ahead of him, and then went on to Louisville, to meet Hunter's mother and his two brothers.

The staff of the *National Observer* had never laid eyes on Hunter when he showed up at the offices in the Washington suburb of Silver Spring, Maryland. In tropical shirt, aviator shades, shorts, and cigarette in a holder, he was out of place with the necktied *Observer* staff. Hunter said the editors met him like a visiting dignitary. "I came home as a man who'd been a star," he said. "All the editors met me and treated me as such."

The editors took him out for drinks at the Hay Adams, and arranged for him to speak at the National Press Club. Face-to-face, they recognized that their star writer was an oddball. Out of courtesy as much as anything else, Hunter was offered a cubicle job in the features section. "I offered to put him on the staff," editor Bill Giles said. "He clearly had a lot of talent. He wasn't interested. He wanted to go to San Francisco because in those days it was the place young people went." Ridley would have welcomed Hunter in his department. But others on the *Observer* breathed sighs of relief when Hunter said thanks but no thanks. He could best contribute to the *Observer* as a writer, and wanted to return to the West. His diabolical plan was to persuade Philip Graham to add the *National Observer* to his stable of publications and install Hunter Thompson as his editor. He never got a chance to present his idea to the publisher.

Chapter 6

STRANGER IN A STRANGE LAND

There is no human being within 500 miles to whom
I can communicate anything—much less the fear and
loathing that is on me after today's murder. . . .
I want to kill because I cannot talk.
—*HST, November 22, 1963*

I t was odd, being home. After a year on smuggler's boats and sleeping in
wooden huts, Hunter was back in Louisville, in his bedroom. He felt
strange.

He and Sandy were a beautiful young couple. When Hunter talked
about his ambitions, he sometimes wished he had taken the turn toward
conventional life, to be the insurance agent, like his father, whose primary goal in life was providing shelter for his family, doing the lives-of-
quiet-desperation thing.

But that wasn't in his genes. He got married to please his mother.
The idea of marriage came as a surprise to Sandy. They were staying at
Ransdell Avenue. Hunter came home and called to her upstairs and told
her to put on a skirt because they were going out. She dressed as well as
she could, considering she had her arm in a sling from a horseback riding
accident two days before.

It was May 19, 1963. They piled into the car, Hunter and Sandy in back, brothers Davison and Jim up front. Sandy wanted to know where they were going. "Jeffersonville, Indiana," Hunter announced matter-of-factly. *Why*, Sandy wanted to know. "Oh," Hunter shrugged, "to get married." Indiana allowed for quickie marriages and Kentucky did not.

Sandy passed the Thompson audition. Jim, by now a pre-teenager, was a fan of his new sister-in-law: "Sandy appealed to all of us because she seemed to be so direct, so down-to-earth, and honest. Very beautiful, too. I thought, 'She's a great person for Hunter. She'll probably settle him down.'"

Later, the marriage was consummated in the backseat of the car. For Hunter, the marriage "merely put the stamp of law on a worthy and time-tested relationship."

Hunter didn't care for his new mother-in-law, Leah Conklin, and hated Sandy's father—who had abandoned the family long before and whom Hunter never met. He wanted to be the most important person in Sandy's life and did not like competition. But he did not refuse Leah Conklin's wedding gift: a Rambler. Hunter immediately hatched a plan for a cross-country honeymoon, and set off first for a week at the Conklin home in Deland, Florida. As he unpacked his trunks and sifted through his notes, he was able to spin off a few more South American articles for the *Observer*. Some of his best South American writing, including his stories on the Incas and the lingering vestiges of colonialism, appeared after his return to the states. He did an *Observer* piece about a folk-music festival in Kentucky, reviewed several new novels, and concluded that American literature was in decline. The *Observer* also published his hilarious memoir "When the Thumb Was a Ticket to Adventures on the Highway," in which Hunter bragged that he held the record for hitchhiking in Bermuda shorts.

As the article appeared, Hunter and Sandy, now joined by Agar, drove cross-country. Their eventual destination was Las Vegas, where Hunter was credentialed by the *Observer* to cover the Sonny Liston–Floyd Patterson heavyweight fight on July 22, 1963. Liston knocked out Patterson in the first round, but Hunter did not file a story. It would not be the last time Hunter contracted to cover a fight and did not deliver.

Paul Semonin had returned from Africa and was back living in Aspen. He'd invited Hunter and Sandy to visit (the "living is easy," Semonin said by way of inducement). It was added to their itinerary, but a planned short stay turned into a longer residency.

Hunter and Sandy fell in love with Colorado, staying with Semonin for two months, before renting a ranch house about fifteen miles away, in the village of Woody Creek. "These Rockies make the Santa Lucias look like a public park," he wrote Jo Hudson, out in Big Sur. "Deer are big as hell around here. And Elk are fantastic."

The hunting, like the rest of life in Woody Creek, had Hunter sounding like a satisfied man. Had he bought into it, that 2.5-kid Rotarian American Dream? Sandy was soon pregnant, and in Woody Creek Hunter had found something he didn't realize was possible for him: contentment. He kicked around ideas for *Observer* pieces with Ridley, but balked at anything that would take him away from Sandy and Woody Creek for too long. "Christ," he wrote Ridley, "my life is genuine pleasure for the first time since I left Big Sur nearly two years ago. I have a dog, a woman, guns, whiskey, plenty of time to work and a [garbage] Disposall."

Though the Woody Creek rental was the first real home in two years, another move was hanging over his head. They had the place through the fall, but in December the rent was due to increase, and he and Sandy didn't want to leave.

To get more money, he needed more work, and that would mean he needed to do more than contributing book reviews to the *Observer*. "I'm in no position now to take a protracted tour," he pleaded to Ridley. "Sandy would border on a breakdown if I mentioned leaving for a month." Still, sitting at home was not his thing. He itched to get back into the fray.

Now that he was stateside, he saw the *National Observer* regularly and took pride in being part of the publication. His analysis of his time in South America had been published in an August issue of the *Observer* and after rereading his piece about six times, he said, "I feel like a writer again."

His homecoming had energized him, and he set aside fiction for a while. He toyed with the idea of writing a quasi-memoir of his time as a South American correspondent, with all of his articles included to bulk up the book. He thought of another nonfiction book, one to be drawn from a correspondent's tour of Mexico, which Ridley wanted him to do. After a piece on Aspen's skiing industry appeared in the *Observer,* he kicked to the curb a publisher's suggestion that he write a book on ski bums. He wanted to write nonfiction, but he wanted it to be significant nonfiction. "I have always looked at [journalism] as a way to get somebody else to pay for my continuing education," he said. The ski-bum story idea didn't impress him; it would be the journalistic equivalent of a one-liner.

America in the early 1960s was too interesting, he thought, and writing fiction seemed like self-indulgent literary masturbation. He had more or less decided to put aside writing novels for a while when President Kennedy's assassination on November 22, 1963, galvanized his resolve.

Hunter awoke to the news at Woody Creek and immediately responded as a journalist, going into Aspen to get some sense of people's reaction to the assassination. Angered by what he found—largely, unconcern—he poured his feelings into letters to Paul Semonin and William Kennedy. "I am trying to compose a reaction to the heinous, stinking, shit-filled thing that happened today," he wrote Semonin. "Now, President Johnson. Jesus. Mother. Fuck. Where do we go from here?"

To Bill Kennedy, now working part-time on a newspaper in Albany, New York, while writing fiction, he wrote, "I am afraid to sleep for fear of what I might learn when I wake up. There is no human being within 500 miles to whom I can communicate anything—much less the fear and loathing that is on me after today's murder. . . . I want to kill because I cannot talk."

Since he wanted to commit himself to journalism full-time, Hunter began to reconsider the *National Observer*'s offer of a desk job. He had also long admired the *Reporter*, a biweekly that was held in high regard by journalists. At the time, one scholar noted, it was "rated only behind *Time, U.S. News,* and *Newsweek* as the most referred to of all magazines used in [the] work of reporters." Getting published in the *Reporter* would get his work in front of the best in his business. Hunter approached correspondent Dwight Martin about getting on the small, prestigious staff. By way of audition, he did an analysis of race relations in his hometown, which he saw as part of a larger series of political profiles of American cities. While in Louisville for his wedding, he had talked to several people about the city's evolving race relations, and he now followed up with phone reporting and turned his observations into a piece on the city's racial problems ("A Southern City with Northern Problems"). Despite its subject—framed as a journey home—the piece was not personal in the way many of his *Observer* articles were; he simply contrasted the public stance of official Louisville with the resentment of the city's blacks, who said their reality clashed with the portrayal of race relations offered by the city's clerisy.

Despite Hunter's big plans and the by-mail rapport he developed with Martin, the regular, long-term relationship he'd hoped to develop with the *Reporter* didn't happen. A regime change forced out Martin, and by early 1964 he was gone. "*The Reporter* don't dig me at all no more," Hunter whined to Bill Kennedy.

The *National Observer* had launched his career, but Hunter had resisted signing any sort of exclusivity contract with the newspaper. With Sandy pregnant, he didn't rove much, but while they lived in Colorado, he wrote a score of pieces for the *Observer* that didn't require significant travel. He also began regularly contributing book reviews. He reviewed *A Singular Man*, by J. P. Donleavy, giving himself a chance to finally praise in print a writer who had so greatly influenced him.

Given a fairly free hand to pick his assignments and given the whole western half of the country to roam, Hunter chose to write about misfits and outcasts. He wrote about the leftover beatniks, frustrated miners, deer hunters, and Indian rights activists.

Hunter's articles in that period weren't known for their arresting openings. Classic opening paradigms, such as an arrogant golfer on a South American rooftop, did not present themselves. He worried that he had lost his way. Perhaps his muse had cashed the check and moved on. He often used pedestrian methods to begin his articles: asking questions or using blind quotes, which immediately raised the question of who was speaking. He wasn't writing breaking news for a traditional newspaper, and the leisurely way he built his stories was standard practice for magazine writing. Slow to build, Hunter often saved some of his best material for deep in the story.

His writing in many cases reverted to standard feature-writing techniques. The adventurousness and the wild tone of the South American articles are subdued. He did an article on Marlon Brando's attempt to help a group of Indians regain their fishing rights in Washington. Wipe off the byline, and it could easily be mistaken for an Associated Press dispatch for the Sunday features wire; good, but nothing noteworthy in its style.

It's no surprise that the best pieces were those which tugged at him emotionally. As a longtime admirer of Ernest Hemingway, his pilgrimage to Ketchum, Idaho, was nearly as much about Hunter as about its subject. The resulting piece was part travelogue, part literary criticism, and part elegy, as Hunter delivered a benediction on the writer-adventurer whose influence on his work was considerable: "Perhaps he found what he came here for, but the odds are huge that he didn't. He was an old, sick, and very troubled man, and the illusion of peace and contentment was not enough for him—not even when his friends came up from Cuba and played bullfight with him in the Tram. So finally, and for what he must have thought the best of reasons, he ended it with a shotgun."

Hunter had made the 700-mile trip from Aspen and was exhausted when he finally arrived at Hemingway's home. Given an opportunity to look through the house, his adolescent talent as a vandal reemerged, and he took a huge set of elk horns from above the entrance to the home. He stashed them in his car, keeping the horns for the rest of his life. "Forget running with the bulls or reeling in marlins or slaughtering rhinos," Hunter said years later. "I had Hemingway's horns, and with that came an immense literary responsibility. It was now 'Fuck you' to the competition. I had broken from the pack, and there was no turning back."

In the spring and with much reluctance, Hunter left the Woody Creek home and, with Sandy eights months pregnant, moved to Glen Ellen, California. It made sense for work. San Francisco, fount of oddball stories, was only fifty miles down Highway 101, across the Golden Gate Bridge. But after six months of near-paradise in Woody Creek, Hunter found it difficult to muster energy for another move.

He hauled a trailer through the mountains and the desert with the little Rambler. There, in the driveway, with his pregnant wife and all of his worldly belongings, he discovered that the owner of the home he arranged to rent had had a change of heart. Hunter found somewhere else to live—a shack, he called it—and plotted revenge on the reneging landlord. The voodoo knowledge he had picked up back in Puerto Rico might come in handy.

But he gave Glen Ellen a chance and took to referring to the home there as Owl House, perhaps in tribute to the idyllic Owl Country Club back home, to which he had escorted so many Louisville debutantes. Or maybe it was because Wolf House—Jack London's old home—was right across the street. That was one of the reasons he came to Glen Ellen in the first place. In any case, the action was heating up in the Bay Area (the Berkeley Free Speech Movement was in its early stages), and Glen Ellen was perfectly positioned for Hunter's excursions to San Francisco and Berkeley. "Berkeley, Hell's Angels, Kesey, blacks, hippies . . . I had these connections," Hunter said. "I was a crossroads for everything." But the trip from Colorado had nearly killed the Rambler, and Hunter was once again desperately in need of money and a reliable automobile.

In the casual atmosphere of Woody Creek, Hunter had quickly made friends and found bartenders and merchants willing to extend him credit. California was almost another country (he called it the Brazil of North America), and Glen Ellen wasn't very exciting (California was merely "Tulsa with a view"), so it was back to the old practice of pawning his belongings to make household ends meet.

He made friends with a local orthopedic surgeon named Bob Geiger, and when Hunter's landlord began snorting about evicting his crazy-writer tenant, Geiger and his wife took the Thompsons in as guests in their home in Sonoma. Geiger said Hunter was a pleasant but somewhat offbeat roommate. "He collected flies on flypaper and sent them off to the editor of *Time* magazine in New York," Geiger said. "Some grudge, I suppose." To create a balance of power and pedigree in the house, Hunter sent five bucks off to an ad he'd seen in the back pages of a magazine and received his mail-order doctor-of-divinity degree. He began referring to himself as *Dr. Thompson* and punctuated remarks with this afterword: "I am, after all, a doctor." Friends picked up on the joke, and he was "the Good Doctor" for the rest of his life. He frequently phoned Geiger's office just so he could leave a message that "Dr. Thompson called."

Hunter felt that a comeback was on its way, a tacit admission that he had lost his way as a writer since returning from South America. He claimed he had spent more time in South America defending his country than earning a living, but now, as he saw America becoming mired in Vietnam, he wondered whether he would still be able to mount such an impassioned defense.

"I can't speak the language here," he complained to Paul Semonin. He had found his voice as a writer, or so he had thought, south of the equator. He still thought of himself as a drifter, young and on the road, but when he opened his eyes, he saw his young wife and now, their son. Juan Fitzgerald Thompson was born on March 24, 1964. Hunter was about to turn twenty-seven. He had always planned to die by that age, yet here he was with a wife and a son. For the first time in his life, Hunter was a man with responsibilities. Being a husband and a father was more burden than joy in his precarious financial state.

He announced his son's birth to Semonin: "I have a son named Juan. Ten days old. Not a cent in the house and no cents coming in. I am seriously considering work as a laborer. They don't give scholarships to my type. Beyond that, I am deep in the grips of a professional collapse that worries me to the extent that I cannot do any work to cure it."

Hunter had an office in the *Wall Street Journal*'s San Francisco bureau, but couldn't bring himself to join the cubicle crowd. "I would wander in on off hours drunk and obviously on drugs, asking for my messages," Hunter recalled. "They liked me, but I was the Bull in the China shop." Being on the same continent as his editors might not be a good thing. After several serious story ideas were vetoed, a frustrated Hunter finally asked Ridley what the *Observer* wanted from him. Ridley suggested travel stories.

Friction between writer and editors had been building, and there had been a lot of arguing over his assignments. In South America, Hunter was, as an *Observer* headline had called him, "footloose." Now Hunter wanted to write about San Francisco. Much as he sometimes loathed the area, as a resident, he sensed that it would explode with news and cultural shifts in the next couple of years. He had a duty as a journalist to stay near the Bay Area, but felt isolated. "I am in the same condition here as I was in Woody Creek, only in less colorful and pleasant surroundings," he said. "I have no conversations except on chance meetings in San Francisco. Once a month at best."

He wanted to get closer to the action, so he moved his family to San Francisco at the end of the summer in 1964. They settled into a hundred-dollar-a-month apartment at 318 Parnassus, in the Haight-Ashbury neighborhood, two blocks away from Golden Gate Park and Kezar Stadium, home of the 49ers.

Pro football was vastly different in the 1960s. It had yet to become the mechanized big business that made it into an economic juggernaut. "I remember going to my first 49er game in 1965 with 15 beers in a plastic cooler and a Dr. Grabow pipe full of bad hash," Hunter wrote. "The 30,000 or so regulars were extremely heavy drinkers, and at least 10,000 of them were out there for no other reason except to get involved in serious violence."

Turned out that the Parnassus apartment would be prime seating for a cultural revolution. But the *Observer* wasn't interested in those sorts of stories. San Francisco was a little too weird for the typical elbow-patched English professor who read the *Observer*. Feeling at the end of the road as a journalist, Hunter wrote a letter to President Johnson—on stationery from the Holiday Inn in Pierre, South Dakota—offering his services as the next governor of American Samoa. Hunter told the president he was mainly concerned with finding a quiet place to rewrite *The Rum Diary*, which he had decided to enliven with an interracial sex scene that would shock readers. Instead of just tossing Hunter's letter into the oddball file, presidential assistant Larry O'Brien (later to head the Democratic National Party during Watergate days) wrote back, promising serious consideration. Hunter thought he had a realistic chance for the appointment.

The Republicans descended on San Francisco for the presidential nominating convention. Senator Barry Goldwater of Arizona headed the party's ticket and made his famous vow to the delegates: "Extremism in the defense of liberty is no vice." Hunter was on the convention floor for the *National Observer*. He recalled feeling afraid because he was the only person in the building not applauding and stamping his feet in approval of Goldwater. Elect Goldwater, Hunter thought, and there will be another American revolution.

Other members of the *Observer* staff came to report on the convention, and Hunter got very drunk—so drunk, in fact, that the editors sent a letter of reprimand. If he was going to represent the newspaper, he had to get his act together. Editor Bill Giles had faith that he would. "He always struck me as a very solid citizen."

Relations with the *Observer* were becoming strained, and things hadn't taking off at the *Reporter* either. On top of all that, Hunter had been dealing with house guests all summer, including his mother and thirteen-year-old brother, Jim. Other guests came, rang up huge long-distance phone bills, then left. He wanted to escape to American Samoa—and he did, in his fantasies. But when he came back to reality, he was another broke writer at a dead end.

Hunter tried driving a cab, but was fired. He lined up at five each morning in the Mission District with the vagrants and winos who earned booze money by handing out fliers for grocery stores. "I was the youngest and healthiest person there," he recalled, "but nobody would ever select me. I tried to get weird and rotten looking." Still, he was never picked. Donating blood brought in small change.

He kept trying the *Observer*, but whatever article Hunter proposed, the editors shot down. They wanted froth, he said, but he wanted to give them substance. He didn't want to be typecast as the California kook reporter. The strain between correspondent and newspaper grew intolerable. At the beginning of fall 1964, the quarrels became open warfare over a piece on the Free Speech Movement at the University of California at Berkeley. He wasn't telling the editors what they wanted to hear: that the student unrest was nothing more than a high-level tantrum by a bunch of spoiled rich kids.

Hunter sensed that it was something significant. What became the Free Speech Movement began when students returned from the South after taking part in the Mississippi Freedom Summer voter-registration drives. When students began setting up tables on campus to enlist participants for civil rights demonstrations, campus officials shut them down. Only the student chapters of the Republican and Democratic parties could stage membership drives on campus. All that fall, war raged between student protesters and university officials. Students borrowed a tactic from the civil rights movement and staged a sit-in at Sproul Hall, home of the administration.

"I saw it coming," Hunter said. "There was a great rumbling—you could feel it everywhere. It was wild, but Dow Jones was just too far away." Hunter was sent off to report on election day on the Idaho–Montana frontier. He got in some hunting, so the trip was not a total waste.

He was depressed. He pondered whether he wanted to get involved in political activism. The Berkeley crowd tugged at his conscience. Paul Semonin had become a committed Marxist, and he and Hunter exchanged impassioned letters, Semonin pushing Hunter toward radical politics. For the moment, Hunter stayed on the fence.

The *Observer* editors pushed Hunter toward something lightweight, and he tossed them the idea of a cross-country train trip. He planned the trip to coincide with the Christmas holidays, which meant Dow Jones would pay for his family trip to Louisville for Christmas. The *Observer* went for it, and he ran up a widescreen expense report. But after sixty-five hours on a train—hell for Hunter and his family—the *Observer* wasn't happy with the resulting story, which it deemed unusable.

In a way, the rail story (which he titled "Dr. Slow") was a prototype for what would become known as a Hunter Thompson story, minus the sex, drugs, and rock 'n' roll. Hunter came off as a man befuddled by even the slightest wrinkle in his travel itinerary and unable to cope with the simple realities of getting along with others. Part literary reflection, part mad-dog screed at the foibles of modern life, "Dr. Slow" was in the end a diary of an insane cross-country trip with club cars full of people whose sole purpose was making Hunter's life miserable. Infants howled like fiends, and annoyingly talkative fellow travelers made suicide more attractive with every jolt from the rails. All in all, it was a funny piece and in keeping with the sort of stories Hunter had been sending the *Observer* for the last couple of years.

But some members of the *Observer* staff were sharpening their knives. There had always been a faction on the staff that believed Hunter made up stories and quotes. It was nearly impossible to fact-check him when he was in a remote South American village, but closer to home, the office minions who disliked Hunter took their case to editor Bill Giles, an avowed Hunter fan.

"Some of the phrases sounded familiar," Giles said. "There was some discussion that it came from a writer who did the same sort of thing, going cross-country on trains, in the twenties." Though Giles did not find smoking-gun proof, there was enough of a staff rebellion that in the name of office harmony, he acquiesced and killed the piece. "There was an abrupt end," he said, to the *Observer*'s relationship with Hunter Thompson.

Hunter always told a different story about how he left the *Observer*. "My final reason for leaving was because I wrote this strongly positive review of [Tom] Wolfe's *Kandy-Kolored Tangerine-Flake Streamline Baby*. The feature editor killed it because of a grudge. I took the *Observer*'s letter and a copy of the review with a brutal letter about it all to Wolfe. I then copied that letter and sent it to the *Observer*. I had told Wolfe that the review had been killed for bitchy, personal reasons." (As Hunter explained to a friend, "Somebody on the *Observer*—in a reject position— had worked with Wolfe on the *Washington Post* and hated the air that he breathed.")

Dan Greene was on Cliff Ridley's feature desk at the *Observer* and recalled the hot Friday afternoon when an angry call came in from Hunter Thompson. "Cliff abruptly hangs up," Greene said, "grimly strides over to my desk, inhales through his trademark cigarette holder, dramatically clears his throat, and then declares, in a deep, theatrical baritone, 'I believe Hunter Thompson just called me a pig-fucker.'"

Hunter had been reading Wolfe's work and was jazzed by Wolfe's flashy prose, and the distinctive psychedelic Edwardian style that went along with it attracted a lot of attention. Wolfe was on television talk shows, featured in magazine articles, and becoming, by default, spokesman for this new kind of nonfiction writing called the New Journalism. Back in North America, Hunter had been reading Wolfe and Jimmy Breslin and Gay Talese and saw himself for the first time as part of the gang, even though everyone else seemed to be in New York while he was in a rattrap with a wife and a dog and a kid in California.

He'd written Wolfe a simple fan letter before, but when he sent the review, he was at ease and sure of himself. He wrote colleague to colleague. Wolfe wrote back immediately, wanting to see Hunter's work, and thus was their long-distance friendship born.

Whatever the cause, Hunter stopped working for the *Observer* by the summer of 1965. Before the *Observer* breakup, Hunter and his family had gone to Louisville for Christmas. They went on to New York, to see the McGarrs and other friends in the city. Hunter reunited with his old friend Charley Kuralt, who was becoming famous over at CBS News. Kuralt heard Hunter's tales of woe and lent him enough money to get the landlord and the electric company to back off. Kuralt and his wife, Petey, treated Hunter and Sandy to a night on the town, which was particularly important to Sandy, Hunter said, since she was stuck home most of the time, doing the devoted-wife-and-mother act.

Hunter had also hoped to hook up with Carey McWilliams, editor of the *Nation*. California fascinated Hunter and he thought McWilliams's 1939 book *Factories in the Field* best showed the Golden State's cruel underbelly for thousands of migrant workers. Hunter was also working on compiling his photographs for what he dreamed would be a book called *The Californians*. The outsiders in California culture fascinated Hunter, and after reading McWilliams's book, he thought he and the editor had a lot in common. McWilliams had written Hunter just before he left on the trip, mostly to say he admired his work in the *National Observer*, and sniffing around to see whether he might have something to submit to the *Nation*.

Hell, yes. Hunter was thirsting for new markets. He had been depressed, feeling that his writing career was dead, and trapped in a crumbling marriage with the *National Observer*. His other marriage wasn't so great either, and now he was a father on top of everything else. *Trapped*. It was a lot of stuff for a footloose malcontent to deal with. Life was uninspired, and he needed that letter from McWilliams as his kick in the ass.

The *Nation* wouldn't pay the kind of money he would get from *Playboy* or the *Saturday Evening Post*, but those magazines didn't seem interested in what Hunter wanted to write. The *Nation* was another story. It had a long and distinguished history as a liberal journal with a stellar roster of contributors. He respected McWilliams and admired the *Nation* for stirring up trouble. "The *Observer* has taken great pains to keep me doing harmless, nonpolitical stories and I am now casting around for other founts of cash," he wrote McWilliams. He tried to give McWilliams some idea of his desperate situation: "I am long past the point of simple poverty and well into a state of hysterical destitution."

Hunter peppered McWilliams with story ideas: the Free Speech Movement, a spin-off from the cross-country train trip, a screed on what he called the final collapse of the myth of San Francisco. He also pumped an idea from one of Sandy's many drudge feed-the-family jobs. She worked as a phone solicitor for a dance studio that instructed its employees to avoid interesting black people in the program. They hung up on "recognizably black" people. If they learned only after making their pitch that the sucker on the line was black, they had to back out of the deal gracefully.

Interesting, but not enough for McWilliams to want a story. He liked the Berkeley story, and Hunter would eventually publish his account of the Free Speech Movement in the *Nation* in late summer 1965. The magazine's liberal audience no doubt found Hunter's sympathetic account more palatable than the *Observer*'s more cautious copy editors would have. The article was prophetic in its speculation about where the students would go and the scope of the movement they were inspiring.

But it was an idea that came *from* McWilliams, the suggestion that Hunter look into the story of an outlaw motorcycle gang, that piqued Hunter's interest. The story changed the trajectory of his life.

Chapter 7

AMONG THE ANGELS

I'm 27, married, one child, broke, holder of many pawn tickets,
fighting eviction, etc. I guess you've heard the story before.
—HST, *applying for a grant in 1965*

Twenty-seven. Hunter had always thought he would die at twenty-
seven. He was obsessed with death and wrote about it all of his life,
thinking about his own and how it would come. It would be "vehicular, of course," he said. He even had the place in mind. When he had been
stationed at Eglin Air Force Base and drove home to Louisville or up to
Illinois to see Kraig Juenger, he roared up U.S. 31, through the middle of
Alabama, and around Iron Mountain. On those long, solitary drives, he idly
wondered what it would be like to go straight, to not turn the wheel and
follow the contour of the road. He would "come down that mountain road
at a hundred and twenty and just keep going straight right there, burst out
through the barrier and hang out above all that . . . and there I'd be, sitting
in the front seat, stark naked, with a case of whiskey next to me, and a case
of dynamite in the trunk . . . honking the horn, and the lights on, and just sit
there in space for an instant, a human bomb, and fall down into that mess
of steel mills. It'd be a tremendous goddam explosion."

His time in California changed the texture of his death fantasy. Maybe it wouldn't be in a car . . . maybe instead—a motorcycle . . . *yes*, that's more dramatic. "I think that's the way to go out, running the Big Sur highway on a big cycle with no lights and keep turning it over until the engine goes off in a wild scream and on one of the curves you keep going straight over, then turn on the headlight for the surf, and hold tight."

To his friend Paul Semonin, he was more explicit. "Suicide (is) the only logical human act," Hunter wrote.

As he wrote to a friend in 1965, "The one thing I insist on is that I can't be croaked, except when I give the word."

Hunter Thompson wrote suicide notes all his life.

"In 1965 Hunter was living in San Francisco," Carey McWilliams wrote in his autobiography, "having decided, as he put it . . . 'to fuck journalism' and was dead broke at the time. Then one day he got a query from me enclosing a report of the California Attorney General's office on motorcycle gangs and an offer of a hundred dollars for an article. I felt sure the subject would intrigue him."

McWilliams began working for the *Nation* in 1951. The magazine was the stalwart voice of American progressivism. Its roster of contributors included Albert Einstein, Martin Luther King Jr., Gore Vidal, Langston Hughes, Leon Trotsky, I. F. Stone, and Jean-Paul Sartre. McWilliams became editor in 1955, and in his twenty-year stewardship the magazine resumed its place as an important American publication, presenting the philosophy of the New Left to a mainstream audience. In 1965, he invited Hunter Thompson to become a contributor.

Motorcycle gangs were big news in 1965, and the California attorney general, Thomas Lynch, commissioned a report to look into the problem. Many blamed the mess on Marlon Brando, who glorified gangs when he starred in *The Wild One*, a 1953 feature that contributed to Brando's iconic status, from the opening scene in which he leads his fellow cyclists, like killer bees, into an unsuspecting small town. The film was based on a 1947 incident in Hollister, California, in which a motorcycle gang terrorized residents. Now that film seemed quaint compared with the descriptions of depravity in the news stories about the Hell's Angels.

Hunter latched onto the story immediately. He made a few calls and found that the minions who had put together the report (called the Lynch

Report) hadn't even spoken to any members of the motorcycle club. All the sources were cops.

"This one is right up my alley," Hunter assured McWilliams.

Hunter immediately made connections with the Angels. Several magazines had run stories filled with leather, chains, beer, and gang rapes, and, again, most of the sources were cops. No one had really talked to any members of the motorcycle club. "I can't imagine doing a story without their point of view," Hunter told McWilliams.

Hunter learned that *San Francisco Chronicle* reporter Birney Jarvis had once been a member of the Hell's Angels—and still was, in a way. Once an Angel, always an Angel, even if you have a real job. Jarvis liked Hunter and offered to introduce him to the gang.

They met at the DePau Hotel Bar, near the docks, around midnight on March 26. Hunter introduced himself: "Look, you guys don't know me, I don't know you. I heard some bad things about you. Are they true?" Despite Hunter's sport coat and wing tips (still trying to look the part of a respectable Dow Jones journalist), the Angels liked the novelty of a writer with the balls to talk to them.

"I recall some hairy moments," Hunter said. "There was talk of setting me on fire and whipping my head with chains. They wanted to teach the press a lesson and I was the only journalist they had access to. After much drinking and shouting, I convinced them that the *Nation* didn't share the same prejudices as *Time* and *Newsweek*, and that any article I wrote would be based on my own experience and not on rabid police reports."

Massive amounts of alcohol brought them all to the same level. "They were a bit off-balance at first," Hunter recalled, "but after about 50 or 60 beers, we found a common ground, as it were. Crazies always recognize each other."

When the bar closed, Hunter invited several Angels—including Frenchy, Filthy Phil, and Ping-Pong—back to his apartment, to continue the drinkfest. Hunter splurged on a case of beer and some cheap wine, while Sandy huddled with baby Juan in the bedroom. Hunter and the Angels did the ritual dance of acquaintance in the living room with *The Freewheelin' Bob Dylan* as background music. The Angels stayed, drinking and talking with Hunter, until dawn. "My wife was very pretty and very vulnerable when the Angels came over," Hunter said. "Things went well for the most part, but I recognized that they could go next door and kill somebody."

It was a ceremony frequently repeated. Within a week of McWilliams's letter, Hunter was regularly staying up all night with the Angels. For the price of beer and wine, Hunter was getting enough material to make five stories. He already realized what a bargain McWilliams would get for the *Nation*'s hundred dollars.

A couple of days after getting the assignment, Hunter met Hell's Angels leader Ralph "Sonny" Barger. Although he wasn't the club founder, Barger symbolized the Angels to the rest of America. After leaving the military in 1956, he had returned home to Oakland and faced a Robert Frost sort of crossroads: go this way and become a beatnik, go this way and become a motorcycle rider. Barger always said he made the right choice, since the beatniks faded into the hippies and the hippies just faded away.

"I don't think we're rebelling against anything," Barger said. "All we're doing is trying to live our lives, ride our motorcycles and have fun. When people try to stop us, we react to whatever is happening at the time."

Hunter first met Barger at the Box Shop, a garage owned by Frenchy. They circled each other for a bit and slowly began to develop a relationship. Barger was intelligent and literate and backed up arguments with evidence, not just force. He was not immediately impressed with Hunter, whom he regarded as a hillbilly. Still, he respected Hunter for having the courage to come face-to-face with the Angels, and he gave him his consent for the piece.

"Sonny was a very powerful leader, charismatic in a quiet way," Hunter said. "We weren't friends, but there was a mutual respect that he acknowledged. We made our peace with each other."

Barger spent a lot of time with Hunter in the weeks he wrote the *Nation* piece. "He acted like a tough guy," Barger recalled. "If we were over at his house, he would shoot his guns out the window." Barger remembered Sandy Thompson as "a nice lady," kind of fidgety and quiet, but polite to the Angels.

The article was done within a month and held the press accounts and the Lynch Report up to reality. *The press says this . . . observation says this*. Hunter kept the story on point, refuting some charges against the Angels, confirming others. "The Motorcycle Gangs: Losers and Outsiders," appeared in the *Nation* on May 17, 1965. Hunter spoke with the voice of authority and always liked to work in shots at the boys in the mainstream press:

We were talking across a pool table about the rash of publicity and how it had affected the Angel's activities. I was trying to explain to him that the bulk of the press in this country has such a vested interest in the status quo that it can't afford to do much honest probing at the roots, for fear of what they might find.

"Oh, I don't know," he said. "Of course I don't like to read all this bullshit because it brings the heat down on us, but since we got famous we've had more rich fags and sex-hungry women come looking for us than we ever had before. Hell, these days we have more action than we can handle."

Elsewhere in the piece, Hunter took another swipe at the straight press: "The difference between the Hell's Angels in the papers and the Hell's Angels for real is enough to make a man wonder what newsprint is for."

Hunter spent so much time around the Angels that for storytelling convenience, he put together quotes from the voice of a collective Angel, a technique Tom Wolfe explored several years later when he developed the "Astronauts' Collective Unspoken," as the communal voice in his "Post-Orbital Remorse" articles in *Rolling Stone*, which formed the genesis of *The Right Stuff*. Hunter created the collective voice of the motorcycle thugs:

This, in effect, was what the Hell's Angels had been saying all along. Here is their version of what happened, as told by several who were there:

"One girl was white and pregnant, the other was colored, and they were with five colored studs. They hung around our bar— Nick's Place on Del Monte Avenue—for about three hours Saturday night, drinking and talking with our riders, then they came out to the beach with us—them and their five boyfriends. Everybody was standing around the fire, drinking wine, and some of the guys were talking to them—hustling 'em, naturally—and soon somebody asked the two chicks if they wanted to be turned on—you know, did they want to smoke some pot? They said yeah, and then they walked off with some of the guys to the dunes. The spade went with a few guys and then she wanted to quit, but the pregnant one was really hot to trot; the first four or five guys she was really dragging into her arms, but after that she cooled off, too. By this time, though, one of their boy friends had got scared and gone for the cops—and that's all it was."

Rather than dignify peripheral characters with names and perhaps slow down the whoosh of his narrative, Hunter seized on a figure's characteristic or habit and used it as his name, "Burr head" being one example. Hunter also would occasionally fly into fantasy, as he imagined scenes that never occurred, much as he might have wanted them to.

McWilliams was pleased with Hunter's article, but after the motorcycle gang story and the piece on the Free Speech Movement, Hunter was done with the *Nation* and its hundred-dollar fees. McWilliams could comfort himself saying the Angels article was "a good but by no means exceptional *Nation* story; we also published, for example, James Baldwin's first published piece."

Within a week of the article's appearance, the mailbox at 318 Parnassus Avenue was jammed with seven book offers. The publishers would have called, but Hunter's phone had been disconnected for nonpayment. Hunter was flabbergasted. As he often said, he would have written the definitive text on hammerhead sharks "and gone swimming with the bastards" for money.

In some cases, the publisher's concept was larger in scope and might require a lot of conceptualizing from Hunter before the money landed in his bank account. Angus Cameron at Alfred A. Knopf saw the Angels as part of an epic story of American "fringe types" in the sixties. Hunter already liked him; Cameron had been the only editor to offer constructive criticism when rejecting *Prince Jellyfish* years before.

Other publishers wanted the usual: book prospectus and sample chapter. The letters were encouraging, but vague when it came to the sort of information Hunter wanted: How much do I get? Hunter followed Dr. Johnson's credo: "No man but a blockhead ever wrote except for money."

Ballantine Books, a paperback imprint of Random House, offered real money. *Sign now*, editor Bernard Shir-Cliff said, *and we'll send you $1,500 immediately*. That was a year's income in Hunter's world. He agreed, got the check, and instantly paid two months rent in advance, then started eyeing motorcycles. If he was going to hang with the Angels, he needed a bike and he wanted the fastest one available: a BSA 650 Lightning. The

Angels weren't known for being faithful, but they never cheated on their Harleys. The BSA did nothing to endear Hunter to the motorcycle gang, but he didn't care.

He was thrilled. At last someone was paying him good money to write a book. He spat back at the editors and agents who had shunned him and reveled in the fact that after eight years of trying, he was finally fairly compensated for his work. He was getting his foot in the door as a Man of Letters, and even though it was in the low-rent form of journalism, that was something. He broke the news to Angus Cameron at Knopf that he had taken the quick money from Ballantine. It *was* Knopf, so Hunter wanted to explain his decision and keep the door open to the prestigious publisher. He still wanted to be a novelist, after all.

"Fiction is a bridge to truth that journalism can't reach," Hunter wrote Cameron. "Facts are lies when they're added up, and the only kind of journalism I can pay much attention to is something like [George Orwell's] *Down and Out in Paris and London*." After tipping his hat to Tom Wolfe's breakthrough articles in *Esquire*, he said, "In order to write that kind of punch-out stuff, you have to add up the facts in your own fuzzy way, and to hell with the hired swine who use adding machines."

The letter to Cameron laid out the approach Hunter used as he began his book: Do the claims of the cops in the Lynch Report have any relationship to the truth? As Edward R. Murrow had done on television with Senator Joe McCarthy a decade before, Hunter planned to duplicate the method he had used in his article: trot out charges, then confirm or refute them.

But that wasn't all he had done in the article. While Hunter had been a strong and forceful presence in the article, he would be even more center stage in the book—a reference point for readers who might not be able to identify with the rowdy, beer-drenched, oil-stained bikers. To write this book, Hunter knew, he would have to become a participatory journalist.

Journalism had been taking itself much too seriously. Since colleges had begun cranking up journalism schools early in the twentieth century, the idea of objectivity had been pounded into the skulls of the students. *Print both sides. Keep out of it. Be fair and objective* . . . the usual drill.

Sometimes, the so-called objectivity didn't work. The battle between Murrow and McCarthy on TV in 1954 was an obvious example. A U.S. senator was running amuck, recklessly tarring people as Communists. He became a fear-mongering firebrand in the early fifties, fertilizing America's already thick postwar paranoia about Commies, nuclear weapons, and the anarchists next door. McCarthy was a creation of the press. All he did was figure out how to manipulate this supposedly objective new animal. He timed his news conferences to match press deadlines, so that his charges—that Humpty Dumpty, let's say, was a dirty, stinking Commie son of a bitch—would make it into the paper but that Humpty Dumpty's denial would have to wait until the next day, when it would be buried in the D section.

Murrow recognized McCarthy's shrewdness and realized that this supposedly new professional approach of modern journalism—objectivity—could easily be manipulated by monsters. On his *See It Now* broadcast of March 9, 1954, Murrow had merely caught the senator in a few lies and pointed out his methods.

Still, a decade later, the titans of American journalism and those teaching in the colleges brayed about impartiality and objectivity. Hunter thought it was hogwash. To write this story, he had to be part of the story.

He went back to the Angels and told them he needed to hang out with them some more for his book. The Angels didn't mind. Many of them had read his piece and admired it. Sure, it was called "Losers and Outsiders," not exactly flattering, but the piece *had* been honest. The club was drawing even more press attention now, from the likes of the *Saturday Evening Post* and *Life*, and *those* reporters still didn't have the decency to come drink with them. Drinking was part of the deal. Hunter promised to buy a keg.

"The club agreed to let him write the book," Barger recalled, "and then it was sort of decided the payment would be a keg of beer. It was a joke. We didn't want his money. All we wanted him to do was write this book." Barger was of the P. T. Barnum school of publicity (any being good), but he also recognized that Hunter's article was simply better written than anything else he'd read on his club. If he was going to cooperate with a writer, it might as well be one with talent.

"I think that the majority of the people really, really got along with him," Barger said. "He was trying to use us—not in the sense that he was trying to take advantage of us. He was trying to use us to make a living. A guy doesn't just come up and say, 'Hey, let me write a book about you,' for the fun of it."

Hunter had the BSA, but the Angels tried to talk him into getting a stripped-down Harley. They even brought a few by his apartment for him to road test. Hunter's neighbors complained about the way the Angels parked their bikes all over the sidewalk. They didn't mind the Angels' partying or the occasional gunshots out the window, but parking, then as now, was critical to San Franciscans.

When Hunter stuck by the BSA, the gang made it clear he wouldn't be welcome on the asphalt with them. Fine, Hunter said. He didn't want to go underground and *be* a Hell's Angel. He just wanted to be *with* them. So he didn't wear the leather jacket or the Angels "colors." He wore jeans and a sport shirt, and while they roared ahead in their Harleys, he followed in his 1959 Rambler Custom.

Hunter's old friend Paul Semonin came for a visit, and Hunter brought him to Sonny Barger's birthday party. "I felt so out of my element, I could hardly drink my beer," Semonin said. "It was like being in a room of Hunter Thompsons."

Life at home was difficult for Sandy and Juan. "Here we are—we're in San Francisco, Juan is an infant, the Angels are sometimes coming over to the house, the apartment, and Hunter sometimes is going out to the bars," Sandy said. Although she was married, she was a single parent.

Sandy maintained the house, tiptoeing around until three o'clock in the afternoon, Hunter's usual waking hour. Keeping a toddler quiet most of the day was hard. If she didn't, she might get slapped. She did her best to make their half of the two-story house in the Haight into a home. When Anne Willis visited from Louisville, she helped Sandy paint the kitchen pink. When Hunter saw it, he was furious. "He didn't like anything with a feminine touch," Willis said. "He had a lamp base that had three elk legs on it, fur rugs and all this crazy stuff. But let Sandy put in one lacy curtain or paint the kitchen pink—he was so mad about that kitchen. . . . It was a constant struggle. They had no money, they had no rent." Sandy fed the family by enlisting friends to help her shoplift. They'd take the baby to the grocery, buy a couple cans of soup, and sneak out steaks in their overcoats. Sandy made it her mission to keep Hunter's life worry-free. Juan might go without milk, but his father blithely ordered shirts from the Pendleton catalog.

Meanwhile, Hunter was becoming the point man for the Angels. While doing a *Saturday Evening Post* story on the gang, journalist William Murray got to know Hunter. Usually collegial with fellow reporters and willing to share information and contacts, Hunter gravitated toward Murray, even though there could be no stronger representative of the establishment press Hunter despised than the *Saturday Evening Post*. Murray had no interest in entering into the manhood dance with the Angels. He wanted a respectful distance. He said Hunter became something of a para-Angel and even shot a hole through the wall of his apartment in an effort to impress the Angels. "But they stomped him anyway."

Hunter's benevolent landlord from Sonoma, Dr. Bob Geiger, came down to San Francisco nearly every night to read and comment on Hunter's manuscript. He liked what he was reading, but questioned the content. "Hunter, why are you writing about these losers?" Geiger asked. "These guys are crazies—you're glorifying them and they're nothing." Hunter just shrugged and said, "This is the way society is going."

A lot of crazies were ending up in the Bay Area. San Francisco was America's prime Bohemia. Almost a republic unto itself, it had always rolled in its cultural niche and flowered into public consciousness with the beatniks and now the hippies. Hippies from Des Moines and Cincinnati and points beyond began to march toward San Francisco, and Bay Area rock became a huge force in youth culture. Hunter loved the bands: the Warlocks (later the Grateful Dead), Big Brother, and, perhaps more than any other band, Jefferson Airplane. He loved the venues the bands played, especially the Matrix, and witnessed the scene from the sidelines as a benign older brother who shared intoxicants with kids. Hair was a line of demarcation then, and Hunter had little of it. Still, the hippies got over the fact that the tall, balding guy looked like a narcotics agent and learned to embrace Hunter's inner weirdo. When his old buddy Gene McGarr visited from New York, they hit the Matrix. Everywhere they went, McGarr said, there was someone else who seemed to be Hunter's best buddy. Hunter traveled with equal ease through the psychedelic tie-dyed hippie world and the leather milieu of the Angels.

Though Hunter downplayed his role in the affair, Hunter was instrumental in bringing two strains of fringe culture together: Hell's Angels and the hippies. Hunter admired Ken Kesey, author of *One Flew Over the Cuckoo's Nest* (1962) and *Sometimes a Great Notion* (1964). Since taking his first few bites out of *Cuckoo's Nest*, Hunter had pegged Kesey as perhaps the best writer of his generation. He'd met the author, who presided Buddha-like over a conclave of oddballs down the coast in La Honda. These Merry Pranksters were patient zero for the species *hippie*—generally quiet and gentle folk who ate LSD the way the rest of us eat potato chips. To celebrate the publication of his second book, Kesey and the Pranksters took their psychedelic Day-Glo school bus cross-country in the summer of 1964, with motor-mouth Neal Cassady (Dean Moriarty of Kerouac's *On the Road*) at the wheel. It was a coast-to-coast freak-out and a defining moment in the birth of the sixties counterculture.

Hunter naturally gravitated toward Kesey. They had much in common: writing, alcohol, and drugs. He had been having a few beers with Kesey during one of the author's regular trips to the city, when Hunter mentioned that he had to go over to the Box Shop to meet up with a couple of the Angels. Would Kesey like to come along?

Never one to pass up a good time, Kesey met half a dozen Angels, who were bent over their bikes, doing their best to make them into even badder ass machines. The Angels could be tough on outsiders. They tested people on first meetings and kept their group pretty much a closed society. But Kesey was different. He was a big, brawny guy, a former athlete from his University of Oregon days in the midfifties, and he had the confidence to match his muscle. The Angels liked him right away. He became their new pal.

Kesey was hospitable, and his party hosting was revered among his friends. Only natural, then, that he invite the Angels back home. He planned a party of bacchanalian proportions for the first weekend of August 1965 at his La Honda compound. He even strung a banner across the entrance to his property: "THE MERRY PRANKSTERS WELCOME THE HELL'S ANGELS." The cops who dogged the Angels watched from the highway as the Angels and their end-of-the-universe-loud chopped hogs entered the hippie paradise.

"It was a horrible, momentous meeting," Hunter recalled, "and I thought I'd better be there to see what happened when all this incredible chemistry came together. And, sure as shit, the Angels rolled in—about 40 or 50 bikes—and Kesey and the other people were offering them acid. And I thought, 'Great creeping Jesus, what's going to happen now?'"

Hunter watched the gentle Pranksters opening their arms to the Angels and handing out tabs of LSD. The drug was still legal then, but Hunter hadn't tried it. Friends had warned him. They said his violent tendencies would come out in full force and things could turn dangerous.

Hunter saw himself as a puppy dog compared with the Angels, and here they were, gobbling acid like jelly beans. The Angels were strictly beer-and-pills people, and Hunter feared what sort of ugliness would descend on the passive denizens of La Honda when the acid kicked in the Angels' collective brain.

The only way to deal with it, Hunter reasoned, was to get "as fucked up as possible." He had brought Sandy and Juan along, but nevertheless decided it was time to experiment with the drug. He took 800 milligrams, and the dose "almost blew [his] head off, but in a very fine way." He was startled by his reaction. "I went completely out of my head and I had a wonderful time, didn't bother a soul."

Thus began Hunter's love affair with acid. "I'd heard all these stories when I lived in Big Sur a couple of years before from this psychiatrist who'd taken the stuff and wound up running naked through the streets of Palo Alto, screaming that he wanted to be punished for his crimes. He didn't know what his crimes were and nobody else did either, so they took him away and he spent a long time in a loony bin somewhere, and I thought, 'That's not what I need.' Because if a guy who seems level-headed like that is going to flip out and tear off his clothes and beg the citizens to punish him, what the hell might I do?"

Turns out . . . *nothing*. "I've gone to the bottom of the well," Hunter said, "and the animal's not down there." Hunter—and also the Angels, for the most part—had a fairly peaceful time at La Honda, as long as you forget about the gang rape.

After a few hours in the company of lysergic acid diethylamide, one young blond woman announced she would sexually accommodate three of the Angels. They went to a building called the backhouse on the Pranksters' compound, and she began servicing the men. Then came the audience and everyone wanted a turn. It was more than the woman had bargained for, but she went along with it. There was no tying down, no threats of life, but the gang thing was *not* her idea. The woman was a guest of Kesey's, and so was her ex-husband, who was then invited into the backhouse, at first to watch, then to participate. As he prepared to enter her, she begged him to kiss her. The Angels cheered.

The Hunter-arranged meeting between the Pranksters and the Angels was the first of many such gatherings. When Kesey asked Hunter to broker the deal, Hunter was at first horrified. "You motherfucking, crazy bastard," Hunter told Kesey. "You'll pay for this from Maine to here." Hunter imagined a horrific confrontation. "I thought they [the Angels] would take the Pranksters apart like cooked chicken. I had been to La Honda and knew they were a gang of innocents playing with fire."

The neighbors in La Honda were nervous, and local police patrolled the periphery of the property, once picking up Hunter and his traveling companion for the day, poet Allen Ginsberg. Hunter was becoming the social secretary for the Angels. When someone wanted to hang with the motorcycle gang, they called Hunter. Ginsberg wasn't above that and was eventually so moved he wrote an ode to his hairy brethren.

Other editors came calling: *Playboy* wanted Hunter to write about the Angels, and so did the *Stanford Literary Review*. Soon he was the leading authority on the motorcycle gang. He still spun off other articles now and then; finally, his piece on the Free Speech Movement was in the *Nation*, and an article on Big Sur broke in a new market for him, *Pageant*, a *Reader's Digest*–sized general-interest magazine.

But the Angels book obsessed him from mid-1965 until the book's publication in February 1967. Shir-Cliff, his editor, pitched it to sister imprint Random House for a hardcover edition. "It had a lot of juice," Shir-Cliff said. Hunter was sending the book in thirty- or sixty-page installments, on faded copy paper. "I would read it immediately and send back a letter, usually of praise. The stuff that was coming in was a little disorganized, but I could see what was going on, and I liked what I saw."

Random House agreed the book should be published first in hardcover. Editor Jim Silberman took over from Shir-Cliff, and Hunter was exuberant. Now he wasn't just writing a cheap paperback. He was in the big time. The additional money from Random House was a bonus.

Sonny Barger said that although Hunter had a bad-ass image, in reality he was all hat and no cattle. "If anything ever happened, he wasn't there to back it up," Barger said, "When we got in the thing with the cops at Bass Lake, he jumped in the trunk of his car. When the stuff happened at Squaw Rock, he didn't even try to defend himself. He was like the average guy you would see in a bar today. They get in there and they *ra ra* and they *MF* everybody, and then somebody hits them in the nose and they run to the cops and say, 'I don't even know why they hit me.'"

But Hunter felt he could run with the Angels and be a tough guy. "By the time I started *Hell's Angels*," Hunter told George Plimpton a quarter century later, "I was riding with them and it was clear that it was no longer possible for me to go back and live within the law."

For the first six months he worked on the book, Hunter was the methodical reporter, gathering information, writing an anthropological study of the Angels along the lines of Eleanor Smith Bowen's observations of the tribes of northern Nigeria. Then, with deadline looming, Hunter panicked. He thought if he didn't make deadline, he would have to pay back the advance to Random House. So he said goodbye to Sandy and Juan and drove down Highway 101 until he found a small motel near Monterey. He moved in with his IBM Selectric, his uppers, and his Wild Turkey, and wrote the second half of the book in four days, fueled by radio rock 'n' roll and McDonald's hamburgers. He wrote for one hundred straight hours without sleep and made his March 1 deadline. Unlike the other big books of the sixties, such as *The Electric Kool-Aid Acid Test*, which Tom Wolfe wrote in a cabin in Virginia, Hunter's *Hell's Angels* was the only book lived and primarily composed in the belly of the counterculture, smack dab in the middle of the social revolution at the corner of Haight and Ashbury.

The seam in the middle of the book isn't hard to find. The first half is crisp, literate, at times nearly academic. Then comes his account of the Fourth of July Angels run to Bass Lake, and he is less the crusty observer and more of the in-your-face participant.

He ended the manuscript with an elegiac piece he would later spin off under the title "Midnight on the Coast Highway." After two-hundred-plus pages about the Angels, he put himself at center stage for the finale, riding his motorcycle along the writhing road at night, no lights and no helmet, presenting himself as the quintessential man on the edge. His former editor Bill Giles at the *National Observer* read that and forgot what a trial Hunter had been. "It was fantastic," Giles said. "That was Hunter Thompson at his best for my money."

Hunter said he wrote the passage immediately after taking the ride. As he remembered it, "My face was still almost frozen, dark red and crusted with tears, not from crying but tears that start coming to your eyes just from the wind. I was so high on that—from coming back—that I sat and wrote the whole thing, right through, and never changed a word of it. It's one of my favorite pieces of writing."

With the manuscript done and in Silberman's hands in New York, Hunter was getting ready for the cranking of the publicity machine, ready to reap the benefits of being a published author. Silberman saw the book as being about more than just a gang of misfits on motorcycles; it explored a major fissure in society between the haves and the never-will-haves. Hunter wrote Norman Mailer, with whom he'd had an odd drunken correspondence for a few years, that he'd appreciate good comments on the book, to help spur sales. "It's a frontal assault on everybody involved or even implicated," Hunter wrote Mailer. "Mainly the press. And the cops. I'm looking for some action when it comes out." Mailer's ventures into journalism had inspired Hunter. As historian Douglas Brinkley said, "Hunter felt that Mailer chopped the wood for him and Tom Wolfe to carve."

To his mother, he wrote another note about his nocturnal life at the kitchen table "beating these rotten keys," and filled with hope at the possibilities of *Hell's Angels.* He'd been evicted from Parnassus Avenue because the neighbors finally got sick of the Hell's Angels visits, and the family was squatting at another apartment two blocks away on Grattan Street. Money was always tight, if there was any. There were also other issues, some related to Hunter's newfound infatuation with LSD. Juan discovered daddy's hiding place for his tabs of acid: tin-foil bundles in the refrigerator. Sandy discovered the LSD in her son's hands before he'd been able to ingest any of the drug. "I shook him and I said, 'Did you take these?' He was too little to know what that meant. I opened the foil and the pills were all there. That was a fright."

Hunter depended on Sandy and his network of friends to keep his head above water. Indeed, when it came time to dedicate the book, he passed over his mother, his late father, Sandy, and Juan. "To my friends who lent me money," he wrote, "and kept me mercifully unemployed. No writer can function without them." But financial hope sprang eternal: "If the book goes big, in hardback as well as paper," he wrote his mother, "I'll be able to relax for a while."

Random House sent Hunter a proof of the book's cover, which he didn't like. "I told Random House, 'You fucking pigs, I'll go out and photograph it myself,'" he told P. J. O'Rourke twenty years later. "I was showing the Angels the cover and it said $4.95—whew, $4.95, that must have been a long time ago. And the Angels said, 'Jesus, $4.95! What's our share? We should get half.' And I said, 'Come on.' I was getting a little careless, you see. I said, 'It takes a long time to write a book. *Nothing*—that's your share.'"

On that day, talking to P. J. O'Rourke, he said it was money that brought about the end with the Angels. On another day, he said the fight started because he was preaching the superiority of his BSA to a Harley-worshipping Angel. On another day, talking to Craig Vetter of *Playboy*, he said it was because he witnessed an Angel named Junkie George (real name: George Zahn) mistreat his girlfriend and then his dog.

As Sonny Barger recalled in his memoir, *Hell's Angel*, "Junkie George got into an argument with his old lady and slapped her. Hey, it happens. Then George's own dog bit him. Junkie George was so pissed off, he kicked the dog too. Hunter walked up to George and told him, 'Only punks slap their old ladies and kick dogs.' This really pissed George off, so he pole-axed Hunter. . . ."

Barger said the beating wasn't as bad as Hunter made it appear when he wrote about it in a postscript to *Hell's Angels*. "He had run around with us long enough to know that he was going to get beat up, but he wasn't going to get hurt," Barger recalled. "George hit him once. We told him, 'That's enough, George.' We picked [Hunter] up and told him, 'Get out of here.' He got in his car and drove off."

Hunter had his stop-the-presses moment. Sandy remembered Hunter calling from the hospital to report the beating and his arrival home a couple of hours later, with his face swollen and turned a few varying colors. He photographed himself in the mirror and retired to bed for four days, then wrote a postscript for the book. It made for a good ending (Hunter quoted Conrad: "The horror! The horror!") and a great promotional angle, the publisher-provided opening question for any interviewer: "So, what exactly was it *like* to be stomped by the Hell's Angels?"

Barger thought Hunter provoked Junkie George so that the beating could be used as a gimmick to promote the book. "The problem I have is that it just really isn't a true story," Barger said, "but it is a very, very good story. He was now able to say, 'I met, I lived with and I was almost killed by the Angels.'"

Barger always complained that Hunter never even delivered on the promised keg in exchange for club cooperation. "Cheap bastard," he huffed in his autobiography. Thirty years after the book's publication, Thompson learned of Barger's complaint and offered—through an intermediary—to buy Barger a keg of beer. "It's thirty years too late," Barger said.

The stomping at the end of the book did turn out to be an eyebrow raiser among reviewers when the Random House hardcover was published in 1967. Most critics remarked on the stunt of riding with the Angels. *Commonweal* called Hunter "a young man of considerable journalistic talent and no little personal courage, since he spent a good deal of his time for a year or more in the company of the Hell's Angels and ended up being stomped by them."

The *New York Times*, the *New Yorker*, and the major newspapers all praised the book and its author. Because of its below-the-salt beginnings as a paperback original, Random House had underanticipated demand, printing 20,000 copies. It sold out quickly. At several of Hunter's book signings, he was faced with every author's and publisher's nightmare: no copies for the author to sign.

"They didn't even print enough to have it on shelves on the day of publication," Hunter said. "So I had to go on a 35-day publicity tour for the book, which was a best-seller before it was published."

Selling out was a sure sign of success for a writer and certainly better than remaindered stacks in some New Jersey warehouse. Yet Hunter saw it as a sign of incompetence, something he could never stand. He finally had a publisher, but his relationship was strained from the start.

During his publicity blast, he had a guest spot on *The Today Show*, where he sat as mute as a toad across from host Hugh Downs. Hunter agreed with his friends that he looked wretched, and he even wrote Downs a note of apology, full of admiration that a man could not only function so early in the day but also host a nationally televised talk show. Hunter also appeared with two imposters to proclaim "I am Hunter S. Thompson" on the venerable daytime game show *To Tell the Truth*, hosted by radio's former Superman, Bud Collyer, and was interviewed for a *New York Times* profile.

Hunter had never been desperate for fame. The publicity apparatus interested him less for putting his face before the public than for getting his work out to readers. As for his image, he seemed more intent on creating mystery about himself. His *Hell's Angels* author photo was in shades of orange, his eyes hidden behind aviator sunglasses. The back-cover author's blurb bragged about the Angels' beating and featured a condensed bio that mentioned his two unpublished novels, his love for Dobermans and for his wife and son. "He is known as an avid reader, a relentless drinker and a fine hand with a .44 Magnum."

How to follow riding with the Angels? He began sniffing around for more magazine assignments to keep the cash coming. Random House had *The Rum Diary* and planned to publish it and schedule another non-fiction book. Hunter had always felt like a writer, and now he had the proof: a book so popular that stores couldn't keep it stocked, and deadlines to write two more. *If this is what it's like to be a published author*, he wondered, *how come I'm still broke?*

Chapter 8

AMERICAN DREAM

So maybe I can write something for you; that's the only thing
I do better than most people. . . .
—*HST, volunteering for Robert Kennedy's campaign*

J im Silberman had invited Hunter to New York to do some of the editing
of *Hell's Angels* face-to-face. He said it would be easier to do it eyeball-
to-eyeball. But he mostly wanted to pick Hunter's brain about his next
project.

Hunter was put up at the Delmonico Hotel. Silberman suggested
they meet at Pete's Tavern in Gramercy Park. It had literary pedigree—
O. Henry had killed himself with drink there. Silberman asked Shir-Cliff
to come along, since he had signed Hunter in the first place. Both editors
were eager to finally meet the thing called Hunter S. Thompson.

They showed up at the packed bar, and after a few moments of study,
picked Hunter out of the crowd: the young but balding man with the
shades and cigarette holder, decamped behind a tumbler of Wild Turkey.
They made introductions and retired to a table. While Hunter ordered
nineteen more Wild Turkeys during the course of the evening, the editors
got to know their new author. He didn't look like a Hell's Angel *or* a hip-

pie. He didn't seem very impressed by the editors, either. After a decade on the fringes of journalism, he'd become cynical and was not cowed by the presence of publishing greatness. Hunter responded to their fawning over *Hell's Angels* with shrugging shoulders and a scowl.

The few problems with the book were organizational, and copy editor Margaret Harrell fixed those. Hunter often said Harrell was the best copy editor he'd ever worked with. "I understood his creative spirit," Harrell said. "My role was to get things done. I kept things oriented toward getting the job done." Harrell said she got along so well with Hunter because they were focused only on his writing and not on the business side of publishing. "I had nothing to do with the money, so I could never owe him money."

Silberman had brought Hunter to New York mostly to see what kind of man he was dealing with and to make sure he stayed with Random House. "Jim loved Hunter's work," Harrell recalled.

The Rum Diary had been languishing with an editor at Pantheon Books, a Random House subsidiary, and so Silberman produced a contract that allowed Hunter to rewrite the novel and to produce another nonfiction work, both books to be published by Random House. The nonfiction ideas they kicked around all put Hunter in the middle of some other motorcycle-gang-like danger: among banditos in Mexico or mercenaries in Africa. *Hell's Angels* worked in part because of the semi-normal-dude-in-danger element, but despite what Gatsby had said, Hunter knew they couldn't repeat the past. But at least those ideas were tangible and clearly defined, with an almost built-in narrative. The final agreed-upon concept for the nonfiction book was the least specific: Hunter would write some hazy polemic on the topic "The Death of the American Dream."

But there it was: a book contract, one that Hunter soon regretted signing. Always at war with agents—he'd been through several in his short career—he had signed the contract without one, since he was waiting for his hastily signed contract with Scott Meredith's agency to expire. Within months of the *Hell's Angels* publication and the publisher's incompetence (as Hunter saw it), he began lobbying to tear it up. He had been victimized, he said.

Hunter, Sandy, and Juan were back in Colorado by the late fall of 1966—first in Aspen and then in a rental house out in Woody Creek that he began calling Owl Farm. Their 1963 idyll at Woody Creek had taken on blockbuster proportions in their memories. The great days of San Francisco were past. Now Gray Line tours took blue-haired sightseers through the Haight-Ashbury district. The magic was over. "By the end of '66 the whole neighborhood had become a cop-magnet and a bad sideshow," Hunter recalled.

Sandy was pregnant again. She had suffered a couple of miscarriages, but with Juan now two and a half, she felt that the time was right for another child. They were away from the Angels and the other craziness of the Bay Area, settled into a cabin in the beautiful Roaring Fork Valley.

As always, there were Louisville connections. Semonin had first come to Aspen, and now so had other old friends, including Jimmy and Billy Noonan. One of Hunter's first acts upon moving to Colorado was serving as best man at Billy's wedding to Anne Willis. Aside from Hunter's putting out his cigarette in the holy water, the wedding transpired without major incident.

Down the road from their rental, Hunter discovered a vacant log cabin. He went there by himself in the afternoons, starting a fire in the fireplace, and just sitting and imagining himself in the home. Sandy discovered who owned the place and charmed the landlord into renting it and another small cabin on the 130 acres for $125 a month. Billy and Anne Noonan moved into the smaller house. This home became Hunter's new Owl Farm.

Hunter and his friends began stealing things to furnish the home, and Sandy finally had a friend, right next door. She, Juan, and Anne would go into Aspen and shop and have lunch, but Sandy always had to be back at three, Hunter's waking hour. Her life utterly revolved around her husband, keeping the house quiet when he slept, feeding him a lavish breakfast when he woke, and tending to his every need at the expense of her own. "I didn't want to be the little wife who badgered Hunter," Sandy said. "I was afraid he'd be angry."

The ideal life ended when Sandy learned she would miscarry, an agony that stretched over several months of enforced bed rest. Hunter hired help to care for Juan and continued his battle with Random House. He stayed tethered to Owl Farm because of Sandy's condition and therefore turned down most freelance work, though he did buy a new motorcycle and a Volvo sedan.

He continued to break into new markets. For the *New York Times Magazine* he wrote a benediction on the hippie scene, which was then just hitting American mass culture, but was essentially already history in San Francisco. His piece was a hit, and *Times* editors kept calling, asking whether he would do other assignments. He begged off because of Sandy. Thanks to Random House publicist Selma Shapiro he'd gotten his foot in the door not only at the *Times* but also at *Pageant*, whose general-interest approach didn't really appeal to Hunter, but which paid well. *Playboy* commissioned an Angels article (never published, but still Hunter was paid), and *Esquire* ran an excerpt from the book.

Mostly, as Sandy endured her ordeal, Hunter spent his time making the cabin into a home, tinkering with *The Rum Diary* and blasting Jefferson Airplane's "White Rabbit" and Bob Dylan's "Mr. Tambourine Man" (which he called the hippie national anthem) into the mountains through his huge custom-made 100-watt stereo system. It was just Dylan, with a murmuring electric guitar, and the louder Hunter played the song, the larger were the spaces in the music, allowing him to crawl inside.

Hunter was the full-time parent during Sandy's bed-rest period. He was always loose with discipline and loved playing jokes on his little boy. Juan—who called his parents Hunter and Sandy, never Mom and Dad—would tell visitors, "Hunter says my name is Dirt Bag." Hunter instructed his friends to play along. For a week, Juan was convinced Dirt Bag was his name. Even when Juan was a toddler, Hunter spoke to him—and joked with him—as he did to his adult friends. He once told his son to bring him his cigarettes or he'd "rip his balls off." When the cigarettes didn't show up, he found Juan hiding in his room, crying.

Much of 1967 was spent waiting. Hunter did not capitalize on the *Hell's Angels* momentum. He waited for his contract with Scott Meredith to expire, so he could sign on with a new agent, Lynn Nesbit. He put off magazine assignments until editors took them to other writers, and what assignments he did take, he turned in hopelessly late. He parried with the editor of the *New York Times Magazine* over a story on Nevada prisons, yet seemed more critical of his work than any editor would be (calling his own story "dull and confusing"), and said he assumed it would be rejected. It was.

That summer, Hunter was in Aspen, drinking with friends in a bar called Daisy Duck when a large Hispanic man rumbled in and announced that he was the trouble they had all been waiting for. Enchanted by this introduction, Hunter offered his hand to Oscar Zeta Acosta, an attorney visiting from Los Angeles. The meeting had been arranged by Michael

Solheim, then an Aspen housepainter, but the former owner of a bar in Ketchum, Idaho, where Hunter had gone to do a story on Ernest Hemingway's final home. Solheim heard something in Acosta's rants and diatribes that reminded him a lot of Hunter's writing. It was the beginning of what would be a profitable friendship, especially for Hunter.

Acosta, nicknamed the Brown Buffalo, was in his early thirties when he arrived in Aspen after his losing campaign for sheriff of Los Angeles County. Voters had given Acosta a first-class pounding (he lost by a million votes), and he came to the mountains for refuge. "But in defeat," Hunter observed, "Oscar managed to create an instant political base for himself in the vast Chicano barrio of East Los Angeles." With a lust for radical politics (he told Hunter he was "long past his puppy-love trip with the law") and huge appetites for food, booze, and drugs, Acosta and Hunter became close friends for the next few years, with Acosta a regular guest at Owl Farm. Acosta was convinced that he would die at thirty-three, as Jesus had. He was already into his thirty-third year when he met Hunter, who was living beyond his self-proclaimed life expectancy of twenty-seven—yet another element for bonding with Acosta. Hunter saw Acosta as the embodiment of menace and articulate rage, a "dangerous thug" with "a head full of Sandoz acid, a loaded .357 Magnum in his belt, a hatchet-wielding bodyguard at his elbow at all times, and a disconcerting habit of projectile-vomiting geysers of pure red blood off the front porch every thirty or forty minutes, or whenever his malignant ulcer can't handle any more raw tequila."

Hunter and Acosta saw themselves as mutually terminal friends for what little time they thought they had left.

Acosta was ready to return to L.A. a couple of days after meeting Hunter, but he wanted to give him a gift to express the bond he felt they'd begun to form. He presented Hunter with a crude, hard-carved mahogany idol he'd obtained in Panama. Acosta had nicknamed it Ebb Tide. It was "an eighteen-inch god without eyes, without a mouth and without a sexual organ. . . . A string of small, yellowed wild pig's fangs hung from its neck." Oddly moved, Hunter hung Ebb Tide over his living room window, where it remained for years. "I've never taken the little bastard down," Hunter wrote, "so he must be paying his way."

Acosta became a frequent visitor to Aspen and even rented apartments for brief spells and labored as a dishwasher and construction worker. He brought his son Marco along, and when they visited Owl Farm, Marco and Juan would sit spellbound in front of the fireplace as Acosta, in a long robe, transformed himself into the Brown Buffalo and delivered fire and brimstone to the frightened children. Even Hunter, a devotee of the Book of Revelation, was flabbergasted by the lunatic power of Acosta's apocalyptic visions.

When Sandy was finally back on her feet in the fall, Hunter traveled to San Francisco to meet the staff of *Ramparts* and write some pieces for the magazine. *Ramparts*, dedicated to the overthrow of the U.S. government, sold more than forty thousand copies each month. Hunter liked both its politics and its journalism and found in editor Warren Hinckle a kindred spirit.

Slowly, he came out of his funk with Jim Silberman at Random House. He had taken back *The Rum Diary* indefinitely for rewrite and polish, and was trying to put a backbone into his vague idea on the American Dream. The Dream obsessed him . . . *but what was it?* Was it Horatio Alger, rags to riches, the idea that you could start with nothing and end up rolling naked in stacks of hundreds? Or was it a dream of freedom? Personal freedom . . . or the concept of freedom that the founders brought into the world?

He saw reflections of the perversion of the Dream in the far right . . . and in the National Rifle Association . . . the Joint Chiefs of Staff . . . all around him, sometimes something positive, as in the local politics in which he quickly became enmeshed. What had happened to the ideals in which he'd been baptized in his youth? Where did Jack Thompson's American Dream go? Would his father recognize this country if he were alive today?

Whatever the Dream would ultimately turn out to be, Hunter knew it would be political. Though he'd gone through long periods of deep skepticism over politics, he had vowed to register to vote again in 1968, just so he could vote against President Johnson, in protest over the Vietnam War. Now, with Richard Nixon on the Republican horizon, it seemed that he would have to back out on that claim. He could not vote for Nixon . . . but he couldn't vote for Johnson either.

An election year was upon him, and as Hunter worked with Silberman to try to clarify the American Dream book, he knew it meant covering the presidential campaign of 1968 from start to finish.

Lyndon Johnson inherited the Vietnam War from President Kennedy and pitched himself in 1964 as the peace candidate. The Republicans nominated conservative Arizona senator Barry Goldwater, who had said, in essence, that the nation needed to quit pussy-footing around in Vietnam: either go ahead and win the war or get out. Johnson cast Goldwater as a trigger-happy madman, and won the election. Johnson preached peace, but starting in 1965 practiced escalation. By the beginning of 1968, there were half a million American soldiers in Vietnam.

Senator Eugene McCarthy, Democrat of Minnesota, announced in late 1967 that he intended to challenge Johnson for the party's nomination. This was unheard of—a pip-squeak senator out in the Midwest challenging the incumbent president of his own party. But McCarthy was fervently antiwar, and he wanted to make sure Vietnam was on the agenda. His campaign was either a fool's errand or a noble crusade. Hunter held the latter view. He wrote McCarthy, sent him a copy of *Hell's Angels*, and offered help, suggesting himself as a speechwriter.

Hunter did not cross over to the dark side of press agentry; he remained a journalist. He used his Random House contract to get credentialed as a political reporter and used an assignment from *Pageant* in February 1968 to get close to Republican candidate Richard Nixon during the New Hampshire primary, the first test of political waters.

"He was just starting his comeback then and I didn't take him seriously," Hunter said. "He seemed like a Republican echo of Hubert Humphrey: just another sad old geek limping back into politics for another beating. It never occurred to me that he would ever be President. Johnson hadn't quit at that point, but I sort of sensed he was going to and I figured Bobby Kennedy would run—so that even if Nixon got the Republican nomination, he'd just take another stomping by another Kennedy. So I thought it would be nice to go to New Hampshire, spend a couple of weeks following Nixon around, and then write his political obituary."

Hunter joined the small pack of journalists trailing the candidates and even made friends with the most conventional of reporters, Bob Semple of the *New York Times*. On Nixon's press bus, he met *Boston Globe* reporter Bill Cardoso, who introduced himself, saying, "Hey, you're the cat who wrote the *Hell's Angels* book." They smoked a joint in the back of the bus to seal their friendship.

In Hunter's view, Nixon was the most vile example of the species *politician*. He'd risen to national prominence in 1948 as the congressman behind the House Un-American Activities Committee investigation of Communists in the State Department. He went on to serve two years in the Senate before being chosen by General Dwight Eisenhower as his running mate in 1952. He served two terms as vice president during a decade of blandness, peace, and prosperity, then lost the presidency to the telegenic Jack Kennedy. Two years later, Nixon's home state rejected him in his quest to be governor. His political career ended with his press-conference claim that members of the press, whom he blamed for his loss, would miss him because they would no longer have fun kicking him around.

Yet six years later, here he was, the front-runner for the Republican nomination. It was probably the most stunning political comeback of the century. To Hunter, Nixon was 175 pounds of pure, compressed evil, but the man also inspired some of Hunter's strongest writing. Hunter wrote to former Jack Kennedy aide Ted Sorensen, raging about Johnson and now offering his services to Robert Kennedy's bid for the presidency. Kennedy was a more likely nominee than long-shot McCarthy, and Hunter wanted to back a winner. "All I really want to do is get that evil pigfucker out of the White House and not let Nixon in," Hunter wrote. "Nixon is a monument to all the bad genes and broken chromosomes that have queered the reality of the 'American Dream.'"

Yet Richard Nixon was Hunter's muse. Hunter's most memorable work was inspired by Nixon's venality. The only meeting between the two men occurred as Hunter covered the 1968 New Hampshire primary. Nixon had an hour's ride following a campaign appearance. After days of campaign speeches, Nixon was tired of politics and wanted to talk football with someone. Speechwriter Raymond Price knew that Hunter was a football junkie as well, and arranged for Hunter to share the backseat of Nixon's limo.

"We were at this American Legion hall somewhere pretty close to Boston," Hunter recalled. "Nixon had just finished a speech there and we were about an hour and a half from Manchester, where he had his Learjet waiting, and Price suddenly came up to me and said, 'You've been wanting to talk to the boss? OK, come on.' And I said, 'What? What?' By this time I'd given up; I knew he was leaving for Key Biscayne that night and I was wild-eyed drunk. On the way to the car, Price said, 'The boss wants to relax and talk football; you're the only person here who claims to be an expert on that subject, so you're it. But if you mention anything else— out. You'll be hitchhiking back to Manchester. No talk about Vietnam, campus riots—nothing political; the boss wants to talk football, period."

It was an odd condition under which to interview a politician, but it was an auspicious beginning to Hunter's career as a political reporter. Nixon enjoyed unveiling his philosophy of the theory and practice of pro football with Hunter. When Hunter described a pass play in the 1967 Oakland–Green Bay Super Bowl, Nixon remembered not only who caught the ball but also where he'd played college ball. Hunter was impressed. "I've never seen him like that before or since," Hunter said of the meeting. "We had a good, loose talk. That was the only time in 20 years of listening to the treacherous bastard that I knew he wasn't lying."

The punctuation on the evening came when the candidate's limo pulled up on the tarmac beside the waiting Learjet. Hunter said his goodbyes, then flicked open his lighter to light a cigarette, within a few feet of the plane's engine. "Watch out!" somebody shouted, and a hand came out of the darkness, pulled Hunter's cigarette from his mouth and crushed it into the runway. "Goddammit, Hunter, you almost blew up the plane," shrieked Nick Ruwe, one of Nixon's aides. Nixon smiled and shook hands with Hunter and climbed on the plane. Ruwe drove Hunter back to the hotel, then sat in the bar with him while they discussed the narrow escape from death.

The Secret Service had not recognized the threat; it was Ruwe who grabbed the cigarette from Hunter's lips. Hunter tried to reassure him: "You people are lucky I'm a sane, responsible journalist, otherwise, I might have hurled my flaming Zippo into the fuel tank."

Ruwe waived off the possibility that Hunter would go down in the flames with the candidate. "Egomaniacs don't do that kind of thing," Ruwe said.

"You're probably right," Hunter replied. "Kamikaze is not my style."

Hunter's assignment from *Pageant* was clearly to do a hatchet job, while exploring the "new Nixon" who had risen from the political ashes to be a serious contender for the presidency. Hunter didn't need to talk to Nixon for the story; it was mostly about Nixon's image-makers and the marketing wizards who were taking over presidential campaigns. If he'd taken a turn down that marketing corridor and explored that theme more fully, he could have written *The Selling of the President*, the brilliant book Joe McGinnis produced from that campaign.

At first, Hunter had imagined that Nixon used sports analogies to appear to be more down to earth, one of the guys, someone all the Joe Sixpacks out there could relate to. Though he was stunned by

Nixon's geekish knowledge of pro football, he still despised the man and said traveling with him was "a nightmare of bullshit, intrigue and suspicion."

Hunter's Nixon article was a slightly cleaned-up version of what he'd been writing to friends and associates (*Pageant* wouldn't let him use "pig-fucker"). He was brutal with the future president, calling him "a foul caricature of himself, a man with no soul, no inner convictions, with the integrity of a hyena and the style of a poison toad." Editing of the piece ("Presenting: The Richard Nixon Doll [Overhauled 1968 Model]") had been ugly. After editors lopped off fifteen pages from his bulky manuscript, he insisted they remove his name from the piece. The magazine refused.

Though Hunter developed a reputation as being some sort of wild-and-crazy, he was actually fairly meticulous when it came to his writing and didn't like it when editors began recklessly slashing his paragraphs. "He was tortured over every fucking word," his friend Gerry Goldstein once said.

But like all writers, he was in search of a great editor. He did not find one at *Pageant*, though he was about to meet two editors who would alter his life and career.

Hunter wrote to one of Nixon's staffers just as the *Pageant* article hit the stands, to prepare him for the piece and, in a way, to thank him. "I went to N.H. with the idea that Richard Nixon was a monster," he wrote, "and although I left N.H. with a strange affection for the man, *as a man* . . . I still tremble at the prospect of 'President Nixon.'"

In his book 1968, writer Mark Kurlansky referred to 1968 as "the year that rocked the world." It was that and a lot of other things. The psychedelia of 1967 and the media-event "summer of love" had given way to a return-to-basics, living-off-the-land/earthen-floor-and-patchouli lifestyle. After out-weirding each other in music, rock bands rediscovered three chords and the truth of the Band's *Music from Big Pink* and Bob Dylan's *John Wesley Harding*. Even the Beatles were not immune, and threw out the synthesizers in favor of the meandering piano in an ode to self-doubt called "Hey Jude." Artists sought authenticity and the eternal verities in the face of a world that had quite literally gone mad.

From his high-altitude perch in the Rockies, Hunter watched the horrors of the year unfold: North Korea seized the *USS Pueblo*; segregationist Alabama governor George Wallace announced his third-party candidacy for president; Senator Eugene McCarthy's strong showing in the New Hampshire primary rattled President Johnson and forced Senator Robert Kennedy to enter the race; President Johnson shocked the nation by going off script at the end of a televised address on the war and saying he would not seek reelection; a million children in Biafra starved to death in the aftermath of the African nation's civil war; civil rights leader Martin Luther King was assassinated in April, and violence erupted in the nation's larger cities; Robert Kennedy was assassinated after winning the California primary.

And it was only June.

President Johnson's withdrawal had cost Hunter $10,000. He had been so infuriated by the president that he was going to put his bile between covers for Ballantine, in a paperback called *The Johnson File*. The surprise announcement ruined that deal.

Hunter was watching Kennedy's California primary victory speech at Woody Creek. He left the room and heard a friend scream from the living room. He ran back into the room to learn of Kennedy's assassination.

Was this second Kennedy death the death of the American Dream? The end had come on television, and Hunter had been out of the room.

By summer, there were more than 541,000 American troops in Vietnam. In the aftermath of King's assassination, his associate, the Reverend Ralph Abernathy, staged a massive demonstration in Washington, erecting a shanty town in the shadows of the Capitol, bringing poverty to the doorstep of the government. Several of the nation's larger universities had limped to summer break after a springtime full of campus activism and building occupations.

So much was happening that even Hunter, he of the gerbil-like metabolism, couldn't keep up. He had to get into the fray and witness the death of the dream up close. He persuaded Random House to get him credentialed to cover the Democratic convention that August. Still puzzled by what he had been thinking when he proposed the concept of his American Dream book, Hunter feared he'd gotten himself into something too "vast & weighty" to be lassoed between covers. Hunter had a feeling he might find what he needed in Chicago. "A presidential campaign would be a good place, I thought, to look for the Death of the American Dream,"

Hunter said. "When Chicago came around, my head had gotten into politics and I thought, well, if we're going to have a real bastard up there I may as well go."

Hunter took his motorcycle helmet because he expected violence. He found it in Grant Park on August 28, as protesters and fellow journalists were attacked and beaten by the Chicago cops and the National Guard, all on orders of Mayor Richard Daley. The helmet came in handy.

That there would be demonstrations and likely violence was no secret in the months leading up to the Chicago convention. The Youth International Party, the Yippies, led by Jerry Rubin and Abbie Hoffman, had promised to bring 100,000 demonstrators to Chicago as a massive statement against the war in Vietnam. All told, there were one hundred anti-war groups in the massive protest. After President Johnson announced he would not seek reelection, demonstrators waited to see whether either of the peace candidates, Eugene McCarthy or Robert Kennedy, would emerge as the nominee. Then Kennedy was assassinated and McCarthy proved himself too esoteric and intelligent to be president, and Vice President Hubert Humphrey ended up being the front-runner heading into the convention.

When the Democrats hit town, things turned bad fast. The night before the convention began, Chicago police moved to drive protesters from Lincoln Park, where they had hoped to camp and demonstrate. When the protesters wouldn't move, police shot tear-gas canisters into their camps and beat them with billy clubs. Clashes continued through the convention and peaked on Wednesday night, as Humphrey was nominated for president. As the protesters tried to move on the convention hall, police attacked them with clubs and tear gas again. The police didn't discriminate, and many innocent bystanders and journalists, including Hunter Thompson, were clubbed. The violence even made it inside the convention hall as CBS reporter Dan Rather was attacked on live television by some of Mayor Daley's thugs. As he dusted himself off, alarmed CBS anchorman Walter Cronkite said, from the safety of his broadcast booth above the convention hall, "If this sort of thing continues, it makes us want to pack up our cameras and typewriters and get the hell out of Chicago and leave the Democrats to their agony." In short, Cronkite was pissed.

By the time the dust cleared, there had been 589 arrests and more than one hundred injuries. "I was treated as brutally as all the other press people," Hunter said. He was "cursed, pushed, chased, punched in the

stomach with a billy club, the whole gig." Years later, he recalled to journalist Curtis Wilkie, "I went to the Democratic convention as a journalist
and returned a raving beast."

The Chicago experience was a turning point in his life, transforming
him into a political radical and intensifying his hatred of authority. "It
permanently altered my brain chemistry," he said. "There was no possibility for any personal truce, for me, in a nation that could hatch and be
proud of a malignant monster like Chicago." He tried to write about the
bloodbath on the streets and produced a manuscript called "Chicago '68,"
but it went unpublished in his lifetime.

Later, an independent commission would call it a "police riot" and put
the blame for the mayhem on Mayor Daley. Daley responded by giving an
across-the-board raise to every member of the police force.

"I have a central incident to work with, now," Hunter wrote Silberman
of *The Death of the American Dream.* "I think I've come out of a fog." He
said the book was "suddenly active" again.

Hunter's cynicism about politics reached monstrous proportions. He
returned to Woody Creek nearly mute. For weeks, he couldn't talk about
Chicago without crying.

Maybe the American Dream he was chasing still had those Horatio
Alger overtones, the self-made man stuff, but maybe it was mixed with
politics. Appalled by the corruption of the Democratic Party and the out-
right evil he saw in the Republicans, he thought maybe it was time for
American politics to reinvent itself.

As he faced the horrifying prospect of the presidential election ballot of 1968 (Richard Nixon, Hubert Humphrey, and George Wallace),
Hunter pondered doing something on a local level. He counseled friends
to vote for Nixon, so that the Democratic Party would be crippled and
forced into change before the next election.

The idea of becoming truly political had been repulsive for Hunter, but
he began to think that getting into politics at a local level might reenergize
him spiritually and artistically. He thought the story of a local campaign
could bring his life and his book into focus. "We'd been beaten in Chicago," Hunter said. "The lesson was very clear. I figured that first, you
change a small town."

Life intervened and the Thompsons were again uprooted, moving to yet another Owl Farm. Hunter was afforded a generous purchase plan for the new place, thanks to owner George Stranahan, who became a lifelong friend because of this and other good deeds. Michael Solheim vouched for Hunter to Stranahan, calling him "a bright and articulate thirty-year-old with a pretty wife who shared his pot." Stranahan agreed. "I rented them [the Thompsons] two houses on 122 acres for $375 a month," Stranahan said. "The rent checks came irregularly, yet often with a handwritten letter full of humor, observation and savage political commentary."

Stranahan's family had founded the Champion Spark Plug Company. While a graduate student at Carnegie Mellon University in the late 1950s, Stranahan headed west for one summer and rented a cabin in Aspen—to fish and write his dissertation, but mostly to fish. The dissertation stalled. Stranahan needed the company of other physicists, but didn't want to leave Aspen, so he founded Aspen Center for Physics in 1962 and brought the scientists to his doorstep. Though he left occasionally to be a professor somewhere, Stranahan kept his home in Aspen and accumulated more property. Also a fine-arts photographer, human-rights activist, philanthropist, beer brewer (the Flying Dog brands), and frustrated delinquent, he was drawn to Hunter and arranged the lease for the three-level house, a smaller cabin nearby, and a stable, and the acreage resting on top of a bluff.

It was a paradise and would be Hunter's home for the rest of his life. His son, Juan, recalling his childhood on the farm, remembered why his father loved it so. "He could go out and sunbathe naked, he could shoot off his guns, he could blow things up and no one was going to give him a hard time about it." When his old friend Porter Bibb visited, he knew why Hunter fell in love with the place. "He had privacy," Bibb said. "He was the master of his domain. He could do anything he wanted."

But it was more than a home; it was a refuge. "Being able to come back to Owl Farm from all the madness and craziness out there was a real relief and a saving grace," Sandy said.

Being in the right place at the right time and knowing Stranahan was what made the 122-acre deal so perfect. Exultant, Hunter canceled his trip home for Christmas and invited his mother and brothers to join him for the holidays. Once again, Sandy discovered she was pregnant.

Chapter 9

EPIPHANY

Unlike most of the others in the press box, we didn't give a
hoot-in-hell what was happening on the track. We had come
there to watch the real beasts perform.
—HST, *"The Kentucky Derby Is Decadent and Depraved"*

Finally, he felt at home. He still carried the oppressive weight of the American Dream book on his back as he limped into 1969, maintaining cash flow by churning out magazine articles.

Stunned by Robert Kennedy's assassination, Hunter struggled to reconcile two aspects of his character. He was a gun owner, yet he also was a pacifist who had admired Bobby Kennedy as he did few other human beings. It was a case of the right hand killing the left hand.

Haunted and puzzled by this contradiction in his character, he approached *Esquire* editor Don Ericson and pitched a story on the National Rifle Association (which Hunter had joined) and the powerful gun lobby. Ericson bit, but what was supposed to be a quick and easy magazine article morphed into an unwieldly, strange manuscript. Hunter went to Washington and interviewed scores of people and soon realized it was becoming a huge project, a literary quagmire to rival *The Death of the American Dream*.

Ericson wanted a detailed journalistic report, something in the 3,000-word range. What Hunter eventually produced was an 80,000-word manuscript. Ericson said it was unmanageable. It was also written in an unusual style. Rather than use the just-the-facts approach the subject would seem to require, Hunter turned it into a long narrative, with himself as the central figure, as the window through which to view America's violent character.

The manuscript was a hybrid of the more sober reporting style of *Hell's Angels* and the frenzied wordplay of *Fear and Loathing in Las Vegas*. It wasn't just a collection of interviews and statistics. It was a narrative with cocktail-party scenes and spelunking into Hunter's psyche. "It's the bridge book," said historian Douglas Brinkley, who would become Hunter's literary executor. "It has a lot of things that are similar to the *Vegas* book, but it's a little more straight journalism than *Vegas*. He thought he was losing his grip on reality. He was doing this assignment for money, and instead this artistic side welled up inside of him." The piece was more serious self-examination than was characteristic in Hunter's work. Devastated by Robert Kennedy's death, he wondered if something was wrong with *him*, considering his love of guns. He also went to Washington, to the headquarters of the National Rifle Association, and began meeting a lot of political sources who would begin to show up in his reporting during the next few years.

"The Gun Lobby," as Hunter titled it, was a fully realized work, not just an overgrown, failed magazine article. It was Hunter in near-top form, writing during what Brinkley called his most brilliant period. "He could type twenty flawless pages without missing a comma or a dash," Brinkley said. "It was extraordinary, the amount of word productivity a day. It's pretty awesome to see his runs of fully realized thinking and writing. It's a different man writing in that period."

Hunter was depressed that *Esquire* passed on his massive manuscript. The gun lobby wasn't a sexy enough subject to sell as a book project. With the country's festering disillusionment in the wake of the latest assassinations, something on the death of the American Dream was far more marketable.

Hunter set "The Gun Lobby" aside and returned to struggling with the American Dream book, occasionally giving thought to combining the work with the Dream book, or at least putting some of "The Gun Lobby" into it. Eventually, he abandoned that idea and back-burnered the manuscript. "It's one Hunter purposely didn't publish," Brinkley said. "He knew it was the golden egg for him, and he had grandiose ideas of what he would get paid for it." (In the last years of his life, he toyed with dusting off the manuscript and selling it under the name "Fear and Loathing at the NRA," but that idea was abandoned.)

Hunter's *Boston Globe* friend, Bill Cardoso, hired him to cover President Nixon's inauguration for the *Globe* magazine. The inauguration would be another link in his American Dream book. As he watched the protesters stage their anti-inauguration, he found himself in the uncomfortable position as the enemy. "In Chicago I was clubbed by police," he wrote. "In Washington I was menaced by demonstrators." It was a different world now. The sixties were essentially over. No one clasped hands and sang songs of peace . . . no "We Shall Overcome". . . . It was another folk song—"Which Side Are You On?"—that took a newer, deeper meaning. *If you aren't for us, you're against us.* Hunter mused about attaining his political adulthood at the beginning of the decade and cheering when Nixon lost to Kennedy. Now, at the ass end of that ghastly decade Nixon was being inaugurated with a splendor that reminded Hunter of the Thousand-Year Reich. Nixon was the "first chief executive to grow from a dropped pile." Like the Kennedy assassination, the scene moved Hunter to consider violence. As the president's car passed, wine bottles, beer cans, and rocks rained down on the limo. He stood next to CBS reporter Joe Benti, who intoned into his microphone, "Here comes the president . . ." Hunter turned on him, "How do you know?" The car's windows were shrouded; Bozo the Clown could be inside, for all they knew. Hunter knew only that when the dust of 1968 had cleared, "another cheapjack hustler moved into the White House." The weekend in Washington was proof that the American Dream was dead. But how did he wrestle that conviction into a book?

"In the sixties, there was a sense of victory," he said, "but it was a false dawn. We had the feeling the bad guys had been driven out and that right had prevailed. But we at least made the generation that came out of the Eisenhower years aware of what they could do."

He continued sending expense reports to Jim Silberman, thanking him for his Random House–funded education. Some element of the American Dream book was barnacled to every magazine assignment he took. He took an assignment from *Pageant* to write about test pilots at the sanctuary for the mad monks of flying, Edwards Air Force Base, in California's high desert. Hunter was again exploring territory that would prove fertile for another writer. Tom Wolfe's 1973 stories on the astronauts grew from a quickie *Rolling Stone* assignment on the final *Apollo* launch, to a saga of the early days of the space program and the seat-of-their-pants daredevils of the skies, the test pilots holed up at Edwards. That would become *The Right Stuff*. But Hunter was there first.

Hunter spent a few days in February at the base and decamped at the Continental Hyatt House (nicknamed the Riot House by Led Zeppelin), the preferred hotel for rock stars visiting Los Angeles. He spent six days at the hotel and was alone much of the time in this monument to noise and excess. He did see Oscar Zeta Acosta, who was trying to radicalize the barrio with his Brown Power Movement politics. Acosta was pressuring Hunter to help him break into the literary world, but Hunter wasn't encouraging. "You're wasting your time trying to communicate in a language you've never mastered and probably never will," Hunter told Acosta.

Acosta kept writing plays and attempts at autobiography that Hunter, as a good friend, would forward to Shir-Cliff at Ballantine or to Silberman at Random House. He wasn't as vicious in his criticism of Acosta to others and generally pushed them to consider his friend's work, noting that it needed heavy editing.

During his days in the city, he briefly saw Acosta and the McGarrs, who had relocated to L.A. But when not reporting, Hunter retreated to his Riot House room and fell into a drugged stupor. He stalked his hotel room, looked down on the Sunset Strip, popped pills, and stared at his enemy, the typewriter. The test-pilot article would not appear. He began to wonder whether he was doing it all the right way. "Trying to mix writing and fucking around with old friends don't work no more," he wrote, frustrated with "this maddening, time-killing late-work syndrome, never getting down to the real machine action until two or three at night . . . half drunk full of pills and grass with deadlines past and people howling in New York."

As he waited for Acosta to come by to take him to the airport for his return to Denver, Hunter ingested mescaline that Acosta had given him, and it was love at first swallow. He loved the drug's elongated reality that opened the spaces around him, giving him more room to explore and hide. It became a regular part of his drug diet.

Back in Woody Creek, he finished the test-pilot article, full of Hunter attitude, yet also exactly what the generally bland *Pageant* wanted. Severely frustrated about the larger work he was supposed to be doing, he wrote Silberman, "One of these days I'll explain how an allegedly talented writer can produce five pages a day for a solid year and finish with nothing at all." He wrote his mother that he had begun to hate the sight of his typewriter.

Davison Thompson followed in the father's footsteps, into a career as a businessman in Cuyahoga Falls, Ohio, outside of Cleveland. Hunter's much younger brother, Jim, did not find an easy path. Virginia kept her older sons updated on Jim's ill fortunes in college. Despite inconsistent income, Hunter usually sent his mother a few hundred dollars a year to help with Jim's University of Kentucky tuition. Hunter managed to make it home to Louisville for most Christmases, but once he settled into his final Owl Farm, he wanted to play host to the rest of his family. He especially wanted to show Jim his life: shooting guns, exploding fireworks, hunting, the drinking and game-playing that defined Hunter. But Jim seemed distant, so much younger that Hunter felt more like a friendly uncle than a big brother. As the Vietnam War ground on, Hunter fretted about his little brother. "I remember thinking I had a tough way to go at 19," Hunter wrote his mother, "but in fact I had a hell of a lot of options that Jim doesn't have in this goddam war-maddened world."

During his visit to Colorado in the summer of 1969, Jim Thompson was always on edge when his big brother was awake. "I used to dread Hunter getting up in the afternoon," he said. "Immediately, he would be grouchy, sleepy and very domineering, from then on." He loved his sister-in-law, but saw that Sandy was a prisoner to her husband's wishes. When Hunter invited friends for male bonding over beer and volleyball, he was furious when Jim didn't participate, calling him a wimp. Jim was uncomfortable in the company of his brother and his rowdy drunks. He spent most of his time with Sandy, and they comforted each other during Hunter's rages.

Virginia Thompson had wanted Hunter to give his little brother guidance or support. Jim had been depressed and had even mentioned suicide. Hunter was supposed to talk things through with Jim during the visit, but instead Hunter remained aloof until he took Jim to the airport. "This suicide business," Hunter said, "you're not serious about that, are you?" Jim was embarrassed and wrote it off to their mother's overconcern. "I downplayed it completely," Jim said. "I didn't want to look bad in his eyes, because he indicated that that was a pretty pathetic thing to do."

Jim returned to Louisville and wrote Hunter a long letter. He was intimidated both by writing to a writer he so greatly admired and by what he had to say. Jim had known for years that he was homosexual. Now, at twenty, it was time to come out.

"I worked on that letter for days," he said in 1992. "I tried to make everything just right. I soft-pedaled everything. It was very diplomatic. . . . He never responded. Nor has he *ever* responded. I never heard any comment. It has never been discussed. *Never* been discussed."

Hunter prepared for fatherhood again. "The thing is due sometime in July," he wrote brother Davison, "and then I plan to have myself castrated."

His articles for *Playboy* had usually fallen through, but in the spring the magazine assigned him a standard-issue personality profile of Olympic medalist Jean-Claude Killy, the French skier who had wowed the world in the 1968 Winter Games. Killy had retired from the sport and was making television commercials for Chevrolet.

Hunter went to the Chicago Auto Show, which turned out to be at the Stockyards Amphitheater, scene of the Democrats' crime the summer before. Dark memories came at him, while he hung out with Killy and the other new Chevy pitchman, football player O. J. Simpson. "What seemed like a quick and easy thing has turned into a complicated monster," he wrote Silberman. He suggested that this assignment too could be part of the American Dream book.

Professional complications aside, Hunter had to admit the rest of life was good. He lived in an isolated mountain retreat with his wife and son, with friends around. Sandy was pregnant again, the cat was pregnant, the dog was pregnant. "It was beautiful at Owl Farm," Sandy remembered. "It was summertime and there were lots of flowers. Everything could not have been happier or more fertile and growing."

Sandy delivered her daughter in July at Aspen Valley Hospital, with Hunter at her side. It had been remarkably painless, and after the birth Sandy remembered the silence. The delivery room grew quiet. For one moment, she saw her daughter, whom they had named Sarah, and then the nurses rushed the baby away. Sandy closed her eyes and kept them closed.

The orderlies took Sandy to a recovery room, and she opened her eyes to look out the window: there was a field of mowed grass and flowers.

Hunter said their daughter was as big as a football player, but she could tell he was trying to protect her. The doctor came in the room, and Sandy turned from the window and saw his face. Their daughter had died.

The pain was excruciating. Sandy looked out the window again. "I could just walk out of here," she told Hunter. "Just walk out of here and then nothing is real. And if that's not real, then my baby didn't die either." She considered briefly the option of going insane. But then, "Hunter looked at me. And he said, 'Sandy, if you need to do that, then you do that. If you need to go away, then you do that. But I just want you to know that Juan and I need you and that we'll be glad when you come back.' And then I just switched. And I came back. And to me, that was one of the most beautiful things Hunter has ever done for me."

Hunter asked about his daughter's body. The doctors said they would "dispose of" it. Furious and heartbroken, Hunter and Billy Noonan broke into the morgue, stole Sarah's body, and buried her on Owl Farm.

Hunter and Sandy limped through the summer and into the fall. Hunter took Sandy to Los Angeles, to Oscar Acosta's home, where they consumed drugs, drank, and generally made such beasts of themselves that Hunter felt the need to apologize to his host. "You got caught in the tides of a sort of honeymoon, 10 years delayed," Hunter wrote. "Even Sandy admits that we both went a bit beyond the pale on all fronts—from running up bills to drugs, to laying bad trips on other people." Gene McGarr was also a little shocked by his old friends' behavior, and he drew an apology: "Sandy has been so generally depressed since that child-death thing that it seemed necessary to get her away to some weird and different scene. . . . It was sort of a long-delayed mescaline honeymoon—an orgiastic Trip that got her back in my world for a while. She was beginning to feel seriously left out, I think, and blowing a Diners Club card is an easy way to stay sane. . . ."

The test-pilot article appeared in *Pageant*, and Hunter, after months of following the skier around, produced what he considered a fine piece on Jean-Claude Killy, for *Playboy*. He sent it to the editors and awaited their response.

Though they had lived in Colorado for only two years, Hunter and Sandy had seen the ugliness of change in Aspen: greedy developers encroached on the wilderness with cookie-cutter condos, and the charming mountain village was becoming a playground for the rich and famous. After finally finding home, Hunter and Sandy bristled at the thought of Aspen spoiled and threw themselves in with the town radicals to stop the destruction.

Then his life and art began to merge. Hunter saw his involvement in local politics as being part of his American Dream obsession. Real change, he thought, needed to begin close to home. So he went to work. The Republican mayor of Aspen was running for reelection, unopposed. It took a couple of days for Hunter to persuade local attorney Joe Edwards to run for mayor on a "Freak Power" ticket. One Saturday at midnight, Hunter called and said, "My man, you don't know me and I don't know you, but three weeks from now, you're going to be the Mayor of Aspen." Edwards eventually agreed to run. The campaign got a late start (mid-October), but Hunter thought Edwards, "a local head and bike racer known as the 'hippy lawyer,'" would help draw the political line in the sand. Much to Hunter's surprise, the usually apathetic hippie brigade took an interest in the campaign and, despite a dearth of political experience, got out the vote.

It nearly worked. Edwards lost the election by one vote. "I suddenly see a bedrock validity in the American Dream," Hunter wrote Silberman, excited again about his book; "the Joe Edwards campaign was a straight exercise in Jeffersonian Democracy." Energized, Hunter thought the grass-roots political angle was what he had been searching for. "What The Book has lacked, all along, is a reason for writing it," he wrote. "But now, in the wake of this virgin political experience, I think I may have that reason."

It had been a rough year, but the political adrenaline restored Hunter and Sandy to life. After two years of drifting and letdown following the success of his first book, Hunter also felt he had a reason to continue wading through the morass of his unfinished book. "It has changed my whole notion of what's possible in America," he said of the first Freak Power campaign.

Playboy **"aggressively rejected"** Hunter's article on Jean-Claude Killy. He'd taken several shots at Chevrolet in the piece, and the magazine, which had been courting Chevy as an advertiser, saw potential ad revenue disappearing. One editor even wrote, in a memo that Hunter happened to see, that "Thompson's ugly, stupid arrogance is an insult to everything we stand for." Another editor said this would be the last time the magazine would solicit a piece from Hunter Thompson.

Furious, Hunter let his bile fly in letters to friends and soon word got to Warren Hinckle in San Francisco, who had left *Ramparts*. With former *New York Times* reporter Sidney Zion, Hinckle was starting a new magazine to showcase the best of the new journalism. Named for a Nottingham hog farmer, *Scanlan's Monthly* would have a short, active life. "What we had in mind was a muckraking magazine," Zion said. "We just went against everything we found wrong."

Hinckle called. Would Hunter let his new magazine run the piece? Hunter responded with a letter in which he tore *Playboy* to shreds ("That whole goddamn magazine is a conspiracy of anemic masturbators"). Hinckle not only ran the article ("The Temptations of Jean-Claude Killy" appeared in the first issue of *Scanlan's Monthly,* March 1970), but he prefaced the piece with Hunter's letter bitching about being blackballed by *Playboy*. Both Hunter and Hinckle went balls to the wall on most things related to journalism. "Hinckle is an editor that would do anything to get a story, including writing bad checks," proclaimed Hunter. "But I liked him as much as any editor I ever worked for. Whatever needed to be done, he would do it."

It's not hard to see why *Playboy* rejected the article. Despite its nudity, *Playboy* in the late sixties was pretty conservative when it came to writing. Most articles were establishment pieces, and the truly innovative nonfiction was in *Esquire*, which had eliminated erotica in favor of literary journalism. Though Hunter might have been harsh in his characterization of the magazine's editors ("scurvy fist-fuckers to the last man"), they were not about to go out on a limb for him. Hunter's original assignment was for a slick-magazine profile on the skier and his life since becoming world famous. But there were two problems with this plan: (1) Killy didn't talk much, and (2) despite the international-playboy image being crafted for him, Killy was not a very interesting person. A straightforward piece on Killy would have been excruciatingly dull. What Hunter did was make himself the centerpiece of the story and write about his difficulty in developing a story from a boring character.

Introducing what became another common technique, Hunter used a confederate—in this case, Bill Cardoso of the *Boston Globe*. Cardoso met him at Logan Airport halfway through Hunter's time spent with Killy, allowing Hunter to start his tale in medias res. Getting off the plane, Hunter looked like "a serious candidate for a drug bust," Cardoso said. The sidekick device helped Hunter introduce himself to readers. With jeans, a sheepskin vest, and love beads, Hunter stood out in the crowd at the airport, and later at the hotel where Killy is first seen, glad-handing ski-equipment retailers in a beer-and-weenie hospitality suite. Hunter's arrival brought the party to a screeching halt (not that that was hard to do). Hunter described the scene as looking like "a cocktail party for the local Patrolmen's Benevolent Association." Cardoso, in his Sancho Panza role, strolled around the dead party, mumbling to Hunter, "Jesus, where are we? This must be Nixon headquarters."

The article focused on Killy's new career as a celebrity huckster. In an extended scene at the Chicago Auto Show, Hunter contrasted performances by Killy and O. J. Simpson. Simpson appeared comfortable, a natural salesman. By contrast, Killy came across as patently insincere ("his voice was pure snake oil") and extremely ill at ease singing the praises of cars he would not consider driving. Hunter revealed that Killy loathed not only Chevrolets but most everything else American. He was there to take the money and run.

Killy came across as a nearly emotionless character until Hunter mentioned the International Olympic Committee's concern about Killy's endorsements and efforts to strip him of his gold medals because he did not fit the true definition of "amateur." Killy's temper flared, and Hunter saw the man inside. He was not a mannequin after all. At this point in the story, Hunter began conveying some sympathy for Killy, a man trapped in an image he could not tolerate. Hunter stood by grimly, watching Killy enduring the handshaking falsity of salesmanship. "Chevrolet doesn't pay him to say what he thinks, but to sell Chevrolets—and you don't do that by telling self-righteous old men to fuck off." Thompson's appearance in the story was justified, as he was the free man by whom Killy could be measured.

Hunter's description of the Chicago Auto Show was one of his best examples of scene-by-scene construction to that point. He kept the focus on himself as he contrasted the garish automobile spectacular in the Stockyards Amphitheater with his last journey to that venue, for the Democratic National Convention the year before. "Chicago—this vicious, stinking zoo, this mean-grinning, Mace-smelling boneyard of a city; an elegant rockpile monument to everything cruel and stupid and corrupt in the human spirit."

While gorging himself on the spectacle of the auto show, Hunter had a chance to have some fun with a few of the grinning dunces in the crowd:

Meanwhile, slumped in a folding chair near the Killy exhibit, smoking a pipe and brooding on the spooks in this place, I am suddenly confronted by three young boys wearing Bass Weejuns and Pendleton shirts, junior-high types, and one of them asks me: "Are you Jean-Claude Killy?"

"That's right," I said.

"What are you doing?" they asked.

Well, you goddamn silly little waterhead, what the hell does it *look* like I'm doing. But I didn't say that. I gave the question some thought. "Well," I said finally. "I'm just sitting here smoking marijuana." I held up my pipe. "This is what makes me ski so fast."

"The Temptations of Jean-Claude Killy" was probably the first piece in which Hunter displayed all of the basic elements of what would define his style: his place at the center of the story; the concern with getting the story as the centerpiece of the narrative; the use of wild flights of fancy (some announced, others spontaneous); and the use of a companion.

Hunter's mixture of fact with fancy may have been with him all along. In hindsight, *National Observer* editors began wondering about his accuracy. Hunter also began to define his position as a political journalist in the Killy piece. Other journalists parroted what politicians and authorities said. Hunter believed his outlaw journalism was the truest form of journalism because he bypassed the usual sources.

As part of his new, liberating style, Hunter included all his struggles whipping the story into shape. He had to deal with a press agent who wanted to make sure that the Head ski logo appeared prominently in the magazine's layout and that Killy's reputation as a great lover was reinforced—he was French, after all. But Killy was not that man. At one point, Hunter exploded with frustration in a phone call with Killy. "As far as I know," writer said to subject, "you don't exist. You're a life-size dummy made of plastic foam. I can't write much of an article about how I once saw Jean-Claude Killy across a crowded room at the Stockyards Amphitheatre." After a pause, Killy laughed and said, "Well, maybe you could write about how hard it is to write about me."

In his innocent way, Killy gave Hunter the approach he needed. The Killy article was the missing link between all that had gone before and the breakthrough that Hunter would make in May 1970.

Scanlan's Monthly was a perfect, but doomed, venue for Hunter's writing. The Killy piece was in the first issue, and from the start the magazine was intent on afflicting the comforted, ready to take a whack at anyone who deserved one. In its short (nine-month) life, *Scanlan's* caught on, with a circulation of 150,000 after six months, but was harassed by the Internal Revenue Service on orders from the Nixon White House. The magazine took pride in being the first publication to call for Nixon's impeachment—long before that became fashionable.

Hinckle didn't mess with Hunter's copy or cut twenty pages, as the *Pageant* editors had with his Nixon article. Reaction to the Killy piece was strong, from readers and from Hunter's friends, who finally saw in one of his articles the voice they heard in his letters or in his kitchen.

Although he was still in a funk over the American Dream book, the reaction to the Killy piece from his friends made Hunter realize he wasn't insane. He had written about himself as a window to seeing this other character in this other world, *and it worked*. People liked it. Suddenly alive with possibilities, Hunter spun off ideas to Hinckle and threw himself into planning for the local elections the following fall. The *Aspen Times* served as the voice of the town's wealthy, and getting coverage for Freak Power was unlikely. Starting an alternative newspaper was prohibitive, so Hunter dreamed up the Aspen Wallposter: his artist friend Tom Benton created designs for one side, and Hunter ranted on back. Folded in fourths, it was the size of a magazine. He produced the first one in March, beginning the drumbeat for that fall's campaign. Hunter was contemplating a run for sheriff of Pitkin County.

But he again lost fuel for the American Dream book. Silberman reminded him that a new decade had begun and that Random House still hoped to publish *The Death of the American Dream* by Hunter S. Thompson. Hunter hated being dragged back into that mess. "I loathe the fucking memory of that day when I told you I'd 'go out and write about The Death of the American Dream,'" he wrote Silberman. "Fuck the American Dream. It was always a lie & whoever still believes it deserves whatever they get—and they will. Bet on it."

Wallposter no. 4, another Benton design, showed a human brain at the bull's eye of a shooting target labeled "The American Dream." It summarized Hunter's feeling about the concept, and the book project. As he kicked around solutions to the mess, Hunter tried to sell Silberman on the idea of using a fictional narrative, told through the eyes of Hunter's alter ego, Raoul Duke. He could do that or put himself center stage, emphasizing his involvement in many of the events he wanted to string together: the Chicago convention, the election, Nixon's inauguration. But would people be interested in what he had to say? "My ego comes through very heavy, even when I try to write the straightest kind of journalism," he said.

Hunter preferred the Raoul Duke approach, putting his fictional protagonist against a background of real events. He also knew that a collection of his magazine articles as a Tom Wolfe–like compilation might just finally put the beast to rest.

The Wallposters interested him far more than his book. During the Joe Edwards campaign the previous fall, he had used the two-fingered peace symbol as the Freak Power rallying cry. Now he conceived a new logo: a double-thumbed fist, clutching a peyote button. It had a little more of the up-against-the-wall spirit and ended up being Benton's side of Wallposter no. 5, titled "Thompson for Sheriff."

While a friend was giving him a haircut, things went horribly wrong and half of Hunter's head was shaved. At first alarmed, Hunter decided to go ahead and finish the job and go into the world with a gleaming, polished skull. He looked like a true freak, a space alien. He also realized that it gave him a talking point in the campaign. The incumbent had a crew cut. Hunter could now take the high road and refer to his "long-haired opponent."

Hunter needed publicity for his campaign, so he went to the office of *Rolling Stone* in San Francisco. The magazine had been started in 1967 by a college dropout and publishing neophyte named Jann Wenner. He had been in some of the same places at the same time as Hunter, but they had not met. Wenner started at Berkeley in 1964 and, as a student intern for the local NBC affiliate, had covered the Free Speech Movement. He'd wandered in and out of the Matrix and the other San Francisco clubs and even shared friends (most notably music journalist Ralph J. Gleason) with Hunter. Wenner's first experience with publishing had come at *Ramparts*, where he worked for Warren Hinckle.

After a modest start, *Rolling Stone* had shot to fame in 1968 by publishing a picture. While his wife was away on vacation, John Lennon of the Beatles had invited Japanese conceptual artist Yoko Ono to his house to spend the night making recordings. After taping an evening full of screeches, howls, farts, and belches, Lennon and Ono decided to consummate their relationship and photograph themselves nude for the eventual release of the recordings of their bodily sounds. It was 1968; people would buy anything with "Beatle" on it.

But the Beatles' regular record company balked at releasing an album with front-and-back nude views of the couple. Eventually, an independent record label released the album, but packaged it in a brown paper bag. No one really wanted to *hear* the album, but they did want to see famous genitals. So Wenner picked up the phone, called John Lennon, and asked for permission to publish the picture in his little quarter-fold newsprint rock 'n' roll magazine. Word got out that you could buy a magazine for thirty-five cents and get both pictures that were on the $5.98 album. The photos made *Rolling Stone* suddenly famous.

Eighteen months later, the magazine had developed a reputation for intelligent writing about popular music. Wenner had wisely avoided radical politics such as those espoused by true underground magazines like the *Berkeley Barb* or the *L.A. Free Press*. As the prototype of the hip young capitalist, Wenner kept his focus on the music and the lifestyle, with only a gratuitous nod toward politics.

Wenner had built a stable of great writers, including Jon Landau, Greil Marcus, J. R. Young, and Lester Bangs. He'd set the magazine up in a loft, and despite knowing nothing about publishing (he claimed to have never even heard the word "demographics" until he'd run *Rolling Stone* for a year), he was remarkably successful. Wenner liked music and drugs, and he found a lot of like-minded readers in the late sixties. "*Rolling Stone* caught on right away," said Michael Lydon, one of the early staff members. "Most things that you work on fade away, but *Rolling Stone* was hot from issue number one."

The straight press took notice. Wenner was called a publishing genius and a spokesman for his generation . . . the sort of phrases that had been trotted out for Bob Dylan. There was grumbling from the ranks of the underground press. The rap against Wenner was that he was the ultimate groupie, that he had started *Rolling Stone* as a way for him to meet the Beatles. One writer called him "Citizen Wenner," equating him with the power-mad publisher in Orson Welles's *Citizen Kane*. He had built the magazine with those writers he had found and nurtured, but once the magazine achieved success, Wenner went after already well-known writers, such as Tom Wolfe and Truman Capote, becoming a literary groupie.

Rolling Stone was still basically a rock 'n' roll magazine when Hunter S. Thompson came calling on its founder and editor. The conduit for the Wenner-Thompson meeting in April 1970 was John Lombardi, then the *Rolling Stone* managing editor. He'd had a nodding acquaintance with Hunter through their shared experiences in the underground-press branch of the freelance world. In 1967, while editing a Philadelphia paper called the *Distant Drummer*, Lombardi had reprinted a piece Hunter had written for the *L.A. Free Press*. It was an essay on his old friend and mentor Lionel Olay, whom Hunter had befriended in his Big Sur days. Hunter admired Olay's take-no-prisoners/no-compromise style. Olay had a self-destructive streak and once turned what was to be a typical candy-coated Hollywood producer profile into a vicious attack (he called the producer a "pompous toad"), getting himself fired from *Life*. After fighting the good fight and serving alongside Castro, Olay had died of a stroke, not yet out of middle age. Hunter's tribute, "The Ultimate Freelancer," was a rumination on personal freedom with Hunter's thoughts on originality, integrity, and intellectual honesty. It impressed Lombardi.

"I literally felt I'd stumbled on the Jim Morrison/Jimi Hendix of hippie print," Lombardi said. He got Hunter's number and called, hoping to obtain reprint rights. "I got his wife Sandy at 1 p.m. She told me Hunter was still sleeping. He called around 5, when I was leaving the *Drummer* office, and we talked until 9 p.m. We got permission to reprint. I remember telling him—about his style—'stasis is death,' and him replying: 'Friends for life.'"

Lombardi approached Hunter again in 1970, not long after he'd landed at *Rolling Stone*, which was chewing up editors and writers. Lombardi didn't last long before leaving for *Esquire*, but made a long-term impact on the magazine by luring Hunter to Wenner's office. Hunter at first was skeptical. *Rolling Stone* had urged caution and restraint in the days after the Chicago Democratic National Convention, when Hunter and the radical press had been urging continued dissent. But Lombardi was persuasive, and Hunter finally admitted that *Rolling Stone* and its national audience would be a great platform. "I got Hunter into *Rolling Stone* when he was losing his bases at *Ramparts* and *Scanlan's*," Lombardi said. He might also have sensed that the politics of *Ramparts* and *Scanlan's* doomed them economically and that the middle-of-the-road *Rolling Stone* might turn into a better and more stable market. Its neutrality certainly gave it a better chance of luring big-name advertisers and staying afloat.

Lombardi warned Wenner that the "Thompson guy" was a little unusual. Hunter made a bad first impression on Wenner by being late. The editor fumed in his oversized straw chair behind his huge round desk. "This better be good," he spat at Lombardi, as he awaited Hunter's arrival.

Then Hunter appeared in the doorway, wearing an aloha shirt, a frosted-blond woman's wig, and clenching in his teeth a cigarette holder, looking like a demented Franklin Roosevelt. He carried a satchel, with hats, wigs, police sirens, knives, flares, and some manuscripts, and he juggled on his knees two six packs as he sprawled on the couch in the editor's office. "He was throwing down a little style on us," copy editor Charles Perry said.

Hunter spoke the way he wrote. He began spewing venom on lawyers, Aspen greed-heads, real-estate agents, developers, phony movie stars . . . virtually all of creation. He was like guitar god Eric Clapton, off on a solo. No one else had a chance to speak. "Oral rock 'n' roll," Lombardi called it.

After a forty-five-minute monologue and guzzling one of the six packs, Hunter got up, inquired his way to the john, and left. Silence fell. Wenner had slumped so far down in his chair that he was nearly horizontal. He turned to Lombardi and said, "I know I'm supposed to be the spokesman for American Youth Culture and all, but what the fuck was *that?*"

In 1970, Wenner was a savvy young businessman and might have realized that Hunter might be the person to bridge his capitalist enterprise with suspicious members of the counterculture. Some felt that Wenner was amassing a huge audience based on *Rolling Stone*'s co-opting of many elements of the radical lifestyle, but none of its politics. Lombardi brought in Hunter as a writer of some credibility and renown. The political angle didn't bother Wenner. After all, it was "freak power," an obviously oddball group, and it was more of an entertainment story than a political one. "Thompson couldn't help himself," Lombardi said. "He was naturally wired to rebel. And rebellion was selling, which is where Jann came in. He was always a rich-kid entrepreneurial type."

So Wenner struck a deal for an article focused on Hunter's campaign that fall for sheriff. Hunter hoped the national attention would lure the freaks out of the mountains to register and vote. Wenner just thought it would draw more readers and pull some of the heat off of him for being politically wimpy. To show some solidarity, Wenner offered to sell the Aspen Wallposters through the pages of *Rolling Stone*.

Hunter was a self-described hillbilly, and Wenner was more cosmopolitan. Hunter had been on his own since he was eighteen, living on financial seeds and stems; Wenner came from a wealthy family. Hunter limped to the finish line in high school, and Wenner had the benefit (for a while) of a Berkeley education. Hunter was better read than Wenner, yet they had enough in common to make for an interesting if wary friendship and a profitable collaboration. Hinckle was a great editor; with Wenner, though, Hunter's work reached a new level.

"The main thing is that I got him and he got me," Wenner said. "I understood his sense of humor. I think he saw in me a lot of stuff that he liked. He saw that his ambitions could be realized in what I was doing. We had mutual goals that were deep and complex. Both of us were pursuing the same agenda. I think I was the best editor around for him. He saw that, just as a technical matter. I just knew how to edit his copy and handle him better than anybody else. I understood the balance of when we had to work and to play and to indulge him. Hunter wanted to find an editor he could be in fine hands with. Everyone wants an editor they can trust, be in good hands with, and take good care of them. He knew I would do that always, with care, craft, and love. Everybody had some level of care, craft, and love for him, but I think mine was just deeper and better. He saw that. This is not to take away from anybody else. He knew I knew what I was doing and wasn't going to let him [get away with it.] Too many people with Hunter were like, 'Oh, Hunter, that's great,' and didn't show the critical eye. We just had a deep understanding about what we were both up to."

Tom Wolfe, who would plant the seeds of two of his finest books (*The Right Stuff* and *The Bonfire of the Vanities*) in *Rolling Stone* said that Wenner's particular genius was coaching writers to do their best work. "You have complete freedom to use whatever style you want. It's either great or he hands it back to you." Wolfe put Wenner in the same class as Clay Felker, who served as editor of *New York* and *Esquire*. "Both of them were also fearless when it came to libel, or the threat or the possibility of libel. Both Clay Felker and Jann Wenner made you feel that you had nothing to worry about. Just go all out. We'll worry about transgressions later." It seemed to Wolfe that Hunter embraced the liberating feeling of working for an empowering editor. "I think its mainly the feeling that they want you to do something unusual. They want reporting, but they want it to have individual flair."

Back home later that month, Hunter was having dinner with Jim Salter, an Aspen resident and screenwriter (*Downhill Racer*), when Salter suggested that Hunter go home to Louisville for the upcoming Kentucky Derby. It seemed like a no-brainer to cover the middle-American version of a rock festival. Immediately, Hunter leaped on the phone and got a wee-hours commitment from a groggy Warren Hinckle to do the piece for *Scanlan's*. It needed illustrations, not photos, Hunter said. There was a special kind of ugliness to the Derby that only an illustrator could capture. Hunter wanted Pat Oliphant, the *Denver Post*'s editorial cartoonist. It turned out that Oliphant couldn't make it, but Hinckle said not to worry; *Scanlan's* had someone else in mind.

Ralph Steadman was born around the same time as Hunter—but across the Atlantic, in Wales. Ralph's bizarre illustrations with distended half-skeletal, half-protoplasmic figures set him apart from other young artists. Though he had ambitions to create paintings, books, operas (all of which he would eventually do), at the moment he was known as one of England's most original magazine illustrators. "I never wanted to be an illustrator," Ralph said. "I wanted to be the creator."

However, he also wanted money, so at that point in his career, Ralph was an illustrator. In April 1970, he was recovering from his first week in America: enjoying the hospitality of acquaintances in East Hampton, New York, who had invited him to use their place as his base of operations for his assault on America. He was finally getting ready to head into the city and start looking for work when the phone rang. It was J. C. Suares, the art director of *Scanlan's*. He invited Ralph to fly to Louisville to meet with Hunter, whom he described as a former Hell's Angel with a shaved head. Ralph took the assignment and was being hustled to the airport for the flight to Louisville, when he realized he didn't have his toolkit. How could he draw without his pens and brushes? Luckily, one of *Scanlan's* editors thought to take him by his apartment on the way to the airport, where he borrowed eyebrow pencils, lipstick, and blush from the editor's wife.

When Ralph got to Louisville, he tried to find Hunter at the hotel where they were both booked, but the writer was not around. Ralph wandered out to Churchill Downs, still not sure whom he was looking for. He had no credentials, nothing to identify himself as a journalist, but he did have a natural willingness to ask directions. He bulled his way into the press area and wandered around for a while, looking for a Hell's Angel. Eventually, a bullet-headed man approached him and asked whether he was the fellow from England. No doubt Hunter and Ralph were the two oddest-looking people in the room—Hunter with his cigarette holder and gleaming scalp, and Ralph with wild locks and a pointed, somewhat accusatory beard.

They sat down with drinks, watched a couple of races, and began building a friendship. "It was my first time in America and I hit a bull's eye," Ralph said. "I met the strangest man in America." They discovered they had a lot in common—perhaps most important, a deep hatred of authority. "At that time," Ralph said, "one was intent on bringing down the establishment and having a better world." Although they shared values, Ralph said they were "as different as a moose is from a crab."

The article that Hunter and Ralph created from their first shared experience ("The Kentucky Derby Is Decadent and Depraved") was the next step after the Jean-Claude Killy piece in building the new guerrilla-warfare journalism that *Scanlan's* encouraged. Unlike the Killy piece, which floated through Hunter's weeks of hanging out with the skier, the Derby article reflected a clear sense of time; Hunter chronicled his adventure from two days before the race until two days after, though "chronicled" might not be the operative word. In the story, Hunter's reality was punctuated freely with fantasy.

From the moment of meeting Ralph, Hunter conjured up images of the crazed whiskey gentry he expected to see out in force at Churchill Downs. Upon his arrival, Hunter had been toying with some of his hometown's denizens, alarming one businessman at the airport lounge ("Call me Jimbo," he had said by way of introduction, giving the piece a Melvillean start), by telling him that he was there to cover the expected Black Panther riot. Jimbo's face twisted into a mask of pain as he envisioned his beloved American institution under attack:

> "No!" he shouted; his hands flew up and hovered momentarily between us, as if to ward off the words he was hearing. Then he whacked his fist on the bar. "Those sons of bitches! God Almighty! The Kentucky Derby!" He kept shaking his head, "No! *Jesus*! That's almost too bad to believe!" Now he seemed to be sagging on the stool, and when he looked up his eyes were misty. "Why? Why *here*? Don't they respect *anything*?"
>
> I shrugged again. "It's not just the Panthers. The FBI says busloads of white crazies are coming from all over the country—to mix with the crowd and attack all at once, from every direction. They'll

be dressed like everybody else. You know—coats and ties and all that. But when the trouble starts . . . well, that's why the cops are so worried."

He sat for a moment, looking hurt and confused and not quite able to digest all this terrible news. Then he cried out: "Oh . . . Jesus! What in the name of God is happening in this country? Where can you get *away* from it?"

"Not here," I said, picking up my bag. "Thanks for the drink . . . and good luck."

The airport-lounge scene seems too perfect, too good an introduction to have simply occurred. It's one of those scenes that made Hunter's warier readers wonder about the ratio of fact to fiction in his reporting. Hunter always believed in William Faulkner's maxim that facts and truth didn't always have much to do with each other.

As he had in the Killy piece, Hunter turned the Derby article into a "process" piece—*getting the story* was the story. From the start, he presented himself as a man behind schedule, unable even to locate his collaborator on the piece, unaware what Ralph Steadman looked like. As he recounted his struggle to get his last-minute press passes, he seemed on the verge of a nervous breakdown. When publicity officers didn't provide what he needed, he threatened them with a blast of Mace.

When Ralph appeared, he provided a great storytelling device: Hunter, who was in his old hometown, had a chance to see the world with the virgin sensibilities of a foreigner. The bouncing-comments-off-a-companion device worked well with Bill Cardoso in the Killy article. The effect was magnified in the Derby article because Hunter and Ralph were such opposites, which is why their collaboration worked. "If he had chosen someone like himself, there would have been two battling maniacs," Ralph said. "I was intelligent enough to know what was happening to me, but I would go along with it. I approached the subject as a stranger, which is an entirely different dimension."

Hunter set the scene for Ralph:

"Just pretend you're visiting a huge outdoor loony bin," I said. "If the inmates get out of control we'll soak them down with Mace. . . ."

The only thing we lacked was unlimited access to the clubhouse inner sanctum in sections "F&G" . . . and I felt we needed that, to see the whiskey gentry in action. The governor, a swinish neo-Nazi hack named Louie Nunn, would be in "G," along with Barry Goldwater and Colonel Sanders. . . .

"That whole thing," I said, "will be jammed with people; fifty thousand or so, and most of them staggering drunk. It's a fantastic scene—thousands of people fainting, crying, copulating, trampling each other and fighting with broken whiskey bottles. We'll have to spend some time out there, but it's hard to move around, too many bodies."

"Is it safe out there? Will we ever come back?" [Ralph asked.]

"Sure," I said. "We'll just have to be careful not to step on anybody's stomach and start a fight." I shrugged. "Hell, this clubhouse scene right below us will be almost as bad as the infield. Thousands of raving, stumbling drunks, getting angrier and angrier as they lose more and more money. By midafternoon, they'll be guzzling mint juleps with both hands and vomiting on each other between races."

In the version of events that became "The Kentucky Derby Is Decadent and Depraved," after Hunter focused on his prerace preparation for horror, he quickly dispatched race-day events and ended with a detailed two-days-later scene, in which Hunter and Ralph suffered epic hangovers. Other, saner events were left out of the story. Southern Gentleman Hunter introduced Ralph to his family. They went to dinner with brother Davison and his wife. Ralph began sketching Davison. Apparently his exaggerated style (no one ever looked pretty in a Ralph drawing) offended Davison and horrified his wife. Hunter was mostly concerned with introducing the recently arrived Englishman to America in the Age of Nixon. He pushed Ralph to find "the face." He vowed the face would be bloated and booze-ravaged, full of horror and bile. They found it, of course, a couple of days after the race. "We didn't really find the decadent and depraved face around us," Ralph recalled. "We looked in the mirror and that's where we saw the decadence and depravity."

The Derby ended up playing a minor, almost off-camera role in the story. In fact, Hunter wound up writing the story not only about trying to write the story but also about trying to guide Ralph's illustrations. The artist's work was hilarious, but monumentally insulting to his subjects. The magazine used Ralph's drawing of the gap-toothed moron as the lead-in for the piece. Ralph had found a lot of horrible-looking people to draw: "The swamp-like humidity of a place like Kentucky brings rivers of sweat pouring over those undulating plains of wobbling flesh, dripping onto polished vinyl floors or down their socks into maroon and white sneakers."

After the race, Hunter and Ralph separately headed to New York, where the *Scanlan's* East Coast office was run by Hinckle's partner Sidney Zion and managing editor Don Goddard. Ralph got there first and was happy to discover that the New York office was above a pub. He finished his work, steadying himself with several pints from downstairs. He shipped his drawings to Hinckle in San Francisco, who called to suggest that a story on the Derby might include a picture of a horse. Ralph promised to get right on it and did so—giving the horse gigantic, distended genitals—before fleeing to England.

Hunter's problems were not so easily resolved. He would rather fly to San Francisco to work with Hinckle, or work at home in Woody Creek. But the magazine decided he should work in New York. Hunter was housed at the Royalton Hotel, on Forty-fourth Street, just off Fifth Avenue, and a copyboy shuttled messages and pages between him and the *Scanlan* office. This odd arrangement puzzled Hunter, but he was under too much deadline pressure to question logistics. For six days, locked into his room with his amphetamines, he wrote a blockbuster full of flashbacks about his return home and the ghosts he encountered. Most of his dive into the past was eventually cut from the article (Goddard slashed four thousand words), but it was the beneath-the-surface background the story needed to float. Eventually, Hunter decided that chronology was his friend, and he pulled together a fairly coherent narrative. It was only *fairly* coherent because, under deadline pressure, Hunter broke from the narrative and started sending the editors scrawled pages ripped from his journal: half-formed thoughts, sketches, semilucid notes. "When I first sent one down with the copy boy, I thought the phone was going to ring any minute with some torrent of abuse," he said. "I was waiting for the shit to hit the fan, but almost immediately the copy boy was back and wanted more. . . . I was full of grief and shame. It was the worst hole I had ever gotten into." Still the editor wanted more. "I was desperate. Ralph Steadman had done the illustrations, the cover was printed and there was this horrible hole. . . . I was convinced I was finished, I'd blown my mind, couldn't work. I was sure it was the last article I was ever going to do for anybody." Hunter couldn't believe what the editors were doing—or rather, weren't doing—with his copy. "They printed it word for word even with the pauses, thoughts and jagged stuff like that," he said. Whereas he had constructed a conventional opening, just at the moment in the narrative when he and Ralph appeared to be spiraling out of control, guzzling Wild Turkey and behaving like madmen, the tone of the article changed. But the stops-and-starts of visions and fantasies matched their actions. Hunter eventually brought it home with a traditionally structured ending, in which he took Ralph to the airport, kicked him out of the car (calling him a "twisted pigfucker"), and offered this benediction: "We can do without your kind in Kentucky."

This was it. Hunter was convinced he would never again work for a major magazine. He also thought that Ralph's drawings would be too repulsive for publication and that he would never be allowed to return to the United States. After the thing was sent off to the printer, Hunter wrote Hinckle an apology. "It strikes me as a monument to whatever kind of limbo exists between humor and tragedy," he wrote. "I wish there'd been time to do it better." To his friend Bill Cardoso, he confessed, "It's a shitty article, a classic of irresponsible journalism." In the aftermath, he realized he had no carbon copy. There had been no time to rewrite . . . no time to look back on what he had written. He was a failure at the craft he had been practicing for more than a decade.

He was wrong. "The Kentucky Derby Is Decadent and Depraved" was hailed as a triumph and brought rabid attention to *Scanlan's*. "I started getting calls and letters," Hunter said. "People were calling it a tremendous breakthrough in journalism, a stroke of genius. And I thought, *What in the shit?*"

The marriage of Hunter's words and Ralph's pictures was a new strain of creative DNA that would thrive for thirty more years. Praising the article, Tom Wolfe celebrated Hunter's "manic, highly-adrenal first-person style." Putting the writer center stage was not always a good idea, Wolfe said, but it worked because Hunter usually casts himself as a "frantic loser, inept and half-psychotic, somewhat after the manner of Celine" and because much of the Derby description comes "in the form of Celine-like fantasies he presents to the artist, Ralph Steadman, in conversation."

Hunter's article was truly different—far above anything to come out of *Harper's*, *Esquire*, or even *Rolling Stone*. "I don't know what the fuck you're doing," Cardoso wrote back, "but you've changed everything. It's totally gonzo."

Finally, Hunter had a name for what he did.

Chapter 10

FREAK POWER

This is our country, too, and we can goddam well control it if
we learn to use the tools.
—HST, 1969

*G*onzo: Perhaps derived from the French Canadian *gonzeaux.* The word had a couple of different meanings, but Bill Cardoso used it in the Boston-bar derivation, referring to the last man standing after a night of drinking. *Gonzo* had a nice ring. Plus, there was an old James Booker organ instrumental out of New Orleans that Hunter used to pick up on WWL late at night. "Gonzo" had been a regional hit and Hunter had liked the demented, loopy tune from the first time he heard it.

Back in Woody Creek, Hunter had brooded over his failure. "The article is useless," he wrote to Ralph Steadman, though he congratulated himself for exciting flashes of style and tone. But then the praise began coming in from readers, and he reconsidered. "The Kentucky Derby Is Decadent and Depraved" provided Hunter his epiphany. When it was published, he remembered "massive numbers" of phone calls, letters, and well-wishes, all saying it was some kind of next step in the evolution of journalism. Hunter, who had his tail between his legs, was stunned.

"I thought, 'Holy shit, if I can write like this and get away with it, why should I keep trying to write like the *New York Times*?' It was like falling down an elevator shaft and landing in a pool full of mermaids."

Getting away with it: one of the central themes of his childhood. Because of his natural charm, wit, and charisma, he had coasted through so many of his childhood troubles. Now he realized he didn't have to reach back and pull out the Dow Jones polish or refrain from stepping into the story. He could write about the slings and arrows of being Hunter, and *people would buy it*.

Though his name did not yet tumble off the lips of American suburbanites, he did arouse the world of journalism. *Scanlan's* was not ubiquitous, like *Life* or *Time*, but it was on the coffee tables of the hip, and Hunter Thompson was drawing notice as the newest of the new journalists. After Tom Wolfe had made his splash in the early sixties, others had followed—including bona fide literati, such as Truman Capote and Norman Mailer. Though Wolfe's nose curled when he heard the phrase "New Journalism," there was no denying that's what everyone called it.

But Hunter stayed apart from the new journalists and tilled his Gonzo sharecropper's claim, working at a parcel separate from the other new journalists. He drew a distinct line of demarcation between himself and . . . those other guys.

"Unlike Tom Wolfe or Gay Talese, for instance, I almost never try to reconstruct a story," Hunter said. "They're both much better reporters than I am, but then I don't really think of myself as a reporter. Gonzo is just a word I picked up because I liked the sound of it—which is not to say there isn't a basic difference between the kind of writing I do and the Wolfe/Talese style. They tend to go back and re-create stories that have already happened, while I like to get right in the middle of whatever I'm writing about—as personally involved as possible."

Hunter was smart enough to see that *Scanlan's* would not last. He knew that the bicoastal operation and Hinckle's and Zion's spendthrift ways were crippling the magazine. Hunter tried to advise Hinckle about over-the-top mismanagement.

But as long as they paid, Hunter was willing to work for *Scanlan's*. Hinckle sensed he had stumbled into a great partnership by putting Hunter together with Ralph. Hunter agreed and was bowled over when a friend suggested the team begin a series called the Thompson-Steadman Report, something that would routinely debunk America's most cherished institutions. It was a brilliant and simple concept, he told Hinckle: the two of them would travel the country "and shit on *everything*," writing "venomous bullshit" about America and all of its most cherished institutions. The Kentucky Derby was just the start. *Mardi Gras . . . the Master's . . . the Super Bowl . . . New Year's Eve in Times Square. . . .* Hunter ticked off a huge list for Ralph, trying to sell him on the idea. Witness all these events, "rape them all, quite systematically," then package as a book on the American Dream, defiled. It might allow Hunter to kill two birds with one stone. He called it a "king-bitch dog-fucker of an idea."

Hunter was exploding with *let's-shit-on-everything* ideas when he should have been cranking up for the sheriff's race that fall. Hunter called in reinforcements—brother Jim had come for the second summer in a row and was keeping Sandy and Juan company. Hunter had not commented on Jim's coming-out letter, but by his invitation showed that he accepted his brother's sexuality. He also needed Jim's help with his campaign. Hunter was sincere about his political ambitions. "I wanted to control my environment," he said.

Finally, in midsummer, Hunter and Ralph compared calendars to see what event they could cover. Ralph suggested the America's Cup yacht race, set for mid-September. Hunter figured he could afford a vacation from his campaign to go watch some sailboats.

In the meantime, Hunter was already overdue for his first *Rolling Stone* assignment, his promised self-blow job on the sheriff's campaign. The idea was to have the piece in print by July, to mobilize an army of freaks to descend on Aspen to get out the vote and scare the hell out of the good citizens. But the story wasn't happening; Hunter was too excited by his reporting breakthrough to concentrate yet on his campaign.

When Ralph returned to the States, he and Hunter set off for Newport, Rhode Island, in the waning days of the summer. What followed was a pointless and mostly nauseated week aboard a schooner in Rhode Island Sound. *Scanlan's* had arranged berths onboard for Hunter and Ralph, and the captain had hired a rock band for a week and run a pirate flag up the mast. While their shipmates partied, the two of them watched the action—or rather, inaction—in the competition. The isolation of the separate crews dulled possibilities for conflict. Two full days were spent waiting for the weather to change. Ralph was sick to his stomach from being on the water. Hunter was fine. "You seem to be having a wonderful time in this nightmare," Ralph told Hunter. "I rely on my medicine to keep totally twisted," Hunter replied, and offered the artist one of his pills.

The LSD nearly blew off the top of Ralph's head. "I started seeing red-eyed dogs emerging from the piano," Ralph said. "My hair felt slick and I felt it coming down on my forehead like Hitler. The psilocybin just gouged out my interior." Luckily, he had an experienced drug user at his side to guide him. By Hunter's account, "Ralph was in an insane condition for three or four straight days." They made a dinghy trip to shore, bought some supplies, and called *Scanlan's* in New York. They learned that the magazine was going out of business. The America's Cup story would be in the last issue, assuming they made deadline.

Fuck deadline. They were still spending *Scanlan's* money . . . time for some real fun. Under cover of darkness, Hunter suggested vandalism. He produced cans of spray paint. He and Ralph rowed up to the hull of *Gretel*, the lead challenger from Australia. He deferred to Ralph: What would he want to spray on the side? Ralph thought for a moment and suggested, "Fuck the Pope." He was in position, shaking the spray cans, when the noise of the ball in the can aroused a security guard. *You there! What are you doing?* Immediately, Ralph dropped the paint cans, and Hunter began rowing back to their schooner. The hull remained virgin.

The assignment was a bust. The *Intrepid*, the last classic wooden yacht to defend the cup, won the race for the Americans, but even if Hunter *had* done a story, he might not have had much use for that information. Results were never that important. No story ever appeared, though Ralph published an abbreviated America's Cup portfolio in his 1976 book *America*. More importantly, he stored away his hallucinogenic visions from his Hunter-guided seagoing acid trip for use the following summer.

Back in Aspen, with his best freelance outlet belly up, there was only one thing for Hunter to do with his time and talent: scare the shit out of the populace. As if his shaved and gleaming skull and teardrop aviator shades hadn't been enough to frighten Aspen taxpayers, Hunter's political platform rattled them to their gonads and kept them tossing in sweaty sheets at night.

Hunter proposed changing Aspen's name to Fat City. *Who in their right mind would want to live in Fat City . . . visit Fat City . . . buy vacation homes in Fat City?* Property values would plummet. He also wanted to jackhammer the streets and replace the asphalt with sod. Automobiles and trucks would be stopped at the city limits, and Fat City would have only foot and bike traffic. For amusement, citizens would visit the public square, to shower spittle on the bad dope dealers, punished there in the stocks.

Bob Braudis, a recent arrival from Boston, had escaped the corporate world for the ski-bum life. Hunter's campaign drew his interest. "Everything he was saying I liked," Braudis said. The incumbent was "a traditional redneck rural sheriff with a bunch of knuckle-dragging deputies." The Aryan old guard in Aspen was made up largely of transplanted Germans who'd settled in Colorado after the Second World War. "They were to the right of Clorox," Braudis said. Enchanted with the Freak Power platform, Braudis signed on as a foot soldier in Hunter's campaign, helping to register the largely apathetic freak vote. His nodding acquaintance with Hunter would develop into a rich thirty-year friendship.

Hunter had been living in Pitkin County for only three years, but he was already known around town, and the mainstream townsfolk regarded him as "a half-mad cross between a hermit and a wolverine." Sure, he'd been tolerated for his blaring rock music, and his love of guns and explosives. All that was well and good, as long as he kept his antics to his acreage up at Woody Creek. But in town in a position of power? No wonder they were losing sleep.

Hunter finally turned in his rant to *Rolling Stone*. It ran October 1, with the cover line "Freak Power in the Rockies" spread across the nose of musician Felix Cavaliere of the Rascals. It was just a month before the election and too late to motivate the nation's freaks to descend on the town. Most of "The Battle of Aspen" (as the article was titled inside) recounted the previous year's Joe-Edwards-for-Mayor campaign and the history of the Freak Power uprising. In 1970, Hunter was doing an end-run campaign, hoping that his over-the-top bid for sheriff would draw attention away from the race the Freak Power ticket really hoped to win, Ned Vare's bid to become county commissioner. Also, Hunter's old Louisville friend and Woody Creek neighbor, Billy Noonan, was running for coroner, because the coroner was the only official with the authority to remove the sheriff from office. "Hunter decided to be a lightning rod," said Michael Solheim, the Freak Power campaign manager. "Ned was a quiet and conservative-seeming person, who in fact had a lot of undercurrents." Solheim was part of the consortium that produced the Wallposter as well as the campaign—a group Hunter named the Meat Possum Athletic Club, in a nod to the Louisville group's Hawks Athletic Club.

In telling the saga of Freak Power, Hunter came as close as he ever would to outlining a political philosophy. He provided an agenda for a generation of artists and writers, from musician Jimmy Buffett to then budding writer Carl Hiaasen. Hunter promoted rage against the machine, declaring war on greed-heads and land rapers. In Hunter's view, the last half of the sixties marked the end of traditional politics. "The old Berkeley-born notion of beating The System by fighting it gave way to a sort of numb conviction that it made more sense in the long run to Flee, or even to simply hide, than to fight the bastards on anything even vaguely resembling their own terms."

To the outsider, Hunter's campaign seemed like purely recreational politics. Let's do this and see what happens. Since Hunter was always known for pranks, maybe this was prankism raised to Cecil B. DeMille scale. But he discovered that a lot of people were mobilized by his campaign, by his charisma, and by what he had to say. They actually believed in him. "We really thought we had the momentum," Braudis said. At that point, Hunter began taking the campaign seriously. Besides, running for office was something serious writers did—Norman Mailer and Upton Sinclair had each tested the waters, and failed.

In October, Hunter asked his old friend Porter Bibb to run the campaign. "I can't do it," Bibb told him. "If you win, it's going to set law enforcement and jurisprudence back a half a century." Other friends did come to help, including Bill Kennedy, his old pal from Puerto Rico. So did Oscar Acosta, who had run for sheriff of Los Angeles County and suffered annihilation at the polls. After the *Rolling Stone* article, the BBC sent a crew to Aspen. The *New York Times*, the *Los Angeles Times*, and *Time* magazine all took notice and even gave him a chance of winning. Even the cautious *National Observer* thought its old correspondent might be on the verge of a political breakthrough: "If Mr. Thompson is indeed elected sheriff, his techniques are likely to be copied by young people elsewhere." The campaign drew so much attention because it seemed like a generational/philosophical/cultural conflict all in one. With people like Acosta stomping around town, the Aspen regulars grew suspicious and terrified. Solheim turned the bar at the Hotel Jerome into campaign headquarters ("That was the hive of political activity," Braudis said). The addition of booze to the other substances

Hunter, Acosta, and the others regularly ingested made the group even louder and more menacing.

Tensions were so high that the incumbent sheriff, Carol Whitmire, called in the Colorado Bureau of Investigation to see what could be done. Freak Power campaign leaders were advised to shut down operations at the Jerome, that there might be violence, presumably from the ardent right-wingers opposed to them. Solheim immediately took Sandy and Juan to his home for safekeeping (Sandy had been the key behind-the-scenes agent of the campaign). Hunter, Kennedy, his old friend John Clancy, and a radicalized former NFL player named Dave Meggysey turned the ranch into a fortified compound, ready to retaliate against any violence. There was a rumor about a plan to torch Owl Farm. Aside from one car full of crazies turned away from the gates, nothing happened.

"You can't put the campaign in the context of any 'normal' political campaign," Meggysey said. "It was being done from a sense of outrage. . . . The point was to take the valley back from the greed-heads."

It was close on election night. Surrounded by supporters and journalists, cameras and lights pressing in on him, wearing his blond bouffant wig, and wrapped in an American flag, Hunter led for a good part of the day, which startled him. In the end, the late returns from the trailer-park precincts sealed a win for the incumbent. "Hunter lost the goddamn redneck vote," said his friend, political operative Dick Tuck. "He got the hippies and the in-town votes. He loved the plastic hippies." Tuck had urged Hunter to work the trailer parks, but the candidate wasn't interested. Still, he had come close: Thompson, 1,065 votes, Whitmire, 1,533 votes. Noonan and Vare also lost their races. "We would have won if we had taken the thing a drop more seriously," Solheim said.

While supporters, some weeping and unable to accept his defeat, sniffled all around him, Hunter—still wearing the wig and flag—withstood the hot television lights and made his concession speech. "Unfortunately, I proved what I set out to prove," he said, "that the American Dream really is fucked. I didn't believe it until now." He ripped off the wig and flashed the smile that made women melt. "I've already made up my mind—this is my last trip in politics . . . at least, this kind of politics."

Other postmortems on the election followed. "If we can't win in Aspen, we can't win anywhere," the *New York Times* quoted Hunter as saying, though at other times, he was more optimistic. "I didn't really want to be sheriff," he said. "I just wanted to own him." He took satisfaction in know-

Hunter was "a cute, jolly, fun kid and he made me laugh," said high school girlfriend Judy Stellings. *From the 1953* Spectator, *courtesy of Porter Bibb.*

Hunter's juvenile-delinquent role models included Marlon Brando and James Dean. *Courtesy of the Filson Historical Society.*

Hunter's serious demeanor in his senior portrait in the Male High yearbook belies his hoodlum nature. *Courtesy of the Filson Historical Society.*

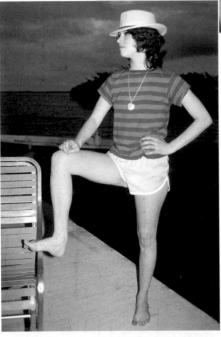

2505

Hunter took refuge in
the Florida Keys at the
end of the seventies
with girlfriend Laila
Nabulsi. While fans
clamored for more
Gonzo journalism,
Hunter savored the
island life. *Photographs by
Tom Corcoran.*

In Jimmy Buffett's borrowed Key West apartment (*top*), Hunter scrutinizes one of his works-in-progress. During one of his stays in the Keys to prepare for his role as Hunter in *Where the Buffalo Roam*, actor Bill Murray (*bottom*) joined Hunter for a spin on the boat Hunter bought with his movie check. *Photographs by Tom Corcoran.*

Tom Corcoran and Hunter at the Bat Tower on Sugarloaf Key,
scouting places where the smugglers of their *Cigarette Key* screenplay
would hide their stash. *Photograph by Tom Corcoran.*

Hunter created wall-sized storyboards and collages to help organize
his work. Here's his wall circa 1983, with a portrait of Juan prominent
(*lower right*). *Photographs by Tom Corcoran.*

Deborah Fuller worked with Hunter for twenty-three years and lived at Owl Farm. He once accidentally shot her while trying to scare a bear away from her cabin, but she lived to tell the tale. *Photograph courtesy of Deborah Fuller.*

Hunter with his Great Red Shark in front of his Woody Creek home in 1994. *Photograph by Christopher Felver / Corbis.*

A nocturnal creature, Hunter did some of his best farming at night on his beloved John Deere. *Photograph by Kevin Simonson.*

Hunter behaved himself at Juan's wedding to Jennifer Winkel, wearing dress clothes and even tolerating a religious service. *Photograph by Louie Psihoyos / Corbis.*

ing he had "scared the piss out of people." Hunter soon had finished a 160-page manuscript about his run for sheriff, but the microscopic detail in his rendering of the Battle of Aspen probably would not have found a large audience. Still, he had begun writing his running autography.

Acosta had come to Colorado to help Hunter as a favor; now he wanted something in return. Acosta had a lot in common with Hunter. They had both endured stretches in the Air Force, they liked drink and drugs, and they were political radicals. Acosta used the GI Bill to get through San Francisco State and law school, passing the bar on his second attempt. But clients didn't line up to hire the large, noisy, drug-addled Chicano attorney, because he might not play well in court. He was still working for the East Oakland Legal Aid Society when Solheim introduced him to Hunter during his 1967 visit to Aspen. He and Hunter had spent time together and become friends, a relationship deepened by their intense correspondence.

By 1968, Acosta had moved to Los Angeles and became active in *El Movimiento*, which hoped to do for Hispanic Americans what Martin Luther King had done for African Americans. White kids protesting the war had leftist attorney William Kunstler to bail them out when they got in trouble. Acosta saw himself as a Kunstler with salsa in his blood. Acosta was seen as a leader of the Chicano-rights movement. If he didn't quite have the stature of Cesar Chavez, he was at least America's second-most-well-known Hispanic activist.

Acosta spoke with the ferocity Hunter poured into his writing. As a limit pusher himself, Hunter liked having Oscar around for his amusement. "You never knew with Oscar what was going to happen next," Hunter said.

Acosta wanted to draw Hunter into a story. He saw conspiracy in the murder of *Los Angeles Times* reporter Ruben Salazar. The police claimed his death was an accident, a natural byproduct of a riot in the barrio. But since Salazar had been deeply critical of the L.A. city government, Acosta felt he had been silenced. Hunter had actually started working on it (and even roughed out a draft) when *Scanlan's* had been a viable publishing concern. Now that *Rolling Stone* was asking Hunter to write regularly, Acosta saw an even better deal. Hunter could come to L.A., do more interviews, update the piece. Getting the story in this hot new magazine, which went into the hands of rich young liberal white kids, would give him the pulpit he needed for the story, and Acosta might finally become a star.

Hunter's deep-seeded loyalty was legendary among his friends. There were few things Hunter would not do for members of his tribe. But he was also drawn by Acosta's passion and his own in-the-marrow sense that there was injustice in this case.

East L.A. was a war zone, and Hunter thought that in the eyes of some, he might be the enemy. Everyone was Hispanic. No matter what Acosta said, his helpers and bodyguards distrusted the gringo writer. Hunter stayed in a flophouse near Acosta's office, but felt he was in danger. He was more afraid of being smacked around by Acosta's associates than he ever had been of the Hell's Angels. Hunter wanted some quality time with Acosta, to nail down a few of the details in the story, but he couldn't do it in the flophouse or in the very pink Beverly Hills Hotel, where they decamped for drinks. Then the perfect solution presented itself.

Not only was it the perfect solution; it was something that someone else would pay for. One of Hunter's old friends from *National Observer* days, Tom Vanderschmidt, had gone on to *Sports Illustrated*. He'd thrown Hunter what he thought might be some quick and easy freelance money: go to Las Vegas, watch a motorcycle race, and gather enough information for a 250-word copy block to go with a photo essay in the magazine. Hunter hadn't yet committed, but he thought maybe what he needed to do was take Acosta to Las Vegas, get the private time he needed, do some nearly robotic reporting, and have Time Inc. pick up the tab. What happened in Vegas didn't stay in Vegas. It became the genesis of Hunter's most famous book, but first things first.

Hunter could finally piece together "Strange Rumblings in Aztlan," his most serious piece of sustained reportage and also the most detailed example of semitraditional journalism that he committed for *Rolling Stone*.

Hunter wrote in takes—one- or two-page blasts of frenzy. These alone were not enough to carry a story. Hunter could live with ordinary passages, as long as those peaks were there. Still, this made it hard to assemble a decent magazine article. In such cases, the editor was a central figure, truly a collaborator in lashing together a story.

Everyone at *Rolling Stone* did double duty. Writers also served as editors. As a writer, David Felton was so slow that he was known as the Stonecutter. Maddeningly methodical, he was nonetheless revered for his work on the other side of the desk. His colleague Timothy Ferris once said that he could learn more from one Felton editorial comment than he could have learned from a year in some high-powered journalism school. He hung up a sign over his desk that said, "David Felton is always right."

Felton had not yet moved to San Francisco and was still working out of L.A., so he drew the duty of editing Hunter's massive Salazar article, not a plum assignment. "He is violent," Felton said. "I've seen him yell at people till they burst into tears, and that's violent." Writer Craig Vetter was Hunter's friend, but shuddered at the thought of working regularly with him. "I would hate to be his editor. He's driven people *out* of journalism. He's made old men of young, robust, and otherwise healthy men."

Hunter's work methods frustrated editors, Felton said, because he produced short bursts, and the editor's job was to find the thread to connect the various passages. It was like assembling a quilt, finding a way to put a bunch of scraps together into something cohesive that served a clear purpose.

Endurance also was an issue. As an experienced user of chemicals, Hunter knew the combinations that would allow him to stay up and work steadily for days. Normal humans like Felton could not keep up. Eventually, Felton crashed and Hunter kept working.

From Felton, Hunter learned about the culture of *Rolling Stone*. There were several warring personalities, with Wenner as the top dog. The editorial staff was a revolving door. Wenner famously fired Ed Ward as music editor because of his messy office.

The first person with real staying power was Charlie Perry. His job title varied, but in the early days he was the man most responsible for getting the magazine out. That meant that when Hunter and Felton sent in parts of the Salazar story over the Mojo Wire, the ancestor of the fax machine, Perry was on the other end of the line, in San Francisco, staying up late to compile the ingredients.

"Hunter's copy came in clean," Perry said. "He was very proud of that and was scrupulous about spelling, particularly about spelling the names of prescription drugs correctly. Much of his writing would come in as bits, as episodes needing to be assembled."

Hunter learned about Perry from Felton, who was terrified of his colleague. Perry was the deadline enforcer, and Felton was always running late. Felton told Hunter that while visiting the San Francisco office once, Perry dangled him from a window for being over deadline. Not quite true, Perry said. "I held him out of the window in the office," he said. "Not all of him, just the top part of his body, his head and shoulders. But it was enough for Felton, and it became a story around the office."

Hunter was summoned to San Francisco to write the final sections of the Salazar piece, supervised by Paul Scanlan, *Rolling Stone* managing editor. The staff got to observe the strange new writer up close. There was no office for him, so he was set up in the record library, with a typewriter on a small table. He worked furiously.

Charlie Perry dropped by for a visit. "I thought I'd stick my head in and introduce myself to the famous author of *Hell's Angels*," Perry recalled. "I said, 'Hi, Hunter. I'm Charlie Perry. How's it going?'" Hunter nearly leaped out of his seat and screamed, "I got momentum! I got this momentum! I'm a train on greased rails! I just need to keep the momentum up!" Perry said, "He sounded so hopped up. I didn't understand why he was being so emphatic. He'd reacted to just hearing my name. Two days later, I passed by the record library and stuck my head in again. I said, 'How are you doing?' And he flinches and says, 'I lost the momentum. I haven't slept, I haven't changed clothes. My feet are rotting.' Then I realized that he had talked to Felton."

Perry was the only editor to ever strike fear in Hunter. At first, although Perry admired Hunter's reportorial skills on the Salazar story, he was not impressed by his writing. "It was a traditional piece," Perry said. "In fact, it was too traditional. If I hadn't gotten paid for reading it, I might not have finished it."

Lombardi and Hunter did the final editing in Wenner's office, each page spread out over the parquet floor. They stared at the pages. Lombardi suggested a change, moving a page around like a king's-knight-to-bishop-three. Hunter grunted his approval.

It was a different kind of article from Hunter, and a surprise to readers of "The Battle of Aspen." While he showed up as the prominent narrator of "Strange Rumblings in Aztlan," it was basically a profile of Acosta, the Chicano attorney crusading for truth and justice. There was little goofing around. This was the story of the death of a Chicano journalist during a racial riot and most Hispanics were convinced that Salazar was the victim of a cold-blooded murder.

The process part of the story is not quite as prominent as in the Killy and Derby articles, but he did bring the audience into the tent to show how he gathered information. At a critical moment, Hunter himself becomes the issue as angry militants debate his value to them and their cause. He deals frankly with his uneasiness.

Hunter's reporting was honest enough to lead him away from the bad-white-man argument made by the militant Chicanos. His mission was not to validate Acosta's claims but to find the truth. Along the way, Hunter stopped to take some of his usual shots, including a swipe at the *Los Angeles Herald-Examiner*, "a genuinely rotten newspaper that claims the largest circulation of any afternoon daily in America. As one of the few remaining Hearst organs, it serves a perverted purpose in its role as a monument to everything cheap, corrupt and vicious in the realm of journalistic possibility."

And again, Hunter portrayed himself as a troublemaker, a screwup, the "frantic loser" that Wolfe described. "It was difficult, even for me," he wrote, "to believe that the cops had killed him deliberately. I knew they were capable of it, but I was not quite ready to believe that they had actually done it . . . because once I believed that, I also had to accept the idea that they were prepared to kill anybody who seemed to be annoying them. Even me."

Despite tensions between the Chicano community and the police and despite the well-founded suspicions of his militant associates, Hunter refused to accept the notion of a murder planned at the highest level of Los Angeles municipal government. The police department issued several versions of the event, methodically discounted by eyewitnesses; the militants suggested that these cover stories validated their accounts. Yet Hunter remained the skeptical journalist, in part because of the ever-changing cover stories from police. In the end, he concluded,

> Ruben Salazar couldn't possibly have been the victim of a conscious, high-level cop conspiracy to get rid of him by staging an "accidental death." The incredible tale of half-mad stupidity and dangerous incompetence on every level of the law enforcement establishment was perhaps the most valuable thing to come out of the inquest. Nobody who heard that testimony could believe that the Los Angeles County sheriff's department is capable of pulling off a delicate job like killing a newsman *on purpose*. Their handling of the Sala-

zar case—from the day of his death all the way to the end of the inquest—raised serious doubts about the wisdom of allowing cops to walk around loose on the street. A geek who can't hit a 20 foot wide ceiling is not what you need, these days, to pull off a clean first-degree murder.

Hunter had taken a step back from the in-your-face style of the Killy and Derby pieces. The Salazar article had the same sensibilities and individual voice, but it was not at warp speed. Acosta enjoyed being cast as a noble attorney, and the article was almost a detective story, in the manner of investigative reporting. By offering readers his prejudices up front, Hunter made all of his biases open and honest. Some were unjustified. In a brief passage on Chicano heritage, he evoked memories of the Alamo, which did not bear on the experiences of California Hispanics. One critic challenged him on this piece: "As usual, Thompson is barely interested in facts." Hunter might have shrugged in reply.

It was also a long story. At twenty thousand words, it was the longest *Rolling Stone* article up to that point and definitely a shock to the magazine's sex, drugs, and rock 'n' roll readers, packaged as it was side by side with a profile of eleven-year-old singer Michael Jackson. No doubt Wenner was infatuated with Hunter Thompson. He had begun treating him like a rock star, giving him a sort of license no other member of the staff could obtain. He withstood ribbing—some good-natured, some mean-spirited—from Hunter and even endured the occasional blast from a fire extinguisher, a favored Thompson toy. The love was somewhat mutual. In spring 1971, things were good between Hunter and Wenner. The editor had just published two solid pieces by Hunter, and though there had been the usual haggling over fees and expenses, Hunter thought he had found a more sturdy home than *Scanlan's*.

He had also been working on something else that he thought might be right for *Rolling Stone*. While working on the Salazar article, which had been an intense and emotional time, he had been writing something else for enjoyment, the way that a skilled athlete would work out before the big game. It was something personal and unusual, something done purely for pleasure.

Chapter 11

MAKING A BEAST OF HIMSELF

When success comes in America, it comes in a golden flood.
—*Ann Charters,* Kerouac

Fear and Loathing in Las Vegas was born that spring afternoon at the Polo Lounge of the Beverly Hills Hotel, when a dwarf waiter walked up to Hunter with a portable phone and said, "This must be the call you have been waiting for all this time, sir."

Or so goes the story.

The lingering question, the one that Hunter was always asked, the one that frustrated, amused, and sometimes angered him: *Is it true?* In a reflective moment he said, "*Fear and Loathing in Las Vegas* is a masterwork. I would classify it, in Truman Capote's words, as a nonfiction novel in that almost all of it was true or did happen. I warped a few things, but it was a pretty accurate picture. It was an incredible feat of balance more than literature. That's why I called it *Fear and Loathing*. It was a pretty pure experience that turned into a very pure piece of writing. It's as good as *The Great Gatsby* and better than *The Sun Also Rises*."

He might have wondered: *I bet they didn't ask Hemingway these ques-*

tions . . . or Fitzgerald . . . or even Kerouac. The comparison is apt: Kerouac claimed an essential truth for *On the Road*, but changed the names and classified it as fiction. Hunter wanted the same for his book, but for some reason it was held journalistically accountable, at least as some sort of distorted reality. In the years since *On the Road*, Hunter had realized what an influential voice Kerouac had been to his generation. Hunter's story would be the twisted buddy saga for the next era.

Hunter and Acosta were in Vegas for the running of the Mint 400 motorcycle race on March 20. The race was lame, and with motorcycles and dune buggies swarming through the desert, there was no way to witness any kind of race; everything was lost in the sand. Hunter and Acosta spent most of their time in bars and casinos and driving the Strip in their rented Great Red Shark. After the long weekend, Hunter had what he needed about Salazar and also banged out 25,000 words on the race for *Sports Illustrated*, which the magazine "aggressively rejected" (Hunter's term). Hunter had written a straight account of the race, leaving out Acosta and drugs, but including lucid reportage about gambling history and the story of how Las Vegas sprung from the desert. It was the same basic story, but told from a sober vantage in a parallel universe. There was no way to salvage a copy block or even a caption from the copy Hunter sent. So he kept going, writing his Vegas thing for pleasure, while finishing the Salazar article.

He hadn't planned to write about his Vegas adventures. In his dark moments, he remembered that he was three years overdue on some bogus bullshit called *The Death of the American Dream*. The project that would become his most celebrated book began with the simple desire to get Oscar Zeta Acosta away from his handlers so that they could have some face time for an interview, hence the Beverly Hills Hotel. While having drinks with Acosta, Hunter recalled that his friend Vanderschmidt had said something about a motorcycle race in Las Vegas, an opportunity for some quick-and-easy freelance money that should be a breeze for a professional writer and an opportunity for a nice expense-account weekend. He called Vanderschmidt, who was out. So Hunter hunkered down over Singapore slings with Acosta. Eventually, the dwarf came bearing the telephone and the deal was set.

The account in *Fear and Loathing in Las Vegas* was a heightened version of reality. While in Las Vegas, Hunter and Acosta talked about Salazar and the merits of Acosta's case against the city. They also took a lot of drugs and ran amuck. The talks informed Hunter's reporting for "Strange Rumblings in Aztlan." The recreational madness gave him the foundation for something he called the "Vegas thing," which he was writing for his own amusement, like a five-finger exercise for a pianist . . . just something to keep loose.

Back in his shabby hotel in L.A., Hunter blasted the Rolling Stones' *Get Yer Ya-Ya's Out!* while he pounded the keys. As the sun came up each morning, he set aside Salazar and began writing something fun. "I've always considered writing the most hateful kind of work," he said later. "Nothing is fun when you *have to do it* . . . . So it's a rare goddamn trip for a locked-in rent-paying writer to get into a gig that, even in retrospect, was a kinghell, highlife fuckaround from start to finish."

During the early stages of the Salazar editing, Hunter showed up at Felton's home one morning, clutching the Vegas thing. "He had these *pages* in his hand," Felton said, "and he was *very excited.*" Felton loved what Hunter was doing, and the first nineteen pages ended up in Jann Wenner's office almost immediately. Shaking with excitement, Wenner told Hunter, "Keep on going."

He had started out writing by hand on Mint Hotel stationery, nervously wondering how to sneak out of the hotel without paying. He retyped them later, but the words maintained their sweaty urgency. The pages were passed around the *Rolling Stone* office. Some whistled admiration, others broke out laughing, some were struck numb. "As soon as you finished it and went home," Perry said, "life was incredibly dramatic. You expected disasters to come rolling out of the alleys, water to be boiling over."

By the time he wrapped up the Salazar article and got the *keep-on-going* message from Wenner on the Vegas thing, he knew he needed more to extend the narrative of his adventure. He first wrote to Vanderschmidt at *Sports Illustrated* to thank him for the assignment and for rejecting what he wrote. "Sooner or later you'll see what your call (to me) set in motion," he wrote. "The Lord works in wondrous ways. Your call was the key to a massive freak-out. The result is still up in the air, and still climbing. When you see the final fireball, remember that it was all your fault."

Though the eventual work focused on two events that seem to come over the course of a long, nightmarish week, there was a month between the Mint 400 and the National District Attorneys' Conference on Drug Abuse. Prosecutors and cops came for three days of fun in Sin City, hoping to learn something about the drug menace. But they didn't recognize that the menace was right there, sitting next to them during the seminars: two experienced drug users, one disguised as a journalist, the other as an attorney.

After a nearly two-month exile from Sandy and Juan, Hunter finally returned to Woody Creek. After the shitholes and McMotels of L.A., he was ravenous to be back home, to make love to his wife, to shower 'til the hot water ran out, to fuck in the snow, to indulge himself with his strange appetites (peanut butter, mayonnaise, and garlic). He was happy. After leaving Vegas and the isolation of the California motel, it took him a while, among the comforts of home, to get back into the crazed rhythm he'd found in exile. "This happens every time I leave the scene of a piece," he lamented in a letter to Tom Wolfe, sending him the first part of the Vegas thing. "What I was trying to get at in this was [the] mind-warp/ photo technique of instant journalism: One draft, written on the spot at top speed and basically un-revised, edited, chopped, larded, etc., for publication. Ideally, I'd like to walk away from a scene and mail my notebook to the editor, who will then carry it, un-touched, to the printer."

Once he got back on track, Hunter knew he was writing something manic and marvelous. He didn't lose the thread or fail to find the jangle when he came back to it. *This* writing wasn't painful. It was like being high. He bragged to Wolfe, king of the wild frontier pushers, that he-disguised as Raoul Duke—was now pushing the limits of whatever new journalism was. "I haven't found a drug yet that can get you anywhere near as high as sitting at a desk writing," he said.

Downstairs at his home, there was a large room with a stone fireplace, a thick rug, and redwood paneling. Hunter set up an old door and two sawhorses and planted his IBM Selectric II front and center. Armed with Dexedrine and bourbon, he worked through the summer of 1971. Hunter ate the tuna-and-bacon and grapefruit-and-eggs that Sandy made him, and they took acid and made love again on the carpet, in front of the fireplace. Sandy was his protoplasm alarm clock. Whenever he finally crashed, it was her job to gently wake him with a whisper in his ear. When he finally woke, she helped him worship with newspapers at the altar of breakfast. Eventually, he headed off to the door desk in the writing room in the basement and worked eight to twelve hours at a stretch.

Hunter hid behind Raoul Duke. Acosta appeared as Dr. Gonzo and was changed to a Samoan, because Hunter liked Samoa and to protect

Acosta's identity—not that any intelligent reader of "Strange Rumblings in Aztlan" couldn't put *dos* and *dos* together.

Midsummer and nearly done, Hunter called Ralph Steadman to ask him to illustrate the story. He gave him background on what brought him together with Acosta, and what he was like. "Oscar is a bit fucked up, by the way," Hunter said. "He suffers from ulcers and self doubt. . . . I asked him to accompany me on a journey to the Heart of the American Dream. I was going to ask you, but after that Rhode Island business, I reckoned you would have had enough. And I needed a lawyer—even a Samoan one."

" 'I thought you said he was Hispanic,' Ralph said.

"Well, he is, Ralph, but for the sake of the story I have written Samoan sounds better. Anyway, what I really called you about was whether you would be up for doing some vicious drawings for it if I send you the manuscript."

When the manuscript arrived in England a week later, Ralph breathed a sigh of relief that he had not been along. What Hunter and Acosta did in Las Vegas (assuming the story was true) might have killed Ralph. Too much time with Hunter could be dangerous. "I often thought I would not come back from going places with him."

Ralph read Hunter's pages and realized it was a brilliant piece, and he also felt that he had, in a way, been there. There was the "shock of recognition," as he called it. Looking from the outside in, Ralph projected himself into the car with Duke and Gonzo. "What I was doing was spewing out the fears and pent-up things that I'd had from the drug [experiences] onto paper. It just poured out." The botched America's Cup assignment had been "a dress rehearsal for *Fear and Loathing in Las Vegas*."

Ralph set aside his current work on *Alice through the Looking Glass* and gave frightening and memorable life to the images suggested in Hunter's writing: two hollow-eyed madmen hurtling through the desert in a car; a horrifyingly naked Dr. Gonzo vomiting into a toilet while a maid screams in terror; Dr. Gonzo again, waving a knife in a bathtub while he awaits electrocution; Raoul Duke sneaking out of the hotel lobby, leaving behind the largest unpaid room-service bill in the history of Las Vegas.

Whatever *gonzo* is, when it's dissected, Ralph Steadman's art is part of its core DNA.

"It's hooliganism," Ralph said of Hunter's story, "but it's the finest kind of hooliganism. It's not mindless idiocy; it's something special. It's got to upset people. It's no good otherwise."

Ralph sent the art to Wenner at the end of September 1971, never realizing that he would never see the originals again. It was copyrighted as part of the planned double *Rolling Stone* issues to feature Hunter and Ralph's work.

"They were fucking beautiful," Hunter said of the illustrations. "I told Wenner right off that nobody could possibly catch the madness of this story & that I refused to let anyone else illustrate it . . . but Jesus! I was overwhelmed when I saw the shit."

Wenner promoted the work, now titled "Fear and Loathing in Las Vegas," with a full-page house ad in the October 28 issue, promising something new and different in the next issue. To draw reader interest, the first two paragraphs of Hunter's manuscript were printed:

> We were somewhere near Barstow, on the edge of the desert, when the drugs began to take hold. I remember saying something like, "I feel a bit lightheaded; maybe you should drive. . . ." And suddenly there was a terrible roar all around us and the sky was full of what looked like huge bats, all swooping and screeching and diving around the car, which was going about a hundred miles an hour with the top down to Las Vegas. And a voice was screaming: "Holy Jesus! What are these goddamn animals?"
>
> Then it was quiet again. My attorney had taken his shirt off and was pouring beer on his chest, to facilitate the tanning process. "What the hell are you yelling about?" he muttered, staring up at the sun with his eyes closed and covered with wraparound Spanish sunglasses. "Never mind," I said. "It's your turn to drive." I hit the brakes and aimed the Great Red Shark toward the shoulder of the highway. No point mentioning those bats, I thought. The poor bastard will see them soon enough.

Charles Perry recalled that "Fear and Loathing in Las Vegas" came in from Hunter as complete manuscript. "In fact, I believe he hired a typist, so that the manuscript would be in near-perfect shape. It was very neat. We edited that in what we later realized was a more leisurely fashion than we would work with him in the future." Wenner agreed. "Hunter didn't need a lot of line editing," he said. "He needed hand-holding. He needed attention."

The article ran in two parts (November 11 and 23, 1971) and was credited to Raoul Duke, even though the manuscript made reference to an associate of Duke's named Hunter S. Thompson.

There was the usual haggling over expenses. The initial investment came from Time Inc., but when *Sports Illustrated* kicked back Hunter's copy as unpublishable, the magazine refused to pay even the minimum expenses, necessitating the hasty retreat from Vegas. When Hunter returned for the drug convention, he was on the *Rolling Stone* dime. He also assumed that it would be okay to turn in expenses for drugs, alcohol, and weapons paraphernalia. He got an advance wired to him in Vegas from David Felton, but it turned out to be his retainer, not expense money. He ran up such a monumental credit-card bill that American Express banned him for life. Carte Blanche and the Diners Club put him on a hit list.

Wenner had started a book division called Straight Arrow, and most of its early titles were from *Rolling Stone* projects. He assumed Straight Arrow would publish *Fear and Loathing in Las Vegas*. But before Wenner could get the book contract signed, Hunter made a deal with Jim Silberman at Random House. It was the Random House money at the finish line, in fact, that had encouraged Hunter to complete the work in the first place.

On the verge of his great breakthrough, Hunter Thompson was once again staring down financial ruin.

He subtitled it "A Savage Journey to the Heart of the American Dream," and he deftly and subtly dealt with themes that would have been so heavy-handed in a ponderous *Death of the American Dream* treatment. He let the anger, despair, and disillusionment lie between the lines.

As historian Douglas Brinkley said of *Fear and Loathing in Las Vegas* many years later, "Hunter was using Vegas as a metaphor for the American Dream in an arch and many ways scathing denunciation of American culture, yet at the same time it's a celebration of American culture."

The plot is simple: Raoul Duke and Dr. Gonzo are speeding across the desert to Las Vegas. With the trunk of their red convertible crammed with drugs (mescaline, LSD, ether, cocaine, nitrates, tequila), they announce they are in pursuit of the American Dream, which they are certain can be found in Vegas. They pick up a naïve hitchhiker and announce their plans to him, all the while admiring the shape of his skull. "We're your friends," Dr. Gonzo smiles at the boy. "We're not like the others." Duke, in particular, has difficulty separating reality from fantasy. Terrified, the hitchhiker escapes when Dr. Gonzo stops the car for a moment.

Duke is a journalist, and he has received a call to cover the Mint 400 motorcycle race in the Nevada desert. As a professional, he is pledged to provide "free lunch, final wisdom, total coverage." But both Duke and Gonzo are so fucked up by the time they arrive in Las Vegas that the simple process of checking into the hotel becomes a terrifying ordeal. Duke sees huge alligators and lizards all around—the people in the lobby have turned into reptiles.

In the madness of Las Vegas, Duke's and Gonzo's odd behavior goes unnoticed or is passed off as mere drunkenness. When they make it outside the next day to cover the race, the scene is chaos. They can't see anything because of the blowing sand, and although thoroughly drugged, the two blend in with the race participants and spectators. Driving around the desert in a press vehicle, they encounter two dune buggies full of "what looked like retired chief petty officers from San Diego," looking for the race. They ask Duke where the racers are. "Beats me," he tells them. "We're just good, patriotic Americans like yourselves." He notes their buggies covered with flags and other symbols of American might. He plays a joke at the expense of the reporters in a press vehicle up ahead. He tells the chief petty officers that if they want a good chase, they should "get after that skunk from CBS News" in the car in front of them. "He's the man responsible for *The Selling of the Pentagon*," Duke tells them. " 'Hot damn!' two of them screamed at once. 'A black jeep, you say?'"

The race is boring, so Duke and Gonzo decide to do their best to terrorize Las Vegas and see if anyone notices them. They bull their way into a Debbie Reynolds show at the Desert Inn, where the entertainer is prancing onstage in a silver Afro wig, gyrating to the big-band sound of "Sgt. Pepper's Lonely Hearts Club Band." "Jesus creeping shit!" Gonzo yells. "We've wandered into a time capsule." Ejected from the show, they manage to blend in with the carnalities of Las Vegas at Circus-Circus, a combination casino and big-tent show:

> Right above the gaming tables the Forty Flying Carazito Brothers are doing a high-wire trapeze act, along with four muzzled Wolverines and the Six Nymphet Sisters from San Diego . . . so you're down on the main floor playing blackjack, and the stakes are getting high when suddenly you chance to look up, and there, right smack above your

head is a half-naked fourteen-year-old girl being chased through the
air by a snarling wolverine, which is suddenly locked in a death battle
with two silver-painted Polacks who come swinging down from opposite balconies and meet in mid-air on the wolverine's neck.

It is too weird, even for Duke and Gonzo. "I think I'm getting the Fear,"
the attorney says. "Nonsense," Duke responds. "We came out here to find
the American Dream, and now that we're right in the vortex you want to
quit. . . . You must *realize* that we've found the main nerve."

They continue their quest for the elusive American Dream through
casino after casino, and eventually run afoul of management. Gonzo
leaves town, catching the first plane he can find heading to Los Angeles. Duke becomes a virtual prisoner in his room, unable to pay his bill,
unable to leave.

Alone in his room, in the city that glorifies American excess and kitsch,
Duke ponders the decline of his generation. He remembers San Francisco in the midsixties and the hope and promise that he felt:

> Strange memories on this nervous night in Las Vegas. Five years
> later? Six? It seems like a lifetime. . . . San Francisco in the middle
> sixties was a very special time and place to be a part of. . . .
>
> History is hard to know, because of all the hired bullshit, but
> even without being sure of "history" it seems entirely reasonable
> to think that every now and then the energy of a whole generation
> comes to a head in a long fine flash, for reasons that nobody really
> understands at the time—and which never explain, in retrospect,
> what actually happened. . . .
>
> There was madness in any direction, at any hour. If not across
> the Bay, then up the Golden Gate or down 101 to Los Altos or La
> Honda. . . . You could strike sparks anywhere. There was a fantastic
> universal sense that whatever we were doing was right, that we were
> winning. . . .
>
> So now, less than five years later, you can go up on a steep hill
> in Las Vegas and look West, and with the right kind of eyes you can
> almost *see* the high-water mark—that place where the wave finally
> broke and rolled back.

Eventually a telegram arrives from Gonzo, announcing a new assignment from *Rolling Stone*, to cover a conference on drug abuse. Duke does

not believe the message at first, but, when confirmed, decides this is the American Dream: getting paid to once again act like madmen.

Duke exchanges the Great Red Shark for the White Whale, a Cadillac convertible, and goes to the Flamingo Hotel, where *Rolling Stone* has reserved a suite for his use. The Mint 400 race had not really been Duke's thing. It required only observation. The drug conference would require participation. "If the Pigs were gathering in Vegas for a top-level Drug Conference," Duke thinks, "we felt the drug culture should be represented."

Gonzo introduces Duke to a new drug—no mean feat, considering Duke's pharmaceutical repertoire. Adrenochrome comes from the adrenal glands of a living human body. They take the drug and watch President Nixon addressing the nation on television, but their minds are so blurred that the only word Duke can make out is "sacrifice . . . sacrifice . . . sacrifice . . ."

The drug convention finally gets under way in a huge ballroom at the hotel. Duke and Gonzo sit amid the packed crowd of law-enforcement officials, their heads spinning from the effects of adrenochrome and mescaline. At the distant podium, a speaker, a so-called expert, is informing the audience about the drug culture. Introducing the crowd to the language of drugs, the speaker says that a marijuana cigarette is called a roach because it resembles a cockroach. Gonzo leans over to Duke and says, "You'd have to be crazy on acid to think a joint looked like a goddamn cockroach."

Duke and Gonzo have decided to pose as undercover narcotics investigators and are dressed conservatively to blend in with the crowd, but the sessions are so tiresome that they soon lose patience, and the pleasure of watching people make idiots of themselves wears thin. The irony is monumental: here is an audience of police officers and district attorneys yammering about the evils of drug abuse, and sitting there, unrecognized among them, are two Picassos of substance abuse. But there is no risk. As Duke says, "These poor bastards didn't know mescaline from macaroni."

Duke muses on what it would have been like attending the convention while using LSD rather than mescaline, but

> there were faces and bodies in that group who would have been absolutely unendurable on acid. . . . The sight of two fantastically obese human beings far gone in a public grope while a thousand

cops all around them watched a movie about the "dangers of marijuana" would not be emotionally acceptable.

In the hotel bar, Duke and Gonzo regale fellow customers with tales
of drugs and crime and say that new Charles Mansons are everywhere,
ready to belly-crawl through window screens and slit throats. On a cruise
down the Strip, Duke and Gonzo horrify tourists and offer heroin to two
cop couples in a convertible.

At one point, the narrative breaks down—or so says the editor's note—
and a transcript of Duke's tape is offered. Now in suburban North Las
Vegas, Duke and Gonzo stop at a taco stand to ask directions from the
minimum wager at the drive-thru window:

> *Att'y:* . . . We're looking for the American Dream, and we were told
>   it was somewhere in this area. . . . Well, we're here looking for
>   it, 'cause they send us out here all the way from San Francisco
>   to look for it. That's why they gave us this white Cadillac, they
>   figure we could catch up with it in that . . .
> *Waitress:* Hey, Lou, you know where the American Dream is?
> *Att'y (to Duke):* She's asking the cook if she knows where the Ameri-
>   can Dream is.
> *Waitress:* Five tacos, one taco burger. Do you know where the Ameri-
>   can Dream is?
> *Lou:* What's that? What is it?
> *Att'y:* Well, we don't know, we were sent out here from San Francisco
>   to look for the American Dream, by a magazine, to cover it.
> *Lou:* Oh, you mean a place.
> *Att'y:* The place called the American Dream.
> *Lou:* Is that the old Psychiatrist's Club?
> *Waitress:* I think so.

Duke muses that perhaps the owner of the Circus-Circus casino has
found his version of the American Dream; as a child he wanted to run
away and join the circus, and now he owns one.

Gonzo returns to Los Angeles and after more ruminations on the
decline of American culture, Duke ponders what he has witnessed about
the media and the law-enforcement establishment. The press is a "gang
of cruel faggots" and journalism itself not a profession, just a home for

"fuck-offs and misfits." It is a "filthy piss-ridden little hole . . . just deep enough for a wino to curl up from the sidewalk and masturbate like a chimp in a zoo cage." As for the district attorneys, they are hopeless losers, worrying about the dangers of LSD when it's no longer a serious issue and is used only by "drug dilettantes" such as himself.

Duke returns the battered Whale to the rental agency and takes a flight to Denver. There he pops into the airport drugstore and asks the woman behind the counter for amyl nitrates. That's not possible without a prescription, she tells Duke. "I'm a doctor," he snarls, rummaging through his wallet until he finds the card identifying him as a doctor of divinity. She agrees to give him the amyls and apologizes: "I hope you'll forgive me, doctor, but I had to ask. We get some *real freaks* in this place." Duke walks out of the airport, a free man in a free country.

Lots of things were at play in *Fear and Loathing in Las Vegas,* and a lot of obscure pronouncements were made about America at the end of the sixties. Hunter said the story came from his subconscious and that people saw more in it than he had put there. Its elegiac tone was appropriate because, as he told Jim Silberman, "We are heading for a far more vicious time." Hunter's tale soon took on the nature of an epitaph on the sixties as the nation lurched through the Nixon era. It was a look back at the promise and hope of the sixties that had been stomped to death somewhere in the middle of 1968.

Duke and Gonzo's version of the American Dream was never clearly articulated, nor was it clear why they believed that dream could be found during a trip to Las Vegas. Cast in the role of searchers, Duke and Gonzo hit the road and after several days, limped home disillusioned and disappointed. What had they expected? What was the Dream aside from the all-expenses-paid strange torpedo they chose to ride? "Buy the ticket, take the ride," Duke intoned at one point. "Don't look back," as Bob Dylan once said.

Two episodes do provide clues about the Dream. They're not part of the chronology and offer a break from the relentless madness of the narrative. One chapter is a flashback to the idyllic sixties, as Duke recalls his early experiences with LSD and an encounter with a Timothy Leary–like character (if not Leary himself, with his "name deleted at the insistence of the publisher's lawyer," a common Hunter phrase). Hunter's San Francisco reverie was an uncharacteristically placid scene, yet it hit the brakes before reaching sentimentality. It was a time Hunter regarded with great fondness, since the nation had turned much uglier in the intervening years. He still held on to the threads of that New Left idealism.

In another chapter, Hunter recalled at length the experience of a Colorado friend who had been traveling around the country "on a sort of early Bob Zimmerman [Dylan] trip." He had passed through Las Vegas, a city of decadence and high life that was supported by the excesses and sins of the nation. Because his friend was free—because he represented what society claimed to respect but actually feared, freedom—he was jailed for vagrancy and beaten. Much like the drifters in the film *Easy Rider*, he was shunned for being the living embodiment of what the nation was supposed to preserve and protect.

Both abstract interludes were fairly short and the words came in bursts, fragments joined by ellipses, delivered in machine-gun cadence. Given these chances to be more explicit, Hunter was still elusive about the Dream and what it all meant. Perhaps the heart of the American Dream was found in the search.

"Raoul Duke" was gone, at least as the author of *Fear and Loathing in Las Vegas*. Hunter stepped from behind his pseudonym when Random House prepared to publish the book, although *Rolling Stone* kept the fictitious alter ego on its masthead as sports editor and Hunter occasionally spun off short pieces under the name. (Wenner turned his office at the magazine into the Raoul Duke Room and held editorial meetings there.)

The book publication was held up because Random House feared that Acosta would sue for defamation of character. He was clearly identified (even if he wasn't named), and prolific felonies were ascribed to his character. Hunter said the lawyers thought the book was "malignant from start to finish." Previously, Acosta had snorted and howled about suing *Rolling Stone*. (His fearsome noise eventually inspired Wenner to publish Acosta's *Autobiography of a Brown Buffalo* with Straight Arrow, in hopes of placating the attorney.)

Random House balked at the crazed noises Acosta made about suing, and publication was postponed as Hunter (by early 1972 already on his next assignment, covering the presidential campaign) tried to reason with him. Part of Acosta's objection had to do with what he considered Hunter's theft of his intellectual property. To Alan Rinzler, Straight Arrow's editorial director, Acosta wrote, "My God! Hunter has stolen my soul. He has taken my best lines and has used me. He has wrung me dry for material." Hunter berated his friend, calling him a "stupid fuck" and questioning his motives for "this cheap, acid-crippled paranoid fuckaround." Acosta claimed he was most upset that Hunter referred to the Dr. Gonzo character as Samoan. Hunter said he was just trying to protect Acosta's identity and save him from "the wrath of L.A. cops and the whole California legal establishment." He said he didn't want Acosta disbarred.

The lawyer didn't buy the writer's argument. "Don't you have any respect for the truth?" Acosta screamed over the phone. "I can sink the whole publishing house for *defaming me*, trying to pass me off as one of those waterhead South Sea mongrels."

Then, in a truly strange turnaround for a man claiming to be libeled by a fictional portrayal, he suddenly demanded that the book's back cover feature a photograph of him sitting next to Hunter in Caesar's Palace, clearly identified as Oscar Zeta Acosta. For years, Hunter kept Acosta's letter releasing him of all *Fear and Loathing*–related claims tacked on the wall in the kitchen at Woody Creek, and demanding that his photograph appear on the cover.

Finally, *Fear and Loathing in Las Vegas* was published by Random House in July 1972.

Hunter was justifiably proud. "We really cracked the buggers with this one," he wrote Ralph Steadman; "we drove them right down to their fucking knees." He urged Bernard Shir-Cliff at Ballantine to buy the paperback rights. Hunter promised that his monetary demands would go up by the hour until the editor gave in. "This book is pure fucking gold," Hunter wrote.

Critics agreed. In the *New York Times Book Review*, writer Crawford Woods said, "Thompson's American dream is a fanfare of baroque fantasy." He wrote, " 'Writing' is as exact a label as the book will carry. Neither novel nor nonfiction, it arrives with fashion's special sanction. Its roots are in the particular sense of the nineteen-sixties that a new voice was demanded—by the way people's public and private lives were coming together in a sensual panic stew, with murder its meat and potatoes, grass and acid its spice. How to tell the story of a time when all fiction was science fiction, all facts lies? The New Journalism was born."

Woods, who lauded Hunter for his poetic madness, said the book was "the funniest piece of American prose since *Naked Lunch*." Tom Wolfe called it a "scorching, epochal sensation." Over the years, comparisons were drawn between *Fear and Loathing* and *The Great Gatsby*. Both books read with astonishing clarity. "There's not one misplaced word," Douglas Brinkley said. "There's no sloppiness." Jay Gatsby and Raoul Duke are pure products of their time, but share a basic philosophical difference. Gatsby believes in the possibilities of reinvention and does not understand why what is past cannot be re-created. Duke, on the other hand, recognizes that the past is dead and cannot be resurrected, giving the ultimate finality to his concept of the American Dream of freedom and possibility.

Hunter dedicated the book to his friend Dr. Bob Geiger, who had done above-the-call duty as a reader of his *Hell's Angels* manuscript back in 1966. He also dedicated the book to Bob Dylan because Vice President Spiro Agnew was braying about drug references in songs and used "Mr. Tambourine Man" as a whipping post. It was, he said, obviously a song about a drug dealer.

"Mr. Tambourine Man" was a constant in Hunter's life. From the first time he heard it in San Francisco, through blasting it through Owl Farm on his huge sound system, to its eventual spot in his funeral service, the song spoke to Hunter perhaps because it was a plea from an artist to his muse: please *take me on a trip . . . I'll come following you*. For Hunter, whose life and livelihood depended on elusive inspiration, it was a love song to the one thing he could not live without.

As the book's epigraph, Hunter chose a statement from Samuel Johnson: "He who makes a beast of himself gets rid of the pain of being a man." Asked about the quote years later, Hunter said, "I'm a suffering person and I've always been. It is a torturous road that we hoe. It's a tough road, particularly if you want to be a criminal."

Chapter 12

TRUTH IS NEVER TOLD
IN DAYLIGHT

I do believe we're heading toward apocalypse—the collapse,
the total shame and impotence of the American Dream.
—HST to J. Anthony Lukas, 1972

H unter was still the new guy on the *Rolling Stone* staff. He'd done
the self-indulgent piece on his sheriff's campaign, then followed
with the huge account of Ruben Salazar's murder and its aftermath. But it was "Fear and Loathing in Las Vegas" that gave Hunter
carte blanche with Jann Wenner. Some of the proles in Wenner's loft
resented the strange new guy who so quickly became the editor's favorite. Whatever Hunter wanted, Hunter got. Wenner recognized the
power of Hunter's voice and wanted more madness, more over-the-top
craziness.

"We loved what Hunter did," Charles Perry said, shrugging off the
office carping as mere whining by no-talents.

So Wenner opened the door. *What do you want, Hunter?*

What Hunter wanted was one of the things Wenner had tried to avoid:
politics.

As soon as Hunter got the go-ahead from Wenner, he packed up a trailer, hitched it to his Volvo 174, and headed for Washington, to set up the National Affairs Desk, in the middle of a blizzard. "Driving across goddamn Nebraska with a huge Doberman, pulling a giant U-Haul trailer, driving through a storm," Hunter remembered. "These big 18-wheelers looming up on me suddenly out of the white. I couldn't go fast enough, couldn't see, blind in the snow. . . ."

He also had serious doubts about what he was doing. Why politics? He was a neophyte who had been radicalized by Chicago 1968, but did he really want to give over a year of his life to *this*? Wenner had given him a telefax machine, which Hunter dubbed the Mojo Wire. Sandy and Juan had come along, and at *Rolling Stone* expense they rented a two-story brick home in the Rock Creek section of the city, an established family neighborhood. It was on the less-fashionable side of Rock Creek Park and most of the movers and shakers were living in Georgetown, but to Sandy it was a step up. She felt that they were finally in the big leagues.

"I was pregnant again," she said. "This was going to be my last shot. I asked the doctor what my odds were. He said, about twenty-five percent. I said, OK. I'm willing to do it. I wanted a child mostly because I wanted another Hunter. I wanted more of that energy on this planet."

The Thompsons rented out Owl Farm and took over the furnished home, maintaining its conventional appearance but for the dining room, which became Hunter's de facto office when he was in town. As the campaign fever began to intensify that fall, the Rock Creek house became more office than home, as journalists dropped by to talk to the new sensation.

"He was dealing with The Heavies," Sandy said. "He was playing with The Players. And he was even winning. But it was taking its toll."

Almost as soon as Hunter settled his family into the Washington house, he flew cross-country for a major *Rolling Stone* editorial conference. The editors were purely a boy's club at the end of 1971. They met for the magazine's first off-site editorial conference at the Esalen Institute in Big Sur in December. For Wenner, it was a power statement, as he had the bureau chiefs from Los Angeles, New York, and London fly in to romp nude in the hot tubs, get high, and contemplate the future of his five-year-old publishing venture. No business types or women (other than Annie Leibovitz, the staff photographer there to document the event) were allowed.

The whole Hee-Haw gang was there: Wenner, Thompson, Joe Eszterhas, Grover Lewis, Charlie Perry, David Felton, Ben Fong-Torres, Jon Landau . . . all of the major players on the staff, knee deep in testosterone. They were mostly there for partying, and at the editorial meetings Wenner pontificated and lulled his charges to sleep. Editor Paul Scanlan said Wenner's diatribes were "the most excruciating eight or nine hours I ever went through." Hunter wore a hospital smock and a robe and drew heavily on his cigarette, inscrutable behind sunglasses. Sometimes, to liven up things, he pulled on one of his trusty blond wigs. He also entertained the staff by screaming, yelling, and throwing furniture when he wanted Wenner's attention. "Everyone egged Hunter on," editor Robert Greenfield said. Alan Rinzler, who ran Straight Arrow, said, "There was almost a macho thing of who could keep up with Hunter, be the craziest, do the most drugs."

The major worthwhile development at the conference was the tacit agreement that Hunter would cover the 1972 presidential campaign. He would do the whole thing, from the frozen-tundra New Hampshire primary though the sweltering political conventions, through the fall full-bore campaign, until the last ballot was counted on election day. "There was a lot of talent in that room," Hunter said years later, "but when it came to politics, I was the only one that raised my hand." Wenner did not have any trouble selling the idea to the rest of his staff, since earlier that year the Twenty-sixth Amendment to the Constitution granted eighteen-year-olds the right to vote. The newly enfranchised voters formed the core of *Rolling Stone* readership. And although Wenner had avoided plying his magazine with radical politics and rhetoric and instead built circulation with serious and detailed music reporting, he figured it might be time to test the magazine's power with its audience. Educating the masses, and perhaps delivering the coveted Youth Vote to his favored candidate, was the sugar plum dancing in Citizen Wenner's head.

Hunter was stoked about the campaign, and if there was dissent among the staff, no one spoke at Big Sur. "When we decided to cover the 1972 political campaigns," Perry said, "there was really no debate about it. Everyone was behind it. Hunter was never resented, because we all admired him so much. His writing was so good." The magazine was already veering away from its bread and butter of music reporting, with long, cultural reporting by Joe Eszterhas and elegant profiles of main-

stream celebrities (Robert Mitchum, Lee Marvin, Paul Newman) by Grover Lewis, all of which helped broaden the reader base.

But politics would really test the *Rolling Stone* audience. It was a fine
line. Though the mainstream media lumped the magazine in with the
underground press (the *Berkeley Barb*, the *L.A. Free Press*), Wenner had
avoided that radical out-of-the-mainstream taint as the kiss of death. He
hoped to make *Rolling Stone* into a tie-dyed *Time* magazine.

He also realized that he'd stumbled into finding a unique voice in modern journalism. Despite *Hell's Angels*, Hunter wasn't yet widely known in
1971. "Fear and Loathing in Las Vegas" had drawn raves when it appeared
in the magazine and Wenner wanted to strike, to tie down Hunter with
a contract. Hunter, who hadn't drawn a regular paycheck since his days
as a *Time* copyboy, came cheap: he got a $1,000-a-month retainer from
Rolling Stone and a deal for a book on the campaign when it was all over.
What he didn't realize is that Wenner would take Hunter's considerable
expenses out of the money promised for the paperback sale of the book.

Wenner knew that Hunter, with his odd worldview and even odder
work habits, might not be a reliable political correspondent, so he assigned
Timothy Crouse to babysit him. The son of playwright Russel Crouse
(winner of the 1946 Pulitzer for drama for *State of the Union*), Crouse was
a Harvard grad with a couple of years on newspapers and a monumental
stutter. The often abrasive Wenner enjoyed exploiting weakness, which
only amplified Crouse's stutter. Because Crouse wanted to be a contributing writer on the staff, he was eager to help Hunter Thompson, hoping
he might learn something. "I didn't know what I was getting into," Crouse
said. He started the campaign as Hunter's babysitter, and he ended up
benefiting professionally from Hunter's generosity and friendship.

The highlight of the Big Sur conference came after hours. Hunter,
Felton, and Leibovitz were speeding up Highway 1 when a state trooper
pulled them over. Hunter was driving, and he had a head full of mescaline. The officer decided to test Hunter's sobriety and asked him to touch
his nose with his finger. Hunter missed. He was on the brink of arrest
when he suggested another test, a feat of daring. The officer agreed and
watched, flabbergasted, as Hunter flipped his sunglasses off the back of
his head and caught them behind his back. The officer let him go.

But the Esalen Institute had had enough of Hunter's antics. After
three days of drinking, screaming, and furniture throwing, the editors of
Rolling Stone were ordered to leave.

Back in Washington, gearing up for the quadrennial masturbatory madness of a presidential campaign, Hunter took stock of his life and work. Still flushed with the success of "Fear and Loathing" in the magazine and awaiting the end of the legal wrangling that would hold up book publication for another six months, he found himself well outside his comfort zone. The hip young journalists knew who he was, and some of them came by Rock Creek to kiss his ring, but as he imagined the next year and all of the simple logistical crises he would face, he realized how important Sandy had become to him—not only as his wife and partner but as the one-woman support system who made it possible for him to be the raving beast Hunter S. Thompson.

"I've grown accustomed to letting her deal with my day-to-day reality & keeping the fucking weasels off my back," he told Wenner. "I need a human buffer to keep well-meaning people from driving me fucking nuts."

Sandy was the one who answered the phone and explained Hunter. *He's still sleeping . . . he's soaking in the tub . . . he's too upset to speak.* She kept the world at bay. But Sandy would not be on the road with him; she was pregnant and had a precocious seven-year-old at home. Out on the road, Hunter would have to exist without her.

And he would be an indentured servant to Wenner and *Rolling Stone.* Hunter was not a man who suffered authority gladly, and his relationship with Wenner, though fond, was also testy. The political stories appeared in the magazine under the "Fear and Loathing" headline. Hunter had given *Rolling Stone* an extremely valuable franchise, and he wanted Wenner to keep that in mind.

The frustration and the rupture in living arrangements and duties took a toll on Sandy. "I had taken up smoking—and drinking a lot," she said. "Here I am pregnant, right? The doctor gave me a prescription for Valium. Hunter was just so much in his own thing, in his own world, that he wasn't aware until I got really outrageous. He didn't know that every single night I was drunk."

Both the pressure of writing biweekly campaign reports and the political passions of the time kept Hunter on edge. Being on the road also led him astray. He'd never been entirely faithful. His visits to San Francisco were often marked by new liaisons with women on the *Rolling Stone* staff. Sleeping with Hunter raised them in Wenner's eyes, made them more valuable employees. On the road, there were scores of young campaign workers and political groupies, and Hunter did not resist.

The politics and his up-close look at the people who were running his country into the ground were enough to drive Hunter insane. Add the deadlines, and Hunter was an impossible brute. "There was a lot of madness," Sandy recalled. "Hunter had begun to get angrier. And more violent. His language was more violent. He was louder. He was tenser."

The 1972 presidential campaign cranked into gear with Democratic hopefuls duking it out for the right to face Richard Nixon in the general election. In the early days of the New Hampshire primary, small clusters of reporters followed the candidates around.

To much of America and certainly those within the bubble of politics, *Rolling Stone* was still a mystery. Some political aides looked at the credentials dangling from Hunter's neck thought Hunter was a member of the rock band (*Noisy bastards, aren't they?*) or that *Rolling Stone* was a fan magazine for the group.

The other gentlemen of the establishment press weren't any warmer to him. They saw him as the odd-looking, ill attired writer from that *Rolling Stone* thing who was constantly late, delaying the press bus's departure. He was noisy, often *on something*, and carrying a six pack.

Political reporting went through a major change in Hunter's generation. When Hunter was growing up, it was difficult to maintain interest in politics. After twelve years—*a lifetime*—of Roosevelt, the nation was presided over first by a haberdasher, then a grandfatherly war hero, who faced the same bald Democrat in the elections every four years. The presidential election of 1960 was a watershed and offered a clear choice. John F. Kennedy drew political teenyboppers into the mix. Clearly, a lot of the young people at JFK's campaign rallies could not vote, but they turned out to cheer the candidate as if he were the new Elvis.

The Kennedy-Nixon election also was a turning point for press coverage of presidential campaigns. Television had stumbled into live coverage of the political conventions in 1952 and slowly gone from being a novelty to a major part of the political process. After the first night of live coverage of the 1952 Democratic convention in Chicago, CBS News producer Don Hewitt was finishing breakfast at a greasy spoon across from the convention hall, trying to figure out how to cure one of his big headaches. While showing someone on the convention floor on camera—Senator Stuart Symington, let's say—how did he tell viewers that they were looking at Symington without interrupting the host, correspondent Walter Cronkite? At that moment, the gum-snapping waitress came up and asked Hewitt whether there was anything else he wanted. Hewitt looked beyond her, to the sign announcing "Today's Specials." *Sure*, Hewitt said, *I want to buy that sign*. He'd figured out that if they could use the letters to put names of delegates on the sign, they could photograph it, drop out the black background and superimpose the name on the picture of the talking head, all without interrupting Cronkite. The lunch-counter invention revolutionized TV coverage for live events.

The 1960 campaign was made for television, with the tousle-haired Kennedy versus the stubbly Nixon, and the televised debates that fall were deciding factors for many voters, who responded to the image of the candidates as much as to the content of their political platforms.

It was also the year that campaign coverage was reinvented by Theodore H. White. For generations, political reporting and commentary had been the property of chin-stroking columnists and snoremongers. The major decisions, according to lore, were made by stogie-puffing pols in smoky back rooms. White was a longtime reporter for *Time* and *Life* magazines who wanted to explain the political process to the masses. He followed the candidates through primary season, then worked the hotel rooms and hallways during the party conventions, and followed Nixon and Kennedy up through election day. When it appeared in 1961, *The Making of the President 1960* was an immediate best-seller, found on all the best coffee tables in America. No journalist had thought to bring average readers into the tent before, and White's innovation changed the way the press reported politics.

In 1960, White had a lot of face time with the candidates. By 1964, more reporters followed candidates through primary season. By 1968, when White was working on his third *Making of the President* book, the crowd was stifling. But White's 1968 volume was surpassed by a book focused on political marketing by twenty-six-year-old newspaper reporter Joe McGinniss. *The Selling of the President* was a book Hunter could easily have written, since his *Pageant* article on Nixon was about rehabilitating the image of a damaged-goods candidate.

By 1972, covering a political campaign had become near-routine; reporters were said to be *doing a Teddy White*. With Hunter and Tim Crouse along for the ride that year, campaign coverage went through more changes, and both *Rolling Stone* writers were to publish books with long shelf lives.

With a sitting president, the Republican nomination was a surety: Richard Nixon, who in 1968 staged the most remarkable political come-back in American history, was in.

The 1972 Democratic race was a free-for-all. First came the shadow candidate, Senator Edward Kennedy of Massachusetts. As the next Kennedy in line for succession, he was wounded by a scandal—his actions following the drowning death of a young woman in his company in 1969. The Chappaquiddick incident, with its implicit infidelity and irresponsibility, damaged Kennedy politically, but he still had something the other candidates did not: the royal bloodline.

Edmund Muskie, the failed vice-presidential candidate from four years before, was the early favorite. There was also former vice president Hubert Humphrey, the senator from Minnesota. Washington Senator Henry "Scoop" Jackson was in the mix as well. Alabama Governor George Wallace, who had run on a third party ticket in 1968, was back to preach his segregationist philosophy to the nation. There were others: Eugene McCarthy, 1968's quixotic peace candidate, making another try; Shirley Chisholm, the black congresswoman from Brooklyn; John Lindsay, the smoothie mayor of New York; and Wilbur Mills, the Arkansas good old boy who ran the House Ways and Means Committee.

In that huge field, the genial and mild-mannered George McGovern did not stand a chance. In 1968, McGovern had picked up the fallen standard when Senator Robert Kennedy, the "peace candidate," was assassinated. In 1972, McGovern's campaign manager, Gary Hart, knew it would be an uphill battle because the candidate was from a small state and had the stage presence of an eleventh-grade social-studies teacher. "It was a complex and complicated time," Hart said. "It was a long-shot presidential campaign in the middle of social revolution involving the Vietnam War, civil rights, gender rights, environmental movement—a lot of the social and cultural revolutions of the 1960s and 1970s."

It was clear from the start, once Hunter's "Fear and Loathing" political dispatches began appearing in *Rolling Stone*, that McGovern was the only candidate Hunter cared about. He admired both the man and his principled politics. Despite the wisdom that put the betting money on Muskie or Humphrey, in the early days of the New Hampshire primary campaign, Hunter followed around McGovern, the only man he felt had the integrity to do what he promised if elected: extricate the nation from the hell of the

Vietnam War. Hunter would rather blow a dead dog than listen to a speech by Muskie or Humphrey. There were times, during the dark-winter-hand-shaking days at factory gates with McGovern when there were only four reporters covering the candidate, and two of them were from *Rolling Stone*.

Hunter could not fathom how the political reporters for the major papers could face a deadline *every day*, when having a story due every other week was killing him. Crouse, with his newspaper expérience, turned out to be a useful and experienced hand-holder. Hunter worked hard, but on his own terms. Deadlines were chaotic, both for Hunter on the road and for the *Rolling Stone* editors in San Francisco. When the pages started spewing out of the telefax machine in San Francisco, they were rarely in coherent order. The first page might have "Insert K" scrawled at the top . . . and then the next page might have no relation to that first page. Spreading the papers over the floor of the Raoul Duke Room and then putting them together in some coherent order usually fell to David Felton or Charlie Perry. As copy chief, Perry had the final duty of packaging Hunter Thompson for readers. "A lot of Hunter's stuff would come in in the form of inserts," Perry said. "There would be no lead, no walk-off, just the inserts, and we'd sort of have to shuffle them around until we came up with a mosaic we liked."

As the campaign grew, Hunter found himself on the press bus with the big-time reporters from the *New York Times*, the *Washington Post*, the *Boston Globe*, and other papers. They resented him from the start: *Slogging to the bus, predawn, to witness the candidate-of-the-day shaking hands at factory shift-change, waiting in the parking lot. Cold, impatient, inhaling bus fumes, anxious about deadline, wondering what-in-the-hell is the holdup. Finally, that noisy thug in the flop hat and the athletic shoes comes down the aisle, bumping the other reporters with his baggage and his trailing six pack. In the backseat, still noisy and unrepentant. You mean, we were waiting for that?*

That was Hunter Thompson, but few of the straight reporters knew who he was. Soon, though, some of the editors of the major dailies were reading Hunter's dispatches and heckling their reporters on the road: *How come you can't write stuff like that?* The reporters read what Hunter wrote about the candidates—things they *thought*, but could never *write* . . . not in a family newspaper . . . and developed a grudging respect for the noisy creature in the back of the bus.

Muskie was the media-anointed favorite when the year began, and he

fulfilled his promise by winning the majority of delegates at the Iowa cau-
cus in January and winning the New Hampshire primary in early March.
The Florida primary, in the second week in March, was to be a bigger
test. Muskie hoped to continue the steamroller leading to his nomination
in Miami. He planned a whistle-stop tour in a train called the Sunshine
Special.

Monty Chitty was a nineteen-year-old student at the University of
Florida who worked as a photographer on the school paper, the *Alligator*.
Early in the winter, he'd applied to be one of two state college students to
ride the Sunshine Special as accredited members of the press. *Anything
to get out of classes*, Chitty figured, and so he made a deal ("either I traded
pot to a faculty member, promised to give up my job as one of the editors, or wrote some idiotic essay") to get one of the seats. He hitchhiked
to Jacksonville the morning of the campaign run, obtained his credentials, and boarded the train. There were a lot of suits and a lot of media
heavies on board ("There's Frank Reynolds of ABC!"), all very friendly,
quick to chat with the two college journalists, especially the "knock-out
brunette" (Chitty's term) representing another school. By noon, after four
hours on the campaign train, Chitty was already jaded. He'd witnessed
the "true underbelly" of network-TV stage-managed news: unloaded cameras, orchestrated events in front of handpicked crowds, loaded up and
doing it again at the next stop. Everything was staged; even the arrival of
the train was reenacted for the cameras. Muskie read the same script at
every stop.

Already weary, Chitty retreated to the open bars for press in one of the
railcars. "As I walk toward the rear through a deserted seating car, block-
ing the aisle is a 10 gallon galvanized tub filled with ice and four kinds of
beer," Chitty recalled. "In the adjacent seat sits this 30-something guy in
shorts, Converse tennis shoes, a Guayabera shirt, safari hat, dark aviator
sunglasses, pinching a long metal cigarette holder with cigarette. He's
looking up at me as I look down at his beer. After about 15 seconds of
looks and silence, he breaks down and invites me to have a beer. I notice
the press credential '*Rolling Stone*' hanging from his neck. We hit it off.
He had hash . . . I had Colombian pot."

Hunter and Chitty quickly bonded, and although Chitty didn't know
Hunter's work, seeing *Rolling Stone* on his press badge impressed him.
Chitty played a supporting role in one of Hunter's campaign adventures
and eventually became his longtime friend and neighbor in Colorado.

The campaign allowed Hunter to show off his story-within-a-story style. His articles were about the agony of reporting and writing a story every two weeks, and much of the folklore and language that would surround the character (or caricature) called Hunter Thompson came from this period, as Hunter constantly portrayed himself as a man tormented by deadlines *lashing together* a story, *feeding twisted gibberish* into the Mojo Wire under *brutal* deadlines, when he was at the mercy of *savage and obscene* editors on the other end of the line.

But his narrative device, in which getting the story became the story, fit his political reporting perfectly. It allowed him to present a scene, then ask the questions readers asked. As he questioned his sources, readers were collaborators piecing together facts. Hunter presented himself as a manic and somewhat inept reporter, a clever way to mask his shrewd style.

The episode with Monty Chitty, which appeared as "The Banshee Screams in Florida," began with Hunter reading a story in the *Miami Herald*, learning he had apparently run amuck on the Sunshine Special and terrorized Senator Muskie and almost everyone else. He used the *Herald* story as an epigraph that hit him squarely between the eyes as he cut up grapefruit (with a machete, of course) for his room-service breakfast at the Royal Biscayne Hotel in Miami Beach.

So Hunter began the story at the end. He called some of his fellow reporters to figure out what had happened. He discovered the Muskie campaign had banned him for giving press credentials to a lunatic. Like a detective who knows the identity of a murderer but must find proof, Hunter worked backward, retracing his steps, figuring out how the mess had happened. It turned out that a thug identified on his press badge as Hunter Thompson of *Rolling Stone* had mercilessly heckled Muskie, pulling on the candidate's pants legs at a campaign stop and shouting wild and obscene comments. After getting a reasonable account of the proceedings from his telephone source (in a conspiratorial note, he told his readers that his source's name "need not be repeated here"), Hunter pieced together a chronology.

A couple of nights before, Hunter and Chitty had met Peter Sheridan, whom he dubbed the Savage Boohoo, in the lobby of a Ramada Inn in West Palm Beach. The Boohoo was drunk and angry, screaming gibberish, railing against Muskie to anyone who would listen. Normally, Hunter said, he would not have paid much attention to this sort of act, but the

Boohoo had a special quality, "the Neal Cassady speed-booze-acid rap—a wild combination of menace, madness and genius." The Boohoo's behavior left Hunter with no choice but to invite him along for a ramble with Chitty. "Don't mind if I do," the Boohoo said in response to the invitation. "At this time of the night I'll fuck around with just about anybody."

Hunter, Chitty, and the Boohoo ended up spending five hours together. Again adopting a conspiratorial tone, Hunter declined to go into much detail: "I'd like to run this story all the way out here, but it's deadline time again and the nuts & bolts people are starting to moan." So he quickly wrapped up the story by confessing that when he heard the Boohoo's sad tale of being trapped in West Palm Beach with no way to get to Miami, he had to intervene. He handed over his press pass for Ed Muskie's Sunshine Special:

> "It's the presidential express—a straight shot into Miami and all the free booze you can drink. Why not? [S]ince the train is leaving in two hours, well, maybe you should borrow this little orange press ticket, just until you get abroad. . . . [A]ll it got me was a dozen beers and the dullest day of my life."
>
> He smiled, accepting the card. "Maybe I can put it to better use," he said.

And, of course, the Boohoo could. Hunter's closing line was worthy of O. Henry. At first look, the article seemed haphazard, but on subsequent readings artful. As in *Rashomon*, the same story was told multiple times before a truth was revealed.

Thirty-five years later, Chitty recalled that the real ending of the story wasn't quite so neat. There was a tacit agreement that Hunter would give Sheridan the credential, but he didn't want to do it overtly. He left Sheridan in the hotel lobby in the wee hours, took the elevator up to his room, then sent his credential back to the lobby in the unoccupied elevator.

That was not the end of the story for Chitty. Three days later, back in his college apartment, Chitty was awakened by pounding on his door. Two faculty members and two fellow *Alligator* staff members were on his doorstep, telling him that the White House called the newsroom looking for him. "Of course, I believe they're tripping on mushrooms," Chitty said. He pulled on some clothes and went to the *Alligator* office to talk to the White House assistant press secretary. Chitty was quick on his feet:

"Yes, I met Hunter Thompson of the *Rolling Stone* magazine. No, that was not Hunter Thompson who boarded the hotel bus Saturday morning taking us back out to the train. Yes, I was with Hunter the entire night before, and I can only imagine this fellow lifted Hunter's press credentials from his jacket that evening. No, that was not Hunter Thompson on the train that day. Yes, this fellow was threatening almost everyone with broken whiskey bottles. Yes, he was screaming lewd and profane language, grabbing every female by the ass aboard the train. No, it was not Hunter Thompson who grabbed Ed Muskie's pants and attempted to pull him from the rear platform in the Miami train station during his final speech. I was standing ten feet away and can swear this fellow who went nuts was not Hunter Thompson."

Nixon's press secretary Ron Ziegler called Chitty again the next day to reconfirm the details. As Ziegler explained, Hunter's White House press credentials hung in the balance. Losing those would have been a crushing blow to Hunter's career as a political writer. "Both Hunter and I lied our asses off to the White House about Peter Sheridan," Chitty recalled. Hunter was grateful, flying Chitty to Colorado to spend time at Owl Farm.

George Wallace, the segregationist candidate, was the winner in Florida, but Muskie still steamed ahead as the front-runner until a Tuesday night in Milwaukee. The Wisconsin primary was expected to provide the exclamation point for Muskie's campaign. After a week of what he considered hellish exile in Milwaukee, Hunter contemplated life under President Muskie. Nixon was the Antichrist, but even if Muskie could beat Nixon would he make any difference?

Just for fun, Hunter decided to use his *Rolling Stone* pulpit to spread a rumor about Muskie and his use of a "rare Brazilian drug" called Ibogaine. Even for a presidential candidate, Muskie had been acting a little weird. When conservative newspaper publisher William Loeb had criticized Jane Muskie, the candidate broke down in tears defending his wife. Hunter had also seen odd flashes of imperious temper as he watched Muskie deal with staff. Why not suggest that it was all the result of the candidate's using a hallucinogenic drug?

"I never said that Muskie was taking Ibogaine," Hunter wrote years later. "I said there was a rumor in Milwaukee that a strange Brazilian doctor had been showing up at his suite to administer heavy shots of some strange drug called Ibogaine. I never said it was true. I said there was a rumor to that effect. I made up the rumor. . . . I didn't realize until about halfway through the campaign that people believed this stuff. I assumed that like the people I was around, and like myself, they were getting their primary coverage of the campaign from newspapers, television, radio—the traditional media."

On Wenner's orders, Hunter was stationed at Muskie headquarters the night of the Wisconsin primary, and Crouse was at McGovern's offices, to cover the candidate's presumed concession speech. But when the numbers came in, a bizarre thing happened: McGovern won. After working nearly two years to build a significant political base in Wisconsin, McGovern scored his first victory of the 1972 campaign.

Wenner heard the returns on the network news and called Crouse immediately. "Don't write a fucking word," he told him. He then called Hunter and told him to go to the McGovern headquarters and file a story.

Instead, Hunter gathered several bottles of his usual supplies and went to sit with Crouse and coach him through his first major story for the magazine, a detailed and lucid analysis of how McGovern cleaned Muskie's clock. Wenner had threatened to fire Crouse for disobeying his orders, but grudgingly admitted that he had another great reporter on his staff.

At that point in the campaign, after the Boohoo incident and the Ibogaine story, straighter members of the campaign press corps finally began to talk to the thug at the back of the bus. Thompson wrote all that great stuff in *Rolling Stone* that they wished they could write: that Ed Muskie "talked like a farmer with terminal cancer trying to borrow money on next year's crop"; that Hubert Humphrey was "a treacherous, gutless old ward heeler," who needed to be castrated, and that "getting assigned to cover Nixon [is] like being sentenced to six months in a Holiday Inn."

"His caricatures were overstated," said political reporter Curtis Wilkie, "but there was truth in them, especially in his portrayal of Muskie and his ferocious temper."

"The brilliance of Hunter and his semi-hallucinogenic reporting was that it got to the truth about things," said William Greider, who covered that campaign for the *Washington Post*. "You could read his account of Muskie, that he was on some strange Brazilian drug, and it spoke the truth about his odd behavior. He would describe these titanic struggles in the McGovern campaign, and maybe he was over the top, but the stories were true in a deeper sense. He was such a brilliant writer that he could leave you somewhat in doubt as to what he was actually describing (it may have been in his own head), yet nevertheless, it was wildly entertaining and on the money."

"Reading Thompson obviously gave them a vicarious, Mittyesque thrill," Crouse wrote. "Thompson had the freedom to describe the campaign as he actually experienced it: the crummy hotels, the tedium of the press bus, the calculated lies of the press secretaries, the agony of writing about the campaign when it seemed dull and meaningless, the hopeless fatigue." As Wilkie said, "His work ethic was not the kind of thing any regular journalist practices. I don't recall him taking copious notes, but he remembered things well."

Now those reporters who had cold-shouldered him wanted to make nice, but Hunter did not suffer hypocrites gladly. He decided to hatch an elaborate revenge ploy and bring Tim Crouse into it. *Study those other reporters*, Hunter told him. "Watch those swine day and night," he advised. "Every time they fuck someone who isn't their wife, every time they pick their nose, every time they have their hand up their ass, you write it down. Get all of it. Then we'll lay it on them in October."

Crouse produced his next major *Rolling Stone* piece on the campaign press corps, which led to a book contract with Random House for *The Boys on the Bus*, published the following year. Again, Hunter's instincts for what makes good books (*Acid Test* for Wolfe, *Selling of the President* for Joe McGinniss, and *Boys on the Bus* for Crouse) were acute.

For his part, Hunter did not want to be one of the boys on the bus. He was disgusted by the game. "Guys write down what a candidate says and report it when they know damn well he's lying," he told *Newsweek*. "Half the conversation on a press bus is about who lied to whom today, but nobody ever prints the fact that they're goddamn liars."

Crouse frequently visited Hunter in his unnatural habitat, the home-away-from home in Washington. "Sandy was an incredibly sweet person, devoted to what she saw as fostering Hunter's genius," Crouse said. "She helped him develop his equilibrium each day he was home."

As a novice writer, Crouse appreciated being the audience for Hunter at work:

> I was in the guest room upstairs with him and saw how he would sit at the card table with a Selectric in front of him, his elbows out to the sides, sitting up very straight, and then he would get this sort of electric jolt and start to type. He'd type a sentence and then wait again

with his arms out, and he would get another jolt and type another sentence. Watching him, I began to realize that what he was trying to do was to bypass leaded attitudes, received ideas, clichés, anything like that and go to something that had more to do with his unconscious and his immediate perception of things. He wanted to somehow get the sentence out before anything could interfere with it in the way of convention or preconception. The idea was that the story would function sort of like an internal-combustion engine, with a constant flow of explosions of more or less equal intensity all the way through.

Hunter became close friends with George McGovern's campaign manager, Gary Hart (later his senator from Colorado), and the campaign's chief political adviser, Frank Mankiewicz. While in his dark period in Wisconsin, staying at a hotel he considered a shithouse, Hunter met attorney Bill Dixon, who helped mastermind McGovern's primary victory. "Hunter showed up with a ten-foot-long length of chain around him and an open drink," Dixon said. "You knew who Hunter was immediately. He was the star of that campaign in the eyes of his fellow journalists."

Mankiewicz was the campaign veteran on the staff. He had run Bobby Kennedy's doomed 1968 presidential campaign and, despite his lofty principles, always reminded himself that politics was a game, an attitude Hunter admired.

Despite Hunter's stories of massive drug and alcohol use and psychic ruptures under deadline pressure, Mankiewicz thought most of those stories were manufactured. "I always thought Hunter was sober and clean," he said. "I assume there must have been episodes where he was wildly drunk or high, but I never saw it."

Though of the same generation, Gary Hart approached Hunter with some caution. He liked him as a person, but was somewhat skeptical of his reporting and what it could do to help McGovern reach the coveted Youth Vote. "He brought the campaign to the attention of a certain sector of the audience, a lot of whom don't vote," Hart said. As campaign manager, Hart wanted the attention and endorsement of the *New York Times*, the *Washington Post*, and all of the establishment papers. As much as he liked Hunter, he kept his work in perspective.

"He didn't do journalism," Hart said. "It was Hunter's view of the world around him. That's what made it so interesting and different. It required him to be in his own writing, and he increasingly portrayed himself as wacko. When he would write about a political event, I couldn't recognize it. Everything, even normal events, somehow had a back story that was unbelievable and over the top and bigger than life. Of course, that meant he had to be all those things." Literary critic Morris Dickstein said Hunter's stories were "wildly erratic yet [he] really gives the impression of having been there."

Dixon said all the other reporters envied Hunter. "Reporters in those days couldn't wait for *Rolling Stone* to come out to read what Hunter had written," he said.

Mankiewicz said Hunter's reporting was "the most accurate and the least factual" account of the 1972 campaign. Indeed, Hunter reported that at one point in the campaign, Mankiewicz leaped from behind a bush and tried to bash in Hunter's head with a ball-peen hammer. Everyone knew that was a joke, right? Hunter thought he made it clear when he was going into flights of fancy. He wrote for his own amusement, and if others came along for the ride, that was all right. Usually, he punctuated his fantasies with a line that was supposed to telegraph his fun to the masses: "Jesus, why do I write stuff like that?"

Dickstein again: "Hunter Thompson learned to approximate the effect of mind-blasting drugs in his prose style. . . . [And] in 1972 he affronted the taboos of political writing, and recorded the nuts and bolts of a presidential campaign with all the contempt and incredulity that other reporters must feel but censor out. The result was the kind of straightforward, uninhibited intelligence that showed up the timidities and clichés that dominated the field. But in high gear Thompson paraded one of the few original prose styles of recent years, a style dependent almost deliriously on insult, vituperation, and stream of inventive to a degree unparalleled since Celine."

Curtis Wilkie covered the campaign for the *Wilmington News Journal* in Delaware and met Hunter when one of his editors suggested that he seek him out and write a profile. They met around the time of the Wisconsin primary and began a thirty-year friendship. As Wilkie calmly toiled to meet his daily deadlines, he noticed Hunter becoming frantic when his *Rolling Stone* stories were due. "His work habits were certainly different from mine," Wilkie said. "Hunter lived by night and I'm a morning person. He showed up for things and did reporting, but much of what he was writing was impressionistic. His stories came to him in visions, not as the result of hard reporting."

And his stories came to him in odd situations. When Iowa Senator

Harold Hughes surprised McGovern by switching his endorsement to Muskie, Hunter tracked down McGovern as he was urinating, and got a candid statement of surprise and disappointment from him. "You never had a dull conversation with Hunter," McGovern said.

"His work habits were as insane as he describes them," said William Greider. "He was extremely tense and serious and overwrought—and also very focused, in a way that only someone with that kind of an observer's eye can imagine. He *did* drink a lot. He *did* do drugs a lot. That wasn't imagined—maybe or maybe not exaggerated, but I doubt it. And yet he had a kind of earnestness as a reporter, which he sustained day after day in kind of excessive ways. You could never be quite totally sure—is he putting me on or is he putting himself on? I think it was probably a little bit of both. You have to be insanely sincere to behave the way he did and to write the way he did."

Hunter knew he had to do things differently. "In Washington, truth is never told in daylight hours or across a desk," he told writer Craig Vetter "If you catch people when they're tired or drunk or weak, you can usually get some answers."

The frenzy of the spring ended, and Hunter went west for the California primary. By this time, he was loose enough with McGovern and his staff to urge Hart to test-drive the new Vincent Black Shadow with him. ("It was as big as a small horse," Hart remembered.) California marked the end of primary season, and Hunter's stomach turned as he watched McGovern shilling for votes. He was actively courting the old guard of the party, the same people who'd turned the police loose on the demonstrators in the streets of Chicago four years before. It was a political reality, but a personal betrayal. "Thompson began to smell the fat cats latching on to the campaign," Crouse wrote, and "had become wholly appalled at McGovern's effort to woo the old party regulars."

Hunter's familiarity had bred certain amounts of contempt. "He had this access to the McGovern campaign that was unusual and would not be repeated again," Wenner said. He had become friends with his sources and come to expect more from them than politics as usual. He shared his broken hopes with his editor, who was himself nearly as frazzled by the campaign as his star reporter. Working with Hunter required maximum participation from editors. It wasn't the word-by-word parsing that Hunter needed. Wenner said that part of Hunter's writing was always good. "Hunter needed *assembly*," he recalled. "He'd write in batches and pieces, and they'd need to be assembled and transitioned. He needed also to be told, 'Keep going in that direction . . . stop going in *that* direction, it's not fruitful.' He needed more guidance because he was working on deadline. He needed a collaborator, a foil. Sometimes he'd need a buddy to work with. You had to discern what it was that was required. I had an intuitive instinct for what was required for Hunter at all times. I could tell where he was going, whether the piece was going to work, and what he would need at a given time. It was just like managing a prizefighter, or like being a road manager. My role with him would range from being a line editor to being a road manager."

Primaries over, a long, hot summer and two political conventions, both in Miami, yawned before him. Washington was not home, though he enjoyed his new friends in politics. He amused them by zipping around town at a hundred miles per hour and living up to the Hunter Thompson Legend, though in private he was the courtly Southern Gentleman that Virginia Thompson struggled to raise. Sally Quinn, the *Washington Post* reporter turned CBS News personality, remembered Hunter as a vulnerable, sweet, and gentle person. "He was never anything but absolutely polite with me," she said. "He was a gentleman. I always thought he was—vulnerable, sad, too."

During that baking-hot summer and just by chance, Hunter was within a couple hundred feet of the biggest political story of the century. While the Democratic National Committee's offices in the Watergate complex were being rifled by political burglars on June 17, 1972, Hunter was downstairs swimming laps in the pool and later enjoying a refreshing tequila at the outdoor bar. He had a knack for being in the right place at the right time.

Fear and Loathing in Las Vegas was finally out in book form, and the other political reporters bought the book and at campaign stops sheepishly asked Hunter to autograph it for them. Suddenly, he was a celebrity on the bus.

"Hunter was beginning to be a cult figure," Gary Hart said. "Other journalists followed him around like puppy dogs. It was like he had some magic that they wanted to capture."

Ralph Steadman flew in from England because Wenner wanted to repeat the "Fear and Loathing in Las Vegas" magic by teaming with Hunter to cover the conventions. Ralph was miserable in the Miami heat, saying his hotel room was fit only for committing suicide. His attitude contributed to his art, as he created especially vicious portraits of the candidates: wheelchair-bound George Wallace spewing bile over an American flag; McGovern urging a convention hall full of lizards to "come home, America"; Nixon at the podium, farting through an ass that is Vice President Spiro Agnew; and the big boys of the press corps all vomiting into their cocktails. The bitterness in Ralph's drawings was reflected in Hunter's prose, as he wrote off the possibilities of true political reform.

The egalitarian nature of the Democratic Party and its desire to be all-inclusive left McGovern to address the nation with his acceptance speech at two in the morning. The Republicans, on the other hand, ran a slickly managed convention, and President Nixon spoke to a prime-time audience and the chants of "four more years" were all heard before the late local news. Hunter also became close with several of the leaders of Vietnam Veterans Against the War, including John Kerry, later to be senator from Massachusetts and a presidential candidate. (Years later, Hunter's writing about the veterans' group was excerpted in a Library of America volume of writing about the Vietnam war the only domestic piece the editors included.)

Hunter covered both conventions and tried to infiltrate a group of young Republicans heading into the convention hall to cheer Nixon. With his sporty attire and close-cropped hair, he could pass as a conservative but for the McGovern button. He tried to rally some of the Nixon Youth to chant hateful slogans at the network television anchormen, in booths hovering over the convention floor. Unfortunately, he was outed by fellow journalist Ron Rosenbaum, who shouted his name when he saw him in the GOP throng.

Hunter felt a sense of doom about the Republican convention. To him, the GOP convention chant of "four more years" had a master-race ring to it: *Nixon über Alles*.

Sandy delivered a son in Washington and was surprised at how good the baby looked, considering all of her drinking. But then the child developed hyaline membrane disease, the disease that had killed President Kennedy's son Patrick in 1963.

"I didn't hold him, but I looked at him," Sandy said. The baby died after one day.

Sandy stayed in the hospital a couple of days to recover. She called Hunter when she was to be released. It was still morning, and he was asleep. She told him not to worry, that she would take a cab. She wanted him to say, *Of course I'll come get you*, but he didn't.

After a season of Hunter's relentless travel, the family was home at Owl Farm. But Hunter came home to crash, Sandy said, not to be her husband. He was also on the party circuit; he was a media star and everyone wanted him. The campaign kicked up again in earnest after Labor Day, and Hunter took Sandy and Juan on one of McGovern's whistle-stop tours of the Great Plains, which proved to be good therapy. "It was the best thing," she said. "He was very tender with me." Getting back home was therapeutic—and she served as campaign manager that fall for a Democrat county commission candidate and made scores of the local phone calls that contributed to McGovern's carrying Pitkin County, the only county in Colorado he won.

Hunter's output slowed in the fall, and his dispatches for *Rolling Stone* weren't as frequent. Relegated to the Zoo Plane, the press plane following McGovern around the country, Hunter watched reporters and camera jockeys get loaded on drink and drugs while accompanying the candidate to speeches in Des Moines, Sioux Falls, and Tacoma. Stuck with a bunch of sloppy drunks—something Hunter despised—he used his charm to woo some of the women aboard. He was not bold in his infidelity. One of his conquests said he approached her with a level of shyness she would expect in a high school sophomore.

Hunter spent the fall stalking McGovern's campaign headquarters in Washington, looking for the villain who was killing the campaign. First, McGovern had taken on as running mate Senator Thomas Eagleton of Missouri, who did not tell McGovern about his history of mental illness and shock treatment. Embarrassed into removing him from the ballot—replacing him with Sargent Shriver, a junior-varsity Kennedy—McGovern never regained his momentum. As he continued to suck up to the party regulars, most of whom Hunter found loathsome, McGovern and his young idealists broke Hunter's heart a little bit, day by day. McGovern was the best hope of his generation, the one man with a chance to take back his country from the greedy and the unprincipled. Finally, in a burst of rage, Hunter wrote the last article of his campaign coverage:

> This may be the year when we finally come face to face with our-
> selves; finally just lay back and say it—that we are really just a nation
> of 220 million used car salesmen with all the money we need to buy

guns, and no qualms about killing anybody else in the world who tries to make us uncomfortable.

The tragedy of all this is that George McGovern, for all his imprecise talk about "new politics" and "honesty in government," is really one of the few men who've run for President of the United States in this century who really understands what a fantastic monument to all the best instincts of the human race this country might have been, if we could have kept it out of the hands of greedy little hustlers like Richard Nixon.

McGovern made some stupid mistakes, but in contrast they seem almost frivolous compared to the things Richard Nixon does every day of his life, on purpose, as a matter of policy and a perfect expression of what he stands for.

Jesus! Where will it end? How low do you have to stoop in this country to be President?

After the disappointing election and unhappy with All Things Wenner—particularly the editor's niggling over expenses and Hunter's being shuttled to the Zoo Plane for the last weeks of the campaign—Hunter resigned from the magazine. He demanded that his name and Raoul Duke's (as sports editor) be removed from the masthead. This would not affect the upcoming campaign book, Hunter promised, but it opened the door for the more formal arrangement that he wanted: as a freelance writer with a contractual agreement with *Rolling Stone*. He did not want Wenner profiting on his image—though Wenner refused to strike the names.

Hunter took his family to Cozumel, Mexico, for a brief vacation to recover from the campaign and to fuel up for finishing the campaign book. For Christmas, Hunter got Juan a kitten and Sandy a mynah bird they named Edward. Hunter coached him to say, "Hi, I'm Edward. Birds can't talk." The important thing was being home. "It always felt good, going back," Sandy said. "Always."

The manuscript of his *Fear and Loathing* campaign book was due on January 1. Wrapped in bitterness and another nut-crunching deadline, Hunter was unable to work at home or in the *Rolling Stone* office on collecting his years' worth of campaign reporting into the book he'd promised Wenner. "I have a powerful aversion to working in offices," Hunter admitted. "I am not an easy person to work with, in terms of deadlines."

Wenner rented a suite for Hunter at the Seal Rock Inn, which advertised itself as "San Francisco's Only Ocean-Front Motor Inn and Restaurant." The suite had a small kitchen, which Wenner's minions stocked with two cases of Mexican beer, four quarts of gin, a dozen grapefruit and "enough speed to alter the outcome of six Super Bowls." Hunter carefully inventoried his supplies in the introduction of his book, another shot of gasoline on the fires of his image. As his editor, Alan Rinzler cracked the whip for two intense weeks; they were determined to beat *The Making of the President 1972* to the bookshelves.

It was mostly a matter of collecting the articles Hunter had written on the run and writing the connective tissue to hold the book together. Here and there he had corrections to make, but mostly he was concerned with narrative flow. The collected pieces read as week-by-week journalism, and he found himself early in the book, in February, making speculations about what would happen at the convention—which, of course, he already knew. But the book's conceit, presenting the illusion of moment-by-moment coverage, worked, conveying the hyper-rush of a presidential campaign witnessed on the run. He also employed the fake editor's note device he'd invented back at Eglin Air Force Base. Since he hadn't written much as the campaign wound down, he covered this section in a supposed transcribed dialogue between Hunter and Rinzler: "At this point, Dr. Thompson suffered a series of nervous seizures in his suite at the Seal Rock Inn. It became obvious . . . that the only way the book could be completed was by means of compulsory verbal composition." The manufactured mayhem added to the book's manic tone. "I would always say, 'Let's talk about the book,'" Rinzler said, "but he would disappear, hop in the car and go down to the local saloon."

He missed his deadline, in part so he could include the Super Bowl in the book. He flew to Los Angeles for the January 14 game between Miami and Washington. He'd been leaning toward Washington, but once he heard that Nixon was for Washington and that the coach, George Allen, was televising prayer meetings with players, he decided that "any team with both God and Nixon on their side was fucked from the start." The Super Bowl epilogue gave Hunter the elegiac device he needed to bring the story of the mad year home, in a cadence that owed much to Hemingway's *A Farewell to Arms*: "Around midnight, when the rain stopped, I put on my special Miami Beach nightshirt and walked several blocks down La Cienega Boulevard to the Losers' Club."

By late February, the presses were rolling with the awkwardly titled

Fear and Loathing: On the Campaign Trail '72. Teddy White was left in the dust. With the prose smoothed out, the book gave a brilliant inside look at a presidential campaign. The decades haven't dimmed the book's relevance. It remains a full-scale portrait of the political process, one part of what Hunter called the American Dream, at work. "His book was just dead on," Curtis Wilkie said. "It was very accurate." Rinzler called it "his smartest book and his greatest intellectual accomplishment." Hart enjoyed the book, but thought its political significance was overblown. "It wasn't about the campaign," he shrugged. "It was about Hunter."

Despite—or because of—the Hunter-centric approach, the book had great influence. "It's the moment we realized that traditional journalism is not sufficient," said Carl Bernstein, who was uncovering the Watergate scandal for the *Washington Post* while Hunter was following the candidates around. "Hunter could not have existed in the mainstream press. The myth of objectivity is what holds us back the most."

But the book was doomed. As a new publisher, Straight Arrow had weak distribution, and most of the first printing was rejected by Wenner because Levison-McNally, the Reno printers hired to print the book, didn't ink the pages sufficiently. *Fear and Loathing in Las Vegas* had sold 18,000 copies in hardback, and Wenner told Hunter he would be happy if Straight Arrow could push half that number of the *Campaign Trail* book.

But the Popular Library paperback of *Fear and Loathing in Las Vegas* was taking off. The book was passed around the nation's newsrooms and stuffed into college-campus backpacks. Hunter's reputation grew with each battered paperback exchanging hands. It was a book *devoured* as much as read, and the faithful committed passages to memory. Hunter's people were paperback people. Eventually, the same thing happened with the Popular Library edition of the *Campaign Trail* book. By the time the Watergate scandal was in full eruption, Hunter was on his way to household-name status.

He was staying afloat. He had not written a best-seller, but he could be satisfied with his three books. He knew they were good, and the critics generally liked them, despite huffing and puffing about his fast-and-loose attitude toward stenographic truth. For all his critical success, he continued to exist the way he had for more than a decade: from job to job, from paycheck to paycheck. It was the lot of the freelance writer: *Buy the ticket, take the ride.*

And whether he wanted to be or not, he was famous.

Chapter 13

CELEBRITY

I have no idea of whether you think you're making a film
about Duke or Thompson. I haven't thought about it until
now and I'm filling with hate and rage, just thinking about it.
I'm never sure which one people expect me to be.
Often, they conflict.
—HST *to BBC television crew, 1977*

The idea was to get some rest and make another run at fiction, some writing that wouldn't require him to catch planes, thrash in distant hotel beds, or march in lockstep with the weasels of the establishment press. But the mind-numbing schedule of 1972 hadn't been a waste; sitting on all those airliners gave him an idea for a short novel set on a coast-to-coast flight.

He wrote Silberman at Random House, suggesting that it was time to deal with the American Dream project and admit that it was dead. *What's next*, Hunter asked his editor. *Do we write it off, or do I have to pay you back?* Hoping that Silberman would forgive the American Dream advance, Hunter offered him *Guts Ball*, his newly conceived "short Vegas-like novel" set on a transcontinental flight. He sent him an audiocassette filled with excited ranting—which, he said, is "about as close as I plan to come to anything resembling a Real Outline."

Though he faced the reality of being in Random House's debt, he also was proud and could not resist gloating a little bit about his newfound status to Silberman. His campaign coverage made him a celebrity, even if it didn't make him rich. In the years since *Hell's Angels*, Hunter had questioned his sanity, and no doubt Silberman and the Random House executives had as well. Maybe everything would pay off after all.

"I plan to force a readjustment in my long-time status (or role)—from RH's House Freak & Subsidized Looney to the role of an actual, profit-churning *Writer*," Hunter wrote. "It's been fun all around—no argument about that—but I get the feeling it's about time we tried to establish a serious relationship. (Which is not to say that I plan to start taking *myself* seriously; all I'm talking about here is my work, as it were. . . .)"

The early spring was a good taking-stock time and also afforded Hunter his first rest and relaxation in three years. "I look forward to as many months as possible of sloth & unemployment," he wrote his mother. "My next project is a weird novel for Random House, [due] around 1975 or so, but between now & then, I have no plans at all—except maybe to run for the U.S. Senate from Colorado, but at the moment, that's only a threat."

But the realities of day-to-day living forced Hunter to again set aside writing a novel. He battled with Wenner over the editor's refusal to remove his name (and Raoul Duke's name) from the *Rolling Stone* masthead. He told Wenner to cut him off, but the $1,000 per month retainers continued arriving. When Hunter figured he had violated the failure-to-produce-anything-in-ninety-days clause of his contract, he insisted the money stop.

Thompson/Duke needed a rest. The fans might have been surprised that he was sunning himself like a bleached lizard on his back porch, recovering. In the public mind, there was no slash between Hunter Thompson the human and Duke the character. They were one.

Sure, Hunter took drugs. He drank a lot—probably enough during a twenty-four-hour span to render a minor-league infield unconscious. But he could hold his liquor. Longtime friends could remember only seeing him truly out-of-control drunk two or maybe three times during the course of a forty-year friendship. His fans knew the character, not the man, and when they approached him, they often felt the need to affect being high if they weren't already. They had assumed Hunter would want them that way. But he hated sloppy, inarticulate drunks. He breakfasted on bloody marys and beer and drank Wild Turkey and Chivas by the tumbler, but he was rarely shit-faced.

As he began to put together freelance assignments to provide the income he needed to make it through 1973, he went to other markets. As he wrote his old friend William Kennedy, "I'm trying to finish my annual reject/effort for *Playboy*." Despite *Playboy*'s earlier vow that he would never again write for the magazine, that banned-for-life policy came before Hunter Thompson grew famous as the Raoul Duke madman character and developed a fan base of stoned freaks, policy wonks, and third-rank journalists, all of whom admired the brass balls of the Duke character.

So of course the *Playboy* editors swallowed their pride. Now that the election was over, what situation could they put him in that was comparable? The editors sent him in April on a deep-sea fishing expedition, a titanic struggle perfectly suited to a mad-dog journalist: *Old Gonzo and the Sea*.

And despite Hunter's feeling that his *Playboy* performance anxiety would render him unable to produce, he did finish the article, though it took over a year to write and eighteen months to appear in the magazine. The piece started out as a report on a fishing tournament requiring a trip to Cozumel, which to Hunter sounded more like R&R than work. It would also allow him to get in touch with his Inner Hemingway and test his testosterone.

He needed a companion. For the Cozumel trip, Hunter brought along Michael Solheim, the Aspen bar owner/real-estate broker/campaign manager who'd first introduced Hunter and Acosta. As "Yail Bloor," Solheim made a good foil for the Duke character, perfect for bouncing back outrageous comments at the protagonist. ("Bloor" was one of Hunter's favorite names from his telephone-prank days, along with "Squane." He had even quoted "Bloor" during his campaign coverage.)

The story again became the struggle to *get the story*. "I'm damned if I can remember anything as insanely fucking dull as that Third Annual Cozumel Fishing Tournament," Hunter wrote. "Deep-sea fishing is not one of your king-hell spectator sports."

But getting fucked up and running amuck was a great spectator sport for Hunter Thompson fans. Moreover, after returning from Cozumel, he was forty pages into the *Playboy* article when all political hell broke loose back in Washington, and he was forced to set aside the fish story.

The break-in at Democratic National Headquarters in June 1972 had turned out to be more than a minor burglary. Treated as a police story by the two *Washington Post* reporters who covered it—Carl Bernstein and Bob Woodward—a trail soon appeared, leading from the Watergate headquarters of the Democrats, to the burglars' point of origin at the White House. Bernstein and Woodward pieced together much of the story before election day 1972, but the majority of the press was too distracted by the campaign horse race to pay heed. The *Washington Post* was pretty much alone on the story, out on a limb that the White House resolutely tried to saw off.

The president's staff had kept the story contained through the election; it was only the following spring, after the burglars had been tried and were awaiting sentencing, that one of the burglars, James McCord, wrote to Judge John Sirica, the man in charge of the Watergate burglary case, saying it was more than a simple burglary. In essence, he said, all that stuff you've been reading in the *Washington Post* is true.

The *Post* had been in a vulnerable spot, shat upon not only by the executive branch but by the establishment press. *If Watergate is such a big story*, the press wizards reasoned, *then who the fuck are Woodward and Bernstein?*

They certainly weren't any of the boys on the bus. Bernstein had been on the verge of getting fired before the Watergate break-in came along, and Woodward was relatively new, by way of Yale, the U.S. Navy, and a small Maryland paper. As nonpolitical reporters, they didn't look for sources in the usual places. They talked to secretaries, office workers, and others political-reporter types disdained. They shared unconventional work methods with Hunter Thompson.

Their stories painted a picture of a corrupt White House full of con men and shysters, presided over by the Felon in Chief. When McCord's letter to Judge Sirica became public, the Columbia University trustees looked over the recommendations for that year's Pulitzer Prizes, which were days away from being awarded. The *Washington Post* was not on the list. Knowing that the Pulitzers would look ridiculous by not honoring the biggest political story of the year (if not the decade or the century), the trustees called *Post* editor Ben Bradlee and said, more or less, *Which one do you want?* After a moment's thought, Bradlee said, *Public service.* The public-service Pulitzer wouldn't go to Bernstein and Woodward; it would go to the newspaper. When the reporters heard about this, they showered and shaved and put on their best clothes and went to Bradlee to ask why. *Boys*, Bradlee said. *No one will ever forget you. But this paper had its cock on the chopping block. The paper needs the award.*

Hunter would have appreciated the appropriateness of the award. What better example of public service than getting rid of Richard Nixon? Hunter had regarded most journalists, especially those who trailed politicians around the country, as imbeciles. He seethed with contempt for almost any representative of the establishment press, and especially for the editors and publishers who kept the charade going. "There was no room in their complacent world for a man who despised mediocrity—who would let nothing stand in the way of the truth," he wrote. "The great American press was a babbling joke—an empire built on gossip and clichés, a final resting place for rumor-mongers and pompous boobs."

Woodward and Bernstein, two fringe characters in their own newsroom, built the story through simple hard work. Hunter admired that.

The Watergate story grew more complex every day, and Hunter watched, fascinated, glued to his television. As the parade of president's men marched before the Senate Select Committee on Watergate, Hunter felt his political stomach rumbling. The televised hearings were more interesting than all of the Super Bowls combined.

Soon he decided to end his Woody Creek exile and return to politics. "I've about decided to make the big move to the Washington Hilton and start fucking around with the Watergate story," he wrote Frank Mankiewicz. "Watergate is about the only thing that interests me right now." Mankiewicz ended up playing frequent host to Hunter when he wanted to do a Washington story. He preferred the company of friends to a hotel, and Mankiewicz always knew when Hunter was on the way. "He never called to ask if he could stay," Mankiewicz said, "but his mail started arriving. When we started getting forwarded mail, we knew Hunter was on the way."

Hunter didn't need to go to Washington to write his first Watergate piece. It came from his soul and the odd mixture of joy and revulsion he felt watching the televised hearings. The first piece appeared under the Raoul Duke byline, though much of the scrambled article ("Memo from the Sports Desk & Rude Notes from a Decompression Chamber in Miami") was attributed to the Hunter persona. It was a bear awakening from hibernation and finding that the president of the United States is packed in a deep barrel of shit. After blasting the dolts in the campaign press corps as lazy and ignorant bastards, he applauded the Bernstein-

Woodward legwork that brought the Watergate story front and center. "I take a certain pride in knowing that I kicked Nixon before he went down," he wrote.

The "Rude Notes" piece was almost entirely focused on building the Duke/Thompson persona. He wrote with fury of being left off the list of enemies maintained by the Nixon White House, one of the early disclosures of the Watergate hearings. Hunter certainly considered himself significant enough to make the list: "How can I show my face in the Jerome Bar, when word finally reaches Aspen that I wasn't on it?" He had, after all, been the only accredited member of the campaign press corps to compare Nixon to Adolf Hitler in writing.

He also added to the Duke/Thompson legend by reporting that "Dr. Thompson" was being held in a decompression chamber, recovering from both the 1972 election and a scuba-diving incident. There was some truth to the scuba-diving accident—he'd been treated for a serious case of the bends in Miami during a Florida vacation. But the locked-in-the-chamber metaphor allowed him to explain his absence. The months he'd been silent seemed like years to his fans. He even prepared his readers for what he believed could turn into a massive failure. Speaking of himself in the third person as Dr. Thompson, he wrote, "Whether or not he will write anything coherent is a moot point, I think, because *whatever* he writes—if anything—will necessarily be long and out of date by the time it appears in print."

The "Rude Notes" piece was mere treading water for Hunter, but for Wenner, it was gold. He could ignore Hunter's resignation; the meal ticket was back, and the Duke/Thompson monster was aroused from its slumber by the spectacle in the Senate hearing room. No need to remove those names from the masthead.

By the time Hunter hit D.C. in mid-July, much of the key testimony was over. But his arrival was news. For the first time, he was face-to-face with huge celebrity. When he entered the hearing room, heads turned, his name was whispered. He often made noisy arrivals, but this was more than he had planned for. *Reporters* were asking for his autograph, the gutless hacks. It was great once again to be sniffing history being made, but it was alarming, even depressing, that he was drawing so much interest away from the grave constitutional proceedings. He retreated to the Capitol Hill Hotel's bar and the homes of friends and watched the hearings on TV, convincing himself that the testimony was much more interesting on the box than in person. In "Fear and Loathing at the Watergate," his first major *Rolling Stone* article since the campaign, he made no mention of his frightening new celebrity status and merely told readers, "There was not a hell of a lot of room for a Gonzo journalist to operate in that high-tuned atmosphere." Though he had White House press credentials, he'd never found them of much use. He didn't long to spend time among the clueless. "When you're covering the White House with a head full of acid, they don't know anything's wrong," he said. "They just think you're a little bit nervous."

Much of the reporting was done poolside at the Washington Hilton, with Sandy and Ralph and Anna Steadman for company. Wenner had flown the Steadmans first to San Francisco for meetings and then to Washington for the coverage. The editor wanted the Gonzo lightning to strike again. Though their time in the hearing room was brief, Hunter still behaved like the consummate journalist. "He was a tireless round-the-clock worker," Ralph recalled. "No lead was too small to follow up, drunk or sober."

But it wasn't Hunter's kind of story. He was not central to the drama, and there was no real struggle to *get the story.* The story took care of itself, and was unfolding through hours and hours of dry testimony. What he *could* offer to *Rolling Stone* readers was his view on the whole affair; when published in September 1973, "Fear and Loathing at the Watergate" was an extended variation on the theme of Richard Nixon as the dark underbelly of the American Dream. Hunter knew how to kick a man when he was down.

"He will go down with Grant and Harding as one of democracy's classic mutations," Hunter wrote, then offered as much feeling as he could muster for the evil man who had inspired some of his best writing: "I have to admit that I feel a touch of irrational sympathy for the bastard. Not as The President: a broken little bully who would sacrifice us all to save himself—if he still had the choice—but the same kind of sympathy I might feel, momentarily, for a vicious cheap-shot linebacker whose long career comes to a sudden end one Sunday afternoon when some rookie flanker shatters both his knees with a savage crackback block."

Hunter was laying odds that Nixon would resign by Christmas.

He knew what his audience wanted—some of the Duke madness. He made much of his conversations with friends, his struggles with deadline, his use of psychedelic mushrooms and the beer du jour (Carlsberg, mentioned so often you smell brewery kickbacks), and fake editor's notes, generous selections drawn directly from his notebooks, and even a fantasized conversation between presidential aides. It was what readers had been waiting for: Watergate getting the 10,000-word Gonzo treatment.

The social highlight of Hunter's Washington visit was a first-anniversary reunion of the McGovern campaign staff, a dinner party at George and Eleanor McGovern's house one year to the day after he had accepted the party's nomination. There were 150 people there, some speeches, and much wine, and finally George and Eleanor bade everyone a sentimental goodbye at the door.

Then a self-selected group, including Hunter, Gary Hart (in from Denver, where he was planning his U.S. Senate campaign), pollster Pat Caddell, and actor/filmmaker Warren Beatty, spun off into Hunter's rented Cadillac. With a politician's careful memory, Hart recalled, "We started on complicated nightly rounds of Washington, and we closed down several bars. It was kind of a movable feast that night and a lot of alcohol was consumed, and I think—I can't testify to it personally—some drugs were probably consumed as well. It was typical Hunter. Why we didn't get stopped by the police, I don't know."

It *is* a mystery. As Caddell remembered the night, Hunter drove with a bottle of Wild Turkey braced between his thighs, barreling over medians and at one point running a patrol car off the road. "Hunter, that was a cop," Caddell yelled. Hunter tossed the bottle from the window and cut a swath through suburbia and interstate construction before finally losing the cop. Caddell remembered looking over at Beatty, pale with fear.

Hart lived to become U.S. Senator from Colorado, and Beatty also survived to fulfill his destiny of making films. But for Hunter's deft hand at the wheel, they could have all ended up as concrete toast on Interstate 95. Hunter's precision driving skills were grafted to the Duke persona.

Though capable of monumental generosity in public, Wenner could be a pernicious penny-pincher with his writers, even legitimate stars. Hunter had always held himself to a high professional standard, at least up to that point in his career, and he wanted the same in all of his dealings. He especially wanted it from Wenner, since his editorial instincts were sharp and because he owned *Rolling Stone*, the best venue for Hunter's writing.

Hunter could be a literary prick tease for Wenner. *It could happen*, he wrote his editor, *I could write regularly for you again . . . but I need evidence of a regular pattern of professional behavior*. Treating Hunter and other writers like serfs to a feudal lord was not the way to build trusting editorial relationships. Ralph Steadman felt himself screwed by Wenner as well, and he complained to Hunter, who passed on Ralph's insight in a scolding rebuke to Wenner. "Ralph put his finger on it very nicely, I think, when he said: 'Jann doesn't seem to realize that every dime he screws somebody out of today might cost him a dollar tomorrow.'" Hunter didn't want to worry whether he would be reimbursed for all of his legitimate expenses. "The haggling is getting pretty goddamn old," Hunter wrote Wenner, "and the most depressing aspect of it all is that we never seem to make any progress."

Two Watergate pieces done for *Rolling Stone*, Hunter spent the fall trying to get his *Playboy* article on the Cozumel fishing tournament whipped into shape. He realized that the style he had found and propagated was so distinct that it polarized his audience. Some loved it and, like junkies, wanted more of the Duke-and-Gonzo bad craziness. Others found it self-indulgent and left the room when Hunter's byline showed up. Yes, he admitted to David Butler, his editor at *Playboy*, he had once been a more conventional and coherent writer. But for good or ill, what he was sending the magazine now, in bursts, was his style. The editors weren't used to the stop-and-start multifax, *insert here/insert there* approach *Rolling Stone* had gotten used to.

Playboy invested a lot in the piece and even provided two secretaries to make transcripts of Hunter's tapes of his fishing-boat yammering. He'd sent fifty pages to Butler, who'd responded that Hunter needed to rein himself in and try conventional storytelling.

"I'm pretty well hooked on my own style—for good or ill—and the chances of changing it now are pretty dim," Hunter shot back. "A journalist into Gonzo is like a junkie or an egg-sucking dog; there is no known cure."

He toiled on the fishing article and generally resided at the bottom of the emotional abyss. All was mundane at Woody Creek, and he sent off a short piece to a friend, calling it "Fear and Loathing in the Doldrums." After a couple of high-octane years, the sudden absence of the itinerary had left a hole in his life that even "the imminent demise of Nixon" could not fill.

He had never really lusted after fame. Wanting to be a writer and wanting to be famous were two distinctly different ambitions, but now, at thirty-four, he found they were wound together, like one of the grapevines on his ranch.

People kept asking things from him. Every request for a dust-jacket blurb for a book set him off. He sweated over the things, spent much time and energy on them. He was beset by a mob, "a goddamn torrent of people who not only want to come out here and move into my house, but also into my head & my crotch."

Where was the payoff for this bullshit? "I find myself getting 'famous,'" he wrote his mother, "but no richer than I was before people starting recognizing & harassing me almost everywhere I go."

The fame left him empty and angry, mostly. It also rendered him intransigent, nearly mute at Woody Creek. Sandy taught at the Community School, Juan was a great kid, living in a boys' paradise at Owl Farm, but something was wrong with Dad.

Famous . . . but still poor, still writing letters to editors, accusing them of welshing on his expenses or his fees. *When would it end? When would he ever be ahead?*

By all accounts, Hunter had never done cocaine before 1973, but when *Rolling Stone* sent him a new edition of Freud's *Cocaine Papers* to review, Hunter felt the need to try it. He'd avoided it before as a rich boy's plaything and classified it as a "jive drug." But after a few snorts, he discovered that he liked it. It amped up his energy. Always nocturnal, with the right number of perfectly timed snorts, he now could stay up for three days at a stretch.

When Hunter was writing, life hummed along smartly on Owl Farm. When he was blocked (that's what he called them, Sandy said, his blocks), then life was hell.

"This is when the cocaine hit," Sandy said. "There was a lot of it being consumed at the Jerome Bar. He would drink there until three or four o'clock in the morning. And he sometimes didn't get up until six p.m. It was just getting later and later."

Looking back, Douglas Brinkley could clearly see when productive-and-prolific Hunter stopped and cocaine-snorting Hunter took over. He went from twenty flawless pages a day to twenty flawless pages a month, if he was lucky. "I think his greatest frustration was when cocaine hit his life," Brinkley said. "He no longer had the ability to produce as he had."

Sandy continued her studies in alcohol, downing by her recollection a half bottle of bourbon a day or a bottle of wine and change. For the first time, she began to suspect that Hunter was unfaithful. While he was in Mexico for *Playboy*, she sorted through his mail. She never opened the personal stuff, but a bulky package caught her eye. She opened it and a tape fell out, along with a note from one of Hunter's friends saying it might be best "if Sandy didn't hear this." Of course she played it. It was nothing dirty, no "smoking gun" in the parlance of the time, but Sandy could tell from the sound of intimate familiarity in a woman's voice on the tape (saying something innocent and wholly expected, such as "Shall I get you some Wild Turkey?") that she and Hunter were together. "I immediately knew," Sandy said. She began to quietly question Hunter's friends, looking for details, but most of them played dumb. She needed something incriminating. Her drinking grew in intensity, and when Hunter returned, he saw that she was reliant on booze for everyday living. He warned her to "get it together." They remained at a marital stalemate for the next few years. The lost children in their marriage depressed Sandy, turning her to drink. Hunter was devastated too, but didn't know how to communicate his despair to Sandy or show her how the deaths had gripped his heart. As an old-school southern gentleman, he didn't think it was right for a man to show such vulnerability to a woman. He too began drinking more and began using drugs to dull pain, not to feed his imagination. And he did indulge in other women. He and Sandy had begun the marital drift.

By year's end, Hunter got Wenner to fund an all-powers conference of Democratic Party heavyweights to discuss the nation at midpassage of the Watergate hearings. The idea was to plan for that joyous day when Richard Nixon would leave the White House by police escort.

The concept was inspired by political organizer Adam Walinsky, who visited Hunter early in the summer to talk about a Thompson-for-U.S.-Senate campaign, an idea Hunter dismissed when Gary Hart announced his intention. Still, Walinsky opened Hunter's eyes to all of the political roadblocks, not just in the next few years, but looking decades out. Politicians were terrible at devising coherent philosophies. That was what Hunter wanted to do: get the best and the brightest minds of his generation, put them in a room and see what they could come up with.

In fact, Hunter thought the project could turn into a book. He'd gotten stalled on his cross-country flight novella, and after almost a year in a mental wilderness, he was excited about something again. The brain power in the room could throw out lots of ideas, and, once the tape of the meeting was transcribed by a battery of minimum wagers, a book manuscript would result. The book would jump-start real political reform in America. That was Hunter's wish.

Wenner was just happy to see Hunter enthusiastic again. "I was serious about getting into national politics," Hunter said. "I'd met a lot of people on the campaign. . . . I knew all the players. . . . I figured if we could get the best people in the party together we could begin to create a national political machine."

Hunter began organizing the event, hoping to hell it would not turn into Thompson's Folly. He got the political couple of the moment, Richard Goodwin and Doris Kearns, to commit to the conference. Goodwin was gold, a former speechwriter for John F. Kennedy, with Camelot credentials and years of respect as a Washington insider. Kearns was a historian and former White House Fellow for Lyndon Johnson, who'd gone to stay with him at his ranch after his presidency, ghostwriting Johnson's memoir, *The Vantage Point*. The guts of the McGovern staff was coming too—Patrick Caddell, Rick Stearns, Sandy Berger. Some Kennedy people were coming as well, most notably David Burke, later CBS News president. There also was a place at the table for the founder of the feast, Jann Wenner.

Though he was looking to the possibilities of a hopeful political future, Hunter's general outlook was grim—too grim, it turned out, for many readers of the *New York Times*. As the hot political reporting commodity of the moment, he was asked to contribute a New Year's Day column for its op-ed page. It was the first official day on the job for the new op-ed page editor, Charlotte Curtis, and so she turned over almost a whole page of the best newspaper on Earth to a madman.

"Fear and Loathing in the Bunker" was a dour look at the world. Instead of exulting over President Nixon's demise, Hunter came across as somewhat melancholy, as if he knew that when Nixon was gone, he truly would not have the evil man to kick around anymore. It was an odd piece for Hunter, more essay than article. The lack of a central event made his writing uncharacteristically tedious, though there were flashes of his unique sense of language. As he described former White House counsel John Dean's testimony in the Watergate hearings, he set the scene: "Here was this crafty little ferret going down the pipe right in front of our eyes, and taking the President of the United States along with him."

As the piece ran on . . . *and on* . . . it became apparent to readers that they had stepped into Bizarro World, with a violently out-of-control columnist. The page was filled with Hunter's bile and rage and also with his sad resignation that all that was left to do was to sweep up after Richard Nixon, "the main villain of my political consciousness for as long as I can remember."

In contrast, as he plotted the liberal think-tank conference—and ever since the days of his boyhood pranks, he realized the importance of careful planning—Hunter's first concern was keeping the meeting top-secret and invitation-only. He selected Elko, Nevada, off Interstate 80 in the northern part of the state, a location so remote and so devoid of possibilities for fun that real work would have to be done.

Finally, he had a full plate again, going from famine to feast in a matter of weeks. He had to wait a few months for the conference to convene, but the planning energized him to get back to writing. He had never lost his passion for pro football and in the fall had even asked George McGovern to intervene on his behalf with his friend Joe Robbie, owner of the Miami Dolphins. Hunter wanted to do a *Campaign Trail*–style book about a season in the National Football League, but didn't want to wade through the rows of press relations people to get the access he wanted. That idea never worked out, and Hunter ended up making pilgrimages to the Bay Area in fall 1973 to stalk the sidelines of the Oakland Raiders practice field with team owner Al Davis. Alas, the Raiders didn't make the Super Bowl.

The Dolphins did. Too bad the Dolphins book didn't happen, because Hunter could have followed the team week by week as it marched to the Super Bowl. The team that had scored a perfect season in 1972 and pounded the Washington Redskins in the Super Bowl kept its powerhouse going with a 12–2 record in 1973. The team faced the Minnesota Vikings in Super Bowl VIII on January 13, 1974, in Houston. Hunter the sportswriter was back in action.

Wenner thought, *Hunter is back.* The stay, however, would be brief.

He was a stone junkie for pro football. More than any other sport, it embodied his fascination with the visceral aspects of the American

Dream. Wenner had brought in a new managing editor whose passion for sports was equal to Hunter's. John Walsh came to *Rolling Stone* from *Newsday*, where he had been sports editor. At first, the office staff in San Francisco didn't know what to make of him. That he was a legally blind albino was not the issue. That he was trying to professionalize the magazine stuck in the craw of some of the old-timers. He also blasted away at the male hierarchy on the staff and put a number of women in key editorial positions. Talented and well-educated women were already on the staff, but they were secretaries and coffee fetchers. Walsh promoted several women from stenographers to department heads during his tenure.

But to Wenner, one of Walsh's major plusses was that he could speak Hunter Thompson's language. When his star writer wanted to talk sports, Wenner was out of his depth. It took John Walsh to explain to Wenner the meaning of a baseball double play.

In October 1973, Wenner hosted a Monday night dinner party to coincide with the Buffalo Bills–Pittsburgh Steelers game and invited Walsh to his home to meet Hunter, who was visiting. "Jann accurately predicted that Hunter and I would bond over sports," Walsh said. "It was Jann's last accurate prediction." Indeed, within a few minutes Hunter and Walsh had developed an elaborate way to bet on the game, a method that involved categorizing the players by race and odd-and-even-numbered uniforms. "Sports brings out his giddiness," Walsh said of Hunter.

Walsh was Hunter's hand-holder for "Fear and Loathing at the Super Bowl." He was able to persuade the accounting department to pay for the cocaine Hunter had purchased to get members of the Oakland Raiders to open up during interviews. Although the actual game played a minor role in "Fear and Loathing at the Super Bowl," it was one of the most cohesive pieces he had written since the campaign, now two years gone. He folded into the piece his comments on the nexus of drugs and professional sports (hence the cocaine), the relatively new phenomenon of the free agent in football, and the impending apocalypse described in one of his favorite pieces of writing, the Book of Revelation. He used flashbacks to the previous fall to salvage his sideline chats with Raiders owner Davis. Davis, he said, looked like a pimp, adding, "The fiendish intensity of his speech and mannerisms reminded me very strongly of another Oakland badass I'd spent some time with, several years earlier—ex-Hell's Angels president Ralph 'Sonny' Barger." Hunter also used the occasion to bring in his fellow NFL junkie Richard Nixon, allowing him to tie most of the major touchstones in his *oeuvre:* Hell's Angels, drugs, and politics. "God, Nixon and the National Football League," Hunter wrote: "The three had long since become inseparable in my mind."

Hunter presented the piece as a battle against deadline. The story began with his dawn sermon on the balcony of his Hyatt House room on Super Bowl morning. He needed to finish a fire-and-brimstone speech before the leech at the bottom of his spine crawled up to the base of his brain and sucked the life from him.

"Fear and Loathing at the Super Bowl" was quick work by Hunter's standards. When the secret Elko meeting convened, the magazine had already hit the stands and Hunter's rabid fans were ready to declare him victorious over the leech.

In between the Super Bowl and Elko, on February 6, Hunter had one of the hottest tickets in the country, catching one of the Denver shows of Bob Dylan's monstrously successful return to performing after an eight-year self-imposed exile. Although the press accounts were ecstatic and Jann Wenner and others heaped over-the-top praise on Dylan, the show left Hunter feeling uneasy. Dylan was the master of subtlety, but these shows were as loud as locomotives and as subtle as a railroad spike to the temple.

Almost immediately after the concert, Hunter left for Elko, arriving a full week before the distinguished guests. He reserved the rooms at the Stockmen's Hotel under the name of the Studebaker Society. The reservations desk wondered whether Hunter and the other car enthusiasts objected to sharing the conference facilities with the players in the state bridge tournament. *That will be fine,* Hunter said. The card players would provide the perfect cover for his top-secret talks.

It was freezing, dead of winter, middle of nowhere, and when the sessions began, Hunter at first was perturbed with his invited guests for being too contentious. After all of his prep work, he turned the session over to Wenner and ran off the first evening with the babysitter brought along to care for Richard Goodwin's son. By Hunter's account, he ate acid and took the girl off to a truck stop fifty miles east, in a town called Wells. In the parts store there, he bought sixteen tire checkers—iron pipes used by truckers to test tire pressure—and when he got back to the meetings the next day (after enduring angry glares from Goodwin and Doris Kearns, who would marry Goodwin the next year), he passed the clubs around the room. "Okay, you bastards," he told them, "If you want to argue, use these."

What Hunter wanted was agreement; he wanted an agenda to be set. "He said he was going to beat us all if we didn't start saying something," Patrick Caddell said.

Hunter had brought together people from the 1968 Kennedy campaign and the 1972 McGovern campaign, and helped heal the wounds between the camps. Wenner was developing a greater interest in politics, seeing it as the rock 'n' roll of the seventies. Soon, in fact, he would sign up Richard Goodwin as political editor of *Rolling Stone* and throw several hundred thousand dollars his way. But as he had earlier wanted to meet the Beatles, the alliance with Goodwin allowed Wenner to achieve his goal of meeting the Kennedys. (He would even sign on the former First Daughter, Caroline Kennedy, to cover Elvis Presley's funeral in 1977.)

Hunter told the group that the country faced "a genuinely ominous power vacuum" that he hoped the great minds in the room could fill. "We kept trying to focus on what to do with the country and politics," Caddell said, "but nobody knew what to do at that point. The hope was we would come up with a grandiose plan, a manifesto."

The conference was most important for the healing it brought between the political camps, and all of the participants developed a fondness for one another. Goodwin and Kearns forgave Hunter his babysitter transgressions. All that being said, Elko left Hunter with an empty feeling.

"It's hard to understand why we didn't come out of there with a platform," he reflected. "I didn't follow up on it much. My role was to make it happen, and I did."

The Elko book never happened, but *Rolling Stone* soon tried to transform itself into a major political player, and that's where many of the Elko ideas eventually appeared.

As for a book, Wenner soon hatched a plan for Straight Arrow to publish a Hunter Thompson anthology, a collection not only of his *Rolling Stone* articles but also of those hard-to-find pieces he'd done for *Scanlan's Monthly* and other publications, before the advent of Gonzo journalism. As long as an advance was involved, Hunter was game.

Though inconclusive politically, the Elko conference did energize Hunter a lot, as he continued to emerge from the campaign decompression chamber and look forward to the next presidential election, in 1976. Back in Aspen and snowbound, Hunter was approached by writer Craig Vetter about doing a *Playboy* Interview. Considering his rocky history with the magazine and his yet-to-be-completed assignment on the Mexican fishing tournament—nearly a year over deadline—the magazine's editors figured he would turn it down. The *Playboy* interview was a sign of arrival in middle-brow America. Was it too bourgeois for Hunter? Hell no, as it turned out. He'd known Vetter for a year and liked him, and he also knew how this worked. There was no fee for being the subject, but the magazine did pay all expenses. It was a golden period for the magazine, "Those were fat days at *Playboy*," Vetter said. The editors didn't balk at Hunter's suggestion that the interview be conducted in Cozumel. But the simple process of the interview turned into a nightmare for Vetter. Hunter brought Sandy and Juan and turned it into a family vacation. Every time Vetter mentioned the word "interview," Hunter changed the subject or found something else to do. Days passed. Sandy and Juan flew to Florida to visit Sandy's relatives. Hunter and Vetter went fishing ("I want to see blood in the water!" Hunter yelled at the guides). Frustrated, Vetter told Hunter he was giving up. They quarreled and broke one of the hotel's glass tables, and Hunter jumped in his rented jeep and rode off into the night. He showed up at Vetter's room at dawn, finally ready to talk.

The interview took most of the year—months, in a variety of locations—to complete, but when it was eventually published, it became a rare, authoritative biographical source. For the first time, readers could get a good look at Hunter Thompson (three striking and moody portraits by photographer Al Satterwhite) and learn the basic facts of his life. Vetter spent months on the project, and the interview did not appear until the November issue, but when he and Hunter left Cozumel that spring, Vetter felt that he had finally broken the back of the beast.

With impeachment looming and the specter of another presidential campaign on the horizon, Hunter went back on the road and, using the Richard Goodwin connection, was able to make a swing through the South with perennial presidential hopeful Senator Ted Kennedy. Kennedy had an overnight stop in Atlanta with the governor of Georgia, then was to make the Law Day speech on May 4, at the University of Georgia in nearby Athens.

Hunter passed up the governor's invitation for an overnight guest room in the executive mansion, staying in a nearby hotel with an ample supply of booze. But he showed up for breakfast the next morning and after some hassles with the security guard who couldn't believe the beer-toting and scruffy man at the gate was a guest of the governor, he was greeted at the back door by Jimmy Carter. Carter was well aware of Hunter; his sons were huge fans of the "Fear and Loathing" political coverage.

Carter had six more months to go in his term and was expected to return to his quiet life as a peanut farmer downstate in Plains. Hunter had no real interest in him, but appreciated his casual blue-jeans hospitality and his willingness to have him as an overnight guest, a privilege rarely offered to a journalist.

But Hunter was there for Kennedy, and they were all headed to Athens for a luncheon ceremony honoring a former secretary of state, Dean Rusk, at which both Kennedy and Carter would speak. Two hundred guests packed the college cafeteria, most angling for a chance to see a Kennedy up close and personal. But what happened that noon was something as close to a political revelation as Hunter would experience.

The event was the usual dull fare, and Hunter shifted through a lunch and a raft of speakers, making quick and surreptitious trips to the Secret Service vehicle outside the cafeteria doors, where he stocked his iced-tea glass from his bottle of Wild Turkey.

He paid little attention to the speeches, until Carter was ten minutes deep in his talk. He had started with the usual self-deprecating remarks expected from a lame-duck governor, but then the tone shifted. Carter's audience—judges, lawyers, the *haves* in the have-and-have-not equation—was trapped, and he was going to give it to them.

"It was a king hell bastard of a speech," Hunter remembered. He sat up when Carter mentioned that Bob Dylan ("a friend of mine," Carter said, and indeed the singer had been a guest at the mansion after his recent Atlanta concert) was one of the guiding political philosophers in his life. He cited several Dylan songs, using "The Lonesome Death of Hattie Carroll" as an example that showed the inequities in modern society. The song told the true story of black maid Hattie Carroll and how the thoughtless act of a wealthy young white landowner cost her her life. As punishment, the young man drew a six-month sentence. That so little value was placed on this woman's life angered Dylan, and Carter. He talked about the dirty politics and the rotten judicial system in Georgia, and how the nation, suffering from Watergate, reflected a horrifying decline in values.

Hunter rarely heard a politician speak such truths in public. He was used to people like Hubert Humphrey, "this shameful electrified corpse," or the president, "Richard Milhous Nixon, who was criminally insane and also president of the United States." Carter, he felt, showed the sort of political courage that Hunter had only read about, usually in stories about Thomas Jefferson or James Madison.

Afterward, he asked Carter for a copy of his speech. The governor showed him one page of legal-pad scratching. The event had been taped, however, and Hunter made a copy from the version recorded by the governor's staff. For two years, he carried the tape and played it for anyone he could persuade to listen to a talk by the former governor of Georgia. Thirty years later, Hunter still had a cassette of Carter's talk in the glove compartment of his Jeep Cherokee.

In the meantime, Hunter agreed to write about the last gasp of the Nixon presidency for *Rolling Stone*, and that required doing time with his mobile National Affairs Desk in Miami, near Nixon's Key Biscayne compound, and in Washington. Richard Goodwin was setting up *Rolling Stone*'s Washington bureau, to aid Wenner's quest to meet more movers and shakers in American politics. The first bureau was the guest quarters at Robert Kennedy's home in McLean, Virginia. The Kennedy children were thrilled when Hunter showed up to talk over impeachment coverage with Goodwin, but not all members of the family were pleased to have an admitted drug abuser hanging around. Jacqueline Kennedy Onassis knew Hunter's reputation and called to check on her children, staying at the Kennedy estate with their cousins. Goodwin sensed it was time for a more businesslike address and found suitable quarters on Pennsylvania Avenue, next to the Executive Office Building.

Hunter could have easily written "Fear and Loathing in Washington" in his Woody Creek kitchen. He didn't need the Washington hotel room ("the National Affairs Suite") or even a cubicle in Goodwin's new headquarters. He didn't cover anything in the traditional journalistic sense and, speaking of traditional journalists, used a lot of his space to attack those who were attacking him, principally the *Columbia Journalism Review*, which had suggested that readers take anything with a Hunter Thompson byline with a tanker full of salt.

"I'm getting goddamn tired of being screeched at by waterheads," he wrote, and the only hope for improvement in that publication would come, he said, when "the current editor dies of brain syphilis."

His analysis of events as the nation headed down the chute to the resolution of its constitutional crisis was cogent and illuminating. The piece gave him another opportunity to shore up his image, with its drug and alcohol references, his denunciations of opponents ("unprincipled thugs"), his over-the-top ejaculations of surprise ("Mother of babbling God!"), his flights of fancy (an escape with Josef Stalin and a quote from Yail Bloor, his fictional creation), and his focus on himself and his tortured journey to print. In this piece, however, he wrote less about the struggle to get the story and more about what the story would be. It was an advance, a preview of upcoming impeachment attractions, and what he expected to happen by the end of the summer.

"It is definitely worth watching," he wrote, "and perhaps even being a part of, because whatever kind of judgment and harsh reality finally emerges will be an historical landmark in the calendar of civilizations. . . . The trial of Richard Nixon, if it happens, will amount to a *de facto* trial of the American Dream."

Wenner gave his meal ticket huge pages to fill with his text, and Hunter, still seething over his treatment by Wenner, charged a thousand dollars per printed page. Always in need of cash and feeling slighted, Hunter put aside trust and began to insist on all agreements in writing. "If I seem to be grinding down a bit hard in this area," Hunter wrote Wenner, "I want to assure you that this is precisely what I mean to be doing, for good or ill, and not without giving adequate thought to the whole situation." Wenner had offered to pay for a secretary to help Hunter, but he couldn't imagine working with anyone except Sandy, so why not put her on the payroll? Still, the financial workings in the editor's mind bothered Hunter. Wenner would pay for a secretary, but haggle over five hundred missing dollars in Hunter's accounting of his story fees.

But Hunter couldn't stay away from Washington, and he couldn't stay away from *Rolling Stone*. Whether or not he was ever a journalist in the conventional sense, he always had the need—almost an addict's need—to be where the news was happening.

Hunter could not keep pace with the events fast enough to make deadlines. People didn't turn to *Rolling Stone* for *real* news anyway. Hunter's fan base was such that his name as a cover line on any subject was a draw. Many of his fans, the stoners in the crowd, merely responded to the outrageousness in his writing. They liked the swearing, the drugs, the apocalypse around every corner. They would have read an essay on sheep farming if it had a Hunter S. Thompson byline. They just wanted to read what "the Good Doctor" had to say.

Hunter's journalistic sense made him want to stay as topical as possible. In early August, at the moment he was preparing to file his next *Rolling Stone* dispatch on the impeachment summer, Nixon surprised everyone with his sudden resignation.

Immediately, Wenner told his managing editor that he wanted a special issue on Nixon. "I want Hunter to write the cover story." Walsh knew it was foolish to think Hunter could produce something that fast. "Just do it," Wenner spat. But Hunter could not be budged. He wrote about the resignation, but on his own time.

So the staff had to find Nixon-related quotes in all of Hunter's past work, recruit some pieces from other staff writers, and raid the photo files. The special issue featured a deeply unflattering portrait of the fatigued president, with a David Felton cover line: "THE QUITTER."

Hunter began pulling together his long analysis of the final days of the Nixon presidency for a later issue, but just as *that* was about to hit the presses, Hunter was cold-cocked again by President Gerald Ford's pardon of his predecessor. This time, he kept the rewritten section on the resignation and slapped several pages of a new beginning on the piece, foaming with fury over good-old-boyism at the highest level. Passionate and gloomy, "The Scum Also Rises" was the ultimate process story for Hunter. The blown deadlines were part of the story, as was how he learned of the pardon in an early morning phone call from his friend Dick Tuck. "Who votes for these treacherous scumbags!" Hunter screamed at Tuck. "You can't even trust the dumb ones!"

Ford timed the announcement of the pardon for a Sunday morning, when heavy-hitter political reporters were out for an afternoon sail or involved in some family grope at a secluded retreat. Hunter worked the surprise attack on the press into his piece as well. He figured it was fitting that his nemesis was causing him so much trouble, even far removed from office. "I was brooding on this and cursing Nixon," he wrote, "more out of habit than logic, for his eerie ability to make life difficult for me."

He was still working on the *Playboy* interview and, with Craig Vetter's assistance, was able to pull together a massive account of the impeachment, resignation, and pardon, and get it ready for readers' hands within two weeks. When he wanted to, Hunter could meet deadlines.

Then came the letdown. It was a smaller version of what had happened after the campaign ended: his life had expanded to contain all of the impeachment . . . and now that was over. "I've got to get out of journalism," Hunter told Vetter. "I've got to get out of politics. I've got to change."

He would not have Nixon to kick around anymore, and he was going to miss him.

"After the Nixon campaign, his genius articles were no longer about politics," Jann Wenner said. "Nixon was this great character. Nixon was the werewolf that came out at night on the White House lawn. That was a great character in Hunter's whole arc."

Hunter finally finished "The Great Shark Hunt" for *Playboy*, and it was set to run in the December issue, following the also long overdue Craig Vetter interview, which ran in November. The resignation caused Hunter and Vetter to reframe the nearly finished interview in order to revise his position on the Nixon presidency and put it in the proper tense. Hunter even helped Vetter write the introduction to the piece, which is why it reads like Hunter or someone trying to imitate Hunter. His desire to always find the right word impressed Vetter.

Vetter had used a description in his introduction of Hunter sitting on a seawall in Cozumel, reading a $1.25 newspaper that would have cost a more sober man 25 cents. As Vetter told writer Peter Whitmer, "Hunter saw that and said, 'No. No . . . it is better if we make it 24 cents.' That's close-in craftsmanship, not something you could ever teach. Hunter, when he is *on* as a writer, line by line, letter by letter, is as good as you can get."

The "Shark Hunt" piece was Hunter's grandest epic in years. After he had spent three years in politcos' back rooms, moving his vision outside was like going from a black-and-white tea-sipping drama to a Cinemascope cast-of-thousands spectacle.

Set up as a story about a fishing tournament, it was, of course, about Hunter Thompson being assigned to write about a fishing tournament. Much of the action has to do with beer, margaritas, drugs, and the inevitability of the blown deadline. His Celine-like companion Bloor (Solheim) speaks in apocalyptic language, just like Hunter Thompson. The cadence and the emphatic tone could make readers believe that Hunter had developed schizophrenia or found an imaginary playmate. Solheim insisted he was on the boat. The story was mostly about the struggle of being Hunter Thompson, of fighting over expenses, incompetence, and injustice, and his liberal references to his life and lifestyle ("Sandy" was used in the story without explanation) made it clear this was a members-only story for his built-in audience. For a man complaining about the agony of celebrity, he wasn't doing anything to stop perpetuating his image as America's premier outlaw journalist.

He also wasn't doing any rewriting. He admitted that he hadn't done a second draft of anything since *Fear and Loathing in Las Vegas*. If readers lapped up whatever he wrote, no matter how many breakdowns and chronological shifts he threw their way, why try for polish? During the political coverage and in the *Campaign Trail* book, he had occasionally resorted to using his notes verbatim, and his disciples loved them, particularly when he threw in a mock editor's note ("at this point, Dr. Thompson was confined to bed at the insistence of his physician . . ."). The device allowed him to get away with cutting corners. It also enhanced his literary mystique and permitted him to market Gonzo journalism as first-draft "free lunch, final wisdom, total coverage." The style itself freed him from having to labor over multiple drafts.

Getting away with it. Though the *Vegas* book showed his capabilities when he did rewriting, Hunter saw that his readers would accept his work without sheen and polish. He also learned that they would show up to hear him speak, even when he had nothing to say.

Tom Wolfe had urged Hunter to get on the speaking circuit back in 1969. "Lecturing is easy, lucrative and a nice ego melon," he wrote, "but I guess it is essentially a form of the worldwide Grand Jackoff." Hunter took the latter part to heart. In the aftermath of his campaign coverage, universities were clamoring for Hunter as an on-campus speaker. It was easy and lucrative (Wolfe was right about that part), but calling what he did a "speech" was inaccurate.

Most of Hunter's speaking engagements were question-and-answer sessions. He had no prepared text, no rant about the state of modern journalism or politics. He just walked onstage to thunderous applause and opened it to questions. For the acolytes in attendance, this was fine. But many people in the academic community had no idea what to ask. They showed up only because the campus paper said a famous writer was speaking.

The evenings Hunter spent on campus were chaotic. The young fans cheered when Hunter was asked about politics and called elected officials "communist buttfuckers." They loved it when he said *fuck* or *cocksucker*, or when he took a gulp from his bottle of Wild Turkey. The true-believer fans asked him about Ibogaine or Oscar Acosta or other such minutiae of his work, and most of the others in the audience sat there baffled, as if they'd walked in on the middle of a lecture on quantum physics, so strange was the babble from the stage.

This is where the character of Hunter S. Thompson . . . or Duke . . . began to emerge as a notorious figure. Bill Dixon, the 1972 McGovern organizer in Wisconsin, had been the first person hired by the House Judiciary Committee for its impeachment proceedings, during the last days of Watergate. He had become great friends with Hunter, and they occasionally traveled together. Dixon was on the road with Hunter in the seventies and remembered seeing him go onstage in a campus auditorium and *become* the character.

"It was the first time I noticed Hunter Thompson dressed up as Hunter Thompson," Dixon said. Something happened to his body as he stepped onstage and bathed in the applause. They were not happy gigs, Dixon recalled. Lost in the Thompson/Duke persona, Dixon said, is the fact that Hunter was at his core quite shy. He needed to be that other character in order to face the crowd and deal with his persona. On his own, he could not have easily spoken to the crowds.

"Hunter did it because he got twenty-five hundred or he got thirty-five hundred or he got four thousand, or whatever it was," Dixon said. "I mean, he did it in the seventies because he needed the money."

"I detested these fucking things," Hunter said. "Since I felt I had nothing to say I refused to even pretend to make a speech. I would, however, answer any and all questions from the audience—preferably in the form of a pile of 3×5 cards submitted in advance."

Sometimes, the drink was not just a prop. On October 22, 1974, just before he was due to travel overseas, he had a speaking engagement at Duke University. The student assistant who picked him up at the Raleigh-Durham airport greeted him with hashish and a bottle of Wild Turkey. Hunter indulged in both. When he showed up at the university auditorium, the audience had been kept waiting forty-five minutes. "I am very happy to be here at the alma matter of Richard Nixon," Hunter said. Immediately, he opened up the floor to questions. He was asked whether he thought former governor Terry Sanford, who had run for the Democratic presidential nomination in 1972, might make another run in 1976. Unaware that Sanford was then president of Duke, Hunter responded, "He was party to the stop-McGovern movement at the convention and he is a worthless pigfucker."

That was it. The speakers committee sent a delegate—a small, blond girl—out to give Hunter the hook. As she escorted him from the stage, he took an ice-filled tumbler of Wild Turkey and threw it up against the velvet curtain, leaving a stain to remind Duke of his visit.

A few students followed him into the parking lot, where he stayed and talked quietly for about an hour. When the university later said it planned to withhold his speaking fee, he said he thought that the parking-lot talk satisfied the contractual agreement to "talk to Duke students." He never got paid.

He did make news, though. The Associated Press ran a brief article on the wire about the Duke debacle, and several other schools canceled his speaking engagements.

In the aftermath of the *Scanlan's Monthly* collapse, Hunter lumped the magazine's attorney, Bob Arum, in with the crowd that "should be hung by their fucking heels & beaten with wire whips." But four years later, Arum was the boxing promoter who persuaded Hunter to drop everything and head to Africa for the Ali-Foreman fight. Arum appealed to Hunter's ego by noting the celebrities who had already obtained press credentials, including writers Norman Mailer and George Plimpton. Hunter's eyebrows arched. Plimpton—now *there* was a man he admired. They had met several years before, during the *Hell's Angels* era in San Francisco, but Hunter did not know him well. Perhaps the "Rumble in the Jungle" between Muhammad Ali and George Foreman would afford the opportunity. So Wenner sent Hunter and Ralph Steadman to Zaire to cover the event. It sounded like another *can't-miss* assignment.

"Gonzo, Gonzo, Gonzo," Ralph exhaled. "How long do you think we can keep doing this kind of Gonzo thing?"

Hunter pondered for a moment. Finally, he said, "I guess we can keep doing this kind of thing until one of us dies." Between the lines: *As long as they'll pay us*.

Ralph gave in. "OK, let's do it again."

They traveled separately, and Hunter shared the Frankfurt, Germany–Kinshasa, Zaire leg of his flight with Plimpton.

Hunter could be stingy with praise. He was fond of Tom Wolfe, once telling him that "with the possible and perhaps fading exception of Kesey, you're about the only writer around that I figure I can learn from." Though he still considered Wolfe too much of a crusty, outside-looking-in reporter to be a true role model, he liked reading his work.

But Plimpton was also a favorite, drawing rare compliments from

Hunter. They shared an important characteristic: both were participants in their stories. Plimpton had been on the course to a traditional career as a Man of Letters and was the first editor in chief of the *Paris Review* in his expatriate days in the early 1950s. But unlike many others of the raised-pinkie tweed set, he liked sports. Working mostly for *Sports Illustrated*, Plimpton, the Harvard-educated stringbean, put himself into potentially terrifying athletic situations: boxing with heavyweight champ Archie Moore, pitching in a Major League Baseball game, duffing his way through eighteen holes on the PGA tour, and, most famously, leading a professional football team through a series of downs. Most of these stunts later became books, the best-known being *Paper Lion*, the story of his life as a last-string quarterback with the Detroit Lions during summer training camp.

Hunter liked Plimpton's willingness to not stand aside as the detached observer, as Wolfe did. Although not directly influenced by Plimpton, Hunter could still be described as someone who had taken Plimpton's idea and plugged it into a 220-volt outlet. That could be another working definition of Gonzo.

They sat next to each other on the long flight into Zaire, and finally began the friendship they'd been promising themselves for years. Plimpton was amused by Hunter's love of gadgets—on that afternoon, a radio the size of a collie so powerful that it picked up news of a clothing sale in Spokane, Washington. Hunter charmed Plimpton with his comic account of the Duke University debacle, and kept him laughing all the way into Africa. The formation of the Thompson-Plimpton Mutual Admiration Society may have been the only positive thing to come from Hunter's visit to Africa.

It was a failed assignment. First, the fight had been postponed, supposedly because George Foreman had been injured while training. Conspiracy theorists said that it was because the fix was in for Muhammad Ali and that he wasn't ready for the fight, so Foreman's camp came up with a ruse to buy time.

Whatever the reason, it meant that many of the journalists who showed up in September to cover the fight had six weeks to kill until the rescheduled fight at the end of October. Hunter's friend from the *Boston Globe*, Bill Cardoso—coiner of "Gonzo"—was now with the short-lived *New Times*, and one of those left with nothing better to do than drink and smoke dope. When Hunter arrived, he immediately joined his friend in those pursuits. By the time Ralph got there, the situation was well out of control. The Intercontinental Hotel also lost Ralph's room reservation, so he had to bunk with Hunter and had no buffer from the madness.

Since the gentlemen of the sporting press had descended on Zaire to cover a boxing match, most of them went about their business. Plimpton and Mailer, though in a separate stratosphere from the daily reporters, did their part by attending press conferences, watching sparring sessions, doing interviews. Plimpton said Hunter "scorned those single-minded reporters who talked shop and gossiped about what had happened that day in the two fighters' camps."

Hunter did none of that. He stayed high most of the time and amused himself. The gathering place for most of the press was the Intercontinental's lobby, so he routinely had the front desk page him by the name of the Nazi war criminal Martin Bormann (and he even signed for room service as Bormann; it was one of his favorite games). He liked to see the looks on the hotel guests' faces when the bellman strode through the lobby with the name of an evil Nazi on his call board.

Most of the sportswriters who stayed for the long gap between the originally scheduled bout and the actual fight were nearly crazy with drink by the time Ali and Foreman put on the gloves. Ralph witnessed Hunter scooping a handful of Nivea skin cream and shoving it into his mouth to ease his sore throat. "This filthy African humidity," Hunter said. "Like sucking on a swamp."

Hunter's major concerns were staying high, avoiding arrest by the authorities, and buying elephant tusks. He assumed having these was illegal, so he pondered how he would sneak them home through his many customs stops.

As far as Plimpton could tell, Hunter had no interest in the fight, and though Ralph was busily doing sketches of the personalities—Foreman walking his dogs, Ali's friend Bundini Brown jiving it up with fellow bar patrons—Hunter never even took notes.

When Ralph came back to the room to get Hunter the evening of the fight, he was horrified to discover that Hunter was in his bathrobe.

"What's going on?" Ralph asked.

"Nothing, Ralph," he said. "The tickets are gone."

"What are you going to do?" Ralph asked, dumfounded.

"I'm going swimming," he said.

Ralph was astonished and watched Hunter empty a pound-and-a-half bag of marijuana into the hotel pool before diving in and floating in the slick green residue.

"This is it, Ralph," Hunter said. "Fuck the fight. If you think I came all this way to watch a couple of niggers beat the shit out of each other in a rainstorm, then you've got another thing coming." Skipping the fight also gave him a good excuse not to write about it.

The next day, Plimpton dropped by Hunter's room to see why his $200 press seat had been vacant during the fight, which Ali had won. Hunter told him about floating in the marijuana pool. The hotel was deserted, he said, except for a man who came to watch Hunter float for a long time. "Maybe he thought I was a corpse," Hunter said. Plimpton asked whether the experience had a kick to it. "It's not the best way to obtain a high," he said, "but a very luxurious feeling nonetheless."

Leaving Zaire provided more drama than the fight Hunter missed. In addition to sneaking out the tusks, he persuaded Ralph to fly with him back to the States. Because Ralph didn't have the proper visa, they expected a snafu in New York. It worked. Hunter used Ralph to distract customs officials while he snuck the tusks into America in his athletic bag. For the rest of his life, the tusks hung above the fireplace at Owl Farm. After twenty-four hours in the no-man's-land lounge at the airport, Ralph returned to England.

Even though Hunter missed the actual boxing match, the Ali-Foreman fight *could* have made a great Hunter Thompson article. As Plimpton said of Hunter's work and tremendous fan base, "Thompson's readers were not interested in the event at all—whether it was the Super Bowl, or politics or a championship fight in Zaire—but only in how the event affected their author. So, in fact, the only reporting Thompson had to do was about himself." All of the problems and paranoia were good feed for a Gonzo story, Plimpton said. As Plimpton wrote in *Shadow Box,* "His *Rolling Stone* readership required very little of the event he was sent to cover, except, perhaps, that everything go *wrong* . . . to the degree that the original purpose of his assignment was finally submerged by personal misfortune and misadventure."

Mailer grumbled that Hunter's fans were too easily pleased and would accept *anything* from their man.

He was right. Hunter could have given his fans a story about a night-mare assignment in a horrible, uncomfortable city. He could have written about smuggling elephant tusks into Kennedy Airport or his intense paranoia about the Zairean officials and their attitudes about drug use. His fans would have accepted anything, and loved it.

But he gave them nothing.

For years, there had been talk of a film deal for *Fear and Loathing in Las Vegas*, but whenever those talks turned serious, the Oscar Problem reared its hairy and unkempt head.

Although Acosta had signed off on book rights, film rights were another matter. Acosta had withheld consent, and the thought of being mired in lawsuits made most filmmakers run off like buckshot deer. "We can do it amicably—through lawyers—or hand to hand," Acosta had written Hunter in 1973. Reexamining the book agreement, Acosta felt that he had been blackmailed. Wenner had published his book (*Autobiography of a Brown Buffalo*) with Straight Arrow, but Acosta said it died too quick a death because of poor promotion. Hunter wrote his mother that all of Acosta's snorting and hollering had "managed to kill any chance of a film sale by his constant threats of a libel suit."

Still, the threads of their friendship had managed to hold together. At the end of 1973, Acosta's letters to Hunter had become desperate. He was backed against the wall, claiming he was living hand to mouth, cashing in food stamps, resorting to thievery. He still saw his association with Hunter as his one ticket out. "I still am looking to you as my only serious white connection for the big contract," he wrote Hunter. What he needed, he said, was "seed money" from Hunter to get his life back on the right track.

Hunter was baffled. After all of the chaos Acosta had caused with the book and movie deals, why did he think Hunter—*always* cash poor— would have something to send his way? "What in the fuck would cause you to ask me for *money*—after all the insane bullshit you've put me through for the past two years?" Hunter shot back. Acosta saw himself as a man in a crown of thorns, but Hunter betrayed no sympathy. "Good luck with your grudge," he said. "No doubt it'll make you as many good friends in the future as it has in the past."

In June 1974, with the country in its final Watergate agonies, Acosta had disappeared, apparently from a smuggling boat off the coast of Mazatlan, Mexico, other circumstances unknown.

Hunter didn't learn of his disappearance until that fall, while he was in Zaire. Sandy had received a letter from Annie Acosta, worried about her brother, whom she had not heard from since April. She told Hunter there were rumors her brother had been shot on the smuggler's boat, returning from Mexico. "I am desperate and seriously fear for his life," she wrote. "Oscar always thought the world of you—hopefully it works both ways." She thought a famous gringo writer might have some pull with the authorities, certainly more pull than a Chicano woman would have. Acosta's son Marco had spoken to his father by telephone in June, just as he said he was about to board the boat for his trip back to the United States. Marco Acosta was fourteen. "I told him I hoped he knew what he was doing by going back on such a small boat," Marco wrote. "He said he hoped I knew what *I* was doing with my life."

For Hunter, who had embraced the doomed-to-die-young pose for himself, it was startling—even horrifying—that early death had come for his friend. Still, there was no body. Acosta was presumed dead, but there was no hard evidence. But Hunter couldn't be naïvely hopeful, as Annie Acosta was. Acosta walked through a dangerous world, constantly on the edge, eating acid "with a relish that bordered on worship" and doing whatever it took to obtain the drugs he wanted to satisfy his needs.

Marco Acosta believed that he would see his father again. Over the years, there were rumored Acosta sightings in India and Mexico and a pretty solid story of him running drugs off the coast of Florida. But these tales never rose above the level of rumor.

Hunter had given up. His friend was dead.

Hunter returned home from Zaire to find that he had been turned into a cartoon character. Garry Trudeau had begun his comic strip, *Doonesbury*, while an undergraduate at Yale. Upon graduation, he took his lampoon of campus politics and lifestyles on a broader scale and turned *Doonesbury* into a syndicated comic strip with a conscience.

Hunter rarely saw the comics. His newspaper of choice was the *New York Times*, which had no funny pages. At first, he was unaware of the character of "Uncle Duke" that Trudeau introduced into the strip in December 1974: a balding, aviator-shade-wearing *Rolling Stone* writer who hallucinated that he was seeing bats.

For Hunter, it was a nightmare of celebrity coming true. The fame that suffocated him and made it impossible for him to do his work had been turned into fodder for the comics. Now, instead of people merely wanting to share joints and get autographs, he was actually heckled by people shouting his name . . . but it wasn't *his* name . . . it was that other guy, that character:

"Duke! Duke! Duke!"

"It was a hot, nearly blazing day in Washington, and I was coming down the steps of the Supreme Court," Hunter recalled. "I'd been inside the press section and then all of a sudden, I saw a crowd of people and I heard them saying, 'Uncle Duke.' I heard the words Duke . . . Uncle . . . It didn't seem to make any sense. I looked around and I recognized people who were total strangers pointing at me and laughing. I had no idea what the fuck they were talking about. I had gotten out of the habit of reading funnies when I started reading the *Times*. . . . I was sort of by myself up there on the stairs and I thought, 'What the fuck madness is going on? Why am I being mocked by a gang of strangers and friends on the steps of the Supreme Court?' Then I must have asked someone and they told me that Uncle Duke had appeared in the *Post* that morning."

To Hunter, there was nothing funny about it. "When you're a famous American writer, you don't think of things like being in the comic strips," he said. "Being a cartoon character in your own time is like having a second head."

It started as a mere annoyance, but soon it became part of the burden of being Hunter S. Thompson. "The wild, crazy man . . . the drug addict . . . this is what people bought," Sandy said. "This is what people wanted. This is not what Hunter wanted when he was younger. This is not who he wanted to become."

Hunter told Ralph, "I'd feel real trapped in this life if I didn't know I could commit suicide at any moment." Ralph saw his friend and collaborator being engulfed by a character he created: "He became a prisoner of his own cult," he said.

Chapter 14

CASUALTIES OF WAR

Does it look like [drugs have] fucked me up? I'm sitting here
on a beautiful beach in Mexico; I've written three books. I've
got a fine one-hundred acre fortress in Colorado. On that
evidence, I'd have to advise the use of drugs.
—*HST to Craig Vetter, 1974*

It might have just been his nature that he required life to be a series of
intense conflicts—in his writing, in his relationships with friends, in
his marriage.

Hunter's relationship with Wenner was like a marriage in which the
partners hate each other but stay together because the sex is so good.
Wenner was furious about the blown assignment in Zaire; it was as if
Hunter had cheated on him. With time, though, he forgave. He always
forgave. *Rolling Stone* was a popular magazine, but it was at its best—
certainly, in terms of sales—when Hunter's name boomed from the cover.
So Wenner forgave; he even signed a reluctant Hunter to a contract for
a projected *Fear and Loathing: On the Campaign Trail '76* for Straight
Arrow Books. Wenner bought into the Jay Gatsby repeat-the-past philosophy, but Hunter, a big fan of Fitzgerald's book, recognized that it was
fiction.

More importantly, there was the anthology Hunter wanted Straight

Arrow to publish. Collecting and preserving the faded clippings in his archive was more important to him than being the acid generation's Theodore H. White. He was proud of his old *Observer* pieces and the two articles for the *Nation*. His obituary for Lionel Olay had appeared in a small, underground magazine and was read by only a few hundred people at most. His *Scanlan's* articles were mere rumors to even the true believers among his fans, since the magazine had such a short life and most librarians didn't bother to preserve copies. Hunter wanted to present his life's work to a larger audience.

But Wenner wanted the repeat of a lightning strike, and what better way to make it happen than by sending Hunter back out on the campaign trail?

Through the penny-pinching on expenses and the blown assignment in Zaire, Hunter and Wenner had a strange symbiotic relationship. When Hunter visited San Francisco, he stayed with the Wenners, sometimes at Jann Wenner's peril. Hunter enjoyed playing with fire extinguishers, and once the editor awoke in the middle of the night with a CO^2 blast in the face and Hunter's cackling above him in the cloud.

But there was not much laughter anymore. Hunter watched how Wenner treated his writers and editors. "He'd say hideous things that you thought were a joke. Then he'd turn around the next day and do it. A lot of writers couldn't stand up to it. He broke their confidence." Wenner admitted to David Felton: "I can be very mean."

Hunter wasn't happy with the changes at *Rolling Stone*. His best ally, John Walsh, had left for the *Washington Post*. After monumental publicity and a few devastatingly boring essays on political science, Richard Goodwin's association with *Rolling Stone* and its supposed big splash in Washington had died on the vine. Wenner's venture into big-time politics was not only costly; it left the magazine and Wenner looking foolish, like a passed-over political groupie.

Many of the best writers on the *Rolling Stone* staff, including the brilliant Grover Lewis, had left. Some, like Joe Eszterhas, found new careers, writing for the movies. Though there were always new writers and new stories that kept *Rolling Stone* timely, the writers who had forged the magazine's swaggering voice and style were gone or, in Hunter's case, silent.

New people and new stories fed *Rolling Stone*. One of the most sensational tales began in the magazine's backyard and became the most significant work of real journalism (as opposed to Gonzo journalism) in the magazine's history.

On February 4, 1974, San Francisco newspaper heiress Patricia Hearst was kidnapped by the radical Symbionese Liberation Army (SLA). Her whereabouts were a mystery, and the nation hung on the tale of the beautiful young woman taken hostage. But a few months later, on April 15—presumably after much brainwashing—she helped the SLA rob a bank and appeared to have bought into radical politics. Now she was Tania, and in diatribes issued to the press, she denounced wealthy fat cats such as her father and vowed to bring death to the fascist insect. The SLA had a violent history, including the assassination of the superintendent of schools in Oakland. In the bank robbery, two innocent bank customers were murdered. The San Francisco Bay Area might have been a comfortable environment for radical politics, but the SLA and its murderous ways were not welcome by the nonviolent radical elite. SLA leader Donald DeFreeze, also known as Field Marshal Cinque, soon took the group back to his hometown, Los Angeles.

A little over a month after Patty Hearst had reintroduced herself to the world as Tania, more than four hundred law-enforcement officers from the FBI and the Los Angeles police closed in on the SLA residence. Two members of the SLA tribe had tried to shoplift from a sporting-goods store and, when that was botched, left in a frenzy, without their van. The van's glove compartment contained a receipt with an address police presumed was their headquarters. There was a siege, a shootout, and a fire; when it was all over, several SLA members were dead, including DeFreeze, by his own hand.

Patty Hearst's body was not found. For more than a year, she was on the run, mostly in the company of former middle-school teachers turned radical couple, Bill and Emily Harris.

The whole Hearst-SLA episode kept America on edge: *Where was she? Was she brainwashed or was she really a terrorist?*

Reporters Howard Kohn and David Weir knew. Friends since college, they had arrived at Jann Wenner's home for wayward reporters. (Kohn had committed major faux pas with the *Detroit Free Press*, much as Eszterhas had with the *Cleveland Plain Dealer*—skirting the facts on a couple of key stories.) Working through deeply anonymous sources, Kohn and Weir pieced together a mammoth, intricately detailed example of narrative nonfiction that hit newsstands and network-news broadcasts just as the FBI finally tracked down Hearst and captured her, along with Bill and Emily Harris.

It was a masterpiece of journalistic timing and the sort of coup that had been the province of the *New York Times*, when it broke the Pentagon Papers stories, or of the *Washington Post*, when Judge Sirica's letter vindicated its Watergate reporting.

It was the greatest story in *Rolling Stone*'s history, and it wasn't by Hunter Thompson. It wasn't his kind of story, anyway. He could not have written about Patty Hearst, because he would play no role in the story.

Although it was a high point for the magazine, Wenner could not fully enjoy his success. Wenner and his mentor, the music journalist and sage Ralph J. Gleason, had stopped speaking a year before. There would have been no *Rolling Stone* without Gleason, but he had removed himself from the equation, so frustrated was he by what he saw as Wenner's mismanagement of people. When Gleason died of a heart attack in 1975, Wenner was left with much unsaid to the man who had been both his benefactor and his spiritual father. He went to console Gleason's widow, yet it was Wenner, shattered and shaking with tears, who needed the comfort.

Hunter was waiting . . . *and waiting* . . . for his $75,000 advance on the 1976 *Campaign Trail* book. When it did not arrive, Hunter finally called Wenner and found that he had sold the Straight Arrow book division and that the advance Hunter counted on was a casualty. Hunter was in a rage, writing Wenner a letter full of bile, fury, and sadness. "I can't conceive of *anything* right now that could effectively remove the memory of you sitting out here in my living room with the fire & the music & the coke (and even Bangkok Fred), acting like a human being while we worked over that proposal of yours . . . and then going back to San Francisco & driving a stake through the heart of the relationship. . . ."

Hunter went into a self-appointed psychic exile in the spring of 1975 and vowed never to speak to Wenner again.

The Vietnam War had consumed nearly all of Hunter's adult life, yet he had been watching it from off-stage, a rare position for him. The war began to wind down, with the Nixon administration's vow that "peace is at hand" just before election day 1972. Apparently, it was not. Finally, by early 1975, it looked as if it was finally ending: the Communist North Vietnamese were poised for the final push to take control of South Vietnam and its capital city, Saigon. The nation that had been split apart by the Geneva Conference in 1954 was about to be reunited under communism.

Hunter wanted to be there. He watched his portable television on the porch of his home in Woody Creek, still brooding like a deposed count. Wounds were fresh from the lost advance for the 1976 *Campaign Trail* book. He was still in never-speaking-to-Wenner-again mode when the phone rang.

"How would you like to go to Saigon?" Wenner asked.

Hunter jumped. "I had to write that piece because the war had been such a player in my life for ten years," he said. "I needed to see the end of it and be a part of it somehow."

He called his journalist friends with war-reporting experience. John Sack had gone to Vietnam for *Esquire* and returned with the article and eventual book called *M*, about a year in the life of a military company. *How do I do this*, Hunter asked Sack. Hunter's main concern, Sack said, was that the government would not credential him, because he was from *Rolling Stone*. Sack was puzzled. "*Rolling Stone* is against the war," Hunter explained. Sack told him, "They're going to talk to you about rock and roll. They're not going to know its editorial position."

Hunter was in the unusual role of novice. During a brief layover in Hawaii on the way to Southeast Asia, Hunter called his old buddy from Middletown and Puerto Rico, Bob Bone. Hunter held on to friends as best he could, and so he had kept track of Bone, and called him from the Honolulu airport. Hunter nervously told Bone he was off to cover the end of the Vietnam War. Bone told him he was crazy; he had no experience as a war correspondent and certainly had no business being in Saigon. Hunter agreed. "But I've got the assignment and so I've got to go."

Some of the danger Hunter brought on himself. When he arrived in Saigon and went through customs, he had $30,000 literally on him. "I got off the plane greeted by a huge sign that said, 'Anyone caught with more than $100 U.S. currency will go immediately to prison.' Imagine how I felt with $30,000 taped to my body." At the request of *Newsweek*, he was carrying the entire payroll for the Vietnam staff because it was the safest way to get the cash into the hands of the writers, photographers, and editors. "I was a pigeon," he said. "I thought we'd all be executed. It was total curfew when we got off the plane, so we were herded into this small room with all these men holding machine guns. There I was with three hundred times the maximum money allowance. We got out and I leapt on a motor scooter and told the kid to run like hell."

Clearly, the city was about to collapse. Hunter attached himself to the friendlies among the press corps, including Philip Caputo of the *Chicago Tribune* and Nicholas Proffitt of *Newsweek*. Both had served in Vietnam as GIs and both were back as journalists. Also working for *Newsweek* was Loren Jenkins, whose friendship with Hunter extended from the early sixties, when he was a teenager living in Aspen befriended by the new crazy writer in town. When Jenkins decided he might want to go into journalism, Hunter was free with advice and the names and addresses of friends who could help. "Consider a year or six months on a small paper that will give you enough freedom to get some good clips," Hunter had advised. Jenkins had listened. Now on *Newsweek*'s staff, he would go on to win a Pulitzer in 1983 for the *Washington Post* and also earn distinction with National Public Radio.

Jenkins was to receive the $30,000 from Hunter, but he held back on delivering the payroll until Jenkins arranged for a lush hotel suite for Hunter. It was not an easy thing to do, but Jenkins came through.

Although Hunter fell into the company of Proffitt, Caputo, and Jenkins, he wasn't fully embraced by all of the reporters. They might have enjoyed reading Hunter's work, but they knew of his habits, which, even if exaggerated for literary effect in his stories, were not good practices when bullets were flying. They didn't want to risk their lives for a drug-addled, slow-to-respond rookie war correspondent. Hunter was a man who conveyed a willingness to embrace imminent apocalypse, and here it was in all of its Technicolor glory.

Hunter was all about attracting attention. While the other war correspondents dressed in olive drab or in the unofficial journalist's uniform—the silk "CBS jacket," made by tailors left from the French colonial era—Hunter wore his usual Hawaiian shirts of brightly colored blooms and his Chuck Taylor high-top sneakers. As he appeared thus attired for his first venture into the war-torn outskirts of Saigon with Proffitt and Caputo, he brought along two hired Vietnamese boys to follow him carrying a cooler full of beer.

Much as Proffitt, Caputo, and Jenkins might have liked Hunter and his work, they did not want to be killed and felt that by taking unnecessary chances and drawing attention to himself, he put them in danger. After a jeep ride into the sticks, Proffitt and Caputo quickly performed a couple of interviews and wanted to jeep it out of there pronto. But Hunter had wandered off. "We debated whether to let the son of a bitch get himself killed," Proffitt remembered. They found him several hundred yards down the road, walking directly toward a Vietcong encampment. They drew up alongside him, grabbed him, and tossed his lanky frame into the back of the jeep.

Back in Saigon, the sense of doom added to the rush of Hunter's usual recreation. The correspondents had set up an opium den in a room at the Continental Palace Hotel, and Hunter satisfied his curiosity with a variety of Vietnamese whores, including several much older than him. He liked the novelty of women from a different culture, women who spoke a different language, women with some years on them.

Not long after arriving in Saigon, Hunter called *Rolling Stone* because his Telex card had been refused. He discovered that Wenner was on a ski vacation, and managing editor Paul Scanlan explained that in a fit of fury after receiving a letter from Hunter, Wenner had taken him off retainer. It was like being fired—and meant losing staff benefits, such as health insurance and life insurance.

Just before leaving home, Hunter had vented about the whole Straight Arrow affair and the cancellation of the $75,000 book advance he'd counted on. "I wrote a serious vicious letter," he said, "finally saying all I was thinking, as I was taking off for Saigon." Then the letter hit San Francisco. "Wenner flew into a rage upon receiving the letter," Hunter recalled. "Getting fired didn't mean much to me—I was in Saigon, I was writing—except that I lost health insurance. Here I was, in a war zone, and no health insurance."

Scanlan restored Hunter's Telex card and expense-account privileges. As it turned out, the firing of Hunter Thompson had not been processed. "The business department had ignored the memo to fire me," Hunter said. "They didn't want to be bothered with the paperwork, so Wenner's attempt had been derailed. The *attempt* was enough," he huffed.

The insurance cancellation was a blow to Hunter's machismo. "He took it very seriously," editor Alan Rinzler said. "Hunter felt as if he had been emasculated by his inability to care for his family." What Rinzler didn't know . . . what Hunter didn't know . . . what few people other than Jann Wenner knew was that Wenner had purchased a huge life insurance policy on Hunter that would make the magazine very rich if something happened to its star reporter. Tom Baker was the *Rolling Stone* vice president ordered by Wenner to take out the policy. "I didn't know you could buy a policy on a guy and not tell the guy," Baker said. "It sounded strange, but that's what Jann wanted, so I called the insurance guy I dealt with, and he did a bit of running around. And I think we did wind up with some kind of policy—an accident policy, moving into a war zone."

The firing was a bone of contention with Wenner for the rest of Hunter's life. Wenner always denied he was serious about the firing. Although they still had a relationship (albeit strained), Hunter never fully forgave Wenner. "Anyone who would fire a correspondent on his way to disaster . . . I vowed not to work for," Hunter said. "It was the end of our working relationship, except for special circumstances. . . . You shouldn't work for someone who would fire you en route to a war zone."

Stuck in Saigon, assignment uncertain, Hunter continued to work in his style. He had more of a country-club approach to covering the war than his peers.

The fall of Saigon was coming, that much was certain. It was merely a question of when. Hunter wanted to witness it, but felt unprepared. He'd left home so suddenly that he did not have all of his gear, though he had brought a tape recorder. Nick Proffitt said Hunter constantly spoke into the recorder, while "drinking beer from the chest and popping some sort of pills, maybe Speed, I don't know what they were. He was washing them down with the beer. He was popping one pill every fifteen minutes. And he was talking into his tape recorder. I looked over and noticed that there was no tape in it." Hunter confessed to friends that he had fallen in love with opium in Vietnam and that might explain his oversight.

Still, Hunter wanted more than a tape recorder and a typewriter. It was the seventies, the era of wiretaps and secret tapes in the White House. Hunter lusted for some serious electronic equipment to allow him to listen to what was going on inside the walls of the U.S. embassy, so he'd know when the big gong was going to sound. So Hunter flew to Hong Kong, to see what gizmos he could find. While he was gone, Saigon fell to the Communists, and the Americans evacuated gracelessly, by means of overladen helicopters lifting precariously from rooftops. "Of course, he missed the evacuation," Proffitt said.

Communications were restored with Wenner. Hunter had been cut off from most of the world, including Sandy. She was frantic that something had happened to her husband. Hunter got word to Sandy (through Paul Scanlan and Timothy Crouse of *Rolling Stone*) that he was fine and that he wanted her to meet him for some "beach time." Wenner paid for her to fly to Hong Kong to be with Hunter.

The visit was supposed to last only a couple of days, so Sandy asked Craig Vetter, neighbor and *Playboy* interviewer, to house-sit, keeping an eye on Juan, who was ten, and the menagerie of animals at Owl Farm. Juan, a prodigy with electronics, had hooked up a system that played loud, frightening noises when the light switches were turned on. "One night," Vetter recalled, "a wolf howl came screaming through the house by his system, then the power to the whole place went down. We got it back on and thought everything was fine." Hunter and Sandy's brief vacation in Southeast Asia extended to nearly three weeks. This, Vetter said, "put me in a pinch and pissed me off." After two weeks, a putrid smell began emanating from the basement. Vetter found a freezer with a rotting "survivalist stash" of meats, along with unmarked items wrapped in foil. Somehow, when power was restored, the freezer did not click back on. Vetter threw out all the spoiled contents of the freezer. When Hunter and Sandy finally returned and Vetter told them what had happened, Hunter nearly suffered a coronary. "My God, I had all the best drugs in the world there," he moaned to Vetter. "A Smithsonian collection: mescaline, sunshine acid, the last of the black beauties." Vetter considered it a "karmic kick in the balls" for making him put his life on hold for three weeks for babysitting duties.

Hunter and Sandy had reunited in the Repulse Bay Resort in Hong Kong, a beautiful old-world hotel. Sandy brought along mescaline, and she and Hunter took the drug immediately upon her arrival and repaired to their hotel bathroom for fun in the tub and sex. When she awoke after a nap, she saw Hunter at the desk, writing. "I remember lying in bed, looking over and thinking, 'Hallelujah! He was writing again!' It had been so long since I'd really seen him writing. And I had a lot of hope."

What Hunter eventually wrote from his time in Southeast Asia was not published in its entirety for another decade. By the mideighties, Wenner was desperate for anything from Hunter, and so he used the ten-year anniversary of the fall of Saigon as an excuse to publish the piece in full. What appeared in the May 22, 1975, issue of *Rolling Stone* ("Fear and Loathing in Saigon") was a fraction of what Hunter put together in the eventual piece that appeared as "Dance of the Doomed" in the May 9,

1985, issue. The first, shorter article was a bare dispatch, augmented by the reporting of another journalist, Laura Palmer.

But the full piece, "Dance of the Doomed," is one of the best examples of pure Gonzo journalism, assembled as much as written. Hunter had been frightened in Saigon, imperiled by street thugs, and certain the world would end at any moment. He braced himself for that end with amphetamines and beer, and the medicine had an effect on him. Landing helicopters became giant locusts. He was nearly killed in a street shooting.

Hunter rolled all of these experiences, including his telegraphed negotiations with Wenner, into his story. Once again, getting the story became the story, and that included his correspondence, cables, transcribed conversations with war correspondents, his hotel tabs, even relevant passages from books (*The Quiet American*, by Graham Greene) that he folded into his narrative. It was at-the-moment, you-are-there reporting, the kind of thing Hunter did best. It gave him a chance (away from his home turf, where he was too famous to freely function) to work as a journalist again. It also showed him in a more reflective mood:

> If there is any one thing that these last wild weeks in Indochina have etched deeply in my brain, it is the discovery of a whole new level of experience—the Big Fix that comes with living and working in the midst of a war. There is nothing quite like it—especially with the luxury of press credentials—and I tried to explain it in my notebook last night here at the airport part in Bangkok, en route from Hong Kong to Laos.
>
> I leaned back on the red plastic couch and signaled the little Thai waiter for another orange pressee as I stared at the big slow-whirling propeller fan above my head and tried to think back on all those frenzied, high-tension moments that I'd just left behind in Saigon . . . wondering which one of them would endure with the strange kind of timeless intensity that would still be pulling my rip cord twenty years from now. . . .
>
> When I think of Saigon, all the details blend together in one long flash that is more a sensation than a memory: an extremely powerful sense of unreality about almost everything that was happening despite undeniable and often brutalizing reality of almost every moment in those last few weeks of the war, when Saigon was

finally surrounded. . . . You could drive to the outskirts of the city and watch a human sea of refugees trying to fight their way through the huge rolls of barbed wire laid across the highway . . . and if your sense of unreality was strong enough, you could walk right up to the barrier and take pictures while South Vietnamese soldiers were firing their M-16's into the air right next to you, or pick your way through the barbed wire, shouting "Bao Chi! Bao Chi!" [Press! Press!] and take pictures from the midst of the chaos on the other side, with truckloads of terrified refugees screaming and shoving all around you.

Wenner said he published everything Hunter sent him in 1975. Hunter wrote more, and Wenner used that in the 1985 version of the story. Still, Hunter did not choose to include the full piece in any of his books, although he did include a truncated version in *Songs of the Doomed* in 1990.

There was further strain the next year, as Hunter began campaign coverage for *Rolling Stone*. But after two days in New Hampshire, in the early stages of its primary, Hunter cashed it in and returned to Colorado. His celebrity was too great; he could no longer work as a reporter in his home country. The Saigon piece was good because he was an unknown on the other side of the earth. He could work . . . he could *report*. On the campaign trail in New Hampshire, he was hounded by autograph seekers. He couldn't repeat the past, even if he wanted to.

But he did make one contribution. As former Governor Jimmy Carter of Georgia emerged as the front-runner, Hunter produced a cover story called "Jimmy Carter and the Great Leap of Faith." It was the sort of thing people expected from him. It began with the news of a roving dog castrator in Coral Gables, Florida, and included all kinds of observations that had nothing to do with politics. Finally, Hunter settled in to tell the story of how he'd met Jimmy Carter two years before when he made the Law Day speech at the University of Georgia. Swilling Wild Turkey while the crowd sat in silence, Hunter was wowed by Carter's deeply moving talk. Hunter seemed more surprised than anyone to say it, but here was an honest man. Compared with Senator Hubert Humphrey or the other wheezing hacks prostituting themselves in a bid for higher office, Carter seemed like a man with integrity. The innocence and shock that Hunter conveyed about his observations made the article as revealing about the writer as it was insightful about politics.

But when it appeared in the magazine, Wenner tagged on a subhead to the cover line of Hunter's article: "An endorsement, with fear and loathing."

"I didn't like it that they put on the cover that I endorsed Carter," Hunter said. "I picked him as a gambler. Endorsing isn't something that a journalist should do."

The cover line caused yet another rift between Hunter and Wenner. It did not, however, keep Hunter from attending the Democratic National Convention in New York. Wenner threw an elaborate party to announce *Rolling Stone*'s self-perceived presence as a player in national politics. Journalists naturally showed up for the free food and booze. Wenner made his splash and showed off Hunter like a prized monkey. To the generation of young political reporters, Hunter was Mount Rushmore, a living god on earth.

For his part, Hunter just wanted a good time and entertained his worshippers by blowing booze over an open Zippo lighter, to send fireballs across the room. With his whoops and fingernails-on-the-blackboard screeches, he was like the class clown, still calling attention to himself. He got to renew acquaintances with friends he'd made on the 1972 campaign trail, including attorney Bill Dixon, who played a major role in the Carter campaign. He introduced him to Monty Chitty, the young student journalist he'd met on the Sunshine Special in Florida during the 1972 campaign. In a few years, Chitty ended up as floor manager of the 1980 Democratic convention. Part of Hunter's art was collecting the right people, putting them all together, and seeing what happened. He also had great political and journalistic instincts. He met CBS correspondent Ed Bradley on the campaign trail and they became comrades. Hunter lobbied hard with his friends at the network (Charles Kuralt, Hughes Rudd, and others) to get Bradley assigned to cover the Carter campaign. He was, and when Carter became president, Bradley became the first black White House correspondent. He also became Hunter's friend for life, first moving into the basement of Hunter's Woody Creek home for six months before buying his own cabin in the Roaring Fork Valley.

Dixon shared the suite with Hunter for the duration of the 1976 convention. "I didn't sleep for three nights," Dixon said. "Hunter had read in the paper where the youngest delegate to the convention, this woman who was eighteen or twenty, was asked by the *New York Times*, 'What are you going to do in New York?' 'All I want to do is meet Hunter Thompson,' she said. So she'd come by, and various coke dealers came by. And they'd surprise Hunter by sending escorts in that he hadn't ordered to do a Bert Parks Miss America thing, and it was crazy, so after three nights I hadn't slept. And so the fourth morning, about eight in the morning, I put my stuff in my carry-on bag and I got it hidden and I'm moving towards the door, and he springs out of his room and says, 'I hear you. You're abandoning me, you're abandoning me.' I said, 'No, Hunter, I ain't abandoning you, man, I'm going down to get some cigarettes.' And he said 'Use room service.' And I said, 'No, I'm going down to get some cigarettes. Don't give me any shit.' I got down, took the first taxi to La Guardia, took the sixty-minute shuttle home to Washington, D.C., got to my house in Alexandria, Virginia, and called the hotel room. It was only about ninety minutes since I had left, and he answers the phone in the hotel room and he says, 'Where are you?' I said, 'I'm home. I can't take it anymore.' But, you know, that was true, I couldn't."

Dixon did not recall a moment during the week they roomed together when Hunter wrote or even took notes.

Somehow, Hunter's marriage was holding together, but it was a series of skirmishes, battles, and truces. The rift between Hunter and Sandy was often in the room with them; at other times, they could make it disappear. There was missed-you sex in Hong Kong, but there were fights in the living room. She still tiptoed around him while he slept away the days and had food ready when he awoke. It was Hunter's world, and she was expected to be his servant, his lover, the mother of his son. She was left to interpret his growls, his arched eyebrows, his moods. She blamed cocaine for many of the changes in Hunter and for the slowdown in his production. He once wrote manically. Now she was startled when she saw him write.

The lifestyle of the character he had created had consumed him. Hunter may have been unproductive, but the fictional him, Uncle Duke in *Doonesbury*, carried on. Hunter despised Trudeau. "He's going to be surprised someday," Hunter said. "I'm going to set him on fire first, then crush every one of his ribs, one by one, starting from the bottom." During speaking appearances on campuses, students showed up to see Uncle Duke as much as they did to see Hunter S. Thompson. "All over America, kids grow up wanting to be firemen and cops, presidents and lawyers, but nobody wants to grow up to be a cartoon character."

Wenner even gave in. When he couldn't get Hunter to write for him, he put him on the cover of *Rolling Stone* anyway, as Uncle Duke in a Trudeau-drawn cover. "If we want to give paranoia full rein," Hunter wrote his friend Sandy Berger, "we could assume this is Wenner's way of getting back at me for some of the things I've said about him, by using Trudeau's strip as some kind of *Rolling Stone* mouthpiece."

Hunter pondered a libel suit. "I'd like to sue for at least $20 million in damages," he wrote Berger. At first, Duke had appeared living stateside, working at *Rolling Stone* for an editor named Yawn and with a colleague with mushroom-cloud hair that looked like David Felton. Eventually, Sandy showed up in the strip in quote boxes, though Trudeau never drew her. Though harmless on its surface, the *Doonesbury* strips were so close to Hunter's bone that he wondered whether someone was spying on him. As his marital problems intensified, but stayed largely within the confines of Owl Farm, the discord was reflected in the comic strip. As the character took on a life of his own, he stepped away from the *Rolling Stone* job and acted out Hunter's fantasy of living in American Samoa. He became a callous, ugly-American womanizer, and Hunter objected to that as much as to watching his marriage play out on the funny pages. The battle with Wenner was also fodder for the strip. In one sequence, Duke learned that he had been wiped from the *Rolling Stone* masthead. "Impossible!" Duke screamed at his assistant. "I'm the Rolling Stone National Affairs Editor! I'm indispensable!" He promised retaliation by outraged fans, but Duke's assistant said he was listed in the obituary column under the headline "Hack writer, presumed dead at 45." Hunter's sin, as portrayed by Duke, was that he was unproductive and quickly becoming an anachronism in the late seventies culture.

The seventies were a disappointment, a betrayal to Hunter, whose ideals were reflected in the nation's founding documents and whose beliefs found flower in the righteous upheavals of the sixties. The trivialities of the seventies were maddening to true believers. From the moment that President Nixon walked across the White House lawn to the presidential helicopter and exile in California, it was as if a switch had been turned off.

The press had brilliantly covered the civil rights movement, helped bring an end to the Vietnam War, exposed the evils of the presidency in the Pentagon Papers, and brought down the most powerful man on the planet with the Watergate coverage. *That* press was gone. Almost immediately, *People* magazine appeared, the *National Enquirer* went mainstream, and the public was treated to the minutiae of celebrity life with the hushed-voiced solemnity once given to space launches, presidential assassinations, and congressional hearings. Networks that once promised gavel-to-gavel coverage of political conventions now offered truncated summaries at the end of the night. Insignificance had won; trivia *über alles*. And all of this came with the monotonous soundtrack of a synthesized disco beat.

Wenner moved the magazine to New York in 1977 and embraced his own celebrity status and collected new friends—mostly movie stars. Rock 'n' roll and politics still appeared in *Rolling Stone* because of Wenner's sentimental attachments, but the magazine became a glossy showcase for movie-star profiles. During his speaking engagements, Hunter was asked why he wasn't writing for *Rolling Stone* very often. He shrugged, saying he didn't like the content of the magazine anymore, particularly the "celebrity shit." He took his distaste for Wenner public. "When you deal with Jann," he told one reporter, "you think of the worst possible results of what you are doing, and the best possible results, and a lot of the time you end up with both."

He toyed with Wenner and abused his *Rolling Stone* expense account. Another Wenner brainstorm—"Fear and Loathing at Mardi Gras"— ended up being an excuse for a classic Hunter fuckaround on someone else's dime. Hunter brought along his friends Bill Dixon, Monty Chitty, and the singer Jimmy Buffett. "Wenner had sent him down there," Dixon recalled, "and Hunter spent . . . Jesus, he spent *thousands and thousands* of *Rolling Stone*'s dollars, and Mardi Gras was over and everyone went home, and Hunter said, 'You gotta stay with me. Someone's gotta stay with me now while I try and write now.'"

But no "Fear and Loathing at Mardi Gras" ever appeared.

"The fun factor had gone out of *Rolling Stone*," Hunter said. "It was an outlaw magazine in California. In New York, it became an establishment magazine, and I have never worked well with people like that." He didn't even like the new environment, as Wenner took the magazine from the funky loft in San Francisco to Fifth Avenue. "It became like an insurance office, with people communicating cubicle to cubicle," Hunter recalled.

Wenner made the move to New York the cover story in an August issue and announced the magazine's presence in the city with authority by creating a huge tenth-anniversary issue in November, the first *Rolling Stone* with a slick cover and the new streamlined logo. Wenner insisted that Hunter write something. Hunter was still the most significant writer to emerge from *Rolling Stone*. The Hunter-Wenner relationship was bound by the slenderest of threads. It took cajoling, ego-massage, and begging to get Hunter to write something. Eventually, he received enormous billing on the cover, and the only other contributor whose name was trumpeted in huge letters on the cover was another Wenner find, photographer Annie Leibovitz, with a huge portrait portfolio in the issue. When Wenner had found her in 1970, she was a novice without a single published picture. She had grown to be one of the dominant photographers in the last part of the twentieth century.

Wenner might have published any rambling and brain doodles his star writer would send in over the Mojo Wire. Instead, he got one of Hunter's finest essays.

Oscar Zeta Acosta had been much on Hunter's mind, ever since he'd received the letter from Annie Acosta three years before. There were rumors of Oscar sightings here and there, but for Hunter there was only one way to make sure he was dead: write about him. "The Banshee Screams for Buffalo Meat" was a memoir of Hunter's friendship that was both fond and brutal and, despite the looking-back tone, avoided all traces of sentimentality. He reexamined his ten-year friendship and speculated on what had happened to Acosta—whether he had indeed died while smuggling drugs or whether he was still out there somewhere. It was a written version of the dance of male bonding, where affection is often displayed by insults. Hunter stacked layers of shit upon his friend in the article, calling him at turns "a dope-addled clown," a "fat spic," a "dangerous thug," and "a stupid, vicious quack with no morals at all and the soul of a hammerhead shark." He concluded, "We are better off without him." The affection was all between the lines, but the vigor of the outbursts jarred readers arriving late to the party. To people who didn't recognize Acosta as the 300-pound, venom-spewing Samoan attorney from *Fear and Loathing in Las Vegas*, the piece was mystifying.

It was more than fond memoir. "I showered the man with libel," Hunter said. "I had figured he was dead, but I had to make sure. I called him every name I could think of, hoping that it would bring him out of hiding. When I didn't hear from him, I knew he was dead."

The certainty of Acosta's death added another name to the growing list of casualties. Hunter went into another funk.

The Oscar Acosta remembrance drew interest from Hollywood. Ironically, since it was Acosta's braying and moaning about libel that kept *Fear and Loathing in Las Vegas* from going into production, the story of Hunter's friendship with Acosta inspired producer Art Linson to buy the rights to "The Banshee Screams for Buffalo Meat" in early 1978. Hunter was startled. "It was a weird idea," he told David Felton. "Actually, it was so weird that it never occurred to me that it would be made."

Sandy and some of Hunter's closest friends urged caution. *Hunter,* they said, *they're going to turn you into a character*—as if he hadn't already been, thanks to *Doonesbury* and his celebrated antics, which contributed to the growth of the monster persona that now overshadowed the barely productive writer.

Sandy was skeptical that the planned film would be, as presented, a testament to the meaning of the sixties. "Bullshit," Sandy told Hunter. "It's not going to be about the sixties, it's going to be about crazy Hunter Thompson. It's not going to be a serious film."

But Hollywood was talking big money, and Hunter had to listen. Even through the years of his greatest *Fear and Loathing* success, Hunter lived from one sporadic freelance check to another. The movie money gave him some financial stability. "I gave Hunter Thompson the only real money he ever had," Linson later said.

Universal Studios flew Hunter and Sandy to California, put them up at the Beverly Hills Hotel, and sweet-talked him into signing the contract, including a fee for serving as a "consultant" on the film.

The British Broadcasting Corporation also took an interest in Hunter and devoted an episode of its *Omnibus* series to Hunter the writer and Raoul Duke the celebrity. Fearing that Hunter might be uncooperative, the BBC flew Ralph Steadman in from Great Britian, with the plan of putting them together at Woody Creek and following them on the long drive to Hollywood, stopping in Las Vegas on the way.

Ralph came with first-time director Nigel Finch. They flew into the tiny Aspen airport on a puddle jumper from Denver. Ralph counseled Finch not to worry. "When I first met him he scared me, but inside he's a pussy cat—a dangerous one—but nevertheless a clumsy, gentle person. He is very gracious to guests. You'll be fine."

Hunter was not at the airport, and they stood outside the homely terminal, awaiting the writer's arrival. Finally, Ralph spotted the Great Red Shark barreling up the road, heading straight for him. Ralph didn't flinch, and Hunter screeched to a stop, spewing asphalt, inches away from Ralph's knees. They greeted each other warmly. "You bastard," Ralph screamed. "You knew what the odds were when you decided to fuck with me," Hunter said.

For the next two weeks, Finch and his crew (alas, not present to film Hunter's entrance) followed him around Owl Farm, through the long car trip, and into the Hollywood maze. Hunter was difficult. Ill at ease because his slowed production was certainly an issue and also disliking his vast celebrity, he put his annoyance on the filmmakers. Although he claimed to be disturbed by the character of Duke/Thompson that followed him like the chains on Marley's Ghost, he did everything he could to reinforce this image. He allowed himself to be filmed swilling whiskey by the tumbler, smoking marijuana, and snorting cocaine. Still, he claimed victim status.

In the film, Finch discussed the whole dichotomy of the Duke/ Thompson character and how it intersected with the real man. Originally, Hunter had created Raoul Duke to allow him to insert his opinion in stories and still make what he wrote appear to be journalism. "[Duke] was a vehicle for quotations that nobody else would say," Hunter said. "It was me—really—talking. Those were my quotes."

But Duke went beyond the status of mere writer's convenience when he became the narrator of *Fear and Loathing in Las Vegas,* an acid-gobbling, whiskey-swilling demon. Now, years later, Hunter had a legion of fans who had never read a word he had written. He was known as *that character*. The stories, even told secondhand, had a power that attracted a crowd drawn to Amazing Drug Tales.

For Hunter, who took himself seriously as a writer, it was an issue that was obviously troubling and contributing to his writer's block. Between snorts of coke and slugs of booze, he was alternately loquacious and surly as he opened up to Finch.

"People I don't know expect me to be Duke more than Thompson," he lamented.

> Most people are surprised that I walk on two legs, and the idea that I would have a wife or a child or even a mother comes as a surprise. People think I'm maybe a violent version of that comic strip.

I am living a normal life. Right alongside me, this myth is growing and mushrooming, getting more and more warped. When I get
invited to speak at universities, I'm not sure if they are inviting
Duke or Thompson and so I'm not sure who to be. I suppose my
plans are to figure out some new identity—to kill off one life and
start another one.

Hunter admitted he was trapped by his identity, both the comic strip
and the public image as well as what he had written to that point. It might
be time to bury the whole concept of Gonzo journalism, he said. "I think
I've taken that form as far as I could take it. I'm starting to repeat myself
anyway. It's not as much fun anymore. It's hard to work on a story now.
I've become part of the story. The first time I went to a press conference
with Jimmy Carter, I had to sign more autographs than Carter signed.
And the Secret Service had no idea who I was. They thought I was an
astronaut. I used to be able to stand in the back and observe stories and
absorb them. Now I can't do that."

So where to now? Hunter seemed generally perplexed. In terms of
his writing, he was treading water—finally getting ready to publish the
mammoth retrospective of his journalism. He sensed that this look back
through his early work had the tone of an epitaph.

"So I'm really in the way—as a person," he told Finch. "The myth has
taken over. I find myself an appendage. I'm not only no longer necessary
. . . I'm in the way. It would be much better if I died. Then people could
take the myth and make films. I have no choice.

In this remorseful mood, Hunter and Ralph visited a Hollywood funeral
home to get an estimate on staging Hunter Thompson's funeral. There was
to be a huge monument built on his Colorado farm, Hunter told the startled mortician. He wanted to erect a long shaft with the double thumbed
Gonzo fist on top. Ralph began sketching in his tablet. Hunter described
how he wanted his ashes to be shot through the tube and blown over the
countryside while a huge loudspeaker played Bob Dylan singing "Mr. Tambourine Man." The dumbfounded mortician did his best to follow along.

The Finch documentary, called *Fear and Loathing on the Road to Hollywood*, showed Hunter trying to avoid the crew's cameras, skulking in
corners near Grauman's Chinese Theater, and crouching in front of cars
in a parking lot, anything to hide from the intrusive lens. It was nearly too
claustrophobic for him to function.

He was definitely in a funk. As journalist Toby Thompson (no relation) wrote of a visit to Hunter in Woody Creek,

> He was a novelist who'd been seduced toward journalism by the promise of the sixties. With that promise shattered, no wonder he and myriad artists were working poorly . . . .
>
> We'd been discussing the writer's predicament when I hazarded this observation: "Everything you publish these days seethes with a contempt you bring to journalism."
>
> Hunter stared at me. "There are not many people who get that," he said. "You're the first who's said it." I figured he was pulling my leg. But his expression was grave.

Back home, Hunter remained a regular correspondent with friends but could not produce articles the way he had. He was searching for that new voice—committed as he was, at the time, to burying the Duke persona.

Sandy continued to blame cocaine for the writer's block, for the lethargy, for the meanness that she saw more and more in her husband. "Hunter is a really, really big human being," she reflected, years later. "He's very kind. He's very compassionate. He's very generous. He's very wise. And on the whole other end of the spectrum, he's very cruel."

From her first recognition of the possibility that Hunter would have an affair, Sandy had tried to shut him away from the world. She jumped to answer the phone, telling friends he was unavailable. Sometimes, she stalked him nocturnally—once standing outside an Aspen condominium screaming, "Come out of there, you son of a bitch." Juan, still a young teenager, was alone at home, caught in the middle. After a few years, Sandy expected Hunter's infidelities, though she was not resigned to them, calling friends long-distance to wail that she could not take it anymore. Friends knew that Hunter was a rake, drifting through a sea of adoring women, but Sandy was the anchor that he needed. Even though she was saintlike in the eyes of many of Hunter's friends, she tired of her role.

Eventually, she took advantage of his periodic absences and began an affair with a man in a nearby town. At the end of the summer in 1978, during a calm in one of Hunter's flights of rage, Sandy quietly said, "Hunter, I want a divorce." He went berserk, and Sandy called the sheriff.

Bob Braudis, the ski instructor who worked on Hunter's sheriff campaign, had moved into law enforcement after a drought caused a bad

During a photo session for the cover of *Better Than Sex* in 1994, Hunter fires a warning shot from his 45 caliber handgun. *Photograph by Louie Psihoyos / Corbis.*

Visiting Kentucky poet Ron Whitehead with Hunter in 1995. Hunter appreciated Whitehead's looking in on Virginia Thompson at her Louisville nursing home. *Photograph courtesy of Ron Whitehead.*

Writer Kevin Simonson knew that when he showed up to interview Hunter he had to play along with the doctor's kitchen games. *Photograph courtesy of Kevin Simonson.*

Actor Johnny Depp dogged Hunter while preparing for *Fear and Loathing in Las Vegas*. At the Woody Creek Tavern, he posed with Hunter and friend/waitress Cheryl Frymire. *Photograph courtesy of Cheryl Frymire.*

Wayne Ewing was a young filmmaker when he began following Hunter around in the eighties, hoping to create a cable television show. That idea fell through, but he produced three films about Hunter, including *Breakfast with Hunter* and *When I Die*, about the preparations for the 2005 blast-off memorial. *Photographs courtesy of Wayne Ewing.*

Hunter's kitchen was his
command post. From his
stool, he wrote, took phone
calls, and held court. *Photograph
by Matthew Hahn.*

In the nineties, Hunter often
stayed put at Owl Farm, where
the host greeted guests such as
Don Dixon in a woman's wig.
Photograph courtesy of DeDe Brinkman.

In New Orleans a month
before his death, Hunter
met with producers Steven
Land (*left*) and Geoffrey
Proud (*right*) to discuss
a cable-television reality
program. Douglas Brinkley
lurks behind Hunter, who
loved the concept. *Photograph
courtesy of Geoffrey Proud.*

Hunter kisses Anita Thompson after their civil ceremony in April 2003. Anita clutches the fee for the marriage license. *Photograph by Louisa Davidson, Associated Press / Wide World Photos.*

Hunter's homemade do-not-disturb sign, which he posted on the door of his cabin. *Courtesy of DeDe Brinkman.*

GOOD MORNING,

I have shot myself in the nuts & am Un-able to come to the door at this time, for reasons too strange to explain except in crude medical terminology...

SO THEREFORE STAY AWAY FROM THIS DOOR UNTIL 12:00 NOON

Do not knock on this door or any other, and do not attempt any form of Entry until NOON. Thank you.

PLEASE WAKE ME AT 2:00 p.m.

Best wishes, HST

Juan Thompson and Anita Thompson co-hosted a legal seminar at Owl Farm in 2006. *Photograph by Jeralyn Merritt.*

The memorial tower for Hunter's second funeral was built to his specifications and rose 153 feet above Owl Farm. *Photo by Ed Andrieski, Associated Press / Wide World Photos.*

Bob Braudis met Hunter during the 1970 Freak Power campaign and later became the multiterm sheriff of Pitkin County, Colorado. *Photograph by William McKeen*

Ralph Steadman imitates Hunter (*top*), and displays his Hunter-inspired art at his home in Kent, England (*bottom*). *Photographs by Joseph Owens.*

Portrait of the artist in repose. Hunter relaxes in his American-flag hammock at Owl Farm. *Photograph by Louie Psihoyos / Corbis.*

year on the slopes. As he moved up the ladder of the sheriff's office, he became better friends with Hunter. He did not take the call, but he knew the situation. "It was ugly," he said. "Hunter had a really dark side to him. It took a police intervention to get her moved out. Some of the rookie deputies showed up with flak vests. They were fighting over stereo components, stupid little things."

As the rookie deputy watched, Hunter burned stacks of paper—Sandy's writing about her life with Hunter. With the deputy as a shield, Sandy and her son left the house.

"I think she had good reasons to leave," Braudis said. "He loved chicks and the only true aphrodisiac is 'strange.' I think Hunter was fucking around and wanted to keep fucking around. He saw this new life with new women, and his little head started thinking."

Sandy and Juan moved into Aspen, and she went to work in a bookstore to support herself. "It was a fiery end," Sandy said. "It had had a fiery beginning. First time it was love. Last time it was fear."

Hunter had long been paranoid that Garry Trudeau had spies who leaked information about his private life because often the Uncle Duke episodes in *Doonesbury* struck too close to home.

In one strip, as Uncle Duke returned home, he asked Zonker, "Where's Sandy?" Zonker replied, "Sandy's gone. And she's not coming back."

Chapter 15

THOMPSON'S ISLAND

My reputation is getting to be real expensive.
—HST, *on a cocktail napkin to Tom Corcoran, 1979*

I n Key West, "occupation" is a fluid thing. Consider Tom Corcoran's
résumé. In 1968, the U.S. Navy sent Corcoran, a young officer, to an
eight-week training program in Key West. He didn't like his quarters,
so he rented an apartment in Old Town. "And I just kind of fell into the
mode," Corcoran said. "Nobody said, 'You should get an apartment and
buy a bicycle,' but I did." After the Navy, Corcoran and a pal made a
cross-country road trip and circled back to Fort Lauderdale. At the end
of their grueling first week working construction, Corcoran and his friend
pondered how to spend their paychecks. Corcoran said, "I know where I
want to drink this beer," and they drove to Key West and had a drink at
Captain Tony's.

Corcoran never looked back. In the early years, it was sometimes tough
to eke out a living in that expensive paradise. "Either you worked for
Southern Bell or you sold tires at Sears," he said. Corcoran did neither,
instead pedaling tacos from a three-wheel bicycle. Tennessee Williams

was a regular customer. "Tennessee had an entourage that looked like the Olympic swimming team," he said. Corcoran also got to know writers Jim Harrison (*Legends of the Fall*) and Thomas McGuane (*Ninety-two in the Shade*), taco aficionados and dispensers of writing wisdom.

Corcoran's college girlfriend and wife-to-be, Judy, moved down from Ohio and began bartending at Captain Tony's. After a few bartending gigs of his own, Corcoran settled in as part of the brain trust running the bar at the Chart Room. Corcoran mixed drinks in the blender and mixed songs on the sound system that conveyed the bar's funky atmosphere. "Within two years' time, we made the Chart Room *the* institution in Key West," he said.

At that bar Corcoran served new arrival Jimmy Buffett his complimentary first beer in town, thus beginning a long friendship and collaboration. "The beer was free," Corcoran recalled. "That's what Jimmy really liked."

Buffett had been chased out of Nashville by music-business types who didn't like his songs. He found his performing identity in Key West, and Corcoran was there at the start, offering more than free beer. "I fed him," Corcoran said. With Judy and his baby son, Sebastian, Corcoran represented family stability. "Jimmy had no money. He came home with me for spaghetti one night, and he picked up my guitar and started strumming a song he was working on. A couple nights later, I couldn't sleep, so I got up and started strumming the guitar, playing that song. I couldn't remember Jimmy's words, so I made up my own." When he shared his lyrics with Buffett, the singer said, "Damn, Corcoran, you've got a song." The result, "Cuban Crime of Passion," was on Buffett's *White Sportcoat and a Pink Crustacean*, the 1973 album that became the blueprint for the Parrothead lifestyle affected by Buffett's soon-to-be legions of fans. He also collaborated on "Fins." ("Fins to the left, fins to the right and you're the only girl in town," a rallying cry for male sharks descending on a bar.) Corcoran had scratched an opening scene on some notepaper, then stuck it in a duffel bag when he went sailing with Buffett. Buffett found the scrap and asked whether he could work with it. The result, recorded in 1979, brought Corcoran decades of royalties.

When Buffett starting making big money, he bought a home in Aspen. He had created a party-boy persona through his music and, much like Hunter, was pursued by fans who confused the man with the image. His new wife, Jane, liked Aspen and felt more comfortable there. Key West was many things, but it was not a good place to raise children—too many temptations: drugs, alcohol, and in-breeding.

Buffett met Hunter, they became friends, and he offered Hunter the keys to his bachelor-era apartment in Key West. He called Corcoran and asked him to look after Hunter during his first trip down. Corcoran knew it could be hazardous duty, but he was still in the young-writer-seeking-experience stage. He was eager to meet Hunter and learn from him.

Hunter was with Sandy when Corcoran and he met. When he came back as a single man, he and Corcoran became confidants and, eventually, collaborators.

Hunter fell in love with Key West. Owl Farm would always be home, but divorce lawyers were quarreling over its disposition. Key West became Hunter's refuge from fame, the long and brutal divorce battle, and his inability to write. Tourists clogged the thin arteries of Key West, but the locals had patented the what-the-hell attitude, which made it a safe haven for writers. Since Ernest Hemingway's arrival in 1928, the city crawled with literary he-man types. In the seventies, these included Harrison, McGuane, Philip Caputo, Shel Silverstein, and the ghost of Papa his own bad self. The air was thick with the macho bonhomie that intoxicated men and often repulsed women. As a live-and-let-live community, it was also welcoming for homosexuals, including writers Tennessee Williams and Truman Capote. The locals, known as Conchs, gave everyone a wide berth.

Painter Russell Chatham befriended Hunter in his Key West years. "In those days, it was kind of a much smaller scene," Chatham recalled. "Hunter was there, and he and Jim Harrison and I fished. That's how we got to know Hunter. Of course, in those days, there was an awful lot of drinking and drugs involved. That colors the experience."

Chatham's huge canvases and lithographs were selling for thousands, and his patrons included an army of Hollywood hipsters led by Jack Nicholson. Chatham and Harrison were close (Chatham created the moody landscape on the cover of *Legends of the Fall*), and he had the sort of income and fame few painters attained. Along with fishing, cooking was a highlight of Chatham's annual trips to Key West, and Harrison routinely spent whole days preparing meals. Hunter usually just observed. "Fucking Hunter couldn't even make himself a cup of coffee," Chatham snorted. "He liked to *eat*. In those days, even though he was doing drugs and drinking, he did a lot of exercise too."

Monty Chitty escaped Aspen for a few months in the Keys each year, and he and Hunter went fly-fishing for bonefish and tarpon. Harrison had just spent four months in Hollywood, learning how to write screenplays. He had recently sold *Legends of the Fall* to Hollywood, thanks to Jack Nicholson. Harrison invited Chitty and Hunter to join him, McGuane, Chatham, and their friend Guy Valedene for dinner—a complicated Chinese meal that took Harrison three days to prepare. From the moment Chitty and Hunter arrived at Harrison's place, Hunter was in the kitchen, asking Harrison and McGuane questions about scriptwriting and agents and the nuances of film storytelling.

"Notorious most his life for living hand to mouth, always searching mail for the next check, Hunter decides then and there that the real money is in Hollywood, writing scripts," Chitty recalled. "This will be his financial salvation."

By four in the morning, dinner deep into digestion, Harrison finally took Chitty aside and begged him to take Hunter home. His relentless questions were driving Harrison and McGuane insane.

As Chatham got to know Hunter, he observed how different he could be from his public image. He learned that Hunter took his work seriously, if not himself, and that he was extraordinarily well-read. "He was a much deeper, more serious person than the public I think even now suspects," Chatham said. "I think anybody who knew him, who actually took the trouble to know him, knows that. But as far as the general public is concerned, I think their view is that he was some sort of loose cannon, did a lot of drinking, took a lot of drugs. That was true, but fundamentally, he was a very serious person."

Key West formed a subculture unto itself. It was originally called Cayo Hueso ("island of bones") when it was a Spanish city, because the first white settlers found it littered with bones from a battle or perhaps from a Calusa Indian burial ground. It was eventually anglicized into Key West, presumably because it is the westernmost island in the Florida Keys. Yet, for a brief period in its history, it had another name. When Commodore Matthew Perry sailed to the island and claimed it for the United States in 1822, he renamed it in honor of the secretary of the Navy: Thompson's Island.

For a man with a Hemingway fixation, Key West was a great place to chase that dream. His borrowed home had a narrow stretch of beach and was just a couple of blocks from Hemingway's estate on Whitehead

Street. Just as Hemingway set the agenda for those who followed in his wake, Hunter was Alpha Dog for his generation of writers. His old friend Ralph Steadman said that Hunter's time in Key West allowed him to indulge in the fantasy of "being Hemingway."

His friend Tom Corcoran shared Hunter's talent of putting the right combinations of people together for friendships to grow. In addition to Corcoran, Hunter hung out with his duplex-mate, Chris Robinson. Robinson and Buffett had been good friends, and when the singer had married in Aspen in 1976, Robinson made the trip and got to know Hunter on his home turf first. "Here comes this guy in a suit, with wing-tipped shoes, semi-bald and short hair, the straightest-looking guy in the world," Robinson recalled. "And he was handing out acid to anyone who wanted some." Another Florida friend at the wedding, Dan Mallard, said Hunter had not officially been invited, because he inspired fear among friends. No one knew what sort of widescreen epic prank he might plan. Even without an invitation he showed up, and in addition to providing the acid, he enlivened the reception by bringing a dog that had been sprayed by a skunk. "He kept the dog under the table," Mallard said. "No one saw the dog, but they sure as hell smelled him."

Hunter and Robinson had prime real estate on the tiny two-by-four island. "We lived right next door to Louie's Backyard, a real-fine four-star restaurant," Robinson said. "Their exhaust fan used to come up right next to the upstairs window of Buffett's place, and I guess the kitchen burned something one time and all of this smell was coming over and so Hunter had this tape of all these S&M sounds . . . erotic orgasm sounds. And Jimmy had these big speakers—100-and-some amp JBL speakers. And Hunter put on the tape and cranked that thing up and aimed the speakers over at the restaurant: *'Oh! Oh! Oooh! Oh my God! Jesus!'* We were just howling, and all those poor people next door were trying to dine."

Day-to-day life as Hunter's housemate wasn't challenging. He was not the outrageous character that Garry Trudeau portrayed. "Hunter would rant and rave up there, but I learned not to try to out-Gonzo Mr. Gonzo," Robinson said. "He would get up in the morning—well, not the morning—he'd get up in the afternoon and watch all of the different stations and read all the newspapers. Then we'd go down to the water and sit there and smoke a doobie together and have a nice conversation. The only time Hunter would get bizarre is when someone would try to out-bizarre him."

Like many Conchs, Robinson held a variety of jobs, eventually becoming a successful fishing guide. Also like many Conchs, he spent time in the drug trade. After getting pinched by the Coast Guard for smuggling a small amount of marijuana ("They *did* drop the charges," he pointed out), Robinson amused himself in a local woodshop trying to figure out some way to keep Coast Guard wives happy while their husbands were out busting dealers. He studied how the woodshop's antique jigsaw worked. It had a steady up-and-down motion that reminded Robinson of vigorous, pile-driving intercourse. With the jigsaw as inspiration, he used scrap parts from bicycles and lamps and constructed something about the size of a clothes dryer, and attached an old metal tractor seat covered in heavy vinyl. He then affixed a latex appendage rising from the center, a dildo with settings for two-, four-, and six-inch strokes. As a decoration on the front of the machine, Robinson carved a mahogany mushroom-shaped penis head. "It kind of looked like that thing in *Clockwork Orange*," Robinson recalled. "It was kind of a sculpture. I called it 'fucktional art.'"

The machine was operated with a handle that allowed the rider to control the speed of the insertion of the dildo. "It came up on a ten-speed sprocket and man, that worked better than we could," Robinson said.

Hunter wasn't known for doing much with his hands other than writing and shooting guns. He was fascinated by Robinson's craftsmanship and admired the assembled apparatus in the woodshop. A few nights later, he came downstairs and pounded on Robinson's door. "Chris! Chris!" he yelled. "I've got this woman upstairs and she's asleep in the bedroom. I want her to find your machine in the living room when she wakes up."

Hunter and Robinson carried the machine from the woodshop and up the narrow covered stairway to Hunter's apartment. When the woman awoke, the presence of the fucking machine achieved its intended effect. It became Hunter's new favorite toy, and he kept it in his apartment for months, inviting over friends in the evenings to watch young women ride it.

"The two-inch stroke was the better stroke," Robinson remembered. "You had good penetration and although it was a shorter stroke, you could put the seat down so it went up farther. It just had enough play in it and had enough noise that the rhythm of the sound got them excited. It was kind of like a freight train: '*Choo Choo!*' We had girls breaking into the house to ride this thing."

Hunter was not always a randy bachelor when he visited Key West.

Although he was still suffering the agonies of divorcing Sandy, Key West was where he began one of the most important relationships in his life.

Laila Nabulsi was a beautiful young woman working on the hottest show on television, *Saturday Night Live*. From its debut on October 11, 1975, *SNL* had defined the weekend for young Americans. It was the epitome of appointment television; people went out of their way to watch the show. Part of the attraction was its cast of Not Ready for Prime Time Players, including Chevy Chase, Dan Aykroyd, and the unpredictable John Belushi. The show quickly earned a place in public consciousness, lobbing catch phrases into popular culture almost weekly.

Laila was a segment producer and a good friend of Belushi and his wife, Judy Jacklin. She often got drafted into Belushi projects, including the skit that he and Aykroyd had created, the Blues Brothers. There were a lot of continuing skits on *SNL*, from the *cheeseburger-cheeseburger* diner to the killer bees and the samurai desk clerk. The Blues Brothers had also been conceived as a one-off skit, but when Aykroyd and Belushi announced they were taking the act on the road during the TV show's hiatus, Laila became road manager. It wasn't a vanity project for hotshot TV stars. Guitarist Steve Cropper and bassist Duck Dunn, two of the greatest musicians in rock 'n' roll history, signed on to be sidemen.

Laila was friendly enough with Belushi that he felt comfortable enough to ask her for favors. One Saturday night in 1977, a couple of years into the show's run, he called to ask her to drop by his apartment and pick up a jacket from his front closet. When she brought it by his dressing room, it was the usual crazed preshow scene. "There was this guy lying on the couch," Laila recalled. "I had no idea who he was. I just remember thinking, 'Uh-oh.' I had this feeling as if a bomb had dropped. I kind of knew from the second I saw him that I would either love him or hate him."

Belushi and Aykroyd had made a cross-country road trip the summer before and invited themselves to Owl Farm. They'd befriended Hunter and even talked of making a film of *Fear and Loathing in Las Vegas* with Aykroyd as Raoul Duke and Belushi as Dr. Gonzo. Nothing came of it, but a friendship began. Hunter once said that Belushi was "more fun in 20 minutes than most people are in 20 years." Now, a year later, Hunter had come to watch a taping of the show. But after meeting Laila, he decided to linger backstage.

"I knew right away that he was the most original person I had ever met," Laila said. "Plus, he had quite a physical presence—tall, very good-looking. He was hysterically funny, but it took me a moment to get his humor. In that first hour that I hung out with him, I remember that he went into the small bathroom in John's dressing room. When he came out I asked if he was okay. I'm not sure why. He said, 'I was weeping,' and I thought he was serious. I really wondered why he would cry and I was intrigued, to say the least. I finally 'got' his sense of humor during the first night I was in his hotel room at the Gramercy Park Hotel. I was sitting in the bedroom and we were talking, and then he would abruptly go into the living room of the suite and start making these awful wailing noises. Then he would come back into the bedroom and continue talking normally. This terrified me—I thought he was really crazy, and sat there trying to appear calm and figure a way out of the hotel room. He did this again, and by the third time he did it I was so scared I yelled, 'Stop that!' He came back into the bedroom, chuckling, and said, 'I'm just looking for my lighter.' I got the whole thing in that moment."

Belushi was also from the broken-mold school of humanity and was one of Laila's close friends, but knowing him and his eccentricities still did not prepare her for the Hunter Thompson Experience. "I had never met anyone who looked like that or acted like that," she said. "He would answer the phone screaming, 'What?' I had never met anyone who did things like that. He was such a wordsmith, and he had a lot of fun with words."

Hunter and Laila spent most of two weeks at Hunter's hotel, the Gramercy Park, and once when she heard him speaking on the phone, there was something in his voice that puzzled her. When he hung up, Laila asked who he'd been talking to. "My wife," he said.

Laila was horrified. She hadn't known who Hunter was when they met, much less known anything about his private life. There had been no mention of a wife for the two weeks they were together, and he certainly didn't act like a married man.

"That was the end of it," Laila said.

A year later, one of her *Saturday Night Live* friends invited her to a party. As she stood in the lobby of the building waiting for an elevator, the door opened and Hunter Thompson fell out. Later, alone together in a bar, he told her that he was in the middle of a divorce. And not long after that, they were at Buffett's place in Key West.

"We were very happy in Key West," Laila remembered. "That's when Hunter and I really started."

Hunter filed for divorce on February 9, 1979.

Laila was his compass, but Hunter could not avoid the complications of a divorce. Sandy wanted to sell Owl Farm and split the profits. Hunter was aghast; he *was* Owl Farm. To argue in court that it was a part of his being, he even used *Doonesbury* strips as examples: Uncle Duke was portrayed at Owl Farm. How could she separate him from his womb? Hunter was still making payments on the farm to neighbor George Stranahan, and the place had a $450,000 market value. Hunter felt entitled to keep it.

They also squabbled over his gun collection, Sandy's lawyers suggesting that it be sold and that she get half the profits. He had a lot of electronic equipment and other personal effects. Sandy wanted to sell everything. Hunter wanted his life to go on as it had, just without Sandy. In the middle was Juan, then fifteen. He lived with his mother, and though his father had been a phantom presence in his early life (Juan was awake and silent when Hunter was asleep, and Juan slept while Hunter worked), they were nonetheless close; Hunter loved his son, and Juan fiercely admired his father.

Sandy felt a rightful claim to a good portion of Hunter's assets. She had been functioning as his editorial assistant/typist/research assistant/caretaker for nearly twenty years. Hunter's income for the last full year of their marriage (1978) was over $100,000, but that was inflated by his movie-contract windfall. He lived mostly hand-to-mouth. Even when he was at his peak of fame in the early and mid seventies, he was constantly badgering editors to be paid for stories and reimbursed for expenses. Since the end of his Watergate coverage, however, he had written only five major articles, including the Acosta eulogy, the two-page dispatch from Saigon, the Jimmy Carter article, "The Great Shark Hunt" for *Playboy*, and a two-part profile of Muhammad Ali that ran in *Rolling Stone* in 1978. It had taken something special to get him back in the magazines. Despite all of the horrors he'd had in dealing with *Rolling Stone*, he accepted Wenner's assignment to write about Muhammad Ali. The resulting two-part "Last Tango in Vegas," allowed Hunter to deemphasize his Duke persona. He had to. Next to a larger-than-life figure such as Ali, all other personalities were subservient. Hunter's ego obtruded, but did not dominate the article, which was a meditation on the nature of supercelebrity and the moat Ali erected around himself. Hunter had spent no face time with Ali in Zaire. In the "Last Tango" articles, he crossed the moat and even did the unthinkable in front of the Champ, smoking and drinking. Ali was amused by the court jester, and the result was one of the most memorable profiles ever written about Ali.

"Last Tango in Vegas" appeared in late spring 1978, and Hunter shoehorned the Ali pieces in at the end of the substantial collection he was preparing for publication. Jim Silberman had left Random House for Simon and Schuster and had his own imprint there, Summit Books. *The Great Shark Hunt*, Hunter's long-delayed anthology, finally appeared in early 1979. Hunter felt he was at last on the crest of a cash wave with his new hernia-inducing book (more than six hundred pages).

The Great Shark Hunt drew a lot of attention and sold rapidly to his built-in audience: all of those fans who had been waiting for something new from Hunter for most of the seventies. Finally, there was a book, though much of it was old. Many of the pieces came from his *National Observer* days, and others were drawn from *Hell's Angels, Fear and Loathing in Las Vegas*, and the *Campaign Trail* book. A few uncollected dispatches—the Kentucky Derby article, the Jean-Claude Killy piece, the Acosta eulogy, and the Ali profile—made the book essential for fans.

The book had apparently been edited by a shovel. It was difficult to figure out the organization, though the seminal Gonzo pieces were in the first section and most of the *Observer* dispatches were in the third section. However, some of his best *Observer* pieces, including his hitchhiking story, were not collected. The fourth section was a mishmash, and the second section appeared to have a political theme. He also threw in a couple of press releases from his Air Force days.

David Felton, his former editor at *Rolling Stone*, called it "probably the worst-edited and most self-indulgent work since the Bible. There doesn't seem to be any order." The early writing, Felton said, was "flat and uninspired." Hunter, who said he used Norman Mailer's *Advertisements for Myself* as his blueprint, didn't seem to mind the criticism; in fact, he appeared to agree with it. "I thought it would be pretty fun to see the development from the Air Force to the Ali piece. It seems like I've been writing the same thing, really, since I was eighteen years old. . . . I'll stand by this," he shrugged. "It's messy. It's fucked up."

Still, *Shark Hunt* drew several strong reviews, with most critics taking the chance to assess the first twenty years of Hunter's published writing. The *New Republic* compared him to Mencken and admired him for writing about moving targets. The *Nation* suggested that Hunter's view of modern America was truer than that of more conventional journalists. And conservative William F. Buckley said Hunter elicited "the same admiration one would feel for a streaker at Queen Victoria's funeral."

The Great Shark Hunt meant money, and Hunter needed it desperately. His paychecks were few and far between, and when Sandy's lawyers asked for their share of the *Shark Hunt* advance, Hunter's attorneys said the money had already been spent. He began a sabbatical from publishing, figuring that anything he wrote while still married would be considered joint property, to half of which Sandy would be entitled.

There was always money from speaking engagements. Hunter was absent in print, but ubiquitous on campus stages, despite the skirmishes he sometimes had there. He drew unusual fans. Many in the audience hung on every word, but had never read one of his books. He was admired for his presumed lifestyle, for the way it was exaggerated and portrayed in his own work and in the *Doonesbury* comic strip. A lot of people might say, "Hunter Thompson is my favorite writer," without having read any of his writing.

He became the preferred Halloween costume of college sophomores. The character of Hunter Thompson had superseded the man and the writer. Hunter was not unaware of this. In the introduction to *The Great Shark Hunt*, he confessed to standing at a crossroads, pondering whether to make a swan dive into the fountain outside the window of his publishers' office, where he was writing his author's note:

> I have already lived and finished the life I planned to live—(13 years longer, in fact)—and everything from now on will be A New Life, a different thing, a gig that ends tonight and starts tomorrow morning.
>
> So if I decide to leap for The Fountain when I finish this memo, I want to make one thing perfectly clear—I would genuinely love to make that leap, and if I don't I will always consider it a mistake and a failed opportunity, one of the very few serious mistakes of my First Life that is now ending.

He was at the continental divide of his life. Suicide was all around. In place of an author photo on the back, there was a Ralph Steadman illustration of Hunter with a gun to his head. The introduction was a suicide note for the First Him, the one who had failed to chronicle the death of the American Dream, the one who had been so suffocated by his own celebrity that he could no longer do his work, the one who was seen as a pied piper for drugs and debauchery. He wanted to get rid of that Him.

So it was no surprise that he found his release on the island that once bore his name. He could spend time in Key West, among his new friends, and not have to perform or become the Beast for audiences who demanded it. In Key West, he and Laila could stroll the streets unmolested. He could drink at the Full Moon. With friends like Chris Robinson and Tom Corcoran, he could do what he could not do when he was on display as Hunter Thompson: he could relax.

Corcoran and his wife, Judy, were both expert at cobbling together livelihoods from of a variety of functions and income sources. Both had been in the Jimmy Buffett orbit and had no trouble circling Planet Hunter. He used his immense charm to lure Judy into working as his de facto secretary, even though she had a job at a rental company. Though he wasn't on a magazine deadline, it was still a lot of work to be him, and he made lists for Judy in the way that he used to plot out Sandy's duties: "Judy: Miami Herald, bank, Visa, booze, screwdriver." On another day: "Beer, Kaopectate, garbage bags, eggs, milk, lighter fluid, Kleenex, toilet paper. *Yell at me*. Say we have to go." Tom was often doing a number of jobs, and that meant that sometimes they needed someone to look after Sebastian, their ten-year-old.

Enter Uncle Hunter. When it was time for Tom to head off for his job du jour and Judy wasn't home from the office, Hunter often pulled up in the Corcoran's postage-stamp yard in his rented cream-colored Buick. Hunter's new toy was a bullhorn. "Sebastian!" he would announce, feedback echoing down the quiet streets. "I have arrived! Turn on the network news!" The Corcorans had no problem with Hunter watching Sebastian at either their house or his place on Waddell, once the sex machine was removed. On one occasion, Tom asked Hunter to put away a pistol, and Hunter was embarrassed about his oversight. Being around Sebastian reminded him of his own son and his shredded marriage.

"Hunter was always 'Doc' to the kids," Corcoran said. "Sebastian felt that Hunter was a guide of sorts, the voice of some kind of weird rationale to have a good life."

Chris Robinson remembered the fun Hunter had with his bullhorn. From the small beach on the property, it was hard to look up into Hunter's apartment because sea grape trees obscured the view. Occasionally, trespassers waded through the shallows and used the private beach. "So this family came over and they were just making noise and they had their kids and their Kentucky Fried Chicken and they were just all talking," Robinson recalled. "So Hunter gets on the bullhorn, and it sounded like such authority: 'Get off the beach or I'll cut your fucking throats!' And those people were looking around, wondering what's going on. And then a little while later, out of the trees: 'Get off the beach or I'll cut your fucking throats!' After about three times, they left. He just loved that megaphone because of the sound of authority."

Laila was close to Hunter for more than twenty-five years and said he might have been at his happiest when he was on the island. "We had lots of quiet times," she said. "Hunter wasn't always performing. We'd listen to music and just be with each other."

Still, being Hunter meant occasionally being noisy. He drove his Buick convertible through Key West's quiet streets well above the speed limit. "He didn't care if people were crossing the street," Chris Robinson said. "He'd be clenching that cigarette holder and he'd be screaming, 'Get out of the way, you bastards!' You know how slow it is in Key West and everyone's just slowly crossing the street and he's just plowing down the street when he was going somewhere."

Good news and more money arrived from Hollywood during one of his Key West visits. Art Linson came through with a check for the film version of Hunter's eulogy for Oscar Zeta Acosta, now to become a movie called *Where the Buffalo Roam*. In addition to the money Hunter earned for selling the "Brown Buffalo" article to the movies, he also got a $25,000 fee as a consultant, which meant that he had to judge whether what was onscreen resembled the real man. Desperate for money in his ongoing divorce war, Hunter didn't seem to care much about the movie, as long as he got paid.

Linson was a successful producer. By 1980, he had made only a few films, most notably the ensemble comedy *Car Wash* and *American Hot Wax*, the biography of rock 'n' roll disk jockey Alan Freed. He went on to produce *Melvin and Howard*, *Singles*, *Fight Club*, and other highly regarded films, but *Where the Buffalo Roam* was his only start-to-finish effort as director.

John Kaye's screenplay telescoped several events in Hunter's life into a short period, with his relationship with the "Oscar" character as the narrative tissue. Character actor Peter Boyle was cast as Oscar Zeta Acosta, infuriating the Chicano community, which wanted the role played by a

Hispanic actor. To quell the anger, the character eventually was changed to Lazslo, a Bulgarian. Boyle, who had thoroughly prepared to play Acosta, was disappointed by the change of ethnicity and by the fact that Lazslo was written as a buffoon.

Actor Bill Murray was cast as Hunter. He was part of Hunter's crowd, since he was in the *Saturday Night Live* cast and close friends with Laila. Preparing for the role, Murray lived with Hunter and Laila, and at times, she said, it was like standing between mirrors. Murray was such an expert mimic that he absorbed Hunter's personality. For nearly a year after finishing the film, Murray still carried many of Hunter's mannerisms.

But superb performances took the film only so far. The buffoonery went beyond Lazslo; the whole script was heavy-handed comedy. Despite Murray's and Boyle's efforts, the film was a cheap cartoon. The deep sensitivity and hurt that Hunter had shown in his epitaph for Acosta was lost in the film version, bogged down in leaden comedy.

Even Garry Trudeau, who had used Hunter's image in his work, was alarmed when someone sent him a draft of the script. Although he didn't know Hunter and they had exchanged only a brief note, he sent him a reprimand: "I don't know how much they paid you to authorize that piece of shit, but it wasn't enough. If you must have your reputation trashed, at least have the integrity to do it yourself." Hunter quickly responded to his nemesis: "What lame instinct prompts you to suddenly begin commenting on my material? You've done pretty well by skimming it the last five years. So keep your pompous whining to yourself and don't complain. You'll get yours." Years later, Hunter was able to show his feelings for Trudeau when late-night television host Conan O'Brien allowed him to machine-gun poster-sized photos of the cartoonist on his program. Hunter responded with relish and obliterated Trudeau's image.

Mocked in print by David Felton for allowing such a weak film to be made from his life, Hunter threw up his hands. "I don't know why people are so concerned about my image," he told Felton. "I'm an egomaniac. *I* should be the one concerned about my image. Why are you and Garry Trudeau so worried about this film hurting me. *I'm* not."

Hunter received his check for the film while he was in Key West and began spending it as fast as he could, and having some fun as well, writing Corcoran a check for two million dollars with "cocaine" in the subject line.

Since he could not get Hunter to write for his magazine, Wenner tried to interest his star byline in doing something for the movies. Wenner was making a *Rolling Stone* film production deal. Hunter had written the voice-over narration for *Where the Buffalo Roam*, and the movies intrigued him. Escaping to screen writing allowed him to leave behind the Duke persona.

But Hunter had never written a screenplay. He'd digested what he'd learned from Harrison and McGuane and also latched on to Tom Corcoran, who was intent on writing for films. He had studied with the best: McGuane wrote and directed the film version of his Key West novel, *Ninety-two in the Shade*, and Paul Schrader, who'd written *Taxi Driver* and *American Gigolo*, had come to Key West to polish the *Raging Bull* screenplay and befriended Corcoran. Hunter realized his buddy Corcoran could help with the technical details, and he agreed to try to jump-start Wenner's first venture into film.

Schrader gave Corcoran good advice, which he relayed to Hunter: "Writing the screenplay is easy. Writing the treatment is the way you sell it. Here's how to do it. Don't write any more than twenty-nine pages. When they [film producers] see thirty pages, they get scared."

Hunter perked up. Twenty-nine pages was nothing. He and Corcoran decided to write about drug smuggling in the Keys, then a profitable, going concern. It was also the sort of film *Rolling Stone* might well produce. Corcoran and Monty Chitty, who was an expert fishing guide, took Hunter out on the flats, through the mangrove channels, showing him how to operate a boat like a smuggler, finding the sorts of places smugglers might use to bring in their dope and wait on the buyers. On the basis of the treatment, Wenner sold the concept to Paramount Pictures. Hunter and Corcoran called the screenplay *Cigarette Key*.

Hunter clipped smuggling stories from the *Key West Citizen* and pinned them on a huge bulletin board Chris Robinson made in his apartment. Hunter didn't want to be dependent on Chitty and Corcoran, so Robinson also tried to teach him to drive a boat. With some of the *Buffalo Roam* money, Hunter bought a seventeen-foot Mako from guide Dink Bruce, whose father had been Hemingway's fishing buddy. Robinson said Hunter knew only one speed: *wide-open*. Robinson advised him, "Hunter, just keep the wheel straight when the boat goes in the air."

One night, after Hunter had been out on the reef doing marine research and eating psychedelic mushrooms, he tried to return to port when his boat got loose in Murray Marina. "It went airborne," Robinson said. "He and Laila had been out there on the reef and it was a full moon and it's really hard to get in at night in that marina. So you have to be kind of straight to get the boat into the marina at night. But Hunter *was* a professional, and he could do all kinds of things while on drugs. So he was backing up to the dock where he was going to leave the boat and Laila was on the back of the boat, and he just was backing up and then kind of hit it in *forward* to stop the boat, but gunned it too much and she fell in the water, the boat just took off. He went over backwards, the motor hit him on the back of the head, and *he* fell in the water and so this boat was in the marina, *loose.* I guess he gave it pretty good throttle as he fell backwards—he didn't *mean* to do that—and the boat, the torque of the engine, will make it turn and go in a circle. So this thing jumped the fuel dock and came back around in a circle, and he's yelling, 'The bastard's trying to get me!' And he had to go down, under water. It ran around several times, knocked consoles off of other boats, just did a massive bunch of damage, and then it got stuck on the fuel dock going, *"Whaaaaaaaangggg!"* And he's screaming at Laila to turn it off and she's mad at him, because she thinks he did it on purpose and finally, after everything's settled out, he got the boat, set it in there, set the center console on it like nothing happened—'cause nobody was at the marina, since it was midnight— and *left.* So when folks came by in the morning, they thought some burglar had gone crazy and vandalized the place—until they saw the bow of Hunter's boat and saw all of the chunks out of it, where it had done all this damage. The marine patrol came over that day, and we had to wake him up. We had to get him up and convince him that it was *very important* that he talk to the marine patrol. He had to do some kind of community service, make some speeches or something."

Hunter and Corcoran both hunched over the typewriter in Buffett's apartment, finishing *Cigarette Key*. "We made up the characters and came up with a few opening scenes and all of that other stuff," Corcoran recalled. "The smugglers [in the story] set up navigational lights in the mangroves that they could operate. They could run through the mangroves by activating these lights. When we started writing the script, his work habits were going down the tubes and his relationship with Laila was building, fast. He was head over heels in love with her and not caring at all about work. And so the work fell to me. I started writing and okaying things with him, and not okaying things with him."

Wenner was excited to hear that the script from Hunter might be arriving via Mojo Wire. He stayed in the office until the wee hours, as the machine slowly belched out the pages. Corcoran took his family on vacation; when he returned, Hunter offered payment for his large part in producing the treatment. "Hunter had bought a Yamaha," Corcoran said. "That was my pay for working on the script—a Sony television and a Yamaha 650." He also got a shared story credit on the screenplay: "By Hunter S. Thompson and Tom Corcoran." (In the end, Hunter delivered the much less powerful Yamaha 400 to Corcoran, who good-naturedly shrugged it off. He eventually noted the short-changing twenty years later in one of his novels.)

The film was never made because Paramount killed the deal. Hollywood was beginning to feel pressure to clean up its act in the early days of the Reagan era, and a movie centered on drug smugglers was a hard sell.

Feeling indebted to Corcoran, Hunter gave him the idea for another film, which he called *The Mole*. "What Hunter dreamed up was an idea about a mole in the CIA who doesn't do anything until he gets to the very top, then he starts raising hell," Corcoran said. "I read a bunch of John le Carré novels really fast, and I wrote a treatment on the thing." Eventually, Corcoran was able to sell that idea to Hollywood, thanks to Tom McGuane, and when he called Hunter to tell him the news, he left a message saying, "*The Mole* had been sold." Hunter called back and asked, "How did you know?" Turns out he had sold a version of the story himself, to the producers of *Where the Buffalo Roam*, who had no intention of filming it. They wanted to keep Hunter under control, and they said if he was a loose cannon on the film set, the deal for *The Mole* would be dropped. Corcoran lost his chance at his first big money as a writer. (He would go on to be a successful mystery writer, with a series of novels set in Key West.)

"He was too naïve in those days to see what they were pulling on him in Hollywood," Corcoran said.

A mass exodus from Cuba began in April 1980 after a plunge in that nation's economy. Over the course of a few months, ten thousand Cubans fled the island, many of them criminals let go by Fidel Castro. Many landed in Key West.

When the migration began, Tom Corcoran's journalistic instincts kicked into high gear. "I hopped on my motorbike and rode up to Garrison Bight and got in touch with a buddy of mine who was a charter captain, and I asked if he had space on the boat and I asked if I could go along," Corcoran said. He made arrangements to photograph the boatlift for *Newsweek.* "I went home and packed and got on the boat, and we were pulling away, and . . . I don't know if I have a photograph of it, or just a photo in my mind: It's my wife and son, who was ten at the time, and Hunter and Laila standing on the pier. We were about fifty yards off the pier at Garrison Bight, and I thought to myself, 'There's something wrong here. Hunter should be on the boat.' I was going off to do something out-landish, to go off and cover this Cuban boatlift, and Hunter's standing on the pier. At that point, I think he was so in love with Laila that he didn't want to give up an hour."

Though he still saw himself on his self-imposed sabbatical, Hunter's instincts required him to be part of an event, or at least *feel* that he was part of it. He began drafting a novel called *The Silk Road.* He did not fin-ish it then, but published three scenes from it a decade later in his *Songs of the Doomed* collection. Still, being so close to the biggest news event of the day and *not* being part of it ate at him. He needed to get back in the game.

As his divorce negotiation neared its end, Hunter was eager to resume work. When he returned to Woody Creek after the divorce, he saw that Owl Farm was a different place, without Sandy's calming presence and Juan roaming around. It was Hunter's home, not fully Laila's, and so it became his warren, as jovially messy as a teenager's clubhouse.

Paul Perry, editor of *Running* magazine, presented Hunter with an opportunity to return to the world of magazine writing, but not with the repeat-the-past baggage he would have at *Rolling Stone.* Perry threw Hunter the assignment to cover the 1980 Honolulu marathon. "Think about it," Perry wrote. "This is a good chance for a vacation." For months, Perry cajoled Hunter by sending him Nike running shoes and eventu-ally flew to Aspen to lobby him. At Woody Creek, Laila had comfortably slipped into Sandy's walking-on-eggshells role while Hunter slept, and she hosted Perry while he waited for Hunter's decision on covering the marathon. Though other editors and members of the *Running* staff told him he was crazy, Perry persevered. "You have something to worry about," Ralph Steadman told him. "Hunter has been known to fall through lately. He hasn't published a story to speak of in about eight years."

But Hunter was ready to reemerge and finally gave in to Perry's pleas. The marathon was over the Christmas holidays. Hunter liked the idea of treating Laila to Hawaii at Christmas. "The winter was coming in Aspen," she recalled. "There was no money. Hunter loved those out-of-the-blue assignments. That was the answer to our problems. The marathon was incidental. It was an excuse." It was "sort of a scam," she admitted. "*Running* magazine was going to foot the bill, and we were going to have this great time." Hunter lured Steadman and his family from England. "The time has come to kick ass, Ralph," Hunter wrote, "even if it means coming briefly out of retirement and dealing, once again, with the public."

The trip turned out to be mostly a soggy nightmare, and the subject of the story did not amuse either man much. Running had become the new sport of the ritualistic liberal. Hunter and Ralph observed the crowded field of eight thousand runners and didn't see many of their kind left. These were the humorless remnants of those they'd walked alongside two decades before. These people were different:

> The same people who burned their draft cards in the Sixties and got lost in the Seventies are now into running. When politics failed and personal relationships proved unmanageable; after McGovern went down and Nixon exploded right in front of our eyes . . . after Ted Kennedy got Stassenized and Jimmy Carter put the fork to everybody who ever believed anything he said about anything at all, and after the nation turned en masse to the atavistic wisdom of Ronald Reagan.
>
> Well, these are, after all, the Eighties and the time has finally come to see who has teeth, and who doesn't. . . . Which may or may not account for the odd spectacle of two generations of political activists and social anarchists finally turning—twenty years later—into runners.

Hunter and Ralph planned to start the race, hop in a cab and ride to a friend's house near the end of the course and join the race just in time to sprint to the finish, and win by cheating. But they discarded that plan and ended up heckling the runners who ran by as they sat on the flatbed of the radio press in front of the leaders, sipping their booze:

"You're doomed, man, you'll never make it."

"Hey, fat boy, how about a beer?"

"*Run*, you silly bastard."

After the race, Hunter and Ralph retreated to side-by-side cabins on the storm-ravaged big island of Hawaii to complete the project. "Hawaii was horrible," Laila recalled. "Bad weather, waves washing onto the porch. . . ." And familiarity bred contempt. Ralph and his wife and young daughter had trouble living next door to Hunter's love nest. Any semblance of a normal family life was lost. Steadman had also injured himself while diving and was in no mood for the usual tomfoolery.

Eventually, Ralph left Hunter in Hawaii and returned to England. They were able to weld together their chronicle of the race for *Running* ("Charge of the Weird Brigade," April 1981), Hunter's first work of original journalism in almost three years. It also was done in a little over two months, not bad, by Hunter standards. But Hunter and Perry had struggled over the manuscript. The copy editors had removed several *fucks* from Hunter's story, and the staff objected to Hunter's use of *nigger*. Perry allowed all of the *fucks* to be reinstated, but tried to persuade Hunter to remove the racist language.

"Why the fuck would I do that?" Hunter asked Perry. "I am a bigot. I'm what they called a 'multibigot.' A unibigot is a racist. A multibigot is just a prick."

The magazine's readers were split when the piece appeared. Some threatened to cancel their subscriptions, though Perry doubted that any of them did. Some were also outraged that a notorious drug abuser was given space in a magazine devoted to the purity of running.

One of the most interested readers was Jann Wenner, who was "jealous beyond belief," according to Laila, that Perry had gotten a coherent article out of Hunter. Other magazine editors began writing Perry, asking whether he would use his magic to get Hunter to write for them.

But the *Running* article wasn't the end of the Hawaii experience. While the Weird Brigade idea was still gestating, Hunter got a letter from Alan Rinzler, the former head of Straight Arrow Books. Now at Bantam Books, Rinzler wanted Hunter to write something for him. An aborted book on Ronald Reagan in 1980 had died on the vine, but not until Hunter had run up a huge expense account in Washington. But Rinzler was a forgiving soul, and this time Hunter pitched a Bantam paperback drawn from the adventures with Ralph in Hawaii. This might be another chance to deal again with the American Dream. It didn't matter to Hunter whether the covers were soft or hard. "We will skulk off the plane in Honolulu with the hopes & dreams of a whole generation in our hands," he wrote Rinzler. "I am already entered in the Marathon & I plan to enter Ralph in the Pipeline Masters surfing competition . . . we will not win these weird events, but we didn't win the Kentucky Derby either."

With deadline met for *Running*, Hunter and Ralph set to work on fleshing out what they had done into a book-length manuscript. But it took two years before *The Curse of Lono* appeared. It *was* a curse. After a while, Hunter began to think of it as "a Ralph book" and resented everything about the project.

Hunter said he couldn't write without Ralph's drawings. A second trip to Hawaii . . . then a third. Hunter couldn't get started. Ralph had to come to Colorado, making daily pilgrimages to Hunter's cabin to pin his new drawings up on the wall, hoping to inspire Hunter to write. No luck. Hunter finagled an all-expenses-paid fact-finding trip to Washington for Ralph and himself, since he felt the work had developed themes about the American tradition of lies and deceit, and what better place to chase that thread of plot. After weeks and thousands of dollars, nothing came of it.

It's not that Hunter was inert; he was partying at Woody Creek. John Belushi came to visit, and even he, with his monumental substance-abuse issues, couldn't keep up with Hunter. He played tapes of punk bands for Hunter, further distracting him from writing. It got so serious that Bantam sent editor Ian Ballantine to Woody Creek four times, trying to coax the book from its author. Ballantine wore a suit to convey that he was all-business and promised to pack up and stop sending money if one grain of cocaine was displayed in his presence.

Despite all of this attention, the book was out of control. The marathon was long forgotten, to end up as a mere subplot. Now Hunter was into fishing and Hawaiian lore and the ancient Hawaiian god Lono.

As Hunter worked on the manuscript, he ranged over wider and wider terrain, and yet the book remained slim and insubstantial. He needed the companion his style demanded, and since Ralph had run back home and no Acosta was around, Hunter invented someone. (He kept Laila largely in the background, using her name only occasionally and now and then making reference to "my fiancée.")

Hunter had introduced Gene Skinner as an apparently real character in "Dance of the Doomed," his fall-of-Saigon article. Skinner was presented as a former agent for the Central Intelligence Agency working for Air America in the last days of the Vietnam War. In *Lono*, he showed up as a shady character on Oahu, a man whose name strikes fear whenever it is muttered. Skinner, clearly a fictional creation, also appears in the abandoned *Silk Road* novel.

Hunter admitted that Skinner was made up. He would be the new Thompson alter ego, but not nearly as nice as Duke and with a different attitude. Hunter described Skinner as "anti-humanist," adding, "What I'm trying to do is to create a character to fit the times." The Skinner character allowed Hunter to take his interior monologues outside. In *The Curse of Lono*, when Hunter arrives in Hawaii, he is met by Skinner at the airport. "I thought you quit this business," Skinner says. "I did, but I got bored," Hunter answers. It was like reading a writer's diary.

Ralph kept sending illustrations and Hunter kept struggling to write, in Woody Creek and in Fairhope, Alabama. Tom Corcoran had retreated there from Key West, convinced that the island city was becoming too expensive and too dangerous a place to raise a child. Tom McGuane had left Key West and settled into homes in Montana and in Point Clear, Alabama. Hunter and Laila thought Fairhope sounded like a good locale to finally put the *Lono* manuscript to rest.

Hunter and Corcoran had a standing appointment for a late breakfast every day at Julwin's Southern Country Barbecue Restaurant. Hunter spread out his new *Lono* fragments over the table and asked Corcoran to help organize what he had. Corcoran read the latest material, while Hunter consumed his standard breakfast:

- ❏ One Pot of coffee
- ❏ One Wild Turkey in a tumbler with only two ice cubes
- ❏ Two bloody marys
- ❏ Two large glasses of orange juice
- ❏ Two Heinekens
- ❏ Four pieces of toast
- ❏ Four whole grapefruit
- ❏ Six eggs
- ❏ Eight sausage links

Hunter always said he liked the "highs" in his writing, the two or three paragraphs that had rhythm and music. The stuff in between just had to connect the highs. A sustained piece of writing was okay, but he preferred the occasional brilliance that was worth waiting for, something that really stood out.

The Curse of Lono was a bunch of scenes in need of connection, but Hunter couldn't find the narrative tissue and required Laila and Tom Corcoran to help him assemble the book, which he had grown to dislike.

"I was outlining it for him," Corcoran said of their spectacular working breakfasts. "He'd written most of these scenes, but they weren't in any order."

Hunter felt that Ralph's part of *Lono* had been easier, which allowed him to finish his work well before Hunter. He also resented Ralph's getting an equal byline on the book. With his apocalyptical, insane drawings, Ralph could lay claim to half of the genetic material of Gonzo, but around the time of *Lono*, Ralph began to feel that Hunter did not appreciate him professionally, while remaining his friend.

To give the book some needed heft, Laila helped Hunter find selections from Mark Twain and from Captain Cook's journals that could be excerpted in *Lono* and, since they were works in the public domain, could be quoted for free. "I did a lot of research, like all the Mark Twain material," Laila said, "and he took a lot of notes. Sometimes he'd write by hand, and then I'd type it up the next day. Sometimes he would be typing and stop and stare at it for a long time, trying to figure out a sentence just to get it absolutely right. He listened to music while he wrote. Music was fuel for him, and helped him get in the right mood to write." Depending on his mood, the Rolling Stones or Bob Dylan provided the perfect fuel.

Hunter and Laila returned to Owl Farm with a still unfinished manuscript. Eventually, Alan Rinzler came to Woody Creek to see whether he could rescue the overdue manuscript. "Hunter was just too tangential," he said. "He was preoccupied with drugs, less so with writing." Rinzler had worked closely with Hunter a decade before and was now appalled by his post-Sandy living conditions—the sloth, the stuffed critters on the wall, the "Hemingway stuff." After three days of work, Hunter finally crashed and Rinzler made his move. "I waited for Hunter to fall asleep and I gathered up all the manuscript, including parts of it that were hand-written on shopping bags and napkins, and I put it all in a big shopping bag and I split. I left. I got on the plane and went back to New York and that was the way the book was published." Nearly three years after Hunter and Ralph had set off for the Honolulu marathon, the book appeared, in November 1983.

The Curse of Lono didn't wow critics. Most said it was acceptable for Gonzo fans but would probably be incomprehensible to those not already singing in Thompson's choir. The immersion in Hawaiian lore and history might baffle his ardent admirers, who might want more Amazing Drug Tales. Yet it was the last section of the book, the head-first dive into the mysticism of the islands, that offered a rare psychic journey into parts of Hunter's brain. As he returned to the harbor, finally with his Hemingway-caliber marlin notched on his belt, he climbed the mast and bellowed "I am Lono," drawing a crowd and making a spectacular entrance. But to some critics, Hunter had fallen into self-parody. The *New York Times Book Review* said that if *Fear and Loathing in Las Vegas* had been the experiment, then *The Curse of Lono* was the control, as he put his more or less "real self" through the motions of Gonzo journalism. *The Curse of Lono* ended up having a shelf life, and eventually a coffee-table sized version with additional artwork was marketed. Actor Sean Penn bought the rights to the book, planning to turn it into a feature film.

Rob Fleder, an editor at *Playboy* and a ferocious admirer of Hunter's writing, secured rights to a book excerpt for his magazine. When he got the *Lono* manuscript, he was appalled at how thin it was not just in girth but in content. The marathon section was excellent, but *Running* magazine had already printed that. Fleder flew Hunter into Chicago, and days of partying and bloated expense accounts ensued. After protracted arguing, Fleder left with a modest and semicomprehensible bit of *Lono*. Fleder was dispirited by the experience, but got what *Playboy* wanted. Hunter's name on the cover still sold magazines.

"After *The Curse of Lono*," Ralph Steadman wrote in a memoir, "Hunter became more circumspect about my involvement in anything to do with Gonzo, as though the very presence of one of my drawings in a journalistic project of his own represented a serious threat to the domination over the world we had collectively created a decade earlier."

Ralph believed that Hunter had trouble acknowledging the role the art played in the character of Gonzo. "It began to bug him," he said. "He wanted to be a great novelist, but half the time he needed my drawings before he could start." For *Lono*, at least, it seemed that Hunter needed to piggyback on Steadman's vision before he could get started.

Hunter took Laila home to Louisville to visit his mother. "She showed me all his newspapers he wrote as a kid and told me stories about him." They stayed at the Thompsons' house in the Highlands, where Hunter had the sudden urge to get married while he was home. "He was going to call the preacher and have him come over, and he had this whole idea that we were going to get married that night. I found out that's how he had gotten married to Sandy, so I didn't want to do the same thing. Certain places would trigger things for him. I think Louisville was full of ghosts for him."

Laila also tried to help Hunter maintain his family ties. She urged Hunter to invite Davison and his family down to Key West when they were staying there. "Davison lived his life a little more conventionally than Hunter," she said. "But he has the same sense of humor and is tall, dark, and handsome."

Eventually, Laila concluded that it was easier to love Hunter than to live with him. His moods, his drinking, his idiosyncrasies . . . eventually, she tired of the daily drama. After more than three years together, Laila left for Los Angeles. She remained friends with Hunter the rest of his life, and near the end he went to her for help. She was the tenacious producer who would finally turn *Fear and Loathing in Las Vegas* into a film. The subsequent women in his life could have no room for jealousy. She was always going to be part of his life. She just couldn't live with him anymore.

Chapter 16

THE GENETIC MIRACLE

Listen, do me a favor. Ask him the one question that is on
everyone's mind: How does he do it? How does he continue
to live the way we did back then and survive?
—*Shopkeeper to journalist prior to meeting HST, 1991*

In the early eighties, Hunter's life began to catch up with him. Part of it was simply aging, the natural process of a boy wonder moving into his midforties. But part of it was the regimen of drink and drugs that was as much a part of his daily life as grapefruit and eggs. Hunter was a genetic miracle, able to withstand all manner of self-inflicted abuse without losing a step. "I never thought I'd make it past 27," he said. "Every day I'm just as astounded as everyone else to realize I'm still alive."

As his old friend Porter Bibb said, "He not only created Gonzo writing; he created Gonzo living." The still-young vigorous Hunter at the end of the seventies gave way to the world-weary, sunken-eyed, and puffier Hunter of the eighties. "I saw myself in the mirror as a grizzled veteran of many wars," he wrote.

He fancied himself an athlete. He still felt young; he'd played football with Sebastian Corcoran in Key West and run his boat through the mangrove at breakneck speed. But as he surveyed his post-*Lono*, post-Laila world, he saw he was closer to fifty than to forty, his body ached more than it used to, and he was living alone in his fortified compound in the Rockies. He didn't do *alone* well.

Occasionally, stories drew him from hiding. At the urging of managing editor Terry McDonnell, he returned to *Rolling Stone* for the first time in five years to cover the 1983 Palm Beach divorce trial of newspaper heir Herbert "Pete" Pulitzer and his much younger wife, Roxanne. The Pulitzer divorce trial was the sort of story that erased the line between traditional journalism and the sleazy tabloid writing that was becoming more mainstream in post-Watergate journalism. But the sex-and-drugs angle was irresistible. When on the first day of the trial, the fawning judge, Carl Harper, stood up and said, "I'm so honored to meet you, Mr. Thompson," Hunter writhed in discomfort.

In his commentary on the Pulitzer divorce, "A Dog Took My Place," Hunter claimed he would amp up his evil side to match the new decade's attitude of nastiness. Wenner was happy to have him back. "It had beautiful stuff in it," he said of the Pulitzer piece. "It was brilliant." Hunter swept down on the epic degeneracy of Palm Beach society like a moral Valkyrie, shrieking of impending apocalypse and Judgment Day.

As he wrote of young Mrs. Pulitzer,

> She was an incorrigible coke slut, [Pete Pulitzer] said, and a totally unfit mother. She stayed up all night at discos and slept openly with her dope pusher, among others. There was a house painter, a real estate agent, a race car driver and a French baker—and on top of all that, she was a lesbian, or at least some kind of pansexual troilist. In six and a half years of marriage, she had humped almost everything she could get her hands on. . . .
>
> Roxanne Pulitzer is not a beautiful woman. There is nothing especially striking about her body or facial bone structure, and at age thirty-one, she looks more like a jaded senior stewardess from Pan Am than an international sex symbol. Ten years on the Palm Beach Express have taken their toll, and she would have to do more than just sweat off ten pounds to compete for naked space in the men's magazines. Her legs are too thin, her hips are too wide, and her skin is a bit too loose for modeling work. But she has a definite physical presence. There is no mistaking the aura of good-humored

out-front sexuality. This is clearly a woman who likes to sleep late in the morning.

More out of outrage than admiration, Hunter delivered a soliloquy on the staggering cocaine use in the Pulitzer house. The coke bill approached nearly half a million dollars per annum. As the product of a modest background, Hunter also couldn't resist the temptation to view the vain and selfish Pulitzers from the point of view of their servants, and even from that of a bartender, who was clearly a fabrication. "I know how those people behave," the bartender wailed to Hunter, "and I know how it makes me feel!" Hunter had the man utter the line that gave the piece its title: "I see those shit-eating grins on their faces *and I feel like a dog took my place.*" This was a giveaway that the barkeep was fiction; Hunter had already used "A Dog Took My Place" as a section heading in *The Curse of Lono*. Hunter knew he was competing with his former self and fretted over this, his first major piece in years. Writing to Jim Silberman, he admitted, "I'm getting too old for this. . . . The Pulitzer thing is a monster. . . . God only knows what will come of it. The NY Times will probably call for my death & strangers might shoot at me on the streets. Fuck them."

In his review of *The Great Shark Hunt*, William F. Buckley had said that after 600-plus pages of Hunter Thompson, he concluded Hunter had no interest in sex because it was not in the book. Hunter's story on the Pulitzer trial was brutal not only in its take-no-prisoners assessment of the major players in the trial but also in that it showed him revealing for the first time his own sexual appetites. At the end of the article, he portrayed himself with two nude women in his convertible, cutting through a brisk and sunny Palm Beach morning on his way to an orgy.

Roxanne Pulitzer was aware of Hunter, but never met him until he was seated next to her at a dinner party just before the trial began. She was startled to look up in court the next day and see her Bermuda-shorts-clad dinner companion in the first row of the press section, where he remained for the trial's duration. She'd read some of his work and knew the hurt he could cause. When "A Dog Took My Place" appeared, she followed a friend's advice and did not read the article. For eight years after the trial, Hunter called to apologize for his brutal assessment of her ("the best piece of ass in Palm Beach"). After years of pleading, Pulitzer gave in and allowed Hunter to throw a party for her during a ski vacation in Aspen. The result of the trial was that Pulitzer lost custody of her two young sons. As Hunter showed her a picture of her he kept tacked up on his wall of fame in his home, he said, "I never thought you would lose your boys." She was touched by his remorse, and they talked about their children and the fact that because of his nasty divorce, he didn't see Juan as much as he wanted. Ultimately, his charm and sympathy got through to her. "He really understood family," Pulitzer said. "I really grew to love him."

When Hunter showed up in the press lounge in August 1984 at the Democratic National Convention in San Francisco, he wore *Rolling Stone* credentials. All the reporters' heads turned to acknowledge his entrance. Visibly agitated, he fooled with the volume on the television, politely and quickly acknowledged his groupies, then tried to find a quiet place to hide and drink a beer.

Bill Greider, the *Washington Post* reporter who'd gone on to be *Rolling Stone*'s political editor in the eighties, hooked up with his old friend during that convention. "We were walking down the street toward the convention hall in San Francisco, and these young kids came up and started talking to him on the sidewalk," Greider remembered. "And Hunter started rocking and rolling, grunting and saying funny things. I thought at first that these kids knew him. He was acting as though they knew him. And then I realized, these were just fans and they adored him. They wanted to touch him. Hunter never got credit for this. Whatever else his brutish moments were like, he responded very generously. I realized in that moment that this was a man who absolutely resonated in the culture and was known in such a way that people could approach him familiarly, as though he was a friend. He would give them that. It takes energy to do that. I find that very appealing. "

He did not write anything for *Rolling Stone* about the convention. The San Francisco excursion was Hunter's last attempt at campaign coverage for a while. He could not be talked into covering the 1988 campaign. "Jann was trying to get him out on the campaign trail, knowing it would be good stuff," Greider said. "I was faxing him these handwritten memos from the Washington bureau, telling him to get out there and rip Bush's lungs out. Something in the Hunter spirit. But he never went out."

Hunter began to deal more frankly with sex and sexual issues than with politics. True, he hadn't written much about sex until the few wink-

wink moments in *The Curse of Lono* and in the Pulitzer story. Russell Chatham believed that Hunter's gentlemanliness would not permit him to write about sex while married to Sandy. Once single, he was free.

Chatham and Hunter partied and fished together in Key West, but they became close friends in San Francisco in the early eighties, when both realized they were sex junkies and they discovered nirvana: the O'Farrell Theater, which Hunter once called "the Carnegie Hall of public sex in America." It began its life in the late sixties as a strip club in one of San Francisco's seedier neighborhoods. Brothers Jim and Artie Mitchell started the business and eventually branched into pornographic films, in 1972 producing *Behind the Green Door* starring Marilyn Chambers. It became one of the first hardcore films to break out of sticky-floor theaters and play in mainstream metroplexes. By the eighties, the O'Farrell was as Hunter had described it: the number-one venue for the sex industry, with expensive sofas on which lap dancers writhed with customers. The dancers did just about anything, masturbating for an audience, masturbating clients, or fellating them. The O'Farrell was a sexual theme park.

Still fervently a bachelor, Hunter was drawn to the fantasyland of the Mitchell brothers. "You've got to go where the girls are and, believe me, that's where they are," Chatham said. "If you were friends with the Mitchell brothers, as we were, you were back in the office with thirty naked girls."

But Hunter did not partake. "Only a freak of passion could have resisted that kind of massive temptation," Hunter said, "and on some nights I come close to caving into it."

The Mitchells berated him for maintaining his observer role. "You are crazy as a goddamn loon not to fuck every one of these girls," Artie Mitchell told him. "They all love you and want to fuck you like animals."

Most of the girls did like Hunter, who was thick with Southern charm and charisma. Debi Sundahl, a star and producer of adult films, said most of the men who came into the O'Farrell were shy and held the women in distanced awe. Hunter radiated confidence, and women were drawn to his comfortable machismo. "He would be talking and engaging their attention," she said, "and then he would throw his arm around them. To me, that's flirting. I never saw him corner anyone or kiss them."

Rob Fleder, the *Playboy* editor who had excerpted *Lono*, came back for more punishment, believing that Hunter could write a great sex article. Hunter sold him the concept for an article on feminist pornography. "Feminist porn was really just couples' films," Hunter said, "Sex films made for couples to which you could take a date. It was a new genre." With the promise of a *Playboy* article as a feeder, Hunter then sold a proposal to Random House for a book called *The Night Manager*. Hunter printed business cards listing himself as the night manager of the O'Farrell and even worked taking tickets on a few occasions. He was borrowing a page from Gay Talese, whose massive book on sex in America, *Thy Neighbor's Wife*, was the result of five years of research, including time Talese spent managing a Times Square massage parlor.

Talese's book wasn't even a decade old, but Hunter saw it as already well out of date. *The Night Manager* wouldn't just be about sex; it would look at the new moral crusaders and the dangerous nonchalance toward the First Amendment he saw under President Reagan and his attorney general, Ed Meese. Meese appointed a commission to investigate pornography and sought to have the distribution of *Playboy*, *Penthouse*, and other adult magazines regulated. Despite all of the efforts at suppression, the O'Farrell and other erotic enterprises were doing well. "This is a time of growth, vigor and profit for the American sex industry," Hunter wrote. "Business has never been better."

As Hunter began his research, he thought the Mitchell brothers made a natural focus. "The only reason I went to see the Mitchell brothers was the chance that they might be interesting enough—for 48 hours—to sustain my interest in the feminist porno story long enough for me to crank out the necessary 6,000 or 7,000 words," Hunter said.

He always needed the big paychecks from publishers, but to maintain cash flow, Hunter still made campus speeches. In the mideighties, he earned $200,000 a year from his every-other-week college talks. He could afford to be an unproductive writer.

During his infatuation with the O'Farrell, Hunter spoke at the College of Marin, north of San Francisco, unaware that his mother was in the audience. She was visiting Jim Thompson, finally at peace with his life and sexuality, and living in San Francisco's Castro district, a homosexual mecca. As the campus talk began, Jim and Virginia Thompson watched Hunter stagger onstage, drink from a bottle of whiskey, and get booed by the audience when he spoke favorably of nuclear energy. It was a typical Hunter Thompson "speaking" engagement: chaotic, disorganized, comprehensible only for true believers. As Hunter left the stage, he saw his mother and brother, who had decided to surprise him at his speech and say hello. They approached him through the crowd. "He looked at me,"

Jim said. "His eyes popped out of his head. Then he looked and saw Mummy, standing right next to me. At that point he went, 'Ho! Jesus Christ!' And just turned, waved his arms and ran with his head down. Just ran past her into the dressing room." Virginia Thompson told Jim, "Hunter will never hurt me again."

In the mideighties, filmmaker Wayne Ewing approached Hunter with an idea to make a television show. Ewing, a cinematographer and director with a home near Aspen, had done a lot of television. After seeing Hunter from afar for a long time, he asked whether he could travel with him to San Francisco to film him at work as the night manager of the O'Farrell. Generally affable, Hunter agreed, and eventually warmed up to Ewing. He liked the idea of a Gonzo television show. Ewing planned to pitch it to the HBO cable network. The freedom of cable would mean Hunter wouldn't have to tone down his language or his drug use, and the idea seemed like a natural. "It took many years to gain Hunter's trust," Ewing said. "After many days and nights at Owl Farm, Hunter knew that I would not call 911 or steal his drugs and women. I was a relatively invisible friend with a camera."

Preserving his life on film was important to Hunter. "He wanted me to record his life just as much as I did. Perhaps I became a surrogate for his notion of Gonzo journalism as a 'reporter with the eye and mind of a camera.'"

Ewing followed Hunter around with a 16 mm camera and became his cinematic Boswell for the last two decades of his life. "The idea was to sell a TV series, perhaps called 'Breakfast with Hunter' or 'The Gonzo Tour,' but for whatever reasons I could never sell it," Ewing said. "We went to Key West for a week and in a week, I was actually able to get Hunter in the presence of the camera for about two hours."

Hunter and his new girlfriend, Maria Khan, stayed at the Sugarloaf Lodge and hooked up with Dink Bruce and other good friends. At one point, as Hunter raced his speedboat over the water, led by a school of leaping dolphins, he screamed, "I'm back! I'm back!"

"What do you mean?" Ewing asked.

"I'm Lono, the ancient Hawaiian god, and I've come back to my people, the dolphins."

Ewing was a regular in Hunter's kitchen, but he didn't always come to work. "For every one night I filmed at Owl Farm there were a dozen where we just gambled on sports and worked on books and columns," Ewing said. "As Hunter once told an interviewer who asked why he allowed me to film so much, 'Wayne makes himself useful around here.' " (Though Ewing never made the sale to HBO or one of the commercial networks, he released a feature film called *Breakfast with Hunter* in 2004.)

Neither the *Playboy* article nor *The Night Manager* ever appeared, but for much of a year, Hunter spent more time in San Francisco and Sausalito than in Woody Creek. At a time when Hunter's reputation was the equivalent of George Jones's in country music—the man who missed more gigs than he made—he was hired in 1985 as a weekly columnist for the *San Francisco Examiner*, at $1,500 per column. Editor David Bergin knew Hunter from a decade before when he was sports editor of the *Washington Star*. Now he'd landed at the *Examiner* and persuaded his publisher, William Randolph Hearst III, to employ the notoriously unreliable Gonzo journalist as a columnist.

The idea seemed insane. Hunter was deadline-challenged. How could he produce a column once a week? He was so legendarily unproductive that many wondered whether he was burned out; was he silent because he had nothing to say or because the drink and drugs had turned his brain into a raisin? From Hunter's side, there was the question of working for a Hearst. He'd once written that Hearst newspapers are "a monument to everything cheap, corrupt and vicious in the realm of journalistic possibility."

Few were more skeptical about the concept of Hunter as a daily newspaper columnist than the *Examiner* staff. A betting faction in the newsroom thought Hunter would go down in flames after the first column appeared, *if* it ever appeared.

Yet somehow the Hearst-Thompson marriage was consummated. Bergin called it "the most intense and wild time" of his long career. During Hunter's first year as a columnist, Bergin said he was so distracted from his day-to-day duties by Hunter that he was eventually fired. "I can't blame him," he said. "I loved editing his stuff. I wouldn't trade it for anything."

The column ran on Mondays, so Hunter had a Friday deadline, which he regarded more as a suggestion than as a firm date. Bergin spent most weekends jabbering with Hunter on the phone, trying to get the column. Will Hearst decided that if he wanted Hunter Thompson as a columnist, he needed to throw more resources his way.

Hearst looked into his newsroom and called David McCumber into his office. It was ten in the morning, but Hearst asked McCumber if he wanted a drink. McCumber thought, *Man, I'm going to get fired.* Then Hearst surprised him by asking if he wanted a new project: managing Hunter Thompson full-time. McCumber agreed. He'd been a Hunter fan for years.

"At that moment," McCumber recalled, "Hunter burst out of Will's bathroom, where he had been listening to the conversation, fixed me a scotch and water and shoved it in my fist, and made one for himself and drank it. And then, for some reason I still don't understand, got down and did ten push-ups in front of me, got up, and shook my hand again and that was the end of it. From that moment, things went quite well."

There was more help, in the form of Maria Khan. She was a journalism student at the University of Arizona when Hunter spoke on campus. Afterward, they met and connected. She became his assistant and soon his girlfriend, establishing an intern-to-girlfriend pattern he followed for many years. George Plimpton visited Hunter during the early days of the *Examiner* column, trying to get him to sit still for a "Writers at Work" interview for the *Paris Review.* The interview wouldn't happen for another fifteen years, but Plimpton recalled Maria's adoring and protective presence. "I thought she was wonderful," Plimpton said. "She had a notebook and wrote down Hunter's conversation." He remembered her often being agitated, "worried about Hunter getting his column in." Hunter referred to her so much in the columns that the skeptics on the *Examiner* staff wondered whether she actually wrote them.

The *Examiner* column gave Hunter latitude. After years in psychic/political exile, he was revitalized by the Reagan/Bush regime. He needed someone to arouse his bile as Nixon had. The problem with Gerald Ford and Jimmy Carter was that they were not loathsome. Hunter was even on record as *liking* Carter. Though Reagan seemed a genial dunce and therefore not worthy of Hunter's most extreme anger, some acts committed by his administration—primarily the Iran-Contra scandal of the mideighties—were sufficient to infuriate Hunter and awaken the sleeping monster in his soul. The monster was Hunter; no Raoul Duke, Gene Skinner, or Yail Bloor was needed as a crutch. Hunter comfortably settled into the role of observer—the Sage of Woody Creek, an outraged and coked-up Mencken for the new era. Reagan's royalist trickle-down let-them-eat-cake attitude aroused his hillbilly anger, which found voice in the *Examiner* columns. He no longer needed to report, as he did in the *Rolling Stone–Campaign Trail* days. He could just unleash his anger, and people loved to read the outrageous invectives he hurled toward Washington.

Hearst aggressively marketed his newspaper and cajoled Hunter into appearing in a television advertisement, in which they stood together at a pistol range. Hearst walked up to an armed Hunter and asked him to become media critic for the *Examiner*. Hunter continued firing, then turned to Hearst and said, "Why not? We'll chase them like rats across the tundra." The final frame of the commercial showed Hunter's target, an obliterated bull's eye.

Hunter's longtime fans sought out the *Examiner* columns in the few publications outside of San Francisco that ran them, usually alternative-lifestyle magazines. But discovering Hunter Thompson was a shared epiphany for a lot of college-age students, much like hearing Bob Dylan for the first time. Books written or songs recorded three decades ago still articulated the majestic rage of youth. Both Hunter and Dylan were so good at congealing that time of life that their early work remained popular with young people long after the creators had ambled into middle age. The old work helped build new audiences. That audience awaited pronouncements from the aging figures. "Twenty-year-olds who never would have thought about buying the *Examiner* started buying it religiously every Monday because of Hunter," McCumber said.

The *Examiner* columns were the closest thing that Hunter had done to real journalism in a long time. Not since his days with the *National Observer* had he written in a generally conventional manner for a generally conventional publication. He also went beyond his column. When the *Miami Herald* broke the story about presidential candidate Gary Hart's womanizing in 1987, Hunter sprang into action on the *Examiner*'s behalf. He'd been Hart's friend for years and traveled in some of the same social circles. He knew that the woman the *Herald* found with Hart was Donna Rice, former girlfriend of rock star Don Henley of the Eagles. Hunter let himself into Henley's Aspen home, where a Polaroid of Donna was still tacked on the fridge. He took the picture and air-expressed it to McCumber in San Francisco. "Thanks to Hunter, we beat the world on a photo of Donna Rice," McCumber said.

Hunter was also masterful at pulling punches. Although not the sort of family paper you might find in Peoria or Dayton (it *was* San Francisco, after all) the *Examiner* was intended for a mainstream audience. Hunter cleaned up his act. In that he resembled comedian Richard Pryor:

known for his profane and brilliant social commentary, Pryor was an artist with ten- and twelve-letter words, which he used as often as he took
breath. On network television, Pryor did his foul nightclub routines but
stopped with precision before uttering obscenities, a masterpiece of control. Hunter's columns for the *Examiner* were like that: classic Hunter
Thompson yammering, but with drugs and obscenity absent. It proved
that those celebrated elements of his work weren't really necessary for
him to make his points.

"You just never knew from one moment to the next what was going to
happen," McCumber said. "That's what made the column work so well.
One week a straight political analysis, very well sourced with politics, or a
completely wacky story." The columns traveled with him. When he spent
the spring fishing at Ramrod Key with Monty Chitty, he filed columns
from Florida. When in Arizona to visit Maria's family, he wrote about
Phoenix politics. When he got into a dispute with his neighbors, that also
fed his columns. Readers were tuning in for Hunter, whose outrageous-
celebrity-persona made his columns read more like the trials and tribula-
tions of one man against the system. The simplest event could become an
epic in his hands. Douglas Brinkley admired the spectacle Hunter could
construct from nothing: " 'Hunter goes to Wal-Mart'—you know there's
drama there," he said.

Hunter still had in his belly the political fire that burned during his
Campaign Trail book. As he surveyed the political scene in the midpoint
of Reagan's second term, he offered this view of Republican history:
"Nixon was genetically criminal. Agnew was born wrong. Ford was so
utterly corrupt that he made millions by pardoning Nixon, and Reagan is
beginning to take on the distinctly Spanish physical characteristics of the
Somoza family, formerly of Nicaragua." As Hunter wrote of the Iran-Contra revelations, "When this one finally unravels, it will make Watergate
look like a teen-age prank, and Richard Nixon will seem like just another
small-time politician who got wiggy on greed and cheap gin."

McCumber was the perfect babysitter for Hunter. Though dedicated
to his newspaper career, McCumber eventually wrote several books,
including *X-Rated* (about the Mitchell brothers) and *The Cowboy Way*.
He said he worked well with Hunter because they had similar interests
and liked the same sort of fun. "One night, at about two in the morning,
we had been talking about a column," McCumber recalled. "I had a '63
Chrysler 300 convertible at the time. We headed across the Golden Gate

Bridge, drove around a little bit. He wanted me to push it a bit. As I did, he opened the passenger door while I drove over the bridge, and knocked over the cones on the side of the bridge. He looked over and grinned at me with this incredible six-year-old-boy grin. I just burst out laughing. It was the most incredible thing I'd ever seen."

One of Hunter's friends from the 1972 campaign, Curtis Wilkie, came to Woody Creek in late 1987 as Hunter was battling a deadline. Wilkie had gone on to become a star political correspondent for the *Boston Globe*, and he took the big-time daily newspaper reporter's amusement in watching Hunter struggle with his deadline.

Hunter was overdue on a column. "Hearst called at some point in the middle of the night, and Hunter quickly turned the phone over to me," Wilkie recalled. Hearst told Wilkie to tell Hunter that his ass would be grass if the column wasn't in Hearst's hands in three hours. "Hunter came back in the room, and I told him what Hearst had said. Hunter said, 'I had a couple of thoughts, but don't like them.' He fished in the trash can and brought out some crumpled-up pages. I looked at them and they were relatively coherent, but they were on different subjects. I said, 'Hunter, we can make this work. Use one as a lead, do a bridge, and then use the other one as the end.' He said, 'Fuck it.' So I ended up writing the 200-word bridge to connect them. We smoothed out the crumpled paper and sent those pages to San Francisco. Somewhere in all of the anthologies of the complete Hunter Thompson, there are 200 words of mine."

It had been fifteen years since Wilkie worked side by side with Hunter covering the 1972 campaign, and he believed that Hunter's reputation . . . *or myth* . . . overshadowed the diligence he brought to his work. "He was not completely irresponsible," Wilkie said. "He was aware of deadlines. When he was cranking it out, he was terrific. He was certainly not a nine-to-five journalist—well, maybe a nine p.m. to five a.m. journalist. He was certainly unconventional. Journalism professors would not hold him up as a paradigm, but Jesus, he was great at what he did." Wilkie was not alone in admiring Hunter's work; the *Examiner* columns were nominated for a Pulitzer Prize for distinguished commentary. Though Hunter didn't win, that sort of acceptance was gratifying for him—as was being named a non-fiction judge for the National Book Awards.

Bob Braudis had been elected sheriff and become close enough to Hunter to have 24-hour-a-day drop-in privileges. "I don't want to be the sheriff," Hunter often said. "I just want to *know* the sheriff." The friendship sometimes put Braudis in an odd position, but he frequently reminded Hunter, "I can be your sheriff or I can be your friend, but I can't be both." Hunter chose to keep the friendship.

During the eighties, Braudis's dropping-in privileges might mean helping Hunter talk his way through writing a column. He used his conversations with Braudis to come up with ideas and sometimes asked him to answer the phone when Hunter sensed it was Will Hearst on the other end. "I was always making up excuses for Hearst," Braudis said. "I'd say, 'Hunter's got diarrhea, he's sick.'" Braudis, a tall and imposing man, could protect Hunter from the outside world both on the phone and in person.

The column kept Hunter too busy to pursue other projects, though he got tingly over an idea Paul Perry sent. He called Perry one day to thank him for the Honolulu marathon assignment, which had led to a book. That was something he hadn't been able to do in a while, he admitted, then asked Perry, "Do you have any other ideas?"

Actually, Perry did. He knew Hunter was secretly concerned about his health, and he admired what Hunter had written about the die-hard humorless troops in the marathon. How about a book on fitness freaks? He even had a title: *The Rise of the Body Nazis*. Hunter loved it. "Any book with 'Nazi' in the title is my kind of book," he told Perry. Perry planned to put Hunter through a fitness regimen and keep track of his progress. Hunter disliked the smugness he saw in the body Nazis. "You don't ever see runners smiling, do you?" he asked Perry. He asked Perry to outline the project, attach his name, and send it to the New York publishing world and watch editors fight over it like junkyard dogs after a scrap of raw meat. "They'll pay me a quarter of a million for that," he said. Hunter's only request was that Jim Silberman not hear about the proposal.

Perry pitched the *Body Nazis* to an editor at Simon and Schuster, who loved the idea and shared it with the editorial board. It was shot down by board member Silberman, Hunter's editor since *Hell's Angels*. Silberman had advanced Hunter $125,000 on an earlier book. He predicted to the board that Simon and Schuster would never see the *Body Nazis* manuscript.

Perry tried to persuade Silberman to accept the *Body Nazis* to satisfy Hunter's obligation. "I don't want this book," Silberman shouted. "I think this is an irresponsible thing for you to do. Don't you know you could kill a person like Hunter?" And so *The Rise of the Body Nazis* never happened. Silberman told Perry to relay a message to Hunter: "If he writes this book, I'll go to the courts and take his ranch away. I'm dead serious."

In the end, the *Examiner* columns were collected in a book that Silberman published with his Summit imprint: *Generation of Swine*. With McCumber's help, Hunter had assembled a sharp anthology, mostly focused on the me-first politics of the Reagan era. The book did not retire Hunter's obligation to Silberman, but it did become a best-seller and was greeted as a comeback. In the *New York Times*, critic Herbert Mitgang said, "He's a little more strident this time out, but if you happen to share his enemies, Mr. Thompson's your man." Mitgang tried to draw some comparisons with the yellow journalism of Joseph Pulitzer and William Randolph Hearst, in whose newspaper his columns appeared. But even those old war lords could not compare with Hunter. "Nearly everything he writes makes yellow journalism pale," Mitgang wrote.

Drawn together, the columns made an impressive case that Hunter had not lost his touch. He quoted himself a good deal, mimicking the "We were somewhere near Barstow on the edge of the desert" opening of *Fear and Loathing in Las Vegas* in several columns ("We were somewhere on the freeway near the San Diego Zoo . . .") and taking a dead lift from the last line of Hemingway's *Farewell to Arms* ("Then I walked back to the hotel in the rain"). Self-references and hat tips to Hemingway, Fitzgerald, and his other favorites were all over the place.

Hunter had never stopped writing, but *Generation of Swine* was greeted as a comeback by fans. Hunter was a faithful letter writer (and, eventually, fax sender) all of his life. But the weekly deadline for the *Examiner* forced him into the long-promised second phase of his career, the post –Raoul Duke era he'd been promising since the introduction to *The Great Shark Hunt*. Journalism, in whatever form it took when it came out of Hunter Thompson, was seductive to him. As he wrote in the introduction to *Generation of Swine*,

> I have spent half my life trying to get away from journalism, but I am still mired in it—a low trade and a habit worse than heroin, a strange seedy world of misfits and drunkards and failures. A group photo of the top ten journalists in America on any given day would be a monument to human ugliness. It is not a trade that attracts a lot of slick people; none of the Calvin Klein crowd or international jet

set types. The sun will set in a blazing sky to the east of Casablanca before a journalist appears on the cover of People magazine.

Hunter had not really been in the political arena for more than a decade. Since the *Examiner* columns didn't circulate widely outside of San Francisco, his long-term fans were heartened, when the collection appeared, to see that he still had a sense of outrage about mean-spirited, royalist politics. "We think of him as a libertine outlaw, but he's actually a moralist," Carl Bernstein said of Hunter's political writing. After years of watching, he never lost the passion or the indignation provoked by the abuses of power, such as he saw in the Iran-Contra stories. "He suffered no falsehood," his friend Gerry Goldstein said.

Generation of Swine earned much better reviews than *The Curse of Lono*, and since his subject was mostly politics and popular culture, it was much more reader-friendly than his venture into island mysticism. Curtis Wilkie reviewed his friend's book for the *Boston Globe* and said Hunter's political writing "has regained the intensity of his work in *Rolling Stone* magazine nearly 20 years ago. . . . He is back in command of his career."

Maria left in 1988. No hard feelings, but she needed to get on with her life. She eventually graduated from the University of Arizona law school and became a well-known political figure in Arizona. McCumber went on to another job. Hunter kept writing for the *Examiner* but was bunkered down even more in his Woody Creek compound. "He became more of a hermit the last thirty years," Douglas Brinkley said. "He was one of the hottest writers in the country, then the comic strip [*Doonesbury*] came along, and that humiliated him. He would have been a different guy without that comic strip. He used to go out dining with friends, but when that comic came along, he retreated into a compound mentality." Unable to travel with the anonymity of a real journalist, he kept working from the kitchen in his home, now with a bank of televisions. In the sixties, he'd struggled along with one station, a CBS affiliate out of Grand Junction, the only thing he could pick up with his antenna. Now, thanks to satellite, he had all-news all-sports all the time at his home. He became more of a *reactor* than a reporter, sort of a high-tech mind-altered Walter Lippmann. Reporters gathered information and reported it; columnists read what the reporters wrote, sat back, thought about it for a couple of days, then told readers what it all meant.

The Ronald Reagan presidency had brought with it a banal *just-say-no-to-drugs* ethos and a scourge on any sexually oriented material. For Hunter, along with his crushing celebrity, his feeling that he did not fit in to his country anymore contributed to a sense of isolation at his Woody Creek home. People were cleaning up their acts, getting haircuts, flying off to the Betty Ford Center to dry out. Rehab was fashionable. As he wrote in 1989, "No once-wild 'party' in Hollywood or Aspen or even Greenwich Village is complete, these days, without the overweening presence of superwealthy, hard-hitting ex-addicts 'recovering alcoholics,' and beady-eyed fat women who never let you forget that they 'used to hang out' with doomed friends and dead monsters like Janis, Jim Morrison, The Stones, or John Belushi, or even me." Hunter mourned the fact that people had given up on fun (at least, his sort of fun) and that they had lost all interest in politics. Was there still room for Hunter Thompson? One of his new mottos, part of the collection of catch phrases he randomly threw into his work to please his fans, summarized his feelings: *Death to the Weird*.

With Sandy long gone and Laila on her way to becoming a film producer and now Maria hitting the *resume* button on her life, Hunter became even more dependent on the small support system that kept his life "humming along smartly" at Owl Farm.

Unlike other writers, who needed monklike solitude to work, Hunter preferred an audience. "He never liked to be alone," Braudis said. "He liked to be surrounded with people." Writing was performance for him, and if he wrote a choice morsel, he didn't tack it up on the bulletin board and read it through binoculars, as Gay Talese did. Hunter liked to *hear* it. He'd read it aloud. Sandy, then Laila, then Maria used to read it aloud. House guests often were handed manuscripts with their welcome handshakes and told to read. It was part of the Owl Farm initiation. If Hunter was on speaking terms with his muse, he could write on the median in the middle of rush-hour traffic or in a busy dentist's office during oral surgery. The rhythm of the world would become part of the rhythm in his writing. "He loved people to read his writing in progress," Braudis recalled. "He'd sit there and listen to it as if it was music. He'd say, *Faster . . . quieter . . . louder*. 'Slower' was his big thing."

Again, unlike a lot of writers, Hunter could not stand to be alone. He needed company; sometimes, he put companions on his payroll.

Hunter had met Deborah Fuller during the gut-twisting process of divorce. Deborah was an artist and was Sandy's friend. For a brief period the women had lived together, and Deborah's apartment was a safe haven for Sandy and Juan after the escape from Owl Farm. As the divorce negotiations raged, the judge urged Hunter and Sandy never to be alone with each other, and to bring a companion for face-to-face discussions. Hunter brought his artist friend, Tom Benton, and Sandy brought Deborah. "It was very disturbing for both of us," Deborah said. But Hunter grew fond of Deborah and never regarded her as an enemy.

While Hunter was with Laila, he had a superb companion and editorial assistant. When she left, and before he met Maria, he began working with Deborah. One night, Hunter asked Deborah to help him. "I hadn't been a personal secretary for anyone before," she said. "It was all a matter of chemistry for Hunter. One night he said, 'I'm on a deadline. I need some help.'"

Hunter loved having Deborah around and they had a brief relationship. When that ended, Deborah continued working with Hunter—often, and for long periods, without getting paid—and became the most important person in running his day-to-day life for twenty-three years. She saw Hunter as a serious writer, intent on every word, working tirelessly and all night while on deadline, cursing and fuming over the political idiocy du jour. She also saw him turn on the Duke personality when it was expected.

For the first several years that Deborah worked for Hunter she lived around Aspen, but by the end of the eighties, she moved into the smaller cabin at Owl Farm, across the drive from Hunter's place. It was the place where Billy and Anne Noonan had lived. For a while during the seventies, when Hunter was traveling a bit, writer Jay Cowan lived in the cabin, understudying Hunter and serving as caretaker for Owl Farm, looking out for Sandy and Juan. When Deborah moved into the cabin, she was able to live rent-free, but was also on call twenty-four hours a day. "It was a godsend on one hand and a curse on the other to be that many yards away," she said. "I was called on a lot in the middle of the night. We were best friends, and he liked to talk through a lot of things with me. I was there and he trusted me. He cursed me severely because I wouldn't always agree with him, but that's what good friends are for."

Hunter called Deborah his majordomo, and her job duties were difficult to specify. She did whatever it took to allow Hunter to be Hunter. When the kitchen became his command post, she made sure that he had everything he needed in reach of his perch. Reference books were to his right, under the window. She made sure the collected works of Hunter Thompson were within reach. Two phones by the typewriter. His newspapers, folded and ready. The TV was never turned off but the remote had to be handy. He was meticulous with files, but when Deborah began working for him, she took meticulous to a higher level. She organized all of his papers into fireproof cabinets and even cataloged his old clothes (Johnny Depp would eventually wear Hunter's quarter-century-old shirts when he played him on film.) She organized files boxes kept on the stove behind Hunter, and here Deborah kept folders of all of the works in progress—articles, columns, fragments. The organization was superb, but also important for Deborah's well-being. She needed rest occasionally and having everything that he needed at his side might keep Hunter from raging in the middle of the night. A common refrain: "Where the fuck is my folder?"

Beyond controlling the geography of the kitchen, Deborah also helped Hunter with the mental preparation to write. She helped protect him from all of the needy strangers and fans. Sometimes she found pilgrims at the Owl Farm gates. One wacked-out fan even made it to the front door, where she found him shivering after spending a night out in the cold. "There were weirdos who would eat acid and come hang on the fence," Deborah said. "I was the watchdog. I tried to treat people in a nice way, but people were so in awe of him. I'd say, 'He's not up. Would you like to leave him a note?' and that took care of most of it."

Although Deborah said Hunter was a procrastinator, she also knew that Hunter had certain rituals before writing—from his use of musical fuel (Dylan was a lifelong favorite), his dietary demands (big breakfasts, egg salads, fruit salads, grapefruit by the score), his need to scream at newspapers and television, his methodical nocturnal swimming, and his beloved conversations with friends. "He liked conversations and ballgames," she said. The friends he invited over to watch games with him would help him shape his ideas. He did not insist on being center stage. "He was an incredible storyteller and an incredible political analyst. A lot of people used to come to Hunter for advice. He preferred one-on-one. He also knew something about practically everything." Cowan, who also did time in Hunter's cabin-across-the-drive, was also impressed with the depth of Hunter's knowledge. "He was, if not the smartest man I ever knew, the smartest man I knew well," Cowan said.

Deborah had to do a lot of juggling as part of her job, and that some-times meant keeping the long hours. Sometimes Hunter would stay up for days. "If he was on a writing roll, he would stay up, because he was having fun," Deborah said. "He would also stay up when he was distraught or having problems with a woman. Every relationship was intense, and they were usually with younger women who were working with him. As he put it, 'I need someone young with the energy to stay up with me.'"

Deborah presided over Owl Farm and often that meant also taking care of his young assistants/girlfriends. The assistants helped Hunter with whatever project was in the works, and Deborah did everything else. "I took care of running the house, running all of the finances," she said. "He was very private. Nobody else paid the bills. He didn't want anyone looking at what his life was. I took care of all of the workers and the clean-ing people and preparing his breakfast and preparing food and setting up all the interviews."

If there was no coherent job description for Deborah Fuller, Semmes Luckett's role was also difficult to nail down. The scion of a prominent Mississippi family, Semmes had come to Aspen in the seventies after dropping out of law school. Semmes was Hunter's man Friday. He was always around for pleasure or for work. He stayed on the Thompson payroll to run errands, driving Hunter where he needed to be, picking up liquor or groceries when Hunter didn't have time. Semmes was a great companion, always there and unimpressed by celebrity. He was an extraordinary old-fashioned southern storyteller and he and Hunter pro-vided mutual amusement.

Because the assistants and girlfriends were a revolving door, Deborah and Semmes provided Hunter's continuity in life.

Hunter was tethered as if by an umbilical cord to Owl Farm (he called it his "psychic anchor"). In 1989, Hunter entered into a range war with neighbor Floyd Watkins, and he used the bully pulpit of his *Examiner* column to make his case for Watkins as the Antichrist. Painting the battle as a Kentucky-mountain Hatfield-and-McCoy feud, Hunter lashed out at the multimillionaire who made his money running collection agencies before retiring to Woody Creek at forty-two. Watkins began building an estate, but nothing like the funky mountain scrub farms his neighbors had. He poured concrete for a sweeping driveway and dammed the creek to construct trout ponds, all part of his master plan to build a fish camp. Hunter referred to Watkins's estate as "a hideous eyesore that only a madman or a werewolf would live in." Not long after work started on the Watkins development, the threats began: late-night phone calls, graffiti on his boundary fence ("Fat Floyd's Fish Farm") and occasional gunfire. Watkins figured Hunter was the culprit, but he didn't have the evidence. It was the Louisville mailbox all over again, and Hunter asked the question he had asked when he was nine: *What witnesses?*

Watkins called the Pitkin County Sheriff's Department, but when no action was taken against Hunter, Watkins lashed out at Braudis, charging him with taking sides against him. Braudis, who described his relationship with Hunter as brotherly, was stung by the criticism.

The war escalated. Watkins claimed it was Hunter who fired automatic weapons through his property at four in the morning and who poured a chemical in his ponds that killed $40,000 worth of stocked trout. Hunter barely avoided felony charges for firing the weapons, but continued his battle.

It wasn't just about concrete and trout. Hunter saw the feud with Watkins as part of the ongoing struggle to salvage what was left of the American Dream of authenticity and originality. Hunter confronted Watkins at a public forum held at the Woody Creek Tavern. "No one is oppressing you," Hunter told Watkins. "We all live in this valley; this is a one-road community. We don't want to see the life of this valley poisoned—that is as bad as poisoning fish." Hunter did not have the energy he once had for conflict. "The greedheads work eight days a week," he wrote. "The trouble is that the greedheads, the real estate developers and the people who want to buy and sell quick and move on work harder than I do. I'm a writer. I'm a lazy person."

The reaction to Hunter's war on Floyd Watkins was a sign of changing times. Hunter faced the possibility that he might be forced to change his ways. "I've told Hunter he can't be out shooting on the road as he used to," Braudis said. "His neighbors are complaining more and more about his peacocks screeching and the gunshots in the night. What is happening now is that the billionaires are pushing out the millionaires. The truth is that Woody Creek has become urbanized in the last twenty years."

The dispute simmered through that fall, and Hunter tried to arouse public sympathy in his favor with his *Examiner* column, but the San Francisco paper wasn't widely circulated in Woody Creek.

Some of the locals began to think that maybe Hunter was getting out of control.

Hunter had a new girlfriend. Terry Sabonis-Chafee was an associate at the Aspen Institute and working on a graduate degree at Princeton. When Hunter mentioned that he needed an assistant, Terry didn't take the job, but suggested that Hunter hire her younger sister, Catherine, then a journalism student at the University of Florida. To Hunter, it seemed like the perfect match. Catherine could even earn internship credit while working for him.

Cat, as she was known, was home with her family in Connecticut for the 1989 Christmas holidays when Hunter called to talk to Terry, then asked Cat to get on the phone. "I'm going to send you plane tickets," he said. "Get out here and see if you can handle it." She went for a long weekend during the holiday break and met Deborah Fuller, in whose cabin she would stay, and Semmes Luckett and David McCumber, who'd flown in for the weekend to work with Hunter. As Cat saw it, Deborah and Semmes were there because they "were sort of the people that could kind of keep him in line and do his bidding, but also that he could be fueling himself with. And he could bully them or not bully them, and they were not going to go anywhere. They would still come back. He needs a lot of handling. It takes a lot to maintain Hunter, and so everybody sort of had a role towards that end."

Jim Silberman was still snorting for a promised manuscript. McCumber was there as a coach. Hunter sat at his perch in his command post/ kitchen and bickered with McCumber. Cat was lying down on the couch, on the other side of the kitchen counter, and for three sleepless days took notes on the negotiations. Hunter wanted to cobble something together out of his archive, the mammoth files in the basement, and fulfill his obligation to Silberman. McCumber wanted Hunter to try harder. It worried him to see Hunter not care.

Three days of no sleep and taking notes. "There was a lot of yelling back and forth," Cat recalled. "I started nodding off. It had been forty hours with no sleep. Hunter started getting angry that I was nodding off and he bashed his typewriter, and it came over the counter at me. I was cocky, so I didn't move and didn't react, and he laughed and said, 'I don't really have a choice, do I? You're hired.'"

The long weekend was a preview of coming attractions. McCumber was being paid by Hunter, not Silberman, and his primary purpose in the spring of 1990 was to motivate Hunter to produce another book. In February 1990, after writing about being run down by a tractor toting a bush-hog, Hunter stopped writing the column. He was tired of the weekly deadline, and without that pressure he stalled.

"McCumber would beg and plead," Cat said, "and Hunter just turned into a child and became indolent and refused to do a thing." McCumber came for the weekend (taking time away from his day job as editor of the Santa Barbara *News-Press* in California), and sometimes he and Hunter didn't even talk to each other. Finally, McCumber returned to California. Cat stayed at Deborah's cabin and was there, talking to McCumber on the phone, when Hunter walked over to see what was going on. When she said she was giving McCumber a "progress report" on what Hunter had been doing since his last visit, Hunter flew into a rage. "I don't want to be sensational, although living with Hunter was always sensational," Cat said. "He went back to the house and came back with an ax and hacked through the power lines at Deborah's house."

Other college interns probably didn't see their employers approaching them with an ax. Figuring it was a little out of the ordinary, Cat and Deborah packed up quickly and went to stay with one of Deborah's friends in Aspen. Eventually, Hunter coaxed both of them back to work. He never explicitly apologized but said, "I was making high drama out of nothing. Come back and let's get some real work done." They did. That they would return a week after he approached them with an ax spoke well for his charisma.

Hunter and McCumber struggled over what his book was to be. Even now, Hunter wanted to write fiction. Occasionally, Hunter thought of dusting off *The Rum Diary* or *Prince Jellyfish*. There were scattered short stories he'd written in the Big Sur era. He had a fan base now, and most anything with his name on it would sell to the loyal legions.

His following was such that publishers were beginning to think someone might want a book *about* Hunter Thompson. When a publisher approached me in 1989 to do such a book, I wrote to tell Hunter what I was up to. He was game to cooperate, on the condition that it wouldn't mean more work for him. He got my phone number, and we exchanged messages and faxes throughout the spring of 1990, as I peppered him with questions about his life and career. There really wasn't an accurate chronology of his life available, so a lot of my questions were of the *what-did-you-do-then* variety. Turns out those questions helped him get started. "I used your questions to develop a timeline and framework," Cat said. "The book was a combination of questions you asked as a framework, mixed with his original pieces." With McCumber's help poring through the archives, Hunter began to construct the first of his autobiographical collages. It would be a fairly easy book to assemble, since he could use manuscripts he'd been storing in the basement for twenty or thirty years.

But it threatened to add to his literary-identity problem. By now, he was fully a prisoner of his persona. The character he created had taken over, and he couldn't lay it all at the feet of Garry Trudeau. In fact, his attorney and friend Gerry Goldstein said he got to the point where he began to appreciate Uncle Duke. "To some extent he was flattered by Trudeau," Goldstein said. "He once told me, 'He hasn't said anything about me in a week—let's sue the bastard.'" Suing Trudeau for defamation would be fruitless, Goldstein told Hunter. "Besides, how could you defame Hunter?"

Fans knew the outlines of his life, so Hunter thought it would be easy—for the purpose of his pending book—to revisit scenes of his former triumphs. He could dust off some things that were unpublished, and he could connect the dots by pulling a few things out of a southerly orifice. The autobiographical collage became a working model for several of his books that followed, making it official: Hunter was repeating himself. "Gonzo," he once sighed to a reporter. "I wish I'd never heard the word."

Always pressed for a definition of his style, he came up with this one in the last year of his life: "What it's all about, really, is what you can get away with. If you're a writer, that means writing about what you want to write about."

It was easy for him to slip into that character and play the Gonzo role. "He would retreat into it," Cat said. "He was always at his best when he wasn't doing that. The constant nonwriting that went around him—I think it was kind of helpful as a way of being able to pull him off track and organically remind him of places he had been. If you could catch him as being his most himself, if you could capture that, he could return to it and produce good stuff out of it. But he fell away from that and got caught up on what he was supposed to be and what he was expected to say."

He needed to be pressed, and it was difficult for Deborah or Cat or even McCumber to do that. He would walk over them. "One thing about Hunter," Cat said, "is that he had a different persona for different people. He was at his most lovely, most lucid, most brilliant, with the people for whom he had the most professional respect, like Tom Corcoran, David Halberstam, Ed Bradley, and many others. When he was really spinning out of control on us, we would hope against hope that someone for whom he had to prove himself would call or come by."

McCumber helped Hunter go through the archives, finding clean copies of Hunter's early stories and putting them together in chronological order. After the initial growling and snarling, Hunter and McCumber quickly began assembling the book that became *Songs of the Doomed*. "That was so much fun, that project," McCumber said. "Just the idea of pulling work together from five decades and figuring out how to make it hang together as a book—that was a pleasure."

Once he seized on the approach to the book and learned that it would satisfy Jim Silberman, Hunter couldn't stop working. McCumber remembered Hunter working nine days without sleep. "We were in the war room, finding manuscripts, when we found the original of *The Rum Diary*," McCumber recalled. "It was an *honor* to be entrusted to the history of his writing."

Cat was charged with helping Hunter create the new material for the book, most of which would tie together the disparate excerpts from long-lost works. "A lot of it was dictated," she said. "A lot of that older stuff in the book—it was the first time he'd looked at it since he'd written it. He handed me *The Rum Diary* and said, 'Mark everything in it that you think can stand alone.' So I sat there with Post-It's, marking sections to be pulled out. He hadn't read the book in years."

Since the book was taking the form of tiptoeing through his history as a writer, Hunter also saw it as an opportunity to retire that other debt to Silberman: the ill-fated American Dream book from the sixties. For a time, "American Dream" was the working title of *Songs of the Doomed*, but eventually he bade farewell to the project with *Doomed*'s subtitle, *More Notes on the Death of the American Dream*.

Hunter pushed himself and those around him. "Weeks would go by on this reverse sleep schedule where he would stay up for days and then sleep for anywhere from twenty to twenty-six hours, and then he would stay up for another two or three nights," Cat remembered. "And he would expect you to be on the same schedule. Of course, it was substance supported. At some point coffee ain't going to cut it, and I never would have considered doing any kind of drugs for recreation under any circumstances. But I had to do it in order to keep up. It didn't have any recreational quality to it."

Unfortunately, just as Hunter was making great progress on the book, he suffered a setback: a ninety-nine-day disruption.

Gail Palmer became famous as an actress and director in pornographic films. Her path never crossed Hunter's during his days as a regular at the O'Farrell. When Hunter was spending his term as night manager, she was marrying a wealthy physician in Michigan and settling down to a more normal life. She wanted to be a writer but didn't know any other writers. When her husband scheduled a ski trip to Aspen, she saw her chance to meet the writer she most admired.

She began peppering Hunter with letters and announced she would visit. Deborah penciled the promised date of Palmer's arrival on Hunter's kitchen calendar. The day arrived, and Hunter was wrapped up in watching college basketball on TV with Semmes and a friend named Tim, and with Cat also in the mix. Hunter had read Palmer's letter and seen her visit only as an impending annoyance. She wanted to talk to him about her days in the sex business and how Hunter didn't understand feminist pornography. Hunter could not give a rat's ass what Gail Palmer thought.

But she was in town, and there was a vague understanding that they would meet. To him, she was just another person who wanted to come by and kiss the Gonzo ring. It happened that Semmes was agitated about the sorry state of the women in Aspen, so Hunter thought he came up with the solution to kill a couple of birds: he would invite Palmer to his house and therefore meet this perceived social obligation (he was a gentleman, and did not want to be rude) and also find a suitable dancing and drinking partner for sad-sack Semmes. When Palmer called, Hunter had him handle the negotiations. Since she claimed she wanted to interview Hunter, Semmes was able to finesse things and get Palmer's husband to stay back at their condo. She would come alone by taxi.

When she arrived, Hunter was immediately repulsed by her loud and abrasive manner. She had to be the center of attention, and Hunter knew that there could only be one of those at a time. And all Hunter cared about that evening was the Georgetown game. "I wanted to clear the house and unwind for a night," he said. Semmes and Tim had been lobbying to watch the Grammys, since Jimmy Buffett was scheduled to perform. "I didn't want to watch the fucking Grammys," Hunter said. Cat didn't care.

But now there was an irritant in the room, and she refused to shut up. "Be quiet," Hunter told her repeatedly. She didn't respond. He told Semmes, "She has to be quiet here." Still her shrill voice disrupted Hunter's peace. Semmes and Tim had won the battle of the television and were watching the awards show, waiting for Buffett. Palmer continued to babble, asking Hunter about his sex life. "All right," he said. "Here's a story I just wrote."

He handed Palmer the manuscript for "Screwjack," a story from deep in the groin, filled with carnivorous lust. After a few pages, she put it down and told Hunter he was a pervert. He forced her to keep reading, but the brutality of the story wounded her and had its intended effect: she quieted.

Hunter was disturbed that she kept leaving the room to call her husband. He thought she might be a cop or had some police connection, but Gentleman Hunter continued to play host. After he ran out of margarita mix, he made blenders full of a cranberry juice and tequila concoction. They were well into the fourth pitcher when the trouble began. She had become that thing that Hunter most hated: the sloppy drunk.

Palmer began to pester Cat. "Who are you to Hunter?" she asked. She told Cat to leave, that she was in the way. Tim left, and although Hunter begged him to take Palmer, he refused. His wife would not understand, he said. Semmes also left, without his presumed dance partner. But Palmer stayed.

Hunter tried to call her a cab from the kitchen phone, but she pulled it from his hand. He tried again and actually reached the cab company, but she grabbed the phone again before Hunter could give the address. And then a third time. Finally, she came at him in the kitchen, and he shoved her back, screaming, "Get the fuck away!" She hit her hip on the kitchen counter. He was especially angry that she was in his sanctuary, his kitchen, where he sat at his perch and pounded away at his IBM Selectric and orchestrated his house full of guests. *How dare she?*

Palmer was furious that he had shoved her and so came at him again, and again he shoved her, hitting her on her shoulders with the palms of his hands. She was propelled back and fell to the floor. She pulled herself up and sat against the refrigerator. The duel was over.

"I want you out of here," Hunter said. To Hunter, she was "one more groupie who was unusually determined." Later, he was able to summarize what about her had enraged him so much. "She had a hideous penchant for coming in my area, hassling me, and she was very stupid," he said.

She went to the porch and waited for a cab. Fifteen minutes later, she was gone.

It was over, or so Hunter believed. But later in the week, he was in his kitchen when a neighbor appeared at his window, croaking warnings. "They're going to come search your house," the neighbor said. "They're gonna come get you with a search warrant."

In a preemptive strike, Hunter and his support system of Deborah, Cat, Semmes, and David McCumber (making another pep-talk visit) sprang into action, trying to rid the house of anything incriminating. "It was daunting to clean the place," McCumber said. "We missed some things, as the world knows now. We missed some pot that Hunter thinks fell behind the fridge sometime in the seventies. But it was a heroic effort."

Palmer's husband was furious when his wife returned from Hunter's in the wee hours, with tales of shoving and screaming and obvious drug use. She claimed Hunter had roughly twisted her left breast and nearly forced her into his hot tub. Palmer may have fertilized her tale a bit, but her husband went to the sheriff's office to file a complaint. Since Braudis had been criticized for his handling of Hunter's dispute with Floyd Watkins, he turned the case over to the district attorney's office to avoid any further conflict-of-interest claims. On February 26, five days after Gail Palmer's visit, six investigators conducted an eleven-hour search of Hunter's home, finding small quantities of substances suspected of being cocaine and marijuana. Pending lab tests, the DA's office didn't file drug charges, but did charge Hunter with sexually assaulting Palmer. He posted $2,500 bail and was free to go home and fume.

To Hunter, this was the long-overdue punishment from the conservative faction in Pitkin County. He called it a "lifestyle bust," and though he was furious, he still had a sense of humor about it. When told that the search of his home didn't reveal much evidence of drugs or wrong-doing, Hunter smiled. "I don't know if that helps my reputation or hurts it," he told reporters.

For ninety-nine days, Hunter was unsure whether he would face jail time. If convicted of all charges, he could be sentenced to sixteen years in prison. On the advice of his attorney, he surrendered to authorities, allowing himself to be arrested and released. He later came to believe it was a bonehead move. Before filing the sexual-assault charges, the DA's office hadn't even bothered to interview the other people on the premises.

After having a few days to think about it, Palmer and her husband urged the DA to drop the charges. The district attorney decided to pursue the case anyway. At a hearing in April, Hunter was hit with five felony charges. At that point, he began to turn the tables. This wasn't about an alleged sexual assault or a few seeds and stems left in the carpeting, he said. "This is a political trial," Hunter declared. "I am a writer, a professional journalist with serious credentials in Crime, Craziness, and Politics. . . . I am looking forward to going to court."

Hunter embraced martyrdom and actively solicited monies for defense funds. In England, his friend Ralph Steadman was sympathetic and even managed to persuade the *Guardian* to do a feature on Hunter's troubles. Ralph created a drawing and sold prints to help raise money for Hunter. He advertised the defense fund in *Punch*, but still it wasn't enough for Hunter, who berated his friend, "Do you think this is funny? Just another Gonzo joke? No, Ralph—this is deadly serious. They want to put me in prison." Ralph felt his friendship tested and wrote back, offering an accounting of the five thousand pounds he had amassed on Hunter's behalf. "Please don't bitch at me," he wrote. "I am a REAL friend of Hunter S. Thompson. Maybe you just need RICH friends." Though he had worked hard to help Hunter, Ralph was embittered by the experience. "Our long twisted friendship faltered," he recalled. "Not one word of thanks. That was never his style."

Even as the case against him crumbled, Hunter grew more combative. "This is a *Fourth Amendment* case," he wrote attorney Hal Haddon. "It is not about sex or drugs or violence. It is about police power." The more the district attorney tried to skulk away from the case, the more apocalyptic Hunter became. His friends George Stranahan and Michael Solheim bought a full-page newspaper ad that said, "Today: the Doctor; Tomorrow: *You.*" (The text was by Thompson.) A carload of sex performers from the O'Farrell road-tripped from San Francisco to sashay around the Pitkin County Courthouse in bikinis, carrying signs of support.

The case of *The People of the State of Colorado vs. Hunter S. Thomp-*

son was dismissed on May 30, 1990. The judge granted the request by Hunter's attorneys to throw out the case, because of prosecutorial incompetence. The case should never have been brought, the judge said.

Outside on the courthouse steps, an exultant Hunter met the press. He was proud that he had stood up and changed the focus of the trial to Fourth Amendment issues. "We've grown accustomed to letting anyone with a badge walk over us," Hunter said. "We are all, in all of our houses, a little safer than we were yesterday."

The ugly incident provided *Songs of the Doomed* with its coda. Hunter was still tinkering with the manuscript, and Silberman was lathering for it. Eventually, during a rare Hunter nap, Cat took the manuscript down to Aspen and sent it off by Federal Express. Hunter was incensed, but a day later, when Silberman called and said he was sending a check, Hunter poured champagne for Cat, Semmes, and Deborah. Another deadline nightmare had ended. A few months later, he added a final author's note: "I have changed constantly all my life, usually at top speed, and it has always been with the total, permanent finality of a thing fed into an atom smasher. My soul and my body chemistry are like that of a chameleon, a lizard with no pulse."

The book was an assemblage of five decades of his life, interspersing fragments of his early writing with his dictated-to-Cat reminiscences. For the 1950s section, he pulled three chapters from *Prince Jellyfish,* sandwiched them between stories of Jersey Shore, Pennsylvania, and his early days in New York. He used a portion of *The Rum Diary* in his sixties section, along with dictated reminiscences of Ken Kesey, the Hell's Angels, and the 1968 Chicago Democratic convention.

He included excerpts from his best work in the seventies section, including the "high-water mark" passage from *Fear and Loathing in Las Vegas* that he considered some of his best writing. He used a shortened version of "Dance of the Doomed," and threw in a memo to Jim Silberman about the ill-fated *Death of the American Dream* book. In the eighties section, he used letters, some *Examiner* columns that hadn't made it into *Generation of Swine,* and his coverage of the Pulitzer divorce trial. He also used two chapters and an outline from *The Silk Road,* his story of lowlifes in the Florida Keys during the time of the Mariel boatlift, but his distance from that event is reflected in the text. He was not part of it, only a peripheral witness, and one constant in all of his writing was his need to be in the center of the maelstrom.

The last section of the book, called "Welcome to the Nineties," began with one of the false editor's notes he'd been using since his days at Eglin Air Force Base. Writing in the guise of his publisher, he explained,

> Publishing Dr. Thompson has never been an easy job, but this recent episode was over the line and sent demoralizing shock waves through the whole organization, which for many years has stood behind him like a tall and solid rock. We lived in his shadow and endured his terrible excesses—clinging always to the promise that he would sooner or later make sense of his original assignment: *The Death of the American Dream.* . . .
>
> So it was with a sense of shock, fear, and betrayal that we received the news that he was about to go to prison for a sudden, unexplainable outburst of cheap crimes, misdemeanors, and stupid felony loss leaders that made no sense at all. And it made people *angry*.
>
> Tom Wolfe, after all, had never disgraced his publisher. . . .

Hunter dedicated the book to David McCumber ("the doctor of deadlines") and to Catherine Sabonis-Chafee, "My Top Gun, who did most of the work and endured more real fear and loathing in ninety-nine days than most people see in a lifetime and laughed like a warrior in the constant shadow of doom, jail, and pure craziness . . . well, well, well. . . . The infamous 'woman called Cat' turned out to have solid gold balls."

Cat's internship was finished. Hunter wanted her to stay, to help on his next book. That was his usual reaction when he worked well with someone. "I just couldn't even consider it, because there was a difference between doing what you have to do to kind of get through something, and *choosing* it knowing what it is, and like knowing all of it," she said. She'd had enough, and her boyfriend's family was building a home in the Bahamas. She needed escape from working and living with Hunter.

"For a couple of years, I was fairly traumatized by it," she said. "It can take years and years to get to a point of any kind of reconciliation with him, because he could be a very abusive person, and yet he also had this incredible sense of people. Within minutes of being around somebody, he could bore right into their essence.

"I was just doing it and I liked doing it, and I never really considered leaving. I was just there, in some ranch somewhere in Colorado and very isolated. When I think about it, it's pretty frightening. I never regretted going, but once I knew what it was, there was no way I was putting myself in that situation again. There was no sum of money that would have made it worthwhile."

Cat had kept a journal, part of her internship requirements. Most of the jottings were notes from conversations, some doodles, and general things-to-do lists. "He stole it from me as I was leaving," she said. "He said I had no right to it and that he didn't trust my 'loyalty' enough for me to have it. A couple of times, in the years after, he sent me photocopies of single pages, just to remind me that it still existed."

Sitting on a Bahamian beach that summer, she didn't look back on the six months with Hunter as a nightmare. "I was fascinated by the chance to watch somebody this brilliant and to be able to watch him, to be right there all the time. That made it kind of worth it."

Cat was decompressing, relaxing in a still-under-construction beach house with her boyfriend, when the phone rang. Someone was trying reach Hunter.

"He had forwarded his calls," she said. "I was answering the phone for him in the Bahamas."

Chapter 17

HOMECOMING

I think it was Oscar Wilde that said you destroy the thing
that you love. It's the other way around—
what you love destroys you.
—*George Plimpton, 1996*

Cheryl Frymire came from a family farm in Pennsylvania, not far from Jersey Shore, where Hunter had spent a miserable month as a reporter in 1957. She grew up in a close-knit family, but decided to search for adventure in Aspen, where she worked in a travel agency and then in a four-star restaurant, waiting on Kennedys and movie stars. But she wanted something less snooty and switched jobs, landing at Hunter's favorite restaurant, the Woody Creek Tavern, in 1986. She wore a prairie skirt and a high-necked sweater her first day, and Hunter, who ate at the tavern most days, was immediately suspicious, thinking she might be an undercover narcotics agent. For her part, she didn't have a clue who he was. He was just that weird guy who sat at the table in the corner, underneath the mounted buffalo head.

"When they introduced me to him, I thought he had gotten struck by lightning because of the way he talked," she said.

The Woody Creek Tavern was a small restaurant and post office in a trailer park, made from logs and with a Coca-Cola sign on the roof. Inside, the walls were festooned with pictures, bumper stickers, newspaper clippings, and funky local art. The tavern served salads, burgers, ribs, chicken, Mexican food, and other typical bar fare.

"He'd come in every day after getting his mail at the post office next door," Frymire recalled, "and sort through his mail at his table in the corner, under the buffalo. People told me he was a little bit difficult, and sometimes he would just want to be alone, and sometimes you just had to learn to be able to cope with the mood swings. You could tell if he was in a good mood and if he wanted to chat."

Though Frymire's conservative churchgoing ways didn't seem to gibe with Hunter's up-against-the-wall rebellion, they became friends. "He had a pretty tender spot for me, and I for him," she said. "I had to earn his respect."

Over their twenty years of friendship, Hunter frequently hosted Frymire at Owl Farm and asked her to sit with him at the restaurant while he went through his mail. "Look here, Cheryl," he'd say, looking over a page in a lingerie catalog. "Let me buy you a few things." The other servers shied away from him because of his elaborate, complex orders and his constant demand for a variety of condiments.

Even his appetites were theatrical. "He would come in and get a tall whiskey and a malted beer. He liked drinking these shots that we made with Bailey's Irish Cream and Jameson's Whiskey called a 'Biff.' He would want an extra spicy bloody mary, and in the summer he wanted gin and lemonade too and wanted all these things on the table at the same time."

He never told Frymire about his miserable experience in Jersey Shore, but he often asked about her life back on the farm and her father. Though they never met, they passed greetings through Cheryl. "How's the doctor?" her father asked on the phone. Hunter responded by sending off autographed books to Pennsylvania. "Cheryl's father is Amish," he'd say, if there was an audience in the tavern. He wasn't, but it was Hunter's little joke.

"He knew that I had a conservative side to me, and he appreciated that," she said. "He honored the fact that I was a Christian." Now and then, he asked her to read the Bible to him, especially passages from the Book of Revelation. "I have stolen more quotes and thoughts and purely elegant little starbursts of writing from the Book of Revelation than anything else in the English language," Hunter wrote. "I love the wild power of the language and the purity of the madness that governs it and makes it music."

Frymire was pianist at the First Baptist Church in Aspen and performed hymns during services.

"I want to hear you sing," Hunter told her. "What would they do if I came?"

"They'd probably ask you to leave because you'd be smoking," she told him.

She also was afraid some of the holier-than-thous would shun him. One parishioner had told her, "How can you tolerate him? He is despicable." Frymire responded, "He is a human being who needs love, and I love him."

Hunter realized he would create too much commotion if he showed up at church, so Frymire recorded herself singing her original songs as well as some classic hymns, including "Amazing Grace." He snapped the cassettes into his Walkman and listened when he was alone. Frymire believed that Hunter was spiritual but masked it.

"I secretly worship God," Hunter wrote near the end of his life. "He had the good judgment to leave me alone to write a few genuine black-on-white pages by myself."

Hunter made a lot of promises about work. On the *Songs of the Doomed* dust jacket, he said his next book would be *99 Days: The Trial of Hunter S. Thompson,* but after devoting the last section of *Songs of the Doomed* to the trial, there wasn't a lot left to say.

He also said that his next major work would be his "long-awaited sex book." With his usual sense of approaching apocalypse, he announced, "I am now working on my final statement—*Polo Is My Life,* which is a finely muted saga of sex, treachery, and violence in the nineties, which also solves the murder of John F. Kennedy." It was eventually scheduled for publication, but delayed . . . and delayed.

There were the other lost books along the way, from *Prince Jellyfish* and *The Rum Diary* up through *Guts Ball, The Silk Road,* and *The Night Manager.* Only the fragments in *Songs of the Doomed* were published in his lifetime.

He did publish *Screwjack* in 1991, a limited edition of three hundred numbered copies signed by Hunter, produced by a Santa Barbara publisher. The book, which sold for $300, collected three short pieces in an exceedingly slim volume. Many members of Hunter's longtime fan base whined that the cost put the book well out of reach and was an attempt to appeal to the "rich friends" Ralph Steadman had warned about, the movie stars who had begun to cuddle up to Hunter as their eccentric mascot.

But perhaps Hunter thought two of the stories were too brutal for mass consumption. "Mescalito" was simply a memoir of his first experience taking mescaline, when he was holed up in the Continental Hyatt House in Hollywood on assignment for *Pageant*. (It had already appeared in *Songs of the Doomed*.) "Death of a Poet" began as something comic wrapped around two of Hunter's obsessions, betting on pro football games and inflatable dolls. It ended in ghastly tragedy as the central character, F. X. Leach (another favorite pseudonym of Hunter's) committed suicide by sucking the metallic popsicle. The title story was odd and disturbing, with an undercurrent of bestiality. Though it marked a bold step outside of the usual Hunter S. Thompson fare, he kept it tethered to his persona by assigning the works (in his introduction) to Raoul Duke, signaling that the real Uncle Duke was back and that it would not be pretty. He still smarted over William F. Buckley's review of *The Great Shark Hunt*, in which he had postulated that Hunter had no interest in sex. In part, *Screwjack* was written to refute that notion. Once, after listening to it read aloud in his kitchen, Hunter chortled at the conclusion of the story, "Let's see what Bill Buckley thinks about *that*."

Screwjack was obviously not intended for a mass audience. The stories were meant to provoke and didn't enhance Hunter's nearly nonexistent reputation as a writer of fiction. When it came time for real money, Hunter turned to his meal ticket. Though he'd written sporadically for Jann Wenner in the last several years, he felt indebted to him. Wenner had assigned reporter Mike Sager to write about his 1990 trial, producing two major pieces for the magazine and drawing solicitations for Hunter's defense fund. He could not allow this great favor to go unrewarded.

In early 1992, Hunter published "Fear and Loathing in Elko" in *Rolling Stone*, but the story had nothing to do with the political conference. Instead, it was a long fantasy in which Hunter recalled wild nights in Endicott's Motel with the controversial Supreme Court nominee Clarence Thomas. Thomas's confirmation hearings dragged through the fall of 1991 with a long inquiry into Anita Hill's charges that he sexually harassed her and tried to get her to watch pornographic films. It was a story made for Hunter's brand of political commentary, but he chose to present it as a tall tale. When Raoul Duke (resurrected as narrator of the story) comes across Thomas in a horrific automobile accident, the judge is in the company of two prostitutes. Eventually, Hunter and the judge ended up with F. X. Leach, the doomed figure from "Death of a Poet," but in this mutation of the story, Leach did not commit suicide.

The Elko piece was Hunter's longest work for *Rolling Stone* in years and one of his most sustained attempts at fiction. A sentimental tone crept into the article and hinted he was in the mood for a full reconciliation with Wenner (he'd addressed the piece to him as a letter). It lacked the astonishing wordplay of Hunter's earlier work and had a feeling of having been phoned in. Though he did not want to return to *Rolling Stone* full-time, Hunter did make himself available and, as a presidential election year neared, knew what the editor would ask.

Hunter was a political junkie, but had avoided becoming the new Theodore H. White. "I would have been locked into national politics as a way of life," Hunter said. "There's no way you can play that kind of Washington Wizard role from a base in Woody Creek. I'd have had to move to Washington, or at least to New York . . . and, Jesus, life is too short for that kind of volunteer agony." Hunter could shoot guns and blow up appliances and stalk his property naked in Woody Creek. Those activities were generally frowned upon in New York or D.C.

American politics had changed since Hunter's 1972 campaign coverage. The primaries that Hunter and Timothy Crouse had covered so doggedly were much less important by 1992. The political conventions, which had real excitement in the sixties, were reduced to overproduced coronations by 1992. After a brief frenzy of campaigning in the late winter, former Arkansas governor Bill Clinton was set to be the Democratic nominee, facing incumbent President George Bush, who had gone from grandpa-like popularity in the aftermath of 1991's Gulf War to flat-lining by the next year. A chimp could have beaten Bush in the 1992 election, and there *was* a chimp in the race: eccentric Texas billionaire Ross Perot. The major question of the 1992 presidential campaign was how and to what extent Perot's third-party bid would gum up the works.

The most participation that Wenner arranged for his star reporter's contribution to campaign coverage was a July 31 group interview with Clinton, clearly on the verge of becoming the nation's first rock 'n' roll president. The editor secured the back room at Doe's Eat Place in Little Rock, and

Wenner brought Hunter together with other *Rolling Stone* heavyweights. William Greider, one of 1972's "boys on the bus" had become *Rolling Stone*'s political editor, who crafted thoughtful essays that probably shot over the head of much of the readership. Also at the table was the *Rolling Stone* contributor who had been filling the cultural-commentary void left by Hunter: P. J. O'Rourke, a conservative satirist who'd become famous while writing for the *National Lampoon*. His vicious pieces in the eighties mocked the image of the ugly American so grim thirty years before and provided a refined version of Gonzo for the Reagan years. Hunter never let politics stand in the way of friendship, and though some longtime *Rolling Stone* writers bitched about O'Rourke's conservatism, but Hunter often said that O'Rourke, Tom Wolfe, and Maureen Dowd of the *New York Times* were the best writers in American journalism. At one point, Hunter packed up a pair of his sunglasses and sent them to Dowd, with a note that said, "You wear these—I'm no longer the star."

At Doe's, Hunter was the first to sit, and so he chose a chair at what he figured was the far end of the table, expecting Clinton to sit at the other end. "But no," Hunter said. "The creepy bastard quickly sat down right next to me, about two feet away, and fixed me with a sleepy-looking stare that made me very uneasy. His eyes had narrowed to slits, and at first I thought he was dozing off."

Greider was the serious, hard-nosed political journalist in the room, and he carried the weight of the interview. Wenner wanted his magazine to back a winner, and he fawned over the candidate. O'Rourke, as a Republican, was there for comic relief, and Hunter was a largely mute presence. He was not enamored of Clinton, because of the candidate's cop-out response when asked about his marijuana use in the sixties. Instead of answering "of course," as any honest member of his generation would have, Clinton said, "I didn't inhale," then further embarrassed himself by blaming asthma for his inability to enjoy dope. Dishonesty infuriated Hunter. Hunter also was wary because he still felt the burn from the 1976 Carter "endorsement" cover line Wenner had slapped on his article, and he could tell Wenner was giddy over Clinton.

As they sat around the table, Hunter picked up a strange, distant attitude from Clinton. Clinton clearly wanted nothing to do with Hunter. "He treated me like a roach from the get-go," Hunter said later.

"He is utterly unswervingly sincere and genuine," Greider said of Hunter. "He went down there [to Arkansas] believing that we were making the transaction to deliver the *Rolling Stone* vote to Bill Clinton in exchange for certain things. He was crushed when Clinton dissed him, as he did, quite deliberately. Clinton had come prepared to make it very clear that he was not with Hunter Thompson on drugs and police. Hunter knew that and was really hurt."

Clinton was the cover boy of *Rolling Stone's* special college issue in September 1992, and, like a mini-*Rashoman*, Greider, O'Rourke, and Hunter all gave their versions of dining at Doe's with Clinton. Wenner published a full-page appeal to readers, urging them to vote for the first presidential candidate of their generation now that the "rare possibility of real change has arrived." Greider's piece was the serious political analysis, O'Rourke was the lovable opposition, and Hunter was world-weary and ever wary, punctuating a number of sentences with "bubba," a nod to the good-old-boyness of the candidate.

Hunter was not a fan of the Democratic candidate. "He thought Bill Clinton was a whore-hopper," Douglas Brinkley said. A man serious about his presidential candidacy should behave better. But despite these reservations about Clinton, Hunter did not refrain from announcing that he intended to vote for him:

> Let's face it, Bubba. The main reason I'll vote for Clinton is George Bush, and it has been that way from the start. . . . There is no way around it (for me) and no reason to apologize for it. George Bush is a dangerously failed president and half-bright top-level nerd, who has spent the last four years avoiding grocery stores and gas stations while he tried to keep tabs on the disastrous fallout from the orgy and greed and short-selling that was the "Reagan Revolution."

Biographers descended on Hunter in 1992. I published my book on his work in 1991. In the following year, three publishers invested in books on Hunter aimed at a mass audience. E. Jean Carroll was a former Indiana University cheerleader who became a contributing editor at *Esquire* and sex-advice columnist for *Elle*. She also published several books, including *Female Difficulties*, *A Dog in Heat Is a Hot Dog*, and *Mr. Right, Right Now: How a Smart Woman Can Land Her Dream Man in Six Weeks*. Carroll's book *Hunter* was an adventurous romp through his life, presented tongue-in-cheek as the dissertation of her alter ego, Laetitia

Snap, a scientist supposedly studying Owl Farm peacocks. In Carroll's fanciful episodes, Hunter imprisoned Tishy Snap, who ended up bearing his child. Even the chapters that alternated with the Tishy Snap episodes were unorthodox: huge chunks of interviews with no narration of his life. She drew, however, several terrific stories from Hunter's old friends.

Paul Perry's *Fear and Loathing* and Peter Whitmer's *When the Going Gets Weird* were more conventional biographies, though each had major gaps in Hunter history. Both writers had Hunter connections; Perry had assigned the 1980 Honolulu marathon story, while editing *Running* magazine, and Whitmer profiled Hunter in 1984 for *Saturday Review*.

Hunter was horrified by this sort of attention, which he considered an invasion of privacy. He asked friends not to speak to Carroll, and many did not. Several of those who did came to regret it.

Laila Nabulsi said she and Hunter regarded Perry's *Fear and Loathing* as "a real betrayal. It's kind of the understanding that what happens in the kitchen stays in the kitchen. You don't come in unless you say, 'I'm going to write about this' and then we never would have let him stay in the house."

Whitmer's book came last. Although it was the most detailed, chronicling several generations of Hunter's ancestors, it got the least attention. Much of it concentrated on alcohol and drug stories.

"He hated all those unauthorized biographies," Laila said, and he resented his friends who cooperated with the writers, no matter how unwittingly. Perry even managed to get a cover illustration out of the much-too-kind Ralph Steadman, since Perry had worked with both of them on what became *The Curse of Lono*. "You have caused me a lot of trouble," Hunter wrote Ralph. He was furious about "these cheap, soon-to-be-buried gossip books."

Carroll's book dwelled on Hunter's personal life and sexual history and shined a light into areas he'd have rather kept in the dark or saved until he felt like writing about them. For a man whose work rose directly from his life, it wasn't just that he felt the biographers invaded his privacy; they also co-opted his best material.

The harmonic convergence of publicity made Hunter withdraw, and he became almost gun-shy with interviewers.

Ralph tried to get back into Hunter's good graces by arranging for him to write about the royal family for the *Observer*. After much negotiation, Ralph lured Hunter and his new girlfriend, Nicole Meyer, to London in September 1992. But the trip was miserable. Hunter suffered back pain, and the resulting article, which appeared just in time for the new year, had to be coaxed from him and read as if it had been dictated and linked with paragraphs from the editor. There was no face-to-face encounter with the royal family, instead, as expected, a lot of struggling to do the assignment and get the story. He believed that the British were out to snatch him, flog him, and throw him into a dungeon. A long sidebar by Ralph attempted to explain Hunter to English readers. Though he had devout English fans, Hunter's pure American humor did not always travel well.

But Hunter did not travel well himself, at least not on the campaign trail. He covered the 1992 campaign mostly by watching television. Now that CNN had been loosed upon the world, Hunter felt plugged in; the all-news network negated any need to be on the bus, or jogging after the candidates. Someone else could do that. Thanks to the fax machine, the successor to his Mojo Wire, Hunter could reach out and touch almost anyone, especially CNN vice president Ed Turner, as well as James Carville and George Stephanopoulos, the brain trust running the Clinton campaign. Between CNN and the fax, Hunter burrowed deeper into the role of reactor rather than reporter. He was unenthusiastic about the campaign and the candidate. "It's almost embarrassing to talk about Clinton as if he were important," Hunter wrote. "I'd almost prefer Nixon. I'd say Clinton is every bit as corrupt as Nixon, but a lot smoother."

Aside from the trip to the United Kingdom, Hunter made one other major trip in the fall—home to Louisville, to see his mother and to speak at a literacy festival. He threatened to move to Paraguay if George Bush was reelected. "It's been 12 years of the most oppressive, red neck, stupid . . . greedhead politicians in this country," he told the audience.

Although he announced his intention to vote for Clinton, Hunter did not sound like much of a fan. "He is the Willy Loman of Generation X, a traveling salesman from Arkansas who has the loyalty of a lizard with its tail broken off and the midnight taste of a man who's double date with the Rev. Jimmy Swaggart."

On March 25, 1993, Hunter's youngest brother, Jim, died of complications from AIDS.

Hunter and Jim had been distant for years. Because of the twelve-year age difference, they had never really been close, though Hunter had written Jim frequently as Jim played the roulette game of being draft fodder during the Vietnam War. He'd brought Jim out to Owl Farm, hoping to turn him into a Hunter clone, but it didn't take. Even after Jim wrote his heart-wrenching letter to his big brother confessing his sexual preference, there had been no talk about it. Because he was so much younger than Hunter and Davison, Jim had been left to care for their mother, whose alcoholism incapacitated her and forced him to be her caregiver. The obligation put a strain on his schooling, and he was in and out of the University of Kentucky. Eventually, Virginia went to the Episcopal Church Home on the outskirts of Louisville, a relatively spectacular hotel-like institution. Hunter and brother Davison footed the bill.

Jim drifted to California, where he could live openly as a gay man, residing at the intersection of Haight and Ashbury in San Francisco, where his famous brother had witnessed the madness and majesty of the midsixties. He held a number of jobs, and friends said he was at his happiest while working as a clerk in a health-food store.

He shared leftist politics but little else with Hunter and came to believe that his brother avoided him because of his sexuality. As Hunter grew more famous and made money off of his lifestyle and image, through *Where the Buffalo Roam* and countless film options on *Fear and Loathing in Las Vegas*, Jim's resentment mounted. He eventually criticized Hunter for betraying the liberal ideal of tolerance. Hunter, he said, couldn't even tolerate his own brother's sexual identity. After Jim's death, however, Hunter would occasionally list the government's lack of support for AIDS research as part of the litany of failures by the Reagan and Bush administrations.

Douglas Brinkley earned his doctorate in American diplomatic history at Georgetown University and settled into a comfortable academic career, establishing himself as a respected history professor as a very young man, with his biography of former secretary of state Dean Acheson and a variety of interests that squeezed *eclectic* until it screamed for mercy. Brinkley became an extremely popular professor at Hofstra University, around an hour's drive from New York City, and created a class called "An American Odyssey" that he took on the road in 1993. He loaded up twenty-seven college students on two buses and took them from the Long Island campus all the way to the West Coast, criss-crossing the country, meeting writers in their natural habitats, and gorging on American popular culture. It fit with his belief that history was best experienced outside the classroom.

He wasn't one to publish his work in monographs, merely to impress other scholars. He was emphatic about reaching a mainstream audience.

Woody Creek was on the itinerary. Brinkley had not met Hunter before, but he'd written and asked whether the class could visit. Hunter said he would gladly entertain the young professor and his twenty-seven charges. He instructed Brinkley to park the buses at the Woody Creek Tavern and order some cheeseburgers. He'd be down.

Hunter made an entrance for the students, driving up in a jeep and carrying in a ice-rattling tumbler of Chivas Regal. He took measure of the audience, seizing on one student whose hair was dyed blue. "You'd better be good," Hunter said. "Otherwise you come off as a rank asshole with blue hair." The student was momentarily taken aback, then said, "I'm good." Hunter grabbed him by the neck and said, "We'll see about that, Sonny Boy."

Later, in private, Hunter gave Brinkley some classroom management advice: "Slap the little bastards around. Take no crap." Brinkley, who thought of Hunter as a counterculture *peace-love-understanding* god, was taken aback. Still, he took up Hunter's invitation to bring all the students up to Owl Farm for "refreshments." The highlight of the visit came when Hunter ordered the students to line up with their copies of his books. One by one, on his order, they leaned their books against a tree as he "autographed" them with a .45-caliber slug. In assembly-line fashion, the students were treated to Hunter's unusual show of affection.

Late that night, before the bus pulled out of Woody Creek, Hunter again took Brinkley aside. Obviously, he liked the young man, who wasn't pretentious and stuffy. He asked Brinkley to help him on his next book, the big book about the 1992 campaign that was turning into the diary of Hunter's love-hate relationship with American politics. Brinkley agreed.

Brinkley and his busload of students drove away, but the visit sparked a creative relationship that was to result in the resuscitation of Hunter's literary career.

Unfortunately, that resuscitation had to wait until after the completion of Hunter's political book, *Better Than Sex*. Although most of the book was about the 1992 campaign, it was not under the deadline gun of *Fear and Loathing on the Campaign Trail* '72. Hunter did not put the extra time to good use. Brinkley, coming in midway through the book, couldn't help either. Even friends realized it was a lesser work. Since *The Curse of Lono*, his books had become pastiches of previously published material.

"The books changed from original prose to reedited columns and letters," Braudis said. "People began to accuse him of not being able to write anything longer than a column."

Better Than Sex was Hunter's most inconsistent book; much of it was made up of faxes and photocopies. Though amusing, it was also the least substantial work he produced, reading like an unedited diary. His comments were punctuated too often with *ho-ho*'s and *Bubba*s. His fans didn't seem to mind; they lined up butt-to-bellybutton to buy the thing.

The story of the 1992 campaign and President Clinton's first year in office was bookended with a short political memoir at the beginning and his obituary for Richard Nixon at the end, one of the best things he ever wrote. The Nixon piece saved *Better Than Sex* from mediocrity.

Nixon had been Hunter's muse during his greatest days as a political reporter, and the old man's death on April 22, 1994, came as Hunter was wrapping up the book. Once again, Nixon came through for him, providing the perfect ending for his book on politics. "Hunter hated Nixon so much that he loved him," Brinkley said.

Hunter and Ed Bradley had come to New Orleans for the Jazz and Heritage Festival (Hunter had a book signing; Bradley was just there for music). They hooked up with Brinkley, who had just moved to the University of New Orleans as the heir apparent to historian and writer Stephen Ambrose's throne as head of the Eisenhower Center for American Studies. The four of them went on a bar ramble. Hunter stuck his head into the St. Charles Tavern and yelled, "Nixon died! Anyone want acid?" Ambrose, whose life had been haunted by Nixon as well, had written a three-volume biography of the man. Hunter and Ambrose got noisily drunk, but Hunter worried that he would not be able to rise to the occasion. "I have to out-Mencken Mencken," Hunter told Brinkley.

Hunter had always respected H. L. Mencken, especially Mencken's obituary for William Jennings Bryan in 1925. Mencken had been with Bryan (and Clarence Darrow) in Dayton, Tennessee, for the trial of schoolteacher John Scopes, charged with teaching evolution. Darrow defended Scopes's right of free speech, and Bryan defended the law requiring the teaching of biblical truth. Mencken had overtly mocked Bryan while he was alive and so when Bryan keeled over a couple of days after the trial ended, he was not going to turn hypocrite and praise in death a man he thought was a fool in life. As he wrote in the *American Mercury*, "There was something peculiarly fitting in the fact that his last days were spent in a one-horse Tennessee village, and that death found him there. The man felt at home in such scenes. He liked people who sweated freely, and were not debauched by the refinements of the toilet." Mencken, long a forceful critic of the South (and most other places; he once said that anyone not living in his hometown of Baltimore was "camping out"), later was revered by generations of Southerners who appreciated his kick in the ass to their intellectual movement in the mid-twentieth century.

Hunter called the Mencken obituary "one of the most hideous things ever written about a dead man in the history of American letters." Reading it the first time was shocking for Hunter. "I had learned in school that Bryan was a genuine hero of history, but after reading Mencken's brutal obit, I knew in my heart that he was, in truth, a scoundrel."

Nixon's death provided Hunter with his "moment." While even Nixon's old opponents and political antonyms praised him, Hunter could not restrain himself. If you could not kick the man when he was down, when could you kick him? He wanted to stand over his grave until he was sure he was dead.

Richard Nixon is gone now, and I am poorer for it. He was the real thing —a political monster straight out of Grendel and a very dangerous enemy. He could shake your hand and stab you in the back at the same time. He lied to his friends and betrayed the trust of his family. . . .

If the right people had been in charge of Nixon's funeral, his casket would have been launched into one of those open-sewage canals that empty into the ocean just south of Los Angeles. He was a swine of a man and a jabbering dupe of a president. Nixon was so crooked that he needed servants to help him screw on his pants every morning. . . .

He has poisoned our water forever. Nixon will be remembered as a classic case of a smart man shitting in his own nest. But he also shit in our nests, and that was the crime that history will burn on his memory like a brand. By disgracing and degrading the presidency of the United States, by fleeing the White House like a diseased cur, Richard Nixon broke the heart of the American Dream.

But Hunter was not thinking only about Nixon's death.

The about-the-author bio on the dust jacket of *Better Than Sex* ended with this line: "He will be gone by the year 2000."

The girlfriends and the assistants came and went. The assistants were always young and beautiful, and Hunter expected that they would eventually become girlfriends. If it didn't happen, he'd shrug and go on.

Deborah ran his life: paid the bills, kept Hunter on point, bought the groceries, made phone calls, cooked the dinner, kept the assistants fed and housed.

He never stopped writing. A typical evening might start around nine o'clock, but he wouldn't actually start writing until four or five in the morning. He filled the time in between by amusing the gaggle of friends in his living room, by driving around in his convertible, playing pranks on friends, waking up other friends with long-distance phone calls, and listening to music—his fuel—at loud volume. At the end of the "play" portion of the evening, usually after his audience of friends had gone home, he would drive to a friend's house, quietly let himself in, and take a long, luxurious swim in his indoor swimming pool while the owner slept. Relaxed, Hunter would get into his bathrobe, drive back to Owl Farm, sit behind the typewriter in the kitchen, and then write. It was not a schedule for a man deep into the cliffs of middle age. But Hunter would never admit that he was aging. He still lived as if he were twenty-two.

He traveled. He spoke on campuses and, occasionally, at semiserious symposiums. His "next book," *Polo Is My Life*, was overdue to Random House. He published tantalizing snatches of it in *Rolling Stone*, but it lingered unfinished. "He had a crush on an exotic woman in the Aspen polo crowd who was married to a very rich man and Hunter thought he could seduce her and they would run away and 'live their lives like dolphins,'" Wayne Ewing said. "But, alas the babe wasn't going to wear the Gonzo brand and instead said, 'Hunter, I can't run off with you. Who would take care of my ponies? Polo is my life.' I always tried to get Hunter to write that story—the autobiographical one about his infatuation with a beautiful woman, and a sport that symbolized wealth and power. It was the Gatsby in him. But he never would go there, except to tell the story of the brush off line that became a great title."

He contributed more for *Rolling Stone* (book reviews, the Nixon obit, a denunciation of Timothy Leary) in the early nineties than he had in all of the years since his 1976 campaign piece. Other than the Nixon obit and "Fear and Loathing in Elko," most of it was seen as lower-level self-imitation. He was, indeed, repeating himself.

"It got to be pretty formulaic," Greider said of Hunter's work. "He would cover different ground, but it would end up with similar rhythms or similar shticks. He was not quite as convincing. It became less compelling."

It had never been easy, but Hunter had the gift of making his work appear so. His legions of stoned admirers probably really thought he took a hundred hits of acid before sitting down to write. But the craftsmanship those close to him saw as he agonized over his words spoke to how much went into making it look like a breeze.

"He really worked hard," Brinkley said of Hunter's work in the sixties and early seventies. "It's unbelievable, the amount of work he did, the thinking and trying to make each sentence count. He wasn't eating acid then. He was eating speed—that was his drug of choice, to keep him writing all night. He was not as much fun as he painted himself to be. He was a work beast, and it shows in the quality of anything he wrote in that period."

But then came fame, and cocaine, and the suffocating persona he had created. In the eighties and nineties, it became even harder to write. "Part of his self-loathing was that his drinking and drugging and embracing fame cost him the ability to lose that gift."

None of this mattered to his ever-multiplying fans, millions of whom were still unborn when *Fear and Loathing Las Vegas* was written. Tattoos of the Gonzo double-thumbed fist showed up on college-student calves; his books were on reading lists; new fans as well as old salivated over those rare morsels thrown their way. Known for his antics and style as much as for his writing, he was still a Halloween costume favorite. Finally, he had attained some wealth and could live comfortably. He had close friendships with his neighbors, including Ed Bradley and actors Jack Nicholson and Don Johnson. He was a friend of and influence on a generation of musicians and writers, including Jimmy Buffett, Warren Zevon, and Carl Hiaasen, who was writing what could be called Gonzo fiction, with his outrageous plots and grand bacchanal punishments handed down to greedheads and land rapers. Then there was the college-age generation of actors who embraced Hunter and became his disciples—Sean Penn, John Cusack, Matt Dillon, and others, many of whom pipe-dreamed of somehow translating his work to the screen. "Aspen had this reverse celebrity worship," Bob Braudis said. "That's one of the reasons the Hollywood celebrities elected to come here. And Hunter, being a celebrity in the journalistic and literary world, was a magnet to them."

Hunter busied himself by designing, with Ralph Steadman, now forgiven, the label for the Flying Dog series of microbrews produced by his neighbor George Stranahan. With another neighbor, actor Don Johnson, he dreamed up the concept of what eventually became Johnson's CBS television series, *Nash Bridges*. He remained a dedicated correspondent, though his letters mostly came beeping through the phone wires as faxes. He never fully embraced computers or the world of electronic mail. In fact, as he readily admitted in interviews, he was surprised to still be alive.

"I set out from a young age to live as short as I possibly could," he had told Australian actor Jack Thompson (no relation) in a 1989 interview in *Studio for Men*. Jack Thompson accused Hunter of being more a romantic than a cynic. "I think you went straight to the point there," Hunter said. "To be a romantic and, you know what people say . . . only the good die young. Well, where does that leave me?"

Brinkley, who came to know Hunter extremely well, observed him at work and play and knew that Hunter had produced a wonderful literary creation—the Hunter Figure, he called it—that was at odds with the real man. Most intelligent readers knew that drug-gobbling Raoul Duke was a fictional creation . . . *didn't they*? Brinkley reiterated that Hunter hated sloppy drunks and those people who felt they needed to be inebriated to approach him. "You don't live into your sixties doing as much heavy drug and alcohol lifestyle as Hunter's had and still be around if you don't know that there's a limit somewhere," Brinkley said. "Hunter doesn't go over the cliff. He races a hundred miles an hour to the cliff, slams on the brakes and stops with the wheels dangling over, but he doesn't go off."

Still, as Hunter entered his later years, he was uncomfortable being enshrined as some kind of totem, even for the counterculture. Hunter in the midnineties was adrift, believing that his writing had been of the first rank but was not as respected as it should be. "We're just a very small band of brothers," he told Jack Thompson, ticking off Conrad, Twain, Coleridge, Fitzgerald, and Hemingway. "I like Hemingway, but I kind of worry about being identified with him."

Hunter's career and reputation were about to be brought back to life by three new acquaintances: a poet, an actor, and a historian.

Ron Whitehead was a poet and professor at the University of Louisville who had organized a series of insomniacathons (performances of music and poetry) all around the country. Deeply influenced by Allen Ginsberg and the other Beat poets, he was invited to New York University in June 1995 to be part of the Jack Kerouac Conference. Tall and lean with more than a touch of the lunatic poet, Whitehead had always taken pride in his counterculture credentials. In the late sixties, he'd worked in one of the few headshops in Lexington, and certainly the only place in Kentucky then where *Rolling Stone* was kept in stock and where ingesting hallucinogens was part of the job description. He'd always been proud to be a product of the same ground that produced Hunter S. Thompson.

Hunter was also on the Kerouac panel that night, and Whitehead finally had the chance to meet him. When they stood together after the presentation, comparing notes on Kentucky, fans streamed up to Hunter to present him with pills and joints. "He pocketed the joints," Whitehead said, "then turned his handful of pills up to his mouth, emptied them there, and washed them down with his favorite drink, Chivas. I wasn't sure I wanted to be around him when all of those pills kicked in. I knew then that yes, by God, he was a pure-blooded and bloodied Kentucky boy."

Hunter asked Whitehead to look in on his mother, now in her eighties. He also issued an open invitation for Whitehead and his family to come see him at Owl Farm sometime. When Whitehead returned to Kentucky, he called Virginia Thompson, who said she would enjoy the visit better if he brought along a bottle of whiskey. Though she vowed not to talk about Hunter, Hunter was practically all she talked about. "Visiting with Virginia was like visiting with Hunter," Whitehead said. "Virginia was a tenth-degree smart ass."

Her room was as comfortable as a fine hotel suite, and the walls were a museum of her family: a painting of Hunter and Davison as boys, with Davison holding a toy airplane and Hunter fondling a book; portraits of the Hunter-Sandy-Juan family in happier times, of Jim, and of Davison and his family in Ohio. Clearly, she was proud of her boys.

Not long after meeting Virginia, Whitehead displayed his work at the Louisville Free Public Library, where Virginia had worked. The politically inspired exhibit provoked a death threat written on the wall of the downtown post office: RON WHITEHEAD WILL DIE ON AUGUST 21, 1995. A confluence of events, including the death threat, postexhibit exhaustion, and the recent death of his grandmother, inspired Whitehead to hit the road with his family, visiting Hunter sooner rather than later.

Hunter welcomed the Whiteheads' midnight arrival by blaring a recording over the countryside of what Whitehead said was "a bear killing and eating what sounded like a baby." Deborah Fuller invited the Whiteheads into the command post kitchen, where Hunter saluted them from his perch. After the usual whiskey and pleasantries, Hunter asked White- head to read the Nixon obituary, and smiled appreciatively as he heard his words read by a performance artist/poet. Hunter wanted to send a copy to former vice-presidential candidate Sargent Shriver, who Hunter said was the only person to comment favorably on the piece. As Hunter started to autograph a copy with a silver Sharpie, the marker jammed.

Hunter began screaming, "Fuck! Fuck! Fuck! What's wrong?"

Deborah rushed over, stood behind him, and draped her arms across his chest, holding him and saying, "It's okay, Hunter, everything's okay." Eventually he quieted, pulled another marker from the kitchen drawer and finished signing the work. Simple frustrations could rouse Hunter's fury.

The visit was short but eventful. Jack Nicholson called three times, furious that Hunter had broken a window at his home and tossed in fire- crackers, scaring the bejesus out of his visiting daughters. Hunter watched a basketball playoff game on which he stood to win a lot of money, as he usually did with his sports bets. ("Hunter would bet on a frog race," Whitehead said.) They discussed firearms, and Deborah stood nearby all along, looking out for Hunter, watching for a spike in his mood.

As Whitehead pointed the car west toward San Francisco and a visit with poet Lawrence Ferlinghetti, he thought about Hunter. Not only was he Kentucky's greatest living contribution to literature; he was "one of the best damn writers of all time, bar none."

Yet back home, it seemed that Kentucky didn't appreciate him. With each mile, Whitehead vowed to do something about it.

By the time actor Johnny Depp came into Hunter's life, he had carved out an unusual career playing roles in art-house films as well as block- busters. Handsome and with teen-idol credentials, he could have easily chosen parts that played off of his good looks. But he masked his features under the heavy makeup of Edward Scissorhands or in the guise of cross- dressing filmmaker Ed Wood. Though only in his early thirties, he had already worked with Marlon Brando and Al Pacino and directors such as Tim Burton and Lasse Halstrom.

As a Kentucky boy, Depp was aware of Hunter Thompson but had not met him. He was visiting Aspen in December 1995, trying to avoid the crowds of Hollywood types who descended during the holidays for ski vacations. A friend asked Depp if he wanted to go to the Woody Creek Tavern to meet Hunter. *Of course.*

Hunter arrived around eleven that night, amid a cacophony of engine noises and the virtual rattling of an electronic saber. He put his cattle prod on the table and drank a few rounds with Depp. Aside from the Kentucky connection, they both had expertise as juvenile delinquents. Back at Owl Farm, Hunter and Depp set off a bomb, bonding over munitions. They became friends.

Several months later, at five-thirty one morning, Depp was in New York, preparing for his day's shooting on *Donnie Brasco*, when Hunter called. "Listen," he said, "if they were going to do a film of the Vegas book, would you be interested? Would you want to play me? Are you in?"

"Of course, I was," Depp said. Laila Nabulsi controlled the rights to the film and, to show how well the book could be dramatized, produced an oral performance of the book for release by Jimmy Buffett's Margaritaville Records. With Harry Dean Stanton as narrator, director Jim Jarmusch as Duke, and Maury Chaykin as Gonzo, the production was a success, though spoken-word recordings didn't need to sell much to be deemed successful. Laila even managed to lure Jann Wenner to play himself and Jimmy Buffett to portray a cop in the desert. The recording was not released until late 1996, when *Fear and Loathing in Las Vegas* celebrated its twenty-fifth anniversary. By that time, Depp was deep into what he called his "soul stealing," in preparation to play Hunter S. Thompson on the big screen.

Other scholars carped about Douglas Brinkley. Nothing infuriates an academic more than a talented and successful colleague. Brinkley was both. His chronicle of his spring semester cross-country trip with students, *The Majic Bus*, was in the paws of consumers before finals in the fall. That was another thing he did that irritated his peers: *he produced*. He was a bookwriting machine and was by the midnineties under the wing of Stephen Ambrose, one of America's most successful historians, at the University of New Orleans' Eisenhower Center. Though Brinkley was too polite (not to mention too busy) to deal with critics, Hunter did it for him. In one of their daily phone conversations, Brinkley had told Hunter that one of his colleagues at the university—a creative writing professor he had never met—had written to National Public Radio to complain about Brinkley. Somehow Brinkley found time in his life to serve as a public-radio commentator on poetry, and this outraged the English professor, who thought a historian was unqualified. After hanging up with Brinkley, Hunter wrote—without Brinkley's knowledge or consent—a letter to the English professor. "You are a jealous little jackass & you should be killed," Hunter declared. "The stupid, vengeful, half-bright muttering in yr. letter to NPR is a shame & an insult to every writer or reader who ever called English their first language. . . . There are powerful people . . . who want to beat out your teeth & shit on your chest."

Brinkley had not played a major role in *Better Than Sex*, but he helped Hunter attain the reputation he thought he deserved as a great and under-appreciated American writer. All it would require was a trip to the Owl Farm basement and some diligent editing.

Hunter S. Thompson came home on December 12, 1996. Ron White-head organized Hunter S. Thompson Day and booked Memorial Auditorium for the event. Thrilled, Hunter asked Bob Braudis to come along to get him through his three day visit. Braudis drove Hunter around town, to visit his mother and to see other friends. At a liquor stop, two burly red-necks ("biceps like your thighs, bib overalls") watched Hunter go into the store and asked Braudis in perfect Kentucky slack-jaw, "Was that Hunter Thompson?" Braudis grinned and introduced them when Hunter came out. "He gave them ten great minutes of their lives," he said. "They talked about guns. He loved the fans. If he didn't get attention for a day or two, he'd do something stupid."

Johnny Depp and Warren Zevon came to pay tribute, as did David Amram, the composer and Kerouac collaborator from Hunter's days at the Cuddebackville cabin. They chatted during rehearsals, with Hunter taking occasional breaks to spray his friends with fire extinguishers. He and Amram talked about their old days, mused on the fate of the man-ager of the Huguenot Superette, and talked about their careers. Then Hunter leaned forward, nearly whispering. "My mother will be here," he told Amram. "I hope she approves of my behavior. She is a librarian, as you know. She always encouraged me."

With Virginia Thompson in the front row—eighty-eight, sitting in a wheelchair—the city of Louisville paid tribute to the man who claimed to be its Billy the Kid. With the star-power of Johnny Depp, Ron White-head arranged the Hunter tribute. The mayor proclaimed it Hunter S. Thompson Day, and the governor declared Hunter, Depp, Whitehead,

Brinkley, Zevon, and Amram to be Kentucky Colonels. Hunter even got the key to the city.

Forty degrees and raining, yet the place was packed for the homecoming. Hunter wanted to prove Thomas Wolfe wrong. Whitehead wanted to show Hunter that he was loved.

Behind the scenes, there was chaos. Whitehead thought he had secured financial backing from the University of Louisville, but a week before the event, the university had backed out. Poetry hadn't made Whitehead rich, and he couldn't afford to underwrite the presentation, especially since all of the out-of-town celebrities were staying at Louisville's finest hotels and required limousine service.

"Ron, you're going to have to suck it up," Brinkley said when Whitehead called him. "It's too late to turn back. If you follow through with this, it'll certainly be one of the biggest events in Hunter's life. You've got to do this, Ron. If you do, you'll probably prove to the world what you're made of."

Whitehead did suck it up, and the show went on. Singer Warren Zevon sang a couple of his songs that Hunter loved, "Lawyers, Guns and Money" and "Hula Hula Boys." Former mayor Harvey Sloane, also a friend of forty years, paid tribute to Louisville's native son. "It's about time we recognized our greatest literary talent, don't you think?" Sloane asked the crowd, drawing applause. "Finally, Louisville, we've done it." Roxanne Pulitzer read from Hunter's coverage of her divorce trial. Johnny Depp read the "high-water mark" passage from *Fear and Loathing in Las Vegas*, chewing gum all the while. Douglas Brinkley lectured the crowd about Hunter's place in literary history.

Juan Thompson paced backstage, hearing the tributes to his father boom through the sound system. He was scheduled to speak, but just before he was to go on, he took Whitehead aside. He wasn't an extrovert; speaking in public didn't come naturally.

"I don't think I can do this," he said. "I'm nervous."

Whitehead had edited the text for Juan. "Your piece will be the most precious part of the night," Whitehead told him. "It will mean more to your dad than anything anyone else says. You've got to read it. You have no choice."

Juan stood nervously at the microphone, wearing a suit and tie, looking down on his grandmother in the front row, knowing that his father lurked behind him somewhere.

"What was it like to have Hunter Thompson as your father?" he began. He'd heard the question his whole life. "What can I say? What I can tell you is what I learned from my father and what I respect and admire in him. I've learned that the surface truth is rarely the real truth, and as a result I've become cynical about the motivations of corporations, politicians and law enforcement. Above all, it makes me think and pay attention.

"He demands in everything that he does that you set aside your habits and perceptions and pay attention to what is happening right now and deal with it. That's where the fun and excitement are, in not knowing what's going to happen."

Juan smiled to himself, then continued, "So what am I saying? I am proud of this man. I respect and admire his vitality, his courage, his insight, his perverse resistance to security and predictability, his deliberate disregard for propriety, his ability to make me see and think differently. Ultimately, I love and respect him because he really *lives*—for better or for worse, for richer or for poorer, he lives his life."

Relieved, finally through the talk, Juan smiled and turned to look over his shoulder. Out of the backstage darkness, his father approached, spraying him with CO_2 from a fire extinguisher. Juan stood, spread his arms in a come-and-get-me gesture, and took the full force of the blast. Hunter set down his fire extinguisher and hugged his son, with tears in his eyes.

On the flight home, Hunter and Braudis were buckled into their seats as the plane lifted off. As it climbed, Hunter let out "a thirty-second, two-octave, head-splitting rebel yell." He turned to Braudis and said, "Just what people like to hear during takeoff." Then, with the plane still at a forty-five-degree angle, Hunter ripped off his seatbelt and lurched up the aisle to the men's room. The United flight attendants watched, dumbfounded.

After Hunter bolted the lavatory door, a flight attendant approached Braudis

"Just what is your friend doing in there?" she asked.

"He's had bad diarrhea all day," Braudis lied.

"Oh, no problem," she said.

A half hour later, Hunter returned, refreshed from a stand-up bath and a shave.

"Any problem?" he asked.

Braudis shook his head.

Chapter 18

MAN OF LETTERS

Try to imagine Hunter Thompson fighting for every last
breath in a hospital bed, hooked up to all sorts of tubes.
That's just not him.
—*Juan Thompson, 2006*

*F*ear and Loathing in Las Vegas turned twenty-five and was welcomed into hallowed literary ground. A Modern Library hardcover
edition was published. As a young reader, Hunter cut his teeth on
the Modern Library. Now he was part of that club. He pointed out that
he fell between Thackeray and Thoreau in the alphabetical listing of its
authors.

The original *Fear and Loathing in Las Vegas* hardcover was a rarity.
The book didn't take off until the paperback publication, so a first edition fetched thousands from collectors. (For years, Jann Wenner battled a
false rumor that he hoarded seven thousand first editions in a warehouse
to be sold on Hunter's death.) This new hardcover featured a picture of
Hunter at Caesar's Palace on the front cover. Oscar Acosta, seated next
to him, was cropped out.

Titled *Fear and Loathing in Las Vegas and Other American Stories,* the
collection made it a primer on Gonzo journalism, including Hunter's
companion piece, "Strange Rumblings in Aztlan," which he had written

simultaneously with *Fear and Loathing*. An essay about the creation of the book, originally intended as jacket copy (but ten thousand words too long), also was included, offering insight into Hunter's thought process and his feeling that since he revised and rewrote the manuscript, *Fear and Loathing* was "a failed experiment" in Gonzo journalism. By definition, true Gonzo went directly from the reporter's brain to the reader's brain without editing. "The Kentucky Derby Is Decadent and Depraved" completed the collection.

The anniversary and the Modern Library publication gave Jann Wenner another chance to celebrate Hunter, and he invited him to New York. When Hunter showed up at the *Rolling Stone* office, he greeted Wenner warmly by blasting him with a fire extinguisher.

Hunter arrived in a blizzard of publicity. He was interviewed on CNN and made appearances in the tabloids, on the arms of movie stars, including Johnny Depp, who was at his side, cataloging Hunter's moves. Tom Wolfe hosted a reception at the Lotos literary club, for which Wenner footed the bill. While Jefferson Airplane's "White Rabbit" and Dylan's "Mr. Tambourine Man" blasted through the tony club, the guests—including Mick Jagger, George Plimpton, and P. J. O'Rourke—feted Hunter.

Hunter removed his safari cap, wrapped his necktie around his head, used his walking cane to tickle patrons, and whooped and screeched like one of his peacocks. Chain-smoking, swilling Chivas, he lived up to Dr. Johnson's motto and made an entertaining beast of himself, wallowing in the attention.

O'Rourke offered a toast: "We're here tonight to do something we've never done and that is to take Hunter seriously, which he richly deserves, despite his behavior and his mode of dress and his headwear this evening. Hunter actually is a serious artist, very possibly the best one that's alive right now in his field, which doesn't really speak very well of the rest of us. But nonetheless, it is a distinction of utmost importance and tonight we are here to celebrate that." He raised his glass: "Here is to Hunter, as the artist, the genius . . . as a man of his time, as someone who PhD's will be written about, as soon as all of us who actually knew him are dead."

But Hunter didn't want to be enshrined or embalmed as a writer whose best work was twenty-five years ago. Douglas Brinkley didn't want that either. During his visits to Owl Farm, Hunter had shown Brinkley his crates of correspondence, carbon copies of the letters he'd saved since high school. He asked Brinkley to go through them and put together a collection of letters, something Hunter planned to call "The Education of a Journalist." Hunter had been wanting to do something with the letters for years, but was overwhelmed by the task. Then Brinkley had showed up in his bus. As Hunter wrote his publisher: "The solution to this problem has emerged . . . in the goy/heroic form of the eminent biographer and literary historian, Dr. Douglas Brinkley of New Orleans . . . who has agreed to be my/our editor on this book. . . ." The crates of material might have overwhelmed a lesser man, but the young professor was up to the task. Here was a valuable cultural resource, Brinkley figured. It wasn't just a collection of correspondence; it was a personal history of America. As a young writer, Hunter had the vision and confidence to make copies of his letters, assuming they would make interesting reading someday. They did.

Brinkley's literary and historical instincts made him intent on *doing something* with the mammoth volume of Hunter's correspondence. "I've always thought of Hunter as a great American writer and his most superb art form being correspondence," Brinkley said. "He was a genius at it."

Brinkley found approximately twenty thousand letters stored in boxes at Owl Farm. Hunter admitted making the carbons not just for his files but with an eye toward eventual publication. "These were the pre-Xerox days," he told Brinkley. "I was anal retentive in my desire to save *everything*." His old friend Porter Bibb said that even as a child "Hunter always knew" he would become famous.

Brinkley was unabashedly a fan: "At his best, he's right up there with Scott Fitzgerald and Ernest Hemingway." Once he latched onto the idea of collecting Hunter's letters and getting Random House on board about the letters, he faced his largest task: motivating Hunter. "The key to being an editor of Hunter was staying on him, being persistent, giving him a big advance, letting him spend a lot of money and getting it out of him because Hunter would have a tendency to not deliver the copy and [you] had to ride him and ride him and ride him."

Brinkley and Hunter combed the files, eliminating five letters for every one included. While in New York to celebrate the *Fear and Loathing* anniversary, Hunter met with Random House editor David Rosenthal, who had offered a contract for the book in 1995. "We realized there was a genius in our midst," Brinkley recalled. "These letters were so good and so smart and so critically acclaimed that people started recognizing, 'My Gosh, it's not just the books. This guy can write and has a mind like you can't believe.'"

Rosenthal was convinced that a Hunter Thompson revival was in the making. "This is the book that launches the reassessment of Hunter Thompson as an important literary-slash-journalist figure," Rosenthal said. "And at the same time, it's a big, commercial book." Rosenthal wanted to title the book *Speed Kills*, to cash in on Hunter's image, but the author and Brinkley were reaching for something more literary and less comic.

Rosenthal showed Hunter a print proof of the proposed dust jacket, a photo of young hitchhiking Hunter in suitcase and shades, a picture taken by his friend Paul Semonin nearly forty years before. Hunter shook his head, admiring his handsome younger self. "I should be dead," he said.

"We'd sell a lot more copies," Rosenthal said.

The Proud Highway was published to phenomenal reviews in 1997, and was announced as the first in a series of three books that Brinkley would cull from the letters. It was, as Rosenthal had predicted, the vanguard of the Hunter Thompson renaissance.

The Modern Library and *Proud Highway* publications energized Hunter. "His self-esteem started going up," Brinkley said. "He saw that he was not a failure. He saw that he did have a role in American literature, and that it was one that was sustainable. People were taking Hunter Thompson seriously, and he loved it."

When Hunter appeared at his book signings, fans mobbed him. He didn't actually sign books, but buyers were given a presigned bookplate. They were allowed to shake his hand and grovel before him and accept his good-natured abuse.

The book was the closest Hunter would come to writing an autobiography. It also was a history of half a century of America, seen through the eyes of the nation's leading outlaw journalist. Hunter had been honored before (the New York Public Library named him a Literary Lion in 1989), but *The Proud Highway* made him into a literal and figurative man of letters, an H. L. Mencken–like sage. Clearly, he hadn't lost it. Though it was a collection of things written thirty and forty years before, the point was made: Hunter deserved to be considered among the top rank of American writers of his generation. The recognition Hunter had long sought was finally coming. On the thirtieth anniversary of its original publication, the Modern Library edition of *Hell's Angels* appeared. The Library of America also selected a piece from Hunter's 1972 coverage of an anti-war demonstration at the Republican Convention for an anthology of writing on Vietnam.

In the meantime, Laila Nabulsi had finally done the impossible: get a film of *Fear and Loathing in Las Vegas* into production. She had gotten Johnny Depp as Duke and Benicio del Toro as Dr. Gonzo. She picked Alex Cox to direct and to write the screenplay with partner Tod Davies. Cox had independent-film credibility as writer-director of the cult films *Repo Man* and *Sid and Nancy*. But a disastrous January 1997 script meeting with Cox and Davies in Woody Creek nearly scuttled the project.

Cox and Davies sent Hunter the script, but it was clear in their meeting—filmed by Wayne Ewing, Hunter's Boswell—that Hunter hadn't read it. They discussed a plot point requiring Duke to fly from Vegas to Los Angeles, only to be brought back on an animated tidal wave. Hunter's jaw dropped. "This is a nasty shock to me," he said. He tried to get it straight: that wonderful speech he wrote ("the high-water mark"), the speech about the idealism of the sixties and the broken hopes . . . they wanted to make *that* into a cartoon? The more he discussed the script, the more furious he became. "That's one of my best fucking things I've ever written and to turn it into some stupid cartoon show . . . I don't like, no," he told Cox and Davies emphatically.

Cox saw the Ralph Steadman illustrations as the model for the film's visual style, and Hunter objected so strongly that Cox and Davies stormed from the house. "Write your own fucking movie, write your own story," Hunter screamed at Davies. "You're a smart girl. Go ahead and do it. Just don't fuck with mine and make it into a cartoon."

Hunter called Laila, blaming her for the concept of turning "Ralph's goddam drawings" into the film representation of Hunter's greatest work. "This is going to be a nasty fucking war," he warned her.

After a couple of months, Laila calmed Hunter down and signed Terry Gilliam as director. Gilliam, who had been a member of Britain's Monty Python comedy troupe, made well-reviewed films such as *Brazil*, which eventually achieved cult status. Gilliam and Tony Grisoni wrote a new screenplay that Hunter approved, and after several delays and an agreement from Johnny Depp to rearrange his movie schedule, the film finally began shooting. Depp had already spent a lot of time with Hunter, but the delay gave him more time to absorb his manners and characteristics by moving into the basement of Owl Farm.

Depp had two brushes with death while living with Hunter. He was bitten by a brown recluse spider while sleeping. Craig Vetter told Hunter, "If that's all that happens after living for a month in your basement, he got off easy." On another night, Depp lay in bed, smoking, looking through the rough draft of *Fear and Loathing*, and reading discarded passages. He set down his cigarette into an ashtray on top of the end table. He took a closer look and realized it wasn't an end table. He ran upstairs and asked Hunter to come down and look at the thing by his bed. "Oh, God, that's where it is," Hunter said when he saw it. "I've always wondered what happened to it." The night stand was a gunpowder keg.

Depp went everywhere with Hunter: into Aspen, into the Woody Creek Tavern, driving the back roads. "He looked like he was a kid up to some trick," Hunter said. "He would be right next to me in the convertible, lighting the cigarette the same way, and it got very peculiar, particularly for my friends around here who didn't know what to make of it. But he was getting into his role."

Depp did not want an impersonation; everyone did those, even college sophomores on Halloween mimicked the guttural voice and the loping walk they'd observed on the David Letterman and Charlie Rose shows. Depp wanted to get at Hunter from the inside. "The man should be sainted for putting up with my continual scratching away at the layers of his life," Depp said. "He stuck it out like a champion and couldn't have been a better friend."

So many celebrities came to the Woody Creek Tavern that even a heartthrob movie star didn't startle the regulars. Most gawkers came for Hunter anyway. Depp became a regular, but fawning fans on the barstools were there to see Hunter. "People just watched him from a distance," Cheryl Frymire said. "No one I think really wanted to upset Hunter. They would just go, 'Is that Hunter Thompson over there?' and just observe him. He treated the tavern as an extension of his domain."

Filming eventually began, but Hunter stayed away, lest he cause a disruption. He showed up one day to film a brief flashback scene in which he played himself at San Francisco's Matrix nightclub. Depp as the young Hunter did a double take when he found the older Hunter sitting at a table.

Back at Woody Creek, the kitchen had always been crowded, but now the clerisy of the young and hip writers, editors, actors, and musicians made a pilgrimage. Brinkley tried to make the case for its being a literary salon. "He was like the Dalai Lama of writers," his artist friend Joe Petro said. Other close friends said the literary pretensions were a little over the top, that frequently the so-called salon was more often filled with Hunter and his betting buddies. "Emerson used to say, 'If you are really great, people will come to you,'" Brinkley said. "Hunter doesn't have to go traveling around the world anymore. Everybody comes through his kitchen. You can be meeting Jimmy Carter or George McGovern there or Johnny Depp or John Cusack or Ed Bradley or Jimmy Buffett. Everybody kind of crosses through Hunter's kitchen." Porter Bibb said, "He's Mohammad and he's the mountain all in one. You have to come sit at his feet." The salon idea worked in reverse. "With two phone calls, he could virtually hook up with anyone in the country," Braudis said, "and I'm talking about the heavyweights." Hunter became friends with Jim Irsay, who shared his love of pro football and literature. Irsay owned the Indianapolis Colts and also the newsprint scroll on which Jack Kerouac had written *On the Road* (he paid $2.5 million for it). In tribute to his kindred spirit, Hunter proclaimed the Colts his favorite pro team.

Hunter did not disappoint visitors to his kitchen. The true friends got the real Hunter, but the acquaintances got Duke. *I'm never sure which one people expect me to be. Often, they conflict.* So he shot his guns, blew up gas tanks, drove his car 110 miles an hour without lights after midnight with his snow cone (Chivas over packed ice) between his legs, screamed, yelled, screeched, squawked. He could amuse by playing the character he professed to hate. But to his close friends, he was still the Southern Gentleman. "He was kind of a beacon for dissent throughout his whole life," said actor John Cusack. "He was a place people could turn to, to get a moral argument from a moral outlaw. . . . Hunter was deeply serious and kind of a deeply moral person who liked orgies."

"No one could ever live up to the image of Hunter S. Thompson, not even Hunter Thompson," Braudis said. "The image of the constantly fucked-up writer was not really the substance of the guy." Braudis amused himself by watching how Hunter drank. "In a three-hour period, I might drink more than Hunter," he said. "But Hunter would drink 24/7. But I never saw him dick-in-the-dirt drunk. He didn't want that to be part of his image. He didn't suffer drunks . . . or people who talked too much . . . or people who interrupted."

Nickole Brown worked for Hunter in 1997, trying to help him assemble *Polo Is My Life*. She met him during the Louisville homecoming, and her former professor Ron Whitehead recommended her as an editorial assistant. When she arrived in Woody Creek, Brown saw that the "book" was a series of boxes, one for each chapter, filled with manuscript pages, peacock feathers, and other things to get him started.

"He always needed a visual stimulus to inspire him," Deborah Fuller said. "He used storyboards marked off with colored tape."

Brown plunged in, doing her best to help Hunter. He offered her drugs; she refused and he never offered again. Once, while driving around, he pulled the car to the side of the road and asked if he could kiss her. No, she said. Hunter grumbled, looked out at the mountains, turned to her and said, "Well, fuck it, then." He took her back to the cabin, and they never spoke about the incident. When her term ended, he sent her off with a glowing reference for graduate school.

Back home in Louisville, there were rumors about Hunter's behavior. Someone said Hunter had held a gun to Brown's head. A *Courier-Journal* reporter called to get the real story. Brown said Hunter was a difficult man to work for—most great artists are, she said—but he was always the perfect gentleman. He had not held a gun to her head or mistreated her in any way, she told the reporter.

A few days after the story appeared, Brown was awakened by the phone in the middle of the night. "What the hell are you trying to do?" Hunter growled. "You'll ruin my reputation."

With *The Proud Highway*, Hunter became a hot property again. When David Rosenthal moved from Random House to Simon and Schuster as publisher, he took Hunter along. Looking into the past had paid off, and Hunter thought it might be time to resurrect one of his novels. After the publication of *Hell's Angels* in 1967, Jim Silberman was going to publish *The Rum Diary* with Random House's Pantheon division. Hunter wanted to do another rewrite, but Silberman seemed intent on going ahead with it, so Hunter had the manuscript stolen. Thirty years later, he finally was ready to work on it. With his new editor at Simon and Schuster, MarySue Rucci, he reworked the forty-year-old story and cut six hundred pages from the thousand-page manuscript. Though there were passages that made Hunter cringe and that he cut, he was generally pleased with what his earlier self had written. It was finally published in 1998. Though critics sharpened their knives, figuring there had to be a good reason why a novel by a best-selling author couldn't get published for forty years, the book came as a pleasant surprise. *The Rum Diary* was a revelation, evidence of both Hunter's promise and his seriousness as a young man. The *Philadelphia Inquirer* said the book showed "a young Hunter Thompson brimming with talent." Some wondered how much fiction there really was in the novel. "Even writing fiction, he was still writing about himself," Ralph Steadman said. "It was him again, doing an assignment in Puerto Rico, doing small-time journalism."

Fear and Loathing in Las Vegas hit theaters on one of the first big weekends of the 1998 summer season. It clearly wasn't a *Star Wars* blockbuster and the release was poorly timed, coming during the kiddie-frenzy time of year. Hunter flew to New York to attend the premiere and asked George Plimpton to accompany him to the theater. As he fidgeted nervously in the back of the limo, the patrician Plimpton read his mind and tried to put him at ease. "Hunter, it's not your medium," he said. "You didn't write it, you didn't do it, you're not in it." *In short: if it sucks, you're not to blame.* Still, Hunter muttered, it was profoundly strange to think about his life on the screen.

After the premiere screening, Hunter stood with Depp and del Toro for the paparazzi and bashed them with bags of popcorn, in classic Raoul Duke style.

When they had a private moment, Depp asked him, "Do you hate me?"

"Oh no," Hunter said slowly. "It was like an eerie trumpet call over a lost battlefield."

Depp said his performance was "less of a job than it was a love letter."

Laila Nabulsi was probably more nervous about the premiere than Hunter. He had entrusted his greatest achievement to her. "Producing *Fear and Loathing* was a crusade, a cross to bear, a cross that I carried for more than ten years," she said. Hunter loved the film.

Audiences and critics did not. The film puzzled Johnny Depp's crazed teen fans who gasped when he removed his hat to show his shaved head. Critic Roger Ebert was rough with the film, which he called "a horrible mess of a movie, without shape, trajectory or purpose."

The film was a financial flop on its initial release. Like all of Terry Gilliam's films, however, it did achieve cult status, and eventually warranted a two-disc special edition for home viewing.

Brinkley continued sorting through Hunter's letters and writing his own books (including a biography of Jimmy Carter). He needed someone to go through the letters with Hunter for the second volume. Hunter had met Anita Bejmuk in 1997, when they were introduced by a mutual friend. Anita had said she wanted to learn about football, and the friend suggested Hunter as the perfect teacher. Anita was twenty-four, had grown up in Fort Collins, Colorado, and attended UCLA but was on an extended break from school, spending a couple of years skiing. Anita volunteered to work on Hunter's second volume of correspondence. She didn't know much about Hunter, other than as the courtly friend of a friend. She had read only one thing he'd written, his 1992 *Rolling Stone* article about Bill Clinton.

"I never had background in publishing or editing, but we just started working on that," Anita said. "Late nights. It was a lot of fun. We just read his letters for a couple months, just every night. That's probably how I fell in love with him, reading his history and seeing what kind of man he was." Brinkley had done the first pass through the boxes of letters, marking those he wanted photocopied. Anita and other assistants were charged with making copies and sending them to Brinkley's university office in New Orleans. There he assembled a rough version of the book and sent it back to Hunter. Anita then read the letters aloud to Hunter. "He would ask what I thought of certain letters," she said. "Sometimes he would say, 'Damn, that's good,' and sometimes he'd laugh and tell a story about what was surrounding that letter. If you misread a word, he would correct it. It was like a parlor trick. People were fascinated: 'How can you remember something from thirty years ago?' It's just that he had such a unique style, he knew that he would not use a word like that."

Soon, Anita's sabbatical from college was about to end. "I was headed back to school and he said, 'Maybe you could stay a few more months,'" she said. "Within a few hours of working with him one-on-one, I fell totally in love with him. He was really a good man and an inspiration to me." They moved in together in 1999.

He took her along for his moonlight swims, and once they were stranded in only boots and robes when their Jeep was stuck in a snowbank on the way back from the pool. He had back pain and sent her off to get help, giving her his robe to stay warm. He stayed in the Jeep, naked, until she returned. They freed the car, then went home for omelets and tequila. He wrote her a short story about that night and presented it to her. He called it "The Polish Girl."

"Leaving the house at all was a major production," Anita said. "He would pack a cooler to go to the gym. Swimming was a big production because he needed towels and snacks and flashlights and Gatorade. We didn't just swim in a regular swimming pool. It was a gorgeous indoor heated pool with glass walls and a glass ceiling and a mosaic. We would swim in ninety-degree water with the lights off, and so we had candles. It was an almost meditative experience, and so there were so many supplies. There was a half-hour preparation to get out of the door and he always had separation anxiety. That would take up half an evening—just to go swimming."

Fear and Loathing in America, the second book of letters, covered a grim period (1968–76: civil rights, Vietnam, Watergate), but years that were great for Hunter's career. He published *Hell's Angels* and produced *Fear and Loathing in Las Vegas* and his monumental *Rolling Stone* coverage of the 1972 presidential campaign. There he was, revolutionizing nonfiction writing and reporting, and yet a lot of the letters were pleas for money from agents, editors, and others.

But there was no whining in the letters. He routinely offered to rip the throats out of editors who welshed on contracts or who were too slow in reimbursing him for expenses. When American Express cut him off after the spending spree that produced *Fear and Loathing in Las Vegas*, Hunter viciously tore into the underling who thwarted him. "After three expensive efforts (to reach you), I got tired of talking to people who could barely speak English—much less understand what I was saying. How would you feel if you kept calling my house for prolonged conversations with my seven-year-old son? He deals with any calls I don't feel like taking."

Friends were used to this treatment. CBS correspondent Hughes Rudd stood up Hunter for a drink when Rudd was hospitalized. Hunter showed concern in his usual way: "Dear Hughes: Fuck off with your excuses about why you didn't show up at Miller's Pub on Thursday night. So you had a fucking heart attack . . . so what? Are you some kind of pansy? Hell, you should have just had the ambulance take you from the Amphitheatre to the Pub, not the hospital. The next time I plan to meet you anywhere for a drink I'll know what to expect."

The book provided insight to all the craft behind making his work look so easy. He shared his early draft of *Fear and Loathing in Las Vegas* with Tom Wolfe. He and Wolfe (whom he called "a thieving pile of albino warts") spent little time together, but corresponded frequently. Wolfe got some of Hunter's best full-force affectionate abuse when he wrote Hunter from Italy, where he was lecturing about the New Journalism in 1971. Hunter wrote back,

Dear Tom . . .

You worthless scum-sucking bastard. . . . Here you are running around fucking Italy in that filthy white suit at a thousand bucks a day laying all kinds of stone gibberish & honky bullshit on those poor wops who can't tell the difference . . . while I'm out here in the middle of these goddamn frozen mountains in a death-battle with the taxman & nursing cheap wine while my dogs go hungry & my cars explode and a legion of nazi lawyers makes my life a goddamn Wobbly nightmare. . . .

You decadent pig. Where the fuck do you get the nerve to go around telling those wops that *I'm* crazy? You worthless cocksucker. My Italian tour is already arranged for next spring & I'm going to do the whole goddamn trip wearing a bright red field marshal's uniform & accompanied by six speed-freak bodyguards bristling with Mace bombs & when I start talking about American writers & the name Tom Wolfe comes up, by god, you're going to wish you were born a fucking iguana! . . .

[T]he hammer of justice looms, and your filthy white suit will become a flaming shroud!

Hunter's continuing struggle with the death of the American Dream was documented in the letters. He tried to wrestle his whole world into this book, and part of the concept eventually led to *Fear and Loathing in Las Vegas*. And yet that still was not what his publisher wanted. Perhaps, three decades later, *Fear and Loathing in America* became that book. He'd been writing his testament all along, but it was hiding in plain sight next to his typewriter.

Anita followed the assistant-to-girlfriend path and moved to Owl Farm, providing him with stability. "I knew Anita would be responsive to the spiritual side—the loving, giving, gracious side," Cheryl Frymire said. "I think it was definitely a high point when they met."

In May 2000, Hunter had accidentally wounded his longtime assistant and full-time caregiver, Deborah Fuller, in a shooting accident. Bob Braudis got a call from Hunter, who explained that he'd seen a bear outside of Deborah's cabin. He tried to call her, but she didn't answer. So he got his rifle and planned to use his "bounce shot"—hitting the ground near the bear, scaring him enough to move but not enough to wound him. At the moment Hunter fired, Deborah opened the door and was struck in the arm.

"Will you come out here?" Hunter asked Braudis on the phone. He was obviously worried about an investigation.

"Have you called an ambulance?" Braudis asked. "Where's Deborah?"

"She's at the hospital," Hunter said.

"Fuck you," Braudis told him. "I'm going to the hospital."

Deborah was fine and more concerned about Hunter's agitated state than about her health. She recovered, but the incident disturbed Hunter. He always prided himself on being a good shot, and now this. *Was he losing it?*

Within three years, Deborah left, after more than twenty years with him. She claimed that the shooting did not affect her decision. "I think she just put her time in," Frymire said. "She cared for him. Working for him was definitely a labor of love. I think these women loved him deeply. They had to love him to work for him as long as they did."

Hunter was often depressed. Friends who dropped in sometimes found him alone, crying. What tortured him, Sandy said, was that he never achieved his potential. Sometimes he took out his anger on women, slapping them. "Hunter had a really dark side to him," Braudis said. "He was self-destructive his whole life." His reckless appetite for women destroyed long-term friendships. If he wanted a woman who was married to a friend, Hunter's needs trumped years of loyalty.

Near the end, he was particularly despondent over politics. His old *Rolling Stone* editor, John Walsh, was with the sports network ESPN. He offered Hunter a weekly column ("Hey Rube") on the Web starting in 2000, and Hunter jumped into covering sports again. Those unfamiliar with his early history might have been surprised that he was now churning out regular columns on sports, but it was a return to roots and also a chance to work with Walsh again, an editor he fiercely admired. Anita said Hunter saw it as a new way of reaching his loyal audience. "He said that sports lovers are just another political bloc, another group of human beings that is not organized," she said. "Hunter said, 'If we help organize them and give them the hint that they are very powerful, they could get involved and take control of their environment.' He looked through the same lens at ESPN that he did at *Rolling Stone*. That's what he was doing in his writing: helping his readers gain more confidence in themselves." But the steady gig also meant relentless deadlines. "There was screaming sometimes," Anita said. "He would get upset when there were too many cooks in the kitchen. He worked the best with one, no more than two people around. He needed a group of people around at the beginning of the night, to help him organize

But then he liked it calm, so his mind could work. We'd keep his drink filled and have a snack around him, so he wouldn't be distracted, so he could stay at the typewriter. That was the trick. The phones would stop ringing around midnight, and that's when he would start to get busy."

Though the ESPN deadlines kept him active and deep into the world of professional sports that he loved, the controversial 2000 presidential election and the terrorist attacks of 2001 skewed his approach to the column. He often filled his acre of cyberspace with anti-Bush political rants. The fury-of-the-seventies Hunter returned. When a young woman in Denver named Lisl Auman was jailed for a murder she did not commit, Hunter went on a rampage, using the bully pulpit of Gonzo to speak out for her case. "Hunter was a fierce libertarian, a stalwart believer that the individual controlled his or her own destiny," Brinkley said. Even low-profile cases, when they stank of injustice, aroused his invective. When a neighbor felt helpless in the onslaught of an encroaching condominium development, Hunter came to her aid and fought the zoning change and stopped construction.

Occasionally, he could muster his old political energy. When Democratic presidential nominee John Kerry came to Aspen for a fund-raiser, he gave Hunter a private interview in his rented Chevy Suburban from the airport to the home of the millionaire hosting the event. As Kerry took the podium, he asked the crowd, "How does *this* sound: Vice President Hunter S. Thompson." The crowd cheered. "Hunter was just glowing," Bob Braudis said.

But he no longer had the stamina for the campaign trail—or for much that required leaving his property. "Hunter privately, with his friends and at home, was a supreme southern gentleman," Anita said. They were happy together ("Anita was his whole life," Brinkley said), and his weekly columns were collaborations. When Deborah left, more burdens fell on Anita—taking care of the man and the writer.

He was retirement age, and his body began to quit on him. "He had a fleet of doctors who admired him, and they knew they weren't going to change him and they worked around him," Braudis said. "He ate a bowl of fruit a day. He didn't want to die. He wanted to prolong his life."

Even the ritualistic swimming, part of his work process, took on more of a therapeutic tone. "We tried to swim more, when writing was less important and health was more important," Anita said. His infirmities also rendered him if not helpless, at least less ambulatory than he had been.

His lifelong writing habits had to change to match his declining health. "When he was younger he was more mobile," Anita said, "so he would get up and walk around more, walk up and down the stairs or go outside and shoot guns. He couldn't do that when he was older, because of his back problems, because of his health problems." Anita became his arms and legs. "He couldn't sit at the typewriter for sixteen hours, like he could in the seventies," she said. "But he believed his skills of observation; his humor and his writing were just as good, if not better. He kept growing. He thought it was very important to keep growing all of your life. That's why he called himself 'a teenage girl trapped in the body of an elderly dope fiend.' He continued to learn. He was curious until the end."

Anita became ever more a caretaker. Despite these burdens, she accepted Hunter's marriage proposal in 2003. He was sixty-five and she was thirty-one. Proposals were nothing new; he'd had other fiancées (Laila, Maria, Terry, Nicole, Heidi) since his divorce from Sandy, but this one was different.

"He came in [the tavern] the day he got her diamond," Frymire said. "He was so excited. I think there were maybe three people there when that happened. I gave them massages as a wedding present."

They married on Thursday, April 24, 2003, at the Pitkin County Courthouse, with Bob Braudis and his wife as witnesses. Hunter punctuated the ceremony with shouts of "*woo hoo.*"

Hunter reported on his wedding for his ESPN readers: "It was done with fine style and secrecy in order to avoid the craziness and drunken violence that local lawmen feared would inevitably have followed the ceremony. . . . Our honeymoon was even simpler. We drank heavily for a few hours with Chris Goldstein and accepted fine gifts from strangers, then we drove erratically back out to Owl Farm and prepared for our own, very private celebration by building a huge fire, icing down a magnum of Crystal Champagne and turning on the Lakers-Timberwolves game until we passed out and crawled to the bedroom."

Things were good again. "Life is humming along smartly out here on the farm," Hunter wrote on his wedding day. He might not have been wealthy, but he was comfortable and Anita knew what she was getting into. Since she was thirty-five years younger than her husband, in taking her marriage vows she had agreed to care for this much-older man and preside over the ceremony of his death. They understood each other and began enjoying what life they would have together.

"He was never loaded," Anita said. "We were not rolling in dough, but we had a good lifestyle. We had to watch our budget. All the trips he went on were always paid by somebody else. We stayed in the best hotels, because of his stature. I never looked at the price tag at the grocery store. I could buy what I wanted. He drove a Jeep Cherokee; I drove a Jetta. We did have a housekeeper that came twice a week. We lived well, but it wasn't what some people think—that he had money for private planes or the ability to travel. The trips were paid for by other people. He was rich in many other ways."

There had always been that joke—the one about how he should really be dead, that his existence was an affront to all modern medical knowl-edge, that he was an anomaly, a genetic miracle. The joke was over.

And it wasn't just the decline of his body that depressed him. He was losing friends. Singer Warren Zevon, the musician who made the rock 'n' roll equivalent of Gonzo, died in 2002. They were friends, shooting bud-dies, and collaborators. (Hunter co-wrote Zevon's song "You're a Whole Different Person When You're Scared.") One of Hunter's closest Woody Creek friends, Oliver Treibick, also died. "He was depressed for a long time," Frymire said. "After Oliver died, that was really tough on him. One of the Woody Creek bartenders died too, Kenny Dimmick. Hunter was losing some close allies, and it really saddened him."

Benicio del Toro once called him "the cherry on the cake of fun," but Hunter began to feel that the fun had stopped. The physical pain, the infirmity, the apparatus of aging and decrepitude—none of it fit with how he saw himself.

The body started to go. Hunter had a hip replaced, but then his spine started impinging on his nerves. He needed carts at airports. Travel became even more of a burden. While visiting Hawaii, he set up a microwave in the hotel bathroom. He made ramen soup, but it was so hot when he pulled it from the microwave that it spilled onto the marble floor. He slipped, break-ing his leg. "He had a cast from his balls to his toes," Braudis said.

Actor Sean Penn chartered a plane to get Hunter back to a clinic in Colorado, and Braudis went to see him. "His mobility and his depen-dence on other people increased," Braudis said. "He hated being depen-dent." When he finally got back to Owl Farm, he had to deal with an army of physical therapists in his home.

"He was talking so much about 'the wheelchair,' " Ralph Steadman said of their phone conversations. "He'd say, 'I'm going to be sitting in this wheelchair, in an old people's home, being watched by old people, do you think I can put up with that, Ralph?' He had an image of being strapped into it, unable to move, and 'Ralph, there's an old lady crawling across the floor towards me, and she's about to fondle my balls.'"

American politics depressed him as well. After four years of George Bush, he threw himself into the 2004 campaign on the side of Democratic presidential candidate John Kerry, and his defeat devastated Hunter. "The jokes disappeared and never came back, replaced by incessant talk of his having fulfilled his life mission," Brinkley said. "Hunter was sharp as a tack, but he could also turn listless on a dime."

And still, he was a prisoner of his persona. "He was trapped by a mythology he created," Cusack said. "I think he would admit that." He continued to enhance that image with his work, with his weekly columns and *Kingdom of Fear*, which had been another tossed-off autobiographical collage in the *Songs of the Doomed* vein. The book reprinted old stories, inserted new ones, and perpetuated the Hunter Thompson/Uncle Duke character.

Even close friends said he was repeating himself. He knew it too. He had worked hard, but too often had taken the easy way out, seeing what he could get away with.

Sandy had moved on. She'd been married twice and found peace and a new life as a yoga teacher. She was a grandmother; Juan had married and there was grandson Will.

Now middle-aged, Juan worked as a computer consultant in Denver, visiting frequently. "I think we've gotten closer as I've gotten older. He was a busy guy when I was a kid. He has unusual hours. He travels a whole lot. So I'd say it's only been the last 15 years or so that we've definitely gotten closer over time."

Because of Juan and his family, Hunter and Sandy were intertwined, even though Sandy tried living in California for a while. She eventually moved to Denver. Talking about her former husband was hard, she wrote: "I have a truly wonderful life and [telling] the Hunter story again and again interrupts the peace, as it did every day of my life when I was with him." Yet she said she loved him and always would. Hunter wrote a note to Sandy and Juan in 2000: "May the right gods fall in love with you, like I did." She could still recall the tender moments. "I asked him if he knew when he was about to become the Monster," she wrote. "He said, 'Sandy, it's like this. I sense it first, and before I have completely turned around he is there. He is me.'"

Sandy tried to keep Hunter deep in the past, but she knew what tormented him. Friends would sometimes come upon him alone, in his salon, crying. Sandy knew why.

"He was a tortured tragic figure," Sandy said. "I do not think that he was a great writer. I think he clearly had great potential, both as a writer and a leader. However, he fell—dramatically and a very, very long time ago. Hunter wanted to be a great writer and he had the genius, the talent, and, early on, the will and the means. He was horrified by whom he had become and ashamed—or I really should say tortured. He knew he had failed. He knew that his writing was absolutely not great. This was part of the torture. And yet, he could never climb back. The image, the power, the drugs, the alcohol, the money . . . all of it . . . he never became that great American writer he had wanted to be. Nowhere close. And he knew it."

He began to say goodbye to all of the places he loved, to Hawaii and Key West. When friends visited, they got emotional farewells. "There was the usual hug," John Walsh said of his last visit to Owl Farm, "accompanied by an unusual tearful goodbye." During the holidays in 2004, he left messages for dozens of friends. Many were traveling or at parties and weren't there to pick up the phone. "He called everybody on his list near the end," Tom Corcoran said. "I got called Christmas Day. He'd just been to a party at [Jack] Nicholson's and had seen Buffett. I was gone; it came through as a message. And I never called him back. I had a million things to do and I thought, 'I'll call him, I'll call him.' It was very nostalgic. He said, 'Jimmy and I talked about doing a book about the old days in Key West.'"

In January 2005, Sean Penn was filming *All the King's Men* in New Orleans, Brinkley's home turf. Hunter planned to write about the production for *Playboy*. "He wanted to go alone, like the old days," Anita said, but the trip ended up depressing Hunter. While there, Hunter wanted to attend the cast-and-crew party thrown by producer and politico James Carville at Arnaud's Restaurant. But Hunter was in a wheelchair and New Orleans was built before the Americans with Disabilities Act had ramped and elevatored the country. There was no way for him to get to the private second-floor dining room, where the party was being held. He sat in the downstairs bar, drinking. Bill Dixon, in town to see his old pal, figured the humiliation was too much for Hunter's pride. "He couldn't get up to the dinner unless four guys grabbed the wheelchair and he wouldn't let them."

Sulking at the downstairs bar, Hunter turned to Brinkley and said, "My time has come to die, Dougie," making a knife-slit motion across his throat. "He didn't like being Hunter at that point," Brinkley said. "It was very difficult for him and they ended up having to call me," Anita said. "It hurt him, I think, because he realized how much harder it was to travel alone. He needed so much help. Doug and Sean were great friends, but they weren't very good caretakers. By the time I got there, Hunter was emaciated, he hadn't eaten in two days. It was awful, it was just awful. He felt very disappointed in himself, that he couldn't take care of himself the way he used to." His ailments also required prescription medication, something new in his pharmaceutical diet. "The painkillers were something unique and they did fog his mind and inhibit his writing somewhat," Anita said. The *Playboy* assignment was abandoned, as were other writing projects.

His depression and his physical pain were sometimes too much for his young wife. Anita needed a break and went to visit her parents. Hunter called Laila and begged her to come. "I went out there and found him not in great shape," Laila said. "His leg was in a cast, and he had a wheelchair to get around the house, which he hated. He was frustrated, angry, and in pain. It seemed the pain pills didn't help much. He was not one to be patient with any physical ailment, so to be dependent, not mobile, and in pain just drove him crazy. This also made it harder to get work done, which he was complaining about a lot. I joked with him that I was the Agnes Moorhead role in *Rebecca*: the stern governess. I took charge of the house and him and started organizing, trying to make things nice for him. I was able to calm him down after a couple of days, and we did end up having a nice quiet night here and there, just like old times. We would be in the kitchen, talking or watching television or being quiet.

"There weren't a lot of people coming around. There were a couple of girls who would come to do physical therapy and grocery shopping. They were lifesavers for me. I don't know why it was so quiet, why people weren't coming around or calling, which was unusual. We didn't discuss it."

Restored, Anita came back and Juan planned a weekend visit, with his wife, Jennifer, and their son, Will. Hunter was "Ace" to his grandson. He'd sent Will a note that said, "Walk tall. Kick ass. Learn to speak Arabic. Love music and never forget you come from a long line of truthseekers, lovers and warriors."

He wrote Anita a note, too, on February 16: "Football Season is Over. No More Games. No More Bombs. No More Walking. No More Fun.

No More Swimming. 67. That is 17 years past 50. 17 more than I needed or wanted. Boring. I am always bitchy. No Fun—for anybody. 67. You are getting Greedy. Act your old age. Relax—This won't hurt."

Juan and Jennifer were just back from a trip to Italy and brought Hunter an orange silk scarf, which he draped over his shoulders. He sat at his perch in the kitchen, surrounded by his son's family, Anita, and friends. He picked up a gun—just a pellet gun, not his .45 caliber—and aimed it across the room, at a gong directly behind Anita's chair. He fired—hitting the gong, but coming too close to Anita.

Anita was furious. "You're in big trouble with me," she screamed, and headed off to the basement guest room for the night. Hunter could hear her crying downstairs, but couldn't walk down there to comfort her. The friends left, Jennifer and Will went to bed, but Juan stayed up, talking deep into the night with his father. Hunter began presenting his son with family heirlooms—jewelry, books, things that were part of Juan's "inheritance." He talked about his death; he wanted to be cremated and his remains blasted from a cannon. Juan knew the story; he'd heard it ever since he was a little boy, still living at Owl Farm.

The next day, Hunter awoke, polished his pistol and resumed the business of being Hunter S. Thompson. He apologized to Anita for coming so close to her with his shot. She accepted the apology, but the thaw had not yet set in. She said she was going to the Aspen Club and Spa. Hunter gave her a look—a "weird look," she said later.

It was late afternoon. After Anita got to the gym and before she began her workout, she called home. When it rang, he hit the speakerphone button. "Hello," she said. When he heard her voice, he picked up, which was rare. Everyone got the speakerphone treatment. He liked having his hands free so he could do other things while he talked. He was the king of multitasking. But he picked up. *That's sweet*, she thought.

They spoke for ten minutes and twenty-two seconds. That's what her cell phone records said. He was funny, as he was most of the time.

"Come home after you work out," he said. "Come home and we'll work on a column." They never said goodbye. It sounded like he put down the phone. Anita heard a sound, something clicking, like something tapping. She listened for a while, maybe a minute, then hung up.

Then Hunter finished loading his .45 caliber pistol, put the barrel in his mouth, and pulled the trigger.

EPILOGUE

Q: If you could meet any person in the world, who would you meet?
A: Hunter S. Thompson; he seemed like a pretty crazy guy.
—*Interview with a college athlete, 2007*

Juan thought a book dropped to the floor. When he came into the room a few minutes later, nothing looked amiss. Hunter was in the kitchen, at his perch in front of his typewriter, but slumped in the chair, as if sleeping. Hunter rarely slept. He fought sleep, sometimes staying up for days, working, making phone calls deep into the night. His friends knew there was real time, and then there was Hunter time. If he had your phone number, you were fair game.

But Juan knew Hunter was not asleep. He had expected this someday, but not today. He found the gun Hunter had fired underneath his stool. Later, deputies found the spent slug in the hood of the oven, which was splattered with blood and brain matter.

There was paper in the typewriter. Hunter had several varieties of stationery. This sheet was for the Fourth Amendment Foundation. He had typed one word in the middle of the page: "counselor."

Juan told his wife and son. Then he called Bob Braudis, who was at a memorial service for one of his deputies.

"Something's wrong with my dad," Juan said.

"Like what?" Braudis asked.

"It's really bad."

"Have you called an ambulance?"

After hanging up with Braudis, Juan got his father's shotgun, stepped outside into the cold, and fired three rounds into the air.

After her workout, Anita was in the health-club bathroom when her friend Robin Smith asked her, "Is Hunter OK?" Word had spread around town once news of the shooting hit the police scanner. "Oh yeah," Anita said. "He's been pretty stressed out lately." But Robin's look scared Anita. Robin insisted Anita check her messages. Her hands shook so much she could barely punch in the numbers. There was a voice mail from Juan, straight and to the point: "Anita, you have to come home now. He's dead."

Rick Balentine was chief of Aspen's Fire Rescue Department. He was playing in a charity poker game downtown when he got a page from medical dispatch. "Hunter shot himself," it said. That's odd, Balentine thought. It's not hunting season. Then Braudis called. Balentine got into his official car and ran code—lights and sirens—all the way to Woody Creek. He arrived the same time as Braudis.

"Juan was in the living room," Balentine said. "The sheriff's deputies were keeping him out of the kitchen. Anita was still at the health club."

It was getting dark as Braudis, Balentine, and the deputies got to Owl Farm. The home became a crime scene.

Braudis thought it best to move Juan, Jennifer, and Will to the other cabin on the property, where Deborah Fuller had lived. Juan first asked a favor. He and his wife bought Hunter the silk scarf they'd found in Florence. The deputies let Juan into the kitchen, and he draped the scarf over his father's shoulders.

Inside, Braudis found his friend: "Hunter sitting on his stool, with his head down, not a lot of visible trauma. Paramedics had the leads on him, and they'd already said he was dead when I got there. The gun was at the bottom of the stool."

The most important thing, Braudis decided, was Juan's family. After they were in the other cabin, he called for grief counseling and a child psychologist. "I let the pros do their thing," he said. "We did all of our forensic shit, but I was at the other house." He asked his girlfriend to call friends and relatives and tell them. "Incoming phone calls were melting the system down." Balentine called Ed Bradley, one of the close friends he shared with Hunter. "He couldn't believe it," Balentine said. "I didn't want him to hear about it on the news."

After getting Juan's message, Anita called Braudis: "She was screaming at me, 'What's wrong. What's going on?' I said, 'I don't want to tell you over the phone.'"

She made the frantic drive out to Owl Farm and pushed past deputies to get to the house. She asked Braudis if she could go in. "I don't recommend it," Braudis said, "but shit, I can't stop you." Balentine had anticipated the request.

"Anita wanted to come in and say goodbye to Hunter before they took him away in the hearse," Balentine said. "I didn't want her to see him or the kitchen in that state. I did what I could to sterilize it." Anita came inside and saw her husband. "He was sitting in his chair when they brought me in," she told a reporter. "I got to hug him and kiss him and rub his legs." He looked as if he were sleeping. "He did not destroy his face," Anita said. "He did it in his mouth. His face was beautiful. It was quick."

The funeral home's hearse showed up, and as the body was being prepared for transport, Bob Rafelson called Braudis. Rafelson was a director (of *Five Easy Pieces*, among many other films) who had been Hunter's neighbor down Woody Creek Road for years. He was celebrating his birthday at home when he got the call about Hunter. He asked to come see the body.

When Rafelson arrived, Hunter was in a body bag. Juan and his wife had drifted back into the house, still in shock. Rafelson knelt down and asked the orderlies to unzip the bag so he could see Hunter's face. He looked for a moment, then stood and turned to Juan. "You know," he said, "property values are going to go down now."

Balentine picked up *Songs of the Doomed* from the kitchen counter, where it rested near Hunter's typewriter. "We need to do what we always do in this kitchen," he said. "Let's have a drink and read."

They found a bottle of Chivas Regal, poured drinks, and held their glasses and stood around Hunter: Juan and Jennifer, Anita, Braudis, Balentine, Rafelson . . . they all took turns. "It was as much religious as anything else," Balentine said. "That was the last time there was actually readings in the kitchen with Hunter."

Anita later called his suicide "a gesture of strength." Juan said, "Maybe he wanted to go out before it stopped being fun."

They drank their Chivas and toasted the late Hunter S. Thompson.

Later, Juan told a reporter, "I've known for many, many years that this is how Hunter would go. It was just a question of when." He told another interviewer, "Hunter, more than most people, lived on his own terms and he was going to do his death on his own terms too. He was going to go out when he was ready to go, the way he wanted to go. He wasn't going to let anybody else decide that for him." In another statement, Juan employed a Hunteresque phrase: "He stomped terra."

"Sebastian saw it on the news," Tom Corcoran said. "He was up and called me in tears. I was in the Keys. And he said, 'What's going on with Hunter?' And I said, 'I don't know. What's going on?' And he said, 'He shot himself.'"

Tom Corcoran had learned a lot from Hunter. When he published his first novel, *The Mango Opera*, Hunter, Jimmy Buffett, and Jim Harrison offered dust-jacket praise to publicize it. To Sebastian Corcoran, Hunter would always be that adopted uncle who played catch with him and used to pull up in the yard, announcing his arrival with a bullhorn.

Corcoran was at his place on Cudjoe Key, working on his next mystery novel. Calls from reporters started coming. "I was interviewed by three different newspapers. And thank goodness I was, because I was the only one who said, 'The man is a genius.' All of the other people said, 'Oh, he was a great guy . . . he barfed on my shoe one time.'"

Back in Louisville, Hunter's childhood friend Neville Blakemore heard the news on National Public Radio the next morning. "My first thought was 'Ah, hell, Hunter, it can't be that bad,'" he said, then briefly considered maybe it was a hoax. Porter Bibb, who now worked in the world of high finance, was in Shanghai. "The local papers had his photo on the front page under the headline, 'American Literary Icon Dead,'" he said, marveling that his childhood friend rated mention in Asia. Paul Semonin woke up to the news at his home in Oregon. In Hawaii, Bob Bone said he was "shocked, but not surprised." Sonny Barger was at his home in Arizona. "I wonder how he made it so long," he said. "His whole life he was on that plunge—a suicidal trip." Cheryl Frymire had moved back with her family in Pennsylvania two months before. She saw the news on the only television station that reached her on the farm. She called the Woody Creek Tavern to talk to friends. "The phones there were ringing off the hook that night," she said. "No one wanted to believe it." In Amagansett, New York, Anne Willis Noonan woke to the news that the best man at her wedding was dead. She cried. "I truly hope he is in a good place, full of peacocks, Dobermans, and it's a dry county," she said.

Former Senator Gary Hart was in Australia. "I was afraid that somehow it had not been a rational act, that he, in a fit of whatever—drugs, hallucination, or something—he'd done something he really wouldn't have done if he'd been more sober or sane," he said. "I didn't understand quite how or why you would do that with your son and his family there." In Montana, Russell Chatham was deeply saddened, but on reflection thought perhaps it should not have been surprising "given the medical problems and the vile political climate."

Ralph Steadman was asleep when he got a transatlantic call from Joe Petro, the printmaker with whom he'd collaborated on Gonzo art. "Take your phone off the hook," Petro told Steadman. "Hunter just shot himself." But Ralph took a call from the *Independent* and wrote a reminiscence for the paper, and was quoted in wire stories saying, "About bloody time. He's been threatening to do it for years." Eventually, Ralph wrote a troubling and touching memoir of their friendship, *The Joke's Over*. "I keep wishing he would have just shot himself in the balls and left that brain intact," he mused after the book was published. "I wish he'd left his mind to function and work on something greater."

Putting Hunter in context was tough. The press reported the death of that crazy dude who took all those drugs and was played in the movies by Johnny Depp and Bill Murray. The madman public image that overshadowed him in life also stalked him in death.

As a historian and Hunter's literary executor, Douglas Brinkley was the leading authority on him and his work. Jann Wenner and the *Rolling Stone* staff, led by editor Corey Seymour, assembled a monumental memorial issue, working against the usual deadline odds, compounded by severe emotional ones. Finally, Hunter's name was moved from the masthead, as he had requested in 1972. It appeared in a place of honor at the bottom of the list of names, alongside Ralph Gleason's. "He was such a big part of my life and I loved him deeply," Wenner wrote in the memorial issue. As soon as the issue was done, he and Seymour began expanding the issue into a book-length treatment called *Gonzo*. When that was finished, Wenner began assembling an anthology of all of Hunter's stories for the magazine. He mused about how their intense partnership in the seventies had cooled. He wondered what Hunter might have achieved "had he not become an alcoholic and a cocaine addict." "I always saw him as an Ambrose Bierce–Mark Twain kind of guy," Wenner mused. "He had that wit and that acid tongue and that gift of hyperbolic language. He could have continued in that direction. He was deeply involved in what America could be and should be. Our love of that was one of the many parts of our bond."

Essayists, friends, and admirers began filling print and cyberspace with postdeath tributes. Some wrote about his large role in chronicling the madness of his times, citing *Fear and Loathing in Las Vegas* as the epitaph for the sixties and its broken hopes. He had always wanted to be known for his fiction, but his journalism nevertheless became his literature. In the end, his epic life became his novel.

Hunter's obsession was the American Dream, something he struggled to write about and never fully defined. "If life is a dream, as some suggest, sometimes beautiful sometimes desperate, then Hunter's work is the terrible saga of the ending of time for the American Dream," Ron Whitehead said. In his heart, Hunter's interpretation might have been close to Sonny Barger's vision: "There ain't an American Dream today like there was fifty years ago. Ten or fifteen years ago, when I lived in Oakland, we would take a trip to San Jose and it was like fifty miles away, and it was an all-day trip down East Fourteenth Street. Things were a lot slower then. It's a much, much faster world now. Because of 9/11, we've lost so many of our freedoms, and started becoming basically a police state. So much of our freedom has been taken away. The American Dream of fifty years ago is totally gone."

Gary Hart said of Hunter, "If he was searching for the American Dream, he was searching for it way out on the margin, not where most people live."

"He could have made a pretty good president," Ralph Steadman said. "People would laugh at that, but he was serious about all of that. I think he was one of the best patriots we've ever had." Hunter was furious with those who confused dissent with disloyalty. "I'm as patriotic as anybody," he said. "I have a long history of writing about this country and I do care what happens to it."

His death came as a shock, but maybe it shouldn't have. He'd been writing suicide notes his whole life. College students mourned. Book sales soared. Fans erected tribute websites. Essayists both praised and denounced his exit. Warren Ellis, the graphic artist whose *Transmetropolitan* books were about a shadow life for Hunter, wrote about Hunter's great influence, then said that the numbness he felt "comes from now finding that he was the kind of man that'd let his family find him like that. I have a personal loathing for suicide. It's stupid and selfish and ugly and cowardly and reeks of weakness."

Hunter's friends faced their grief, replayed their last moments with him, and vented their anger. "I had no signals, no indication that he was contemplating it," Bob Braudis said. The Wednesday before, he was entertaining some out-of-town visitors at a restaurant when Hunter called. When Hunter learned that the visitors were his fans, he asked Braudis to bring them by the farm. For two hours, he gave the guests enough Hunter Thompson stories for a lifetime. "He was *on his game*," Braudis said. "That was the last time I saw him alive."

After Hunter's death, Braudis had to hold things together personally and professionally. "I was the oak tree for the close friends and family," he said. "Then I got fucking pissed. I got really angry." He had to go to California for a funeral. Afterward, he went to Napa Valley. "I got up in the wine country, got fucked up, then I got copacetic with it." Eventually, the anger passed and sadness took over. "I miss him. When shit pops up, like when Deep Throat was outed, I thought, 'What would Hunter say?'"

Numbness, shock, things *left undone and unsaid.* Juan and Anita wrestled with the churning emotions of sudden loss, and the devastating survivor pain of suicide. Anita received thousands of letters from Hunter's devoted fans. "A lot of kids want to be rebels, but a lot of them don't want to be smart rebels, and do it right," she said. But the majority of the letters came from bright kids who seemed to understand Hunter and the need for intelligent dissent, not emotional rant. Hunter had little patience with the dewy-eyed or the uninformed. "When he was gone, it was very *hard*," Anita said. "He had so much to offer. He was so well versed. He could talk about anything. He could bring humor to any dark situation. He was valuable, in so many different ways, to his friends. He was always there for his friends and we certainly have a vacuum." She paused, considering the void left in her life. "At this point," she said, "I would just settle for a three-minute phone call from wherever he is."

Without time to get their wind back, Anita and Juan were both forced to ponder Hunter's legacy, literary and otherwise. The immediate concern was what to do with Hunter's stuff. He had a *lot* of stuff. As a lifelong pack rat, he left behind eight hundred boxes of letters and photographs.

A moving truck backed up to the door of Hunter's home and carted the boxes off to the Denver law firm of Haddon, Morgan and Foreman. Hal Haddon, one of Hunter's close friends, offered the space to the family for the massive task of sifting through Hunter's life in words. Universities began lining up like suitors on prom night, hoping to take the Thompson papers home to their library archives.

As Juan sat on a stool in the middle of the hundreds of boxes, he meticulously indexed the contents. "It's very interesting, now that he's dead, to still be learning about our relationship," Juan said. "What's sad is I can't talk to him about it now. That makes me sad, but I'm very glad that I have this chance to learn more about him." Hunter saved *everything*. "Something that may look like nothing in a box, like a scribbled-on cocktail napkin from Las Vegas, is sort of an interesting artifact," Douglas Brinkley said. "Things like that were key elements of Hunter's work process."

Juan began writing a memoir of life with his father. Anita collected some of Hunter's wit and wisdom for a slim volume called *The Gonzo Way*, and promised Hunter's readers that death would not silence him. The important thing was to develop a publishing strategy, not to dump Hunter's previously unpublished work onto the market. "We're not in a hurry," Anita said. "We don't want to flood bookstores with Hunter's work. That's not the way to do it. And we have to think about these things. There have been some writers, as soon as they died, their estate started pumping out their work. I don't think that's a great tribute, actually."

Brinkley saw *The Gun Lobby* as a complete and fully realized booklength manuscript, something that could easily stand alongside *Hell's Angels, Fear and Loathing in Las Vegas*, and the *Campaign Trail* book. "We have to think through a strategy so that in ten or twenty years, Hunter does not become a dismissed figure, like Ambrose Bierce. So we have to think long-term in publishing his remaining work." Brinkley said that

Juan and Anita were on the same page in this matter: "They want Hunter to look good, in long-term literary reputation." Perhaps pairing the early novel *Prince Jellyfish* with some of Hunter's Fitzgerald-influenced short stories from the fifties would make an entertaining volume, he said. As literary executor, Brinkley was forced to look at the work with an eye toward commercial potential and scholarly value. But he also needed distance; he too had lost a close friend.

Juan's major concern was that his father be remembered as a writer, not as a drug-addled caricature. "People are going to write what they want to write," he said. But he hoped to keep the focus on his father's work and on "not the crazy stories and the crazy things he did."

Juan did not work alone in helping to prop up Hunter's reputation. Two days after Hunter's death, Tom Wolfe wrote his appreciation for the *Wall Street Journal*, including the caveat that he and Hunter had not spent much time together and that he, thank God, was not on Hunter's nocturnal call list. Wolfe noted that Hunter was his candidate for "the greatest comic writer of the 20th Century." Wolfe later said that Hunter really belonged alongside nineteenth-century American humorists such as Mark Twain, Josh Billings, and Petroleum V. Nasby. "All three of them were onstage a lot, and Twain, if you look back at it, Twain was an entertainer. He was the first authentic American voice in literature in the eyes of Europeans. They had all heard about the Wild West and the gold rush and American manners and speech, which was so different. You couldn't find that in literature. In the case of Mark Twain, you found it in the literature, and he was just a great entertainer onstage. Hunter onstage was a performer, but not in words. He always had maniac presentations—throwing things at the audience, throwing a glass of Wild Turkey through a window, and so on. I never saw him out of character in formal situations."

Wolfe said Hunter shared another key characteristic with Twain. "As with Mark Twain, with Hunter you take for granted that it's not all true. In *Fear and Loathing in Las Vegas*, he refers to his Samoan lawyer. He was actually Mexican, but Samoan is a lot funnier." But beyond his comic style and his well-developed persona, Hunter shared a level of celebrity with Twain. "Mark Twain was the best-known American writer in history," Wolfe said. "There will probably never be anyone as well known as he was. He was an international showman. I wonder if there is any writer right now who is better known than Hunter Thompson." Wolfe pondered a moment, and came up with Philip Roth, John Updike, and Norman Mailer. "But outside of the 'litt-tree' world, these are nonpeople, whereas Hunter Thompson is all over the place." Even people who did not read knew Hunter S. Thompson.

But those who did read, Wolfe said, were lucky to live in Hunter Thompson's times. "He was just brilliant," he said. "There are very few writers who could top him. I can't think of any humorist in the whole country who could touch him."

For a long time, Wolfe thought Hunter was a prisoner of his persona. "I said to myself, 'He's trapped himself in this role of having to be the manic clown.' But as I look back on it, that's really not true. That was his particular form of genius. It's a hard act to keep up when you're really not young anymore. But he did. To the bitter end, he was a wild man."

The coroner said death had been instantaneous. Hunter was cremated the next day, and his ashes stored in a bird's-eye maple box. But a scheduled ceremony for the following weekend was canceled (not enough time to arrange), and plans were begun for a memorial. Handling the ceremonies of Hunter's death fell to his young widow and to his son. Many things needed doing, but Anita made certain to attend to one of Hunter's specific wishes: she packed up Hunter's red IBM Selectric II and sent it to Bob Dylan, in gratitude for the forty years of "fuel" his music had provided.

A few days after his father's suicide, Juan called Cheryl Frymire in Pennsylvania and asked whether she would come back to Aspen to sing at a memorial service.

On March 5, a six-hour, invitation-only memorial was held at the Hotel Jerome in Aspen. Life-size cutouts of Hunter greeted the guests—Jack Nicholson, Johnny Depp, Bill Murray, and Jann Wenner, among them. Wayne Ewing's documentary, *Breakfast with Hunter*, played on monitors. Black thong panties with the Gonzo double-thumbed fist on the crotch were displayed on tables, alongside Kleenex and beaded necklaces. Bartenders served beer, liquor, and Jell-O shots. "Everyone there was hand-picked to be Hunter's friend," Frymire said. Hunter's brother Davison came from Cleveland and got to meet these people from the other end of Hunter's life. He saw a familiar face: Porter Bibb, from the old days in Louisville. They got caught up, and at one point Davison asked, "What do you think made Hunter the way he is?" Bibb shook his head. He had no answer. "I thought it was really a strange question for the guy who grew up with him to ask. He didn't have a clue."

The memorial card handed to guests did not have a biblical verse. Instead, it was from *Kubla Khan*, by Samuel Taylor Coleridge:

Weave a circle round him thrice
And close your eyes with holy dread.
For he on honey-dew hath fed
And drunk the milk of paradise.

Jann Wenner spoke, trying to set the record straight about the firing-on-the-way-to-Saigon story. That was all a misunderstanding. "He knew that I would never fuck him over," Wenner later recalled. "That's a rare thing to find in somebody, especially if you're as nutty as Hunter. He knew I was there on every level—as a friend, as an editor, as a comrade." Others offered testaments of love or admiration, with a few bawdy stories. Cheryl Frymire took the stage and sang, a cappella, one of the hymns she had recorded for Hunter at his request, so he could worship in the privacy of his mind:

Amazing Grace, how sweet the sound,
That saved a wretch like me!
I once was lost but now am found,
Was blind, but now, I see.

The memorial at the Jerome, moving as it was, was not the end. There was Hunter's well-documented wish to have his remains blasted from a tower. He'd laid out his specific plans, down to the height of the monument (150 feet), its design (the double-thumbed fist), and the ceremony (his ashes blasted into space through the cannon, while Bob Dylan sang "Mr. Tambourine Man").

Making this pipe dream reality would be incredibly expensive, but Hunter, who collected friends, who put new people together to make new bouquets of friends, who thus created a tribe, had faith it would happen. "I know somewhere in his crooked mind, he knew that I was the only one loyal enough or insane enough to attempt it," Johnny Depp said.

Depp hired Hollywood production companies to build the fist, the tower, and the landscape for the second funeral. At a cost of $2.5 million,

Depp gave Hunter the send-off he wanted. Considering the materials, the labor, the man-hours to construct the monument in California and transport it to Colorado, and then to stage the event on Owl Farm, Depp got a bargain.

The blast-off ceremony was a logistical trial. Depp's planners had to get local governmental approval, obtain the blessings of neighbors, construct the huge tower, choreograph the fireworks, and build a viewing pavilion for the invited guests. To keep the monument as secret as possible, it was covered by a red shroud during construction. There were also pyrotechnic issues. The monument was 150 feet high. The fireworks would go over 200 feet higher, so the Federal Aviation Administration had to get involved to regulate airspace. The site had been specified by Hunter—in the bowl of a valley in front of the bluffs that bounded his land. The ceremony and display were scheduled for August 20. Unfortunately, Colorado was suffering a drought, and a ban on burning was in effect.

Invitations went out late and, to control the size of the event, were limited to 150 guests. Many longtime friends were left off the list, and an article in the *Aspen Free Press* said that "Hollywood hijacked" Hunter's funeral. Anita, sensitive to the issue, put an ad in the newspaper urging people to honor Hunter at the Woody Creek Tavern and an Aspen bar called the Belly Up. Invited guests would be transported to Woody Creek by chartered buses. But none of this planning stopped massive cross-country pilgrimages by Hunter's true believers.

The viewing pavilion was decorated in Hunter style, with a bar, a replica of his refrigerator (stocked with Heineken and Flying Dog), buffalo heads, a stuffed peacock, the *Oxford American Dictionary* open to the entry for *gonzo*, and comfortable furniture that could have fit in Hunter's salon. Huge photographs decorated the room, including one of Hunter's favorites: the picture Tom Corcoran took of him throwing the football to Sebastian in the yard in Key West. Hunter was shirtless, intent as a pro quarterback, young and handsome. He was playing with a young boy, but he looked as focused as Bart Starr or Joe Namath. In the middle of the pavilion was a round bar, serving every alcoholic refreshment known to humanity.

Deborah Fuller came back. Ron Whitehead and his family drove cross-country. Tom and Sebastian Corcoran arrived from Florida, guests of Monty Chitty. Bill Murray, Johnny Depp, Laila Nabulsi, and several other writers and actors made sure to attend. Jann Wenner, Ralph Steadman, and others from the old days at *Rolling Stone* were there. In death as in life, Hunter brought together writers, actors, politicians, and journalists. Bill Dixon was there with his old boss, George McGovern. McGovern's wife, Eleanor, had suffered a heart attack that summer, a few weeks before the memorial, but she insisted her husband attend.

Bob Braudis spoke to the crowd, noting how special Hunter really was. "After all," he said, "even the pope had only one funeral." He tried to remind everyone that Hunter would not want sadness on this occasion. He had spoken to David Amram, who had come to perform, with Lyle Lovett and Johnny Depp. "No tears," Braudis said. "Hunter wrote that when he died there should be a party with all of his old friends, and he wanted to hear the tinkling of ice in glasses."

Surveying the crowd, Ralph Steadman said, "It's like Hunter is our host for the evening, bringing us all together one more time."

Lovett played "If I Had a Boat," one of Hunter's favorite songs. With Johnny Depp and Amram, they played Amram's "Theme and Variations on My Old Kentucky Home." John Kerry waved to the crowd. Anita Thompson read *Kubla Khan*. Jann Wenner described his many collaborations with Hunter, and Ed Bradley told a few of his favorite Hunter stories.

Senator McGovern, the featured speaker, focused on Hunter's *Campaign Trail* book. "At the end of the book, on the last page, Hunter has a list and he says it's 'Ten things I wish I had done during the campaign.' And what he said for number ten was 'I wish I had spent a week on a deserted Caribbean island with Eleanor McGovern.'" The crowd laughed. "I didn't think so kindly of that, but we've stayed in touch over all the years and everything. And when I went to the hospital yesterday to talk to Eleanor—Eleanor insisted that I come—and she said, 'George, since you'll be the last one to talk to Hunter before they shoot his ashes up, tell him I wished I had spent that week with him, too.'"

As the ceremony was about to begin, Juan Thompson drove his father's convertible, the Great Red Shark, to the base of the monument and parked. It was dark now, with a strange low cloud cover and errant raindrops spitting on the spectators, who assembled outside the pavilion to view the spectacle. The drape fell from the shaft of the monument, revealing the dagger. From the top, the drapery crawled upward into the fist, as if being devoured. Finally, the red double-thumbed fist with the electric peyote button was revealed. When the six spotlights hit, several shadows of the fist showed up like a bat signal on the underside of the cloud layer. Someone yelled, "He's here with us!"

The onlookers cheered, as Norman Greenbaum's "Spirit in the Sky" blared from the speakers.

> *When I die and they lay me to rest*
> *Gonna go to the place that's the best*

Then the fireworks began, shooting two hundred feet into the air above the monument as the music echoed through the valley. Three rounds of color and smoke, and then the canister of Hunter's ashes shot into the sky, and his remains fanned across the bluffs and the valley of Owl Farm, just as he had planned. As the smoke slowly drifted across the valley, the crowd applauded the end of the ceremony and Anita Thompson yelled, "We love you Hunter!"

Now the sound system played Hunter's favorite song, Bob Dylan's plea from an artist to a muse:

> *Hey! Mr. Tambourine Man, play a song for me,*
> *In the jingle jangle morning I'll come followin' you.*

Now the ashes drifted, as Hunter must have known they would, back toward the guests standing in front of the viewing pavilion. As the guests stood holding their glasses, the ash floated and settled into their drinks. Tom Corcoran smiled, lifted his glass, and said, "Here's to you, Hunter."

— McKeeN, you shit-eating freak. I warned you about writing that vicious trash about me — Now you better get fitted for a black eye patch, just in case one of yours gets gouged out by a bushy-haired stranger in a dimly-lit parking lot. How fast can you learn Braille? You are scum.

(HST)

NOTES

CHAPTER 1: GETTING AWAY WITH IT

2   **"Hunter came out of the womb":** Sharon Martin, Producer, *Biography: Hunter S. Thompson* (Biography Channel, 2004).

2   **"He was the most charismatic leader":** Gerald Tyrrell, interview with author, June 8, 2006.

4   **"beautifully wild and uncivilized":** Description from Thompson's unpublished novel *Prince Jellyfish* (1959), excerpted in Hunter S. Thompson, *Songs of the Doomed* (New York: Summit Books, 1990), p. 55.

4   **"It was very much a closed community":** Porter Bibb, interview with author, July 24, 2005.

5   **"My dad likes to whip me":** Walter Kaegi, interview with author, January 26, 2006.

5   **"It got us outdoors":** Peter Whitmer, *When the Going Gets Weird* (New York: Hyperion, 1994), p. 30.

6   **"He was passive":** Tyrrell interview.

6   **"I soon became addicted to those moments":** Hunter S. Thompson, *Kingdom of Fear* (New York: Simon and Schuster, 2003), p. 29.

6 **"Louisville was our town":** Tyrrell interview.
6 **"We went all over":** Debby Kasdan Straight, interview with author, July 31, 2006.
7 **"We'd go to his house":** Tyrrell interview.
7 **"Hunter was a sweat to be around":** Neville Blakemore, interview with author, June 2, 2006.
8 **"We'd pack up":** Tyrrell interview.
8 **"In the earlier days":** Gerald Tyrrell, letter to author, August 17, 2007.
9 **"He scared me":** Straight interview.
9 **"a very caring mother":** Kaegi interview.
10 **"Hunter was the first one":** Tyrrell interview.
10 **"Hunter was an extremely good athlete":** Bibb interview.
10 **"I wasn't sure what that meant":** Thompson, *Kingdom of Fear*, p. 10.
10 **"You sweaty swine":** Kaegi interview.
10 **"the pole around which trouble":** E. Jean Carroll, *Hunter: The Strange and Savage Life of Hunter S. Thompson* (New York: Dutton, 1993), p. 19.
10 **"Some had an apprehension":** Kaegi interview.
11 **"It was just a drainage area":** Straight interview.
11 **"He had not just charisma":** Kaegi interview.
12 **"Not prison!":** Thompson, *Kingdom of Fear*, pp. 3–6.
12 **"The mailbox incident":** Ibid., p. 250.
13 **"His dad was a nice and quiet man":** Paul Perry, *Fear and Loathing: The Strange and Terrible Saga of Hunter S. Thompson* (New York: Thunder's Mouth Press, 1992), p. 8.
13 **"Hunter had a real short fuse":** Carroll, *Hunter*, p. 52.
13 **"He was a cute, jolly, fun kid":** Judy Stellings Markham, interview with author, September 14, 2006.
15 **"dangerous as hell":** Tyrrell interview.
15 **"The first time I got high":** Ibid.
15 **"The Athenaeum was kind of":** Paul Semonin, interview with author, August 18, 2005.
16 **"a very unusual social structure":** Bibb interview.
17 **"Even back then":** Markham interview.
17 **"We shared an interest":** Semonin interview.
18 **"We stole cars":** Thompson, *Kingdom of Fear*, pp. 341–42.
18 **"His bedroom was lined with books":** Tom Thurman, director, *Buy the Ticket, Take the Ride* (Starz Entertainment, 2006).
18 **"Where are *you* going":** Whitmer, *When the Going*, p. 62.
19 **"Please don't send him to jail":** *Louisville Courier-Journal*, June 16, 1955.
19 **"He got a raw deal":** Markham interview.

20 **"The police lie"**: Douglas Brinkley, editor's note to Hunter S. Thompson, *The Proud Highway* (New York: Villard Books, 1997), p. xxii.

20 **"I look back on my youth"**: Thompson, *Kingdom of Fear*, p. 33.

CHAPTER 2: SQUARE PEG, ROUND HOLE

21 **"We'll be watching you"**: *Louisville Courier-Journal*, August 18, 1955.

22 **"Louisville is a good place"**: Hunter S. Thompson, interview with author, April 10, 1978.

22 **"I find that by putting things"**: Hunter S. Thompson, *The Proud Highway* (New York: Villard Books, 1997), p. 133.

23 **"Electricity is neutral"**: Hunter S. Thompson, *Songs of the Doomed* (New York: Summit Books, 1990), p. 14.

24 **"I didn't honestly consider myself"**: Hunter S. Thompson, *The Great Shark Hunt* (New York: Summit Books, 1979), p. 303.

24 **"That raucous noise"**: Thompson, *Proud Highway*, p. 20.

25 **"Know anything about sports?"**: Interview with George Plimpton, *Paris Review*, Fall 2000.

26 **"I now have the best deal"**: Thompson, *Proud Highway*, p. 12

27 **"Army cagers cop 7"**: *Command Courier*, April 4, 1957, p. 7.

27 **"Look at the action verbs"**: Hunter S. Thompson, interview with author, March 1990.

27 **"The Spectator is on a well-deserved"**: *Command Courier*, November 23, 1956, p. 8.

28 **"At this point in the chronology"**: Hunter S. Thompson, *Fear and Loathing in Las Vegas and Other American Stories* (New York: Modern Library, 1996), p. 161.

29 **"I have found something"**: Thompson, *Proud Highway*, p. 16.

30 **"He was a wise guy"**: Joe Gonzalez, interview with author, January 6, 2006.

30 **"He made up the craziest stories"**: E. Jean Carroll, *Hunter: The Strange and Savage Life of Hunter S. Thompson* (New York: Dutton, 1993), p. 60.

31 **"We both got onto the newspaper"**: Gonzalez interview.

31 **"It's yours"**: Bill White, interview with author, January 11, 2006.

32 **"Of all the things"**: Thompson, *Proud Highway*, p. 49.

32 **"I don't feel that"**: Ibid., p. 69.

33 **"I don't think you have any idea"**: Ibid., pp. 68–69.

34 **"This Airman"**: Colonel W. S. Evans, memo, Aug. 23, 1957, reprinted in Thompson, *Shark Hunt*, p. 14.

34 **"I'm for the draft"**: Hunter S. Thompson, interview with Charlie Rose, PBS, June 13,1997.

34 **"I don't know exactly what it is"**: Thompson, *Proud Highway*, p. 68.

34   **"The case of THOMPSON VS THE USAF"**: Ibid., p. 72.

34   **"An apparently uncontrollable iconoclast"**: Ibid., pp. 74–75.

CHAPTER 3: THE DARK THUMB OF FATE

37   **"If a man really wanted to bury himself"**: Hunter S. Thompson, *The Proud Highway* (New York: Villard Books, 1997), p. 77.

37   **"The only women under forty"**: Ibid., p. 78.

37   **"It was nice of you to get me"**: Ibid., p. 82.

37   **"I hadn't seen a human being"**: Hunter S. Thompson, *Songs of the Doomed* (New York: Summit Books, 1990), p. 30.

38   **"This romp with the young woman"**: Thompson, *Proud Highway*, p. 94.

38   **"All of a sudden, it was looming"**: Thompson, *Songs of the Doomed*, p. 32.

39   **"If there is a Jesus"**: Thompson, *Proud Highway*, p. 86.

41   **"was probably better read"**: Peter Whitmer, *When the Going Gets Weird* (New York: Hyperion, 1994), p. 93.

41   **"I'm very much into rhythm"**: Hunter S. Thompson, interview with author, March 1990.

42   **"I just want to feel what it feels like"**: Tom Thurman, director, *Buy the Ticket, Take the Ride* (Starz Entertainment, 2006).

42   **"Basically, it's music"**: Thompson interview (1990).

42   **"It was the last time I ever saw"**: Whitmer, *When the Going*, p. 91.

42   **"I think he was enjoying New York"**: E. Jean Carroll, *Hunter: The Strange and Savage Life of Hunter S. Thompson* (New York: Dutton, 1993), p. 74.

43   **"There are people sleeping everywhere"**: Thompson, *Proud Highway*, p. 126.

43   **"Mid-town Manhattan is an unbelievable circus"**: Ibid., p. 116.

43   **"I rode down Fifth Avenue"**: Ibid., p. 121.

44   **"Hunter takes the bag off his shoulder"**: *Rolling Stone*, March 24, 2005, p. 50.

45   **"As far as I'm concerned"**: Thompson, *Proud Highway*, p. 139.

45   **"How many newspapers are there"**: Ibid., p. 142.

46   **"He was already skating"**: Bob Bone, website remembrance.

47   **"Some people find it exceedingly difficult"**: Thompson, *Proud Highway*, p. 157.

48   **"A thousand years from now"**: Ibid., p. 155.

48   **"There was a tiny road side store"**: David Amram, website remembrance.

48   **"He was very lean"**: David Amram, interview with author, May 19, 2006.

49   **"We'd go to the Lion's Head"**: Ibid.

49 **"As far as I can see"**: Thompson, *Proud Highway*, p. 164.

49 **"They ain't throwin' dirt"**: Ibid., p. 174.

50 **"As things stand now"**: *Playboy*, January 2007.

50 **"If you know of anyone"**: Thompson, *Proud Highway*, p. 173.

51 **"He stayed in and out"**: Fred Schoelkopf, interview with author, June 2, 2006.

51 **"He rarely slept"**: Ibid.

51 **"If it hadn't been for Ann"**: Thompson, *Proud Highway*, p. 179.

52 **"You may not appreciate this"**: Ibid., p. 179.

CHAPTER 4: A NATURAL INGRATE

54 **"I had a fiancé at the time"**: *Rolling Stone*, March 24, 2005, p. 52.

55 **"If I were anything but a writer"**: Hunter S. Thompson, *The Proud Highway* (New York: Villard Books, 1997), p. 207.

56 **"a liar, a cheat, a passer of bad checks"**: Ibid., p. 209.

57 **"have the simple goddamned decency"**: Ibid., p. 211.

57 **"I want you to come down here"**: Ibid., p. 214.

57 **"He had a need for histrionics"**: Paul Semonin, interview with author, August 18, 2005.

58 **"I got a call and got some money"**: *Rolling Stone*, March 25, 2005, p. 51.

58 **"If I could think of a way to do it"**: Hunter, *Proud Highway*, p. 217.

59 **"at best, a minor novel"**: Ibid., p. 220.

60 **"I've compromised myself so often"**: Ibid., p. 223.

60 **"That was when I first understood"**: Hunter S. Thompson, *Fear and Loathing in America* (New York: Simon and Schuster, 2000), p. 260.

60 **"I have still not decided"**: Thompson, *Proud Highway*, p. 230.

61 **"I wake up each morning"**: Ibid., p. 233.

61 **"Whatever happens will be all right"**: Ibid., p. 239.

62 **"I am a free man"**: Henry Miller, *Tropic of Cancer* (New York: Grove Press, 1994), p. 66.

62 **"I had the misfortune"**: Henry Miller, *The Air-Conditioned Nightmare* (New York: New Directions, 1945), p. 24.

62 **"The most terrible thing"**: Ibid., pp. 34–35.

63 **"It was one room on top"**: Sharon Martin, producer, *Biography: Hunter S. Thompson* (Biography Channel, 2004).

64 **"For thirty-five dollars a month"**: Joan Baez, *And a Voice to Sing With* (New York: Summit Books, 1987), p. 71.

64 **"We were living in the servants' quarters"**: E. Jean Carroll, *Hunter: The Strange and Savage Life of Hunter S. Thompson* (New York: Dutton, 1993), p. 87.

65 **"The big money is just around"**: Thompson, *Proud Highway*, p. 244.

65   **"It was snowing":** Hunter S. Thompson, introduction to *To Aspen and Back* by Peggy Clifford (New York: St. Martin's Press, 1980).

66   **"When we were in Big Sur":** Carroll, *Hunter*, p. 86.

67   **"He wrote about some baths":** Martin, producer, *Biography*.

68   **"I'm damned if I can figure out":** Thompson, *Proud Highway*, p. 331.

68   **"I am plagued":** Ibid., p. 332.

69   **"A beautiful woman":** Ibid., p. 336.

69   **"When a person spends":** Ibid., p. 333.

69   **"It can be tough":** Lew Sharpley, "It's Tough for a Dog to Have a Globe-trotter for a Master," *Louisville Courier-Journal*, January 3, 1962.

CHAPTER 5: OBSERVER

71   **"We don't need more people":** Edward Scharff, *Worldly Power: The Making of the Wall Street Journal* (New York: New American Library, 1986), p. 176.

71   **"In the beginning":** Jerry Footlick, interview with author, July 11, 2006.

71   **"Bill gave Hunter a contract":** Ibid.

71   **"One complaint we heard":** Ibid.

72   **"the first tourist in history":** *National Observer*, August 6, 1962, p. 16.

73   **"Hunter showed up on Copacabana Beach":** Bob Bone, website remembrance.

73   **"I could toss in a few hair-raising stories":** *National Observer*, December 31, 1962, p. 14.

74   **"Things are not going well here":** Ibid.

74   **"During the Rio days":** Peter Whitmer, *When the Going Gets Weird* (New York: Hyperion, 1994), p. 133.

74   **"They say you never hear the one":** Ernest Hemingway, *Byline* (New York: Charles Scribner's Sons, 1967), p. 275.

74   **"In the morning, before your call comes":** Ibid., pp. 262–63.

75   **"Ten minutes later":** *National Observer*, February 11, 1963, p. 11.

76   **"One of my most vivid memories":** *National Observer*, August 19, 1963, p. 18.

77   **"Hunter's stories were just different":** Footlick interview.

78   **"At first, I couldn't even write":** Tom Wolfe, *The New Journalism* (New York: Harper and Row, 1973), p. 5.

79   **"a pure dull hell":** Hunter S. Thompson, *The Proud Highway* (New York: Villard Books, 1997), pp. 346–47.

80   **"I never felt in some ways":** Paul Semonin, interview with author, August 18, 2005.

80   **"My greatest talent":** Sara Nelson, interview with Hunter S. Thompson, *Book Report*, 1997.

80 **"I'm beginning to think you're a phony"**: Thompson, *Proud Highway*, p. 368.

81 **"Rio was the end of the foreign"**: Peter Whitmer, "Hunter Thompson: Still Crazy after All These Years," *Saturday Review*, January–February 1980, p. 20.

81 **"I came home as a man"**: Hunter S. Thompson, interview with author, March 1990.

82 **"I offered to put him on the staff"**: Bill Giles, interview with author, July 25, 2006.

CHAPTER 6: STRANGER IN A STRANGE LAND

84 **"Sandy appealed to all of us"**: E. Jean Carroll, *Hunter: The Strange and Savage Life of Hunter S. Thompson* (New York: Dutton, 1993), p. 93.

84 **"merely put the stamp of law"**: Hunter S. Thompson, *The Proud Highway* (New York: Villard Books, 1997), p. 383.

85 **"These Rockies make the Santa Lucias"**: Ibid., p. 413.

85 **"Christ, my life is genuine pleasure"**: Ibid., p. 397.

85 **"I'm in no position now to take"**: Ibid.

85 **"I have always looked at"**: Peter Whitmer, *When the Going Gets Weird* (New York: Hyperion, 1994), p. 135.

86 **"I am trying to compose a reaction"**: Thompson, *Proud Highway*, p. 417–18.

86 **"I am afraid to sleep. . . ."**: Ibid., p. 420.

86 **"rated only behind *Time*"**: William L. Rivers, "The Correspondents after 25 Years," *Columbia Journalism Review*, Summer 1962, pp. 4–10.

87 **"*The Reporter* don't dig me"**: Thompson, *Proud Highway*, p. 456.

88 **"Perhaps he found what he came"**: *National Observer*, May 25, 1964, p. 13.

88 **"Forget running with the bulls"**: Douglas Brinkley, "Contentment Was Not Enough," *Rolling Stone*, March 24, 2005, p. 36.

89 **"Berkeley, Hell's Angels, Kesey"**: Hunter S. Thompson, interview with author, March 1990.

89 **"Tulsa with a view"**: Thompson, *Proud Highway*, p. 509.

89 **"He collected flies on flypaper"**: Bob Geiger, remarks at the Aspen Institute, July 21, 2007.

89 **"I can't speak the language here"**: Thompson, *Proud Highway*, p. 451.

90 **"I have a son named Juan"**: Ibid. p. 449.

90 **"I would wander in"**: Hunter S. Thompson, *Songs of the Doomed* (New York: Summit Books, 1990), p. 112.

90 **"I am in the same condition here"**: Thompson, *Proud Highway*, p. 447.

90 **"I remember going to my first"**: Hunter S. Thompson, *The Great Shark Hunt* (New York: Summit Books, 1979), p. 84.

91 **"He always struck me":** Bill Giles, interview with author, July 25, 2006.

91 **"I was the youngest and healthiest":** Craig Vetter, "The Playboy Interview with Hunter S. Thompson," *Playboy*, November 1974.

92 **"I saw it coming":** Thompson, *Songs of the Doomed*, p. 112.

93 **"Some of the phrases sounded":** Giles interview.

93 **"My final reason for leaving":** Thompson interview (1990).

93 **"Somebody on the *Observer*":** Thompson, *Proud Highway*, p. 640.

93 **"Cliff abruptly hangs up":** Dan Greene, "Dow Jones to Gonzo," unpublished recollection accompanying letter sent to author.

95 **"The *Observer* has taken great pains":** Thompson, *Proud Highway*, p. 475.

95 **"I am long past the point":** Ibid., p. 481.

CHAPTER 7: AMONG THE ANGELS

96 **"vehicular, of course":** George Plimpton, *Shadow Box* (New York: G. P. Putnam's Sons, 1977), p. 337.

97 **"I think that's the way to go out":** Hunter S. Thompson, *The Proud Highway* (New York: Villard Books, 1997), p. 512.

97 **"Suicide (is) the only logical human act":** Ibid., p. 468.

97 **"The one thing I insist on":** Ibid., p. 513.

97 **"In 1965 Hunter was living":** Carey McWilliams, *The Education of Carey McWilliams* (New York: Simon and Schuster, 1979), pp. 235–36.

98 **"This one is right up my alley":** Thompson, *Proud Highway*, p. 498.

98 **"I can't imagine":** Ibid., p. 497.

98 **"Look, you guys don't know me":** Craig Vetter, "The Playboy Interview with Hunter S. Thompson," *Playboy*, November 1974.

98 **"I recall some hairy moments":** Hunter S. Thompson, "Motorcycle Gangs: Hell's Angels," *Courier-Journal and Times Magazine*, February 26, 1967, p. 1.

98 **"They were a bit off-balance":** Vetter, *Playboy* interview.

98 **"My wife was very pretty":** Marc Weingarten, *The Gang That Wouldn't Write Straight* (New York: Crown, 2005), p. 135.

99 **"I don't think we're rebelling":** Sonny Barger interview by Paul DeRienzo on Barger's website.

99 **"Sonny was a very powerful leader":** Weingarten, *Gang*, p. 133.

99 **"He acted like a tough guy":** Ralph "Sonny" Barger, interview with author, February 14, 2006.

100 **"We were talking across a pool table":** Hunter S. Thompson, "Losers and Outsiders," *Nation*, May 17, 1965.

100 **"This, in effect, was what the Hell's Angels":** Ibid.

101 **"a good but by no means exceptional":** McWilliams, *Education*, p. 236.

102 **"Fiction is a bridge to truth":** Thompson, *Proud Highway*, p. 529.

103 **"The club agreed":** Barger interview.

103 **"I think that the majority":** Ibid.

104 **"I felt so out of my element":** Paul Semonin, interview with author, August 18, 2005.

104 **"Here we are":** Sharon Martin, *Biography: Hunter S. Thompson* (Biography Channel, 2004).

104 **"He didn't like anything":** E. Jean Carroll, *Hunter: The Strange and Savage Life of Hunter S. Thompson* (New York: Dutton, 1993), pp. 104, 103.

105 **"But they stomped him anyway":** Ibid., p. 105.

105 **"Hunter, why are you writing":** *Rolling Stone*, March 24, 2005, p. 52.

106 **"It was a horrible, momentous meeting":** Vetter, *Playboy* interview.

107 **"as fucked up as possible":** Ibid.

107 **"I'd heard all these stories":** Ibid.

107 **"I've gone to the bottom of the well":** Hunter S. Thompson, *Songs of the Doomed* (New York: Summit Books, 1990), p. 121.

107 **"You motherfucking, crazy bastard":** Martin Torgoff, *Can't Find My Way Home* (Simon and Schuster, 2004), p. 117.

108 **"It had a lot of juice":** Paul Perry, *Fear and Loathing: The Strange and Terrible Saga of Hunter S. Thompson* (New York: Thunder's Mouth Press, 1992), p. 110.

108 **"If anything ever happened":** Barger interview.

108 **"By the time I started *Hell's Angels*":** *Paris Review* interview, Fall 2000.

109 **"It was fantastic":** Bill Giles, interview with author, July 25, 2006.

109 **"My face was almost frozen":** Thompson, *Songs of the Doomed*, p. 115.

110 **"It's a frontal assault":** Thompson, *Proud Highway*, p. 567.

110 **"Hunter felt that Mailer":** Douglas Brinkley, interview with author, October 16, 2007.

110 **"beating these rotten keys":** Thompson, *Proud Highway*, p. 584.

110 **"I shook him and I said":** Carroll, *Hunter*, p. 105.

110 **"To my friends who lent me money":** Hunter S. Thompson, *Hell's Angels* (New York: Random House, 1967), dedication.

110 **"If the book goes big":** Thompson, *Proud Highway*, p. 584.

110 **"I told Random House":** P.J. O'Rourke, "Hunter S. Thompson," *Rolling Stone*, November 5, 1987, p. 232.

111 **"Junkie George got into an argument":** Ralph "Sonny" Barger, with Keith Zimmerman and Kent Zimmerman, *Hell's Angel* (New York: Harper-Collins, 2001), p. 126.

111 **"He had run around with us":** Barger interview.

111 **"The problem I have":** Ibid.

111 **"Cheap bastard":** Barger, *Hell's Angel*, p. 127.

111 **"a young man of considerable journalistic talent"**: William James Smith, "Lessons in Anti-Social Behavior," *Commonweal*, April 7, 1967, p. 96.

112 **"They didn't even print enough"**: Martin, producer, *Biography*.

112 **"He is known as an avid reader"**: Thompson, *Hell's Angels*, jacket copy.

CHAPTER 8: AMERICAN DREAM

114 **"I understood his creative spirit"**: Margaret Harrell, interview with author, February 1, 2007.

114 **"Jim loved Hunter's work"**: Ibid.

115 **"By the end of '66"**: Hunter S. Thompson, *The Great Shark Hunt* (New York: Summit Books, 1979), p. 155.

115 **"I didn't want to be the little wife"**: E. Jean Carroll, *Hunter: The Strange and Savage Life of Hunter S. Thompson* (New York: Dutton, 1993), p. 117.

116 **"dull and confusing"**: Hunter S. Thompson, *Fear and Loathing in America* (New York: Simon and Schuster, 2000), p. 13.

117 **"But in defeat"**: Thompson, *Shark Hunt*, p. 507.

117 **"an eighteen-inch god without eyes"**: Oscar Zeta Acosta, *The Autobiography of a Brown Buffalo* (San Francisco: Straight Arrow Books, 1972), p. 180.

117 **"I've never taken the little bastard"**: Thompson, *Shark Hunt,* p. 509.

119 **"He was just starting his comeback"**: Craig Vetter, "The Playboy Interview with Hunter S. Thompson," *Playboy*, November 1974.

120 **"All I really want to do"**: Thompson, *Fear and Loathing in America,* p. 50.

120 **"We were at this American Legion hall"**: Vetter, *Playboy* interview.

121 **"I've never seen him like that"**: Ibid.

121 **"You people are lucky"**: Hunter S. Thompson, *Fear and Loathing: On the Campaign Trail '72* (New York: Straight Arrow Books, 1973), p. 56.

122 **"a nightmare of bullshit"**: Thompson, *Fear and Loathing in America*, p. 42.

122 **"a foul caricature of himself"**: Thompson, *Shark Hunt*, p. 185.

122 **"He was tortured"**: Gerry Goldstein, remarks at the Aspen Institute, July 21, 2007.

122 **"I went to N.H. with the idea"**: Thompson, *Fear and Loathing in America*, p. 95.

123 **"A presidential campaign would be"**: Hunter S. Thompson, *Songs of the Doomed* (New York: Summit Books, 1990), p. 122.

124 **"If this sort of thing continues"**: Gary Paul Gates, *Air Time: The Inside Story of CBS News* (New York: Harper and Row, 1978), p. 200.

124 **"I was treated as brutally"**: Thompson, *Fear and Loathing in America*, p. 123.

125 **"I went to the Democratic convention"**: Curtis Willkie, "The Gonzo Historie," *Image*, Mary 29, 1988, p. 18.

125 **"It permanently altered my brain chemistry"**: Thompson, *Shark Hunt*, p. 167.

125 **"I have a central incident"**: Thompson, *Fear and Loathing in America*, p. 119.

125 **"We'd been beaten in Chicago"**: Thompson, *Songs of the Doomed*, p. 123.

126 **"a bright and articulate thirty-year-old"**: *Rolling Stone*, March 24, 2005, p. 54.

126 **"I rented them two houses"**: Ibid.

126 **"He could go out and sunbathe naked"**: Tom Thurman, director, *Buy the Ticket, Take the Ride* (Starz Entertainment, 2006).

126 **"He had privacy"**: Sharon Martin, producer, *Biography: Hunter S. Thompson* (Biography Channel, 2004).

126 **"Being able to come back to Owl Farm"**: Ibid.

CHAPTER 9: EPIPHANY

128 **"It's the bridge book"**: Douglas Brinkley, interview with author, October 16, 2007.

128 **"It's one Hunter purposely"**: Ibid.

129 **"In Chicago, I was clubbed"**: Hunter S. Thompson, *The Great Shark Hunt* (New York: Summit Books, 1979), p. 178.

129 **"first chief executive to grow"**: Hunter S. Thompson, *Fear and Loathing in America* (New York: Simon and Schuster, 2000), p. 158.

129 **"another cheapjack hustler"**: Hunter S. Thompson, *Fear and Loathing: On the Campaign Trail '72* (New York: Straight Arrow Books, 1973), p. 86.

129 **"In the sixties, there was a sense"**: Hunter S. Thompson, interview with author, April 10, 1978.

130 **"You're wasting your time"**: Thompson, *Fear and Loathing in America*, p. 167.

130 **"Trying to mix writing and fucking"**: Hunter S. Thompson, *Songs of the Doomed* (New York: Summit Books, 1990), p. 128.

131 **"One of these days"**: Thompson, *Fear and Loathing in America*, p. 162.

131 **"I remember thinking I had a tough"**: Ibid., p. 173.

131 **"I used to dread Hunter"**: E. Jean Carroll, *Hunter: The Strange and Savage Life of Hunter S. Thompson* (New York: Dutton, 1993), p. 121.

131 **"This suicide business"**: Ibid., p. 122.

132 **"I worked on that letter"**: Ibid., p. 118.

132   **"The thing is due sometime"**: Thompson, *Fear and Loathing in America*, p. 173.

132   **"It was beautiful at Owl Farm"**: Carroll, *Hunter*, p. 119.

133   **"I could just walk out of here"**: Ibid.

133   **"You got caught in the tides"**: Thompson, *Fear and Loathing in America*, p. 214.

133   **"Sandy has been so generally depressed"**: Ibid., pp. 275–76.

134   **"My man, you don't know me"**: Craig Vetter, "The Playboy Interview with Hunter S. Thompson," *Playboy*, November 1974.

134   **"I suddenly see a bedrock validity"**: Thompson, *Fear and Loathing in America*, p. 216.

134   **"Thompson's ugly, stupid arrogance"**: Ibid., p. 222.

135   **"What we had in mind was"**: Michael Learmonth, "A Great One Remembered: *Scanlan's Monthly*, 1970–1971," *Folio: The Magazine for Magazine Management*, May 1, 2003.

135   **"That whole goddam magazine"**: Thompson, *Fear and Loathing in America*, p. 223.

135   **"Hinckle is an editor"**: Marc Weingarten, *The Gang That Wouldn't Write Straight* (New York: Crown, 2005), p. 229.

135   **"scurvy fist-fuckers"**: Thompson, *Fear and Loathing in America*, p. 223.

136   **"his voice was pure snake oil"**: Thompson, *Shark Hunt*, p. 83.

136   **"Chevrolet doesn't pay him to say"**: Ibid., p. 85.

137   **"Meanwhile, slumped in a folding chair"**: Ibid., p. 86.

137   **"As far as I know"**: Ibid., p. 90.

138   **"I loathe the fucking memory"**: Thompson, *Fear and Loathing in America*, p. 262.

138   **"Fuck the American Dream"**: Ibid., p. 263.

139   **"My ego comes through very heavy"**: Ibid., p. 266.

140   **"*Rolling Stone* caught on"**: Michael Lydon, interview with author, July 6, 2006.

141   **"I literally felt I'd stumbled"**: John Lombardi, letter to author, February 17, 2006.

141   **"I got Hunter into *Rolling Stone*"**: Ibid.

142   **"This better be good"**: John Lombardi, "Smiling through the Apocalypse," *Miami New Times*, August 22, 2002.

142   **"He was throwing down"**: Charles Perry, interview with author, May 20, 2006.

142   **"Oral rock 'n' roll"**: Lombardi, letter to author.

142   **"I know I'm supposed to be"**: Ibid.

142   **"Thompson couldn't help himself"**: John Lombardi, letter to author, February 19, 2006.

143   **"The main thing"**: Jann Wenner, interview with author, January 15, 2008.

143 **"You have complete freedom":** Tom Wolfe, interview with author, October 28, 2007.

144 **"I never wanted to be an illustrator":** Ralph Steadman, interview with author, November 8, 2006.

145 **"It was my first time in America":** Tom Thurman, director, *Buy the Ticket, Take the Ride* (Starz Entertainment, 2006).

145 **"At that time":** Weingarten, *Gang*, p. 231.

145 **"as different as a moose":** Ralph Steadman, letter to author, February 22, 2007.

145 **"'No!' he shouted":** Thompson, *Shark Hunt*, pp. 25–26.

146 **"If he had chosen someone":** Steadman interview.

146 **"Just pretend you're visiting":** Thompson, *Shark Hunt*, pp. 29–31.

147 **"We didn't really find":** Martin, producer, *Biography*.

148 **"The swamp-like humidity":** Ralph Steadman, *The Joke's Over* (New York: Harcourt, 2006), p. 18.

148 **"When I first sent one down":** Annie Nocenti and Ruth Baldwin, eds., *The High Times Reader* (New York: Nation Books, 2004), p. 79.

149 **"It strikes me as a monument":** Thompson, *Fear and Loathing in America*, pp. 295–96.

149 **"It's a shitty article":** Ibid., p. 295.

149 **"I started getting calls":** Nocenti and Baldwin, eds., *Reader*, p. 80.

149 **"frantic loser, inept and half-psychotic":** Tom Wolfe, *The New Journalism* (New York: Harper and Row, 1973), p. 15.

149 **"I don't know what the fuck":** Carroll, *Hunter*, p. 124.

CHAPTER 10: FREAK POWER

150 **"The article is useless":** Hunter S. Thompson, *Fear and Loathing in America* (New York: Simon and Schuster, 2000), p. 309.

151 **"I thought, 'holy shit'":** Craig Vetter, "The Playboy Interview with Hunter S. Thompson," *Playboy*, November 1974.

151 **"Unlike Tom Wolfe or Gay Talese":** Ibid.

152 **"and shit on *everything*":** Thompson, *Fear and Loathing in America*, p. 319.

152 **"king-bitch dog-fucker of an idea":** Ibid., p. 320

152 **"I wanted to control":** Sharon Martin, producer, *Biography: Hunter S. Thompson* (Biography Channel, 2004).

152 **"You seem to be having a wonderful":** Hunter S. Thompson, *The Great Shark Hunt* (New York: Summit Books, 1979), p. 113.

153 **"I started seeing red-eyed dogs":** Marc Weingarten, *The Gang That Wouldn't Write Straight* (New York: Crown, 2005), p. 235.

153 **"Ralph was in an insane condition":** Thompson, *Shark Hunt*, p. 113.

154 **"Everything he was saying I liked":** Bob Braudis, interview with author, July 19, 2007.

154 **"a half-mad cross":** Thompson, *Shark Hunt*, p. 167.

154 **"Hunter decided to be a lightning rod":** E. Jean Carroll, *Hunter: The Strange and Savage Life of Hunter S. Thompson* (New York: Dutton, 1993), p. 127.

155 **"The old Berkeley-born notion":** Thompson, *Shark Hunt*, p. 155.

155 **"We really thought":** Braudis interview.

155 **"I can't do it":** Martin, producer, *Biography*.

155 **"If Mr. Thompson is indeed elected":** Edwin A. Roberts, "Will Aspen's Hippies Elect a Sheriff," *National Observer*, November 2, 1970, p. 6.

155 **"That was the hive of political activity":** Braudis interview.

156 **"You can't put the campaign":** Carroll, *Hunter*, p. 131.

156 **"Hunter lost the goddamn redneck vote":** Dick Tuck, interview with author, July 5, 2006.

156 **"We would have won":** Carroll, *Hunter*, p. 133.

156 **"Unfortunately, I proved":** *Omnibus: Fear and Loathing in Gonzovision*, BBC Television (1978).

156 **"If we can't win in Aspen":** *New York Times*, November 5, 1970.

156 **"I didn't really want to be sheriff":** Vetter, *Playboy* interview.

157 **"You never knew with Oscar":** Hunter S. Thompson, introduction to the new edition of *The Autobiography of a Brown Buffalo*, by Oscar Zeta Acosta (New York: Vintage Books, 1989).

159 **"David Felton is always right":** Robert Draper, *Rolling Stone: The Uncensored History* (New York: Doubleday, 1990), p. 180.

159 **"He is violent":** Carroll, *Hunter*, p. 141.

159 **"I would hate to be":** Martin, producer, *Biography*.

159 **"Hunter's copy came in clean":** Charles Perry, interview with author, May 20, 2006.

160 **"I thought I'd stick my head in":** Ibid.

160 **"It was a traditional piece":** Ibid.

161 **"a genuinely rotten newspaper":** Thompson, *Shark Hunt*, p. 136.

161 **"It was difficult, even for me":** Ibid., p. 134.

161 **"Ruben Salazar couldn't possibly":** Ibid., p. 142.

162 **"As usual, Thompson is barely":** Gene Lyons, "How Stoned Were You?," *Nation*, October 13, 1979, p. 342.

CHAPTER 11: MAKING A BEAST OF HIMSELF

163 **"This must be the call":** Hunter S. Thompson, *Fear and Loathing in Las Vegas* (New York: Random House, 1972), p. 6.

163 **"*Fear and Loathing in Las Vegas* is":** Hunter S. Thompson, interview with author, March 1990.

165 **"I've always considered writing":** Hunter S. Thompson, *The Great Shark Hunt* (New York: Summit Books, 1979), p. 109.

165 **"He had these *pages*"**: Robert Draper, *Rolling Stone: The Uncensored History* (New York: Doubleday, 1990), p. 176.

165 **"As soon as you finished it"**: Charles Perry, interview with author, May 20, 2006.

165 **"Sooner or later you'll see"**: Hunter S. Thompson, *Fear and Loathing in America* (New York: Simon and Schuster, 2000), p. 376.

166 **"This happens every time"**: Ibid., p. 375.

166 **"I haven't found a drug yet"**: Thompson interview (1990).

167 **"Oscar is a bit fucked up"**: Ralph Steadman, *The Joke's Over* (New York: Harcourt, 2006), p. 70.

167 **"I often thought I would not"**: Ralph Steadman, interview with author, November 8, 2006.

167 **"What I was doing"**: Sharon Martin, producer, *Biography: Hunter S. Thompson* (Biography Channel, 2004).

167 **"dress rehearsal for *Fear*"**: Steadman, *Joke's Over*, p. 63.

167 **"It's hooliganism"**: Martin, producer, *Biography*.

168 **"They were fucking beautiful"**: Steadman, *Jokes' Over*, p. 75.

168 **"We were somewhere near Barstow"**: Thompson, *Fear and Loathing in Las Vegas*, p. 3.

168 **"In fact, I believe he hired"**: Charles Perry, interview with author, May 20, 2006.

168 **"Hunter didn't need"**: Jann Wenner, interview with author, January 15, 2008.

169 **"Hunter was using Vegas"**: Martin, producer, *Biography*.

174 **"We are heading for"**: Thompson, *Fear and Loathing in America*, p. 428.

176 **"My God! Hunter has stolen"**: Mark Hamilton Lytle, *America's Uncivil War: The Sixties Era from Elvis to the Fall of Nixon* (New York: Oxford University Press, 2006), p. 290.

176 **"this cheap, acid-crippled paranoid"**: Thompson, *Fear and Loathing in America*, p. 477.

176 **"We really cracked the buggers"**: Ibid., p. 458.

176 **"This book is pure fucking gold"**: Ibid., p. 470.

176 **"Thompson's American dream"**: Crawford Woods, "The Best Book on the Dope Decade," *New York Times Book Review*, July 23, 1972, p. 17.

177 **"There's not one misplaced word"**: Martin, producer, *Biography*.

177 **"I'm a suffering person"**: *The Criterion Collection: Fear and Loathing in Las Vegas* (commentary track).

CHAPTER 12: TRUTH IS NEVER TOLD IN DAYLIGHT

178 **"We loved what Hunter did"**: Charles Perry, interview with author, May 20, 2006.

179 **"Driving across goddamn Nebraska"**: Hunter S. Thompson, *Songs of the Doomed* (New York: Summit Books, 1990), p. 162.

179 **"I was pregnant again"**: E. Jean Carroll, *Hunter: The Strange and Savage Life of Hunter S. Thompson* (New York: Dutton, 1993), p. 152.

179 **"He was dealing with The Heavies"**: Ibid., p. 156.

180 **"the most excruciating eight or nine"**: Robert Draper, *Rolling Stone: The Uncensored History* (New York: Doubleday, 1990), p. 183.

180 **"When we decided to cover"**: Perry interview.

181 **"I didn't know what I was getting into"**: *Rolling Stone*, March 24, 2005, p. 55.

182 **"I've grown accustomed to letting"**: Hunter S. Thompson, *Fear and Loathing in America* (New York: Simon and Schuster, 2000), p. 454.

182 **"I had taken up smoking"**: Carroll, *Hunter*, p. 152.

183 **"There was a lot of madness"**: Ibid., p. 156.

185 **"It was a complex"**: Gary Hart, interview with author, August 11, 2005.

186 **"A lot of Hunter's stuff"**: Perry interview.

187 **"either I traded pot to a faculty"**: Montgomery Chitty, letter to author, February 16, 2006.

189 **"the Neal Cassady speed-booze-acid"**: Hunter S. Thompson, *Fear and Loathing: On the Campaign Trail '72* (New York: Straight Arrow Books, 1973), p. 108.

189 **"It's the presidential express"**: Ibid., pp. 110–11.

190 **"Yes, I met Hunter Thompson"**: Montgomery Chitty, unpublished recollection sent to author.

190 **"I never said that Muskie"**: Thompson, *Songs of the Doomed*, p. 154.

191 **"Don't write a fucking word"**: Robert Sam Anson, *Gone Crazy and Back Again* (New York: Doubleday, 1981), p. 199.

191 **"His caricatures were overstated"**: Curtis Wilkie, interview with author, August 31, 2006.

191 **"The brilliance of Hunter"**: William Greider, interview with author, July 5, 2006.

192 **"Reading Thompson obviously gave"**: Timothy Crouse, *The Boys on the Bus* (New York: Random House, 1973), p. 332.

192 **"His work ethic was not the kind"**: Wilkie interview.

192 **"Watch those swine day and night"**: Anson, *Gone Crazy*, p. 199.

192 **"Guys write down what a candidate"**: "Catcher in the Wry," *Newsweek*, May 1, 1972, p. 65.

192 **"Sandy was an incredibly sweet person"**: *Rolling Stone*, March 24, 2005, p. 55.

192 **"I was in the guest room upstairs"**: Ibid.

193 **"Hunter showed up with a ten-foot-long"**: Bill Dixon, interview with author, January 18, 2006.

193 **"I always thought Hunter was sober"**: Frank Mankiewicz, interview with author, July 27, 2005.

193 **"He brought the campaign"**: Hart interview.

193 **"He didn't do journalism"**: Ibid.

194   **"wildly erratic"**: Morris Dickstein, *Gates of Eden* (New York: Basic Books, 1977), p. 141.

194   **"Reporters in those days"**: Dixon interview.

194   **"the most accurate and the least factual"**: Mankiewicz interview.

194   **"Hunter Thompson learned to approximate"**: Dickstein, *Gates*, p. 133.

194   **"His work habits were certainly"**: Wilkie interview.

195   **"You never had a dull conversation"**: Tom Thurman, director, *Buy the Ticket, Take the Ride* (Starz Entertainment, 2006).

195   **"His work habits were as insane"**: Greider interview.

195   **"In Washington, truth is never"**: Craig Vetter, "The Playboy Interview with Hunter S. Thompson," *Playboy*, November 1974.

195   **"Thompson began to smell"**: Timothy Crouse, *The Boys on the Bus* (New York: Random House, 1973), p. 335.

195   **"He had this access"**: Jann Wenner, interview with author, January 5, 2008.

196   **"He was never anything but"**: Carroll, *Hunter*, p. 158.

196   **"Hunter was beginning to be"**: Hart interview.

197   **"I didn't hold him"**: Carroll, *Hunter*, p. 160.

198   **"It was the best thing"**: Ibid.

198   **"This may be the year"**: Thompson, *Campaign Trail*, pp. 413–14.

199   **"I have a powerful aversion"**: Ibid., p. 15.

200   **"enough speed to alter the outcome"**: Ibid., p. 16.

200   **"At this point, Dr. Thompson suffered"**: Ibid., p. 422.

200   **"I would always say"**: Sharon Martin, producer, *Biography: Hunter S. Thompson* (Biography Channel, 2004).

200   **"any team with both God and Nixon"**: Thompson, *Campaign Trail*, p. 504.

200   **"Around midnight, when the rain"**: Ibid., p. 505.

201   **"His book was just dead on"**: Wilkie interview.

201   **"his smartest book"**: Martin, producer, *Biography* (2004).

201   **"It wasn't about the campaign"**: Hart interview.

201   **"It's the moment we realized"**: Carl Bernstein, remarks at the Aspen Institute, July 21, 2007.

CHAPTER 13: CELEBRITY

202   **"about as close as I plan to come"**: Hunter S. Thompson, *Fear and Loathing in America* (New York: Simon and Schuster, 2000), p. 522.

203   **"I plan to force a readjustment"**: Ibid.

204   **"I'm trying to finish"**: Ibid., p. 524.

204   **"I'm damned if I can remember"**: Hunter S. Thompson, *The Great Shark Hunt* (New York: Summit Books, 1979), p. 443.

206   **"There was no room in their complacent"**: Hunter S. Thompson, *Songs of the Doomed* (New York: Summit Books, 1990), p. 46.

206 **"I've about decided to make":** Thompson, *Fear and Loathing in America*, p. 519.

206 **"He never called to ask":** Frank Mankiewicz, interview with author, July 27, 2005.

207 **"I take a certain pride":** Thompson, *Shark Hunt*, p. 240.

207 **"How can I show my face":** Ibid., p. 239.

208 **"There was not a hell of a lot":** Ibid., p. 250.

208 **"When you're covering the White House":** Hunter S. Thompson, interview with author, April 10, 1978.

208 **"He was a tireless round-the-clock":** Ralph Steadman, interview with author, November 8, 2006.

208 **"He will go down with Grant":** Thompson, *Shark Hunt*, p. 265.

208 **"I have to admit":** Ibid., p. 281.

209 **"We started on complicated nightly":** Gary Hart, interview with author, August 11, 2005.

209 **"Hunter, that was a cop":** *Rolling Stone*, March 24, 2005, p. 56.

210 **"Ralph put his finger on it":** Thompson, *Fear and Loathing in America*, p. 537.

210 **"The haggling is getting pretty":** Ibid.

210 **"I'm pretty well hooked":** Ibid., p. 538.

211 **"a goddamn torrent":** Ibid., p. 547.

211 **"I find myself getting 'famous'":** Ibid., p. 553.

211 **"This is when the cocaine hit":** E. Jean Carroll, *Hunter: The Strange and Savage Life of Hunter S. Thompson* (New York: Dutton, 1993), p. 176.

212 **"I think his greatest frustration":** Brinkley interview.

212 **"if Sandy didn't hear this":** Ibid., p. 170.

213 **"I was serious about getting into":** Thompson, *Songs of the Doomed*, p. 162.

213 **"Here was this crafty little ferret":** Thompson, *Shark Hunt*, p. 19.

214 **"the main villain":** Ibid.

215 **"Jann accurately predicted":** John A. Walsh, foreword, Hunter S. Thompson, *Hey Rube* (New York: Simon and Schuster, 2004), p. xiii.

215 **"the fiendish intensity":** Thompson, *Shark Hunt*, p. 57.

216 **"God, Nixon and the National":** Ibid., p. 47.

216 **"Okay, you bastards":** Thompson, *Songs of the Doomed*, p. 165.

217 **"He said he was going to beat":** *Rolling Stone,* March 24, 2005, p. 56.

217 **"We kept trying to focus":** Ibid.

217 **"It's hard to understand":** Thompson, *Songs of the Doomed*, p. 165.

218 **"Those were fat days at *Playboy*":** Peter Whitmer, *When the Going Gets Weird* (New York: Hyperion, 1994), p. 213.

218 **"I want to see blood":** Ibid., p. 214.

219 **"It was a king hell bastard":** Thompson, *Shark Hunt*, p. 474.

220 **"I'm getting goddamn tired"**: Ibid., p. 286.

221 **"It is definitely worth watching"**: Ibid., 298–99.

221 **"If I seem to be grinding"**: Thompson, *Fear and Loathing in America*, p. 591.

222 **"I want Hunter to write"**: Robert Draper, *Rolling Stone: The Uncensored History* (New York: Doubleday, 1990), p. 225.

222 **"Who votes for these treacherous"**: Thompson, *Shark Hunt*, p. 301.

222 **"I was brooding on this"**: Ibid., p. 302.

222 **"I've got to get out of journalism"**: Craig Vetter, "The Playboy Interview with Hunter S. Thompson," *Playboy*, November 1974.

223 **"After the Nixon campaign"**: Jann Wenner, interview with author, January 15, 2008.

225 **"It was the first time"**: Bill Dixon, interview with author, January 18, 2006.

225 **"Hunter did it because"**: Ibid.

225 **"I detested these fucking things"**: Thompson, *Fear and Loathing in America*, p. 599.

225 **"I am very happy to be here"**: Paul Perry, *Fear and Loathing: The Strange and Terrible Saga of Hunter S. Thompson* (New York: Thunder's Mouth Press, 1992), p. 202.

226 **"Gonzo, Gonzo, Gonzo"**: Ibid., p. 205.

226 **"with the possible and perhaps"**: Thompson, *Fear and Loathing in America*, p. 338.

228 **"scorned those single-minded"**: George Plimpton, *Shadow Box* (New York: G. P. Putnam's Sons, 1977), p. 253.

228 **"This filthy African humidity"**: Ralph Steadman, *The Joke's Over* (New York: Harcourt, 2006), p. 120.

229 **"This is it, Ralph"**: Ibid., p. 129.

229 **"Maybe he thought I was a corpse"**: Plimpton, *Shadow Box*, p. 251.

229 **"Thompson's readers were not interested"**: Ibid., p. 257.

230 **"I still am looking to you"**: Thompson, *Fear and Loathing in America*, p. 561.

230 **"What in the fuck would cause"**: Ibid., p. 562.

231 **"I am desperate and seriously fear"**: Ibid., p. 596.

231 **"I told him I hoped he knew"**: Oscar Zeta Acosta, *The Autobiography of a Brown Buffalo* (New York: Vintage Books, 1989), p. 201.

232 **"It was a hot, nearly blazing day"**: Annie Nocenti and Ruth Baldwin, eds., *The High Times Reader* (New York: Nation Books, 2004), p. 68.

232 **"When you're a famous American"**: Thompson interview (1978).

232 **"The wild, crazy man"**: Tom Thurman, director, *Buy the Ticket, Take the Ride* (Starz Entertainment, 2006).

232 **"I'd feel real trapped"**: Ibid.

232 **"He became a prisoner"**: Steadman interview.

CHAPTER 14: CASUALTIES OF WAR

234 **"He'd say hideous things"**: Robert Sam Anson, *Gone Crazy and Back Again* (New York: Doubleday, 1981), p. 262.

234 **"I can be very mean"**: Ibid.

236 **"I can't conceive of *anything*"**: Hunter S. Thompson, *Fear and Loathing in America* (New York: Simon and Schuster, 2000), p. 610.

237 **"I had to write that piece"**: Hunter S. Thompson, interview with author, March 1990.

237 **"*Rolling Stone* is against"**: E. Jean Carroll, *Hunter: The Strange and Savage Life of Hunter S. Thompson* (New York: Dutton, 1993), p. 180.

237 **"But I've got the assignment"**: Bone, website reminiscence.

237 **"I got off the plane"**: Thompson interview (1990).

238 **"Consider a year"**: Hunter S. Thompson, *The Proud Highway* (New York, Villard Books, 1997), p. 462.

239 **"We debated whether"**: Carroll, *Hunter*, p. 182.

239 **"I wrote a serious vicious letter"**: Thompson interview (1990).

239 **"The business department"**: Ibid.

239 **"He took it very seriously"**: Peter Whitmer, *When the Going Gets Weird* (New York: Hyperion, 1994), p. 242.

240 **"I didn't know you could buy"**: Robert Draper, *Rolling Stone: The Uncensored History* (New York: Doubleday, 1990), p. 228.

240 **"Anyone who would fire"**: Thompson interview (1990).

240 **"drinking beer from the chest"**: Carroll, *Hunter*, pp. 180–81.

241 **"One night, a wolf howl"**: J. C. Gabel and James Hughes, "Long Live the High Priest of Gonzo," *Stop Smiling*, No. 122 (2005): 51.

241 **"I remember lying in bed"**: Carroll, *Hunter*, p. 184.

242 **"If there is any one thing"**: *Rolling Stone*, May 9, 1985, p. 47.

244 **"I didn't like it that they put"**: Thompson interview (1990).

245 **"I didn't sleep for three nights"**: Bill Dixon, interview with author, January 18, 2006.

245 **"He's going to be surprised someday"**: Hunter S. Thompson, interview with author, April 10, 1978.

246 **"All over America"**: Ibid.

246 **"If we want to give paranoia"**: Hunter S. Thompson, *Fear and Loathing in America* (New York: Simon and Schuster, 2000), p. 658.

246 **"I'd like to sue for at least $20 million"**: Ibid., p. 659.

246 **"Impossible! I'm the Rolling Stone"**: Garry Trudeau, *Action Figure: The Life and Times of Doonesbury's Uncle Duke* (Kansas City, Mo.: Andrews-McMeel Publishing, 2001), p. 29.

247 **"When you deal with Jann"**: Paul Perry, *Fear and Loathing: The Strange and Terrible Saga of Hunter S. Thompson* (New York: Thunder's Mouth Press, 1992), p. 217.

247 **"Wenner had sent him down there"**: Dixon interview.

247   **"The fun factor had gone out"**: Thompson interview (1990).

248   **"a dope-addled clown"**: *Rolling Stone*, December 15, 1977, p. 48.

248   **"I showered the man with libel"**: Thompson interview (1978).

249   **"It was a weird idea"**: David Felton, "Hunter S. Thompson Has Cashed His Check," *Rolling Stone College Papers*, Spring 1980, p. 47.

249   **"Bullshit. It's not going to be"**: Carroll, *Hunter*, p. 209.

249   **"I gave Hunter Thompson"**: Craig Vetter, "Destination Hollyweird," *Playboy*, June 1980.

249   **"When I first met him"**: Ralph Steadman, *The Joke's Over* (New York: Harcourt, 2006), p. 138.

250   **"You bastard"**: Ibid., p. 139.

250   **"[Duke] was a vehicle for quotations"**: Nigel Finch, Director, *Fear and Loathing on the Road to Hollywood* (British Broadcasting Corporation, 1978).

250   **"People I don't know expect me"**: Ibid.

251   **"I think I've taken that form"**: Ibid.

251   **"So I'm really in the way"**: Ibid.

252   **"He was a novelist who'd been"**: Toby Thompson, *The 60s Report* (New York: Rawson, Wade Publishers, 1979), p. 253.

252   **"Hunter is a really, really"**: Sharon Martin, producer, *Biography: Hunter S. Thompson* (Biography Channel, 2004).

253   **"It was ugly"**: Bob Braudis, interview with author, July 19, 2007.

253   **"I think she had good reasons"**: Ibid.

253   **"It was a fiery end"**: Carroll, *Hunter*, p. 201.

CHAPTER 15: THOMPSON'S ISLAND

254   **"And I just kind of fell"**: Tom Corcoran, interview with author, December 20, 2005.

254   **"Either you worked for Southern Bell"**: Ibid.

255   **"Within two years' time"**: Ibid.

255   **"I fed him"**: Ibid.

256   **"In those days, it was kind of"**: Russell Chatham, interview with author, July 26, 2006.

257   **"Notorious most his life"**: Montgomery Chitty, letter to author, January 25, 2006.

257   **"He was a much deeper, more serious"**: Chatham interview.

258   **"Here comes this guy in a suit"**: Chris Robinson, interview with author, June 7, 2006.

258   **"He kept the dog under the table"**: Dan Mallard, interview with author, April 24, 2007.

258   **"We lived right next door"**: Robinson interview.

258   **"Hunter would rant and rave"**: Ibid.

259   **"It kind of looked like that thing"**: Ibid.

260   **"There was this guy lying"**: Laila Nabulsi, interview with author, October 10, 2006.

260   **"more fun in 20 minutes"**: *Rolling Stone*, April 29, 1982.

263   **"probably the worst-edited"**: David Felton, "Hunter S. Thompson Has Cashed His Check," *Rolling Stone College Papers*, Spring 1980, p. 47.

263   **"I thought it would"**: Ibid.

264   **"the same admiration"**: William F. Buckley Jr., "Gonzo's Great Shark Hunt," *New York Times Book Review*, August 5, 1979, p. 1.

264   **"I have already lived"**: Hunter S. Thompson, *The Great Shark Hunt* (New York: Summit Books, 1979), p. 17.

265   **"Judy: Miami Herald, bank, Visa"**: List, from the Tom Corcoran archive.

265   **"Sebastian! I have arrived"**: Sebastian Corcoran, interview with author, June 5, 2006.

265   **"Hunter was always 'Doc'"**: Tom Corcoran, interview with author, June 5, 2006.

266   **"So this family came over"**: Robinson interview.

266   **"We had lots of quiet"**: Nabulsi interview.

266   **"He didn't care if people"**: Robinson interview.

267   **"I don't know how much"**: Postcard, Corcoran archive.

267   **"What lame instinct prompts you"**: Letter, Corcoran archive.

267   **"I don't know why people"**: Felton, "Check," p. 51.

268   **"Writing the screenplay is easy"**: Corcoran interview (2005).

268   **"Hunter, just keep the wheel straight"**: Robinson interview.

268   **"It went airborne"**: Ibid.

269   **"We made up the characters"**: Corcoran interview (2005).

270   **"What Hunter dreamed up"**: Ibid.

270   **"He was too naïve in those days"**: Ibid.

270   **"I hopped on my motorbike"**: Ibid.

271   **"Think about it"**: Hunter S. Thompson, *The Curse of Lono* (New York: Bantam Books, 1983), p. 8.

271   **"You have something to worry"**: Paul Perry, *Fear and Loathing: The Strange and Terrible Saga of Hunter S. Thompson* (New York: Thunder's Mouth Press, 1992), p. 233.

272   **"The winter was coming in Aspen"**: Laila Nabulsi, remarks at the Aspen Institute, July 21, 2007.

272   **"sort of a scam"**: Nabulsi interview.

272   **"The time has come to kick ass"**: Thompson, *Curse of Lono*, p. 10.

272   **"The same people who burned"**: Ibid., p. 55.

272   **"You're doomed, man"**: Ibid., p. 51.

273   **"Hawaii was horrible"**: Nabulsi remarks.

273   **"Why the fuck would I do that"**: Perry, *Fear and Loathing*, p. 246.

273   **"jealous beyond belief"**: Ibid.

273 **"We will skulk off the plane"**: Ralph Steadman, *The Joke's Over* (New York: Harcourt, 2006), p. 178.

275 **"anti-humanist"**: Peter Whitmer, "Hunter Thompson: Still Crazy after All These Years," *Saturday Review*, January–February 1980, p. 60.

275 **"I thought you quit this business"**: Thompson, *Curse of Lono*, p. 28.

276 **"I was outlining it for him"**: Corcoran interview (2005).

276 **"I did a lot of research"**: Nabulsi interview.

276 **"Hunter was just too tangential"**: Peter Whitmer, *When the Going Gets Weird* (New York: Hyperion, 1994), p. 260.

277 **"After *The Curse of Lono*"**: Steadman, *Joke's Over*, p. 174.

277 **"It began to bug him"**: Steadman interview.

277 **"She showed me all his newspapers"**: Nabulsi interview.

278 **"Davison lived his life a little more"**: Ibid.

CHAPTER 16: THE GENETIC MIRACLE

279 **"I never thought I'd make it"**: Richard H. Stratton, *Altered States of America: Icons and Outlaws, Hitmakers and Hitmen* (New York: Nation Books, 2005), p. 77.

279 **"He not only created Gonzo writing"**: Sharon Martin, producer, *Biography: Hunter S. Thompson* (Biography Channel, 2004).

279 **"I saw myself in the mirror"**: Hunter S. Thompson, *Kingdom of Fear* (New York: Simon and Schuster, 2003), p. 131.

280 **"It had beautiful"**: Jann Wenner, interview with author, January 15, 2008.

280 **"She was an incorrigible coke slut"**: *Rolling Stone*, July 21–August 4, 1983, p. 60.

281 **"I know how those people behave"**: Hunter S. Thompson, *Songs of the Doomed* (New York: Summit Books, 1990), p. 225.

281 **"I'm getting too old"**: Hunter S. Thompson, unpublished letter to Jim Silberman, May 25, 1983.

282 **"I never thought you would lose"**: *Rolling Stone*, March 24, 2005, p. 62.

282 **"We were walking down the street"**: William Greider, interview with author, July 5, 2006.

282 **"Jann was trying to get him"**: Ibid.

283 **"You've got to go where"**: Russell Chatham, interview with author, July 26, 2006.

283 **"Only a freak of passion"**: Thompson, *Kingdom of Fear*, p. 25.

283 **"You are crazy as a goddamn loon"**: Ibid.

283 **"He would be talking"**: E. Jean Carroll, *Hunter: The Strange and Savage Life of Hunter S. Thompson* (New York: Dutton, 1993), p. 221.

283 **"Feminist porn was really just"**: Thompson, *Kingdom of Fear*, p. 134.

284   **"This is a time of growth":** Ibid., p. 155.

284   **"He looked at me":** Carroll, *Hunter*, pp. 220–21.

285   **"It took many years to gain":** Wayne Ewing, letter to author, September 3, 2007.

285   **"The idea was to sell a TV series":** Wayne Ewing, website reminiscence.

286   **"For every one night":** Ewing letter.

286   **"a monument to everything cheap":** Hunter S. Thompson, *The Great Shark Hunt* (New York: Summit Books, 1979), p. 136.

286   **"the most intense and wild time":** Carroll, *Hunter*, p. 228.

287   **"At that moment":** David McCumber, interview with author, June 9, 2006.

287   **"I thought she was wonderful":** *Paris Review*, Fall 2000.

288   **"Why not? We'll chase them":** Bill Beuttler, "A Finer Shade of Yellow," *American Way,* June 1, 1989, p. 123.

288   **"Twenty-year-olds who never":** McCumber interview.

288   **"Thanks to Hunter, we beat":** Ibid.

288   **"You just never knew":** Ibid.

289   **"'Hunter goes to Wal-Mart'":** Douglas Brinkley, remarks at the Aspen Institute, July 21, 2007.

289   **"Nixon was genetically criminal":** Hunter S. Thompson, *Generation of Swine* (New York: Summit Books, 1988), p. 190.

289   **"When this one finally unravels":** Ibid., p. 189.

289   **"One night, at about two":** McCumber interview.

290   **"Hearst called at some point":** Curtis Wilkie, interview with author, August 31, 2006.

290   **"He was not completely irresponsible":** Ibid.

291   **"I was always making up excuses":** Bob Braudis, interview with author, July 19, 2007.

291   **"Any book with 'Nazi' in the title":** Paul Perry, *Fear and Loathing: The Strange and Terrible Saga of Hunter S. Thompson* (New York: Thunder's Mouth Press, 1992), p. 255.

291   **"I don't want this book":** Ibid., p. 256.

292   **"He's a little more strident":** Herbert Mitgang, "The Art of Insults Is Back, Gonzo Style," *New York Times*, August 11, 1988, p. 17N.

292   **"I have spent half my life":** Thompson, *Generation of Swine*, p. 10.

292   **"We think of him as a libertine":** Carl Bernstein, remarks at the Aspen Institute, July 21, 2007.

292   **"He suffered no falsehood":** Gerald Goldstein, remarks at the Aspen Institute, July 21, 2007.

292   **"has regained the intensity":** Curtis Wilkie, "The Gonzo Historie," *Image*, May 19, 1988, p. 20.

292   **"He became more of a hermit":** Brinkley remarks.

293 **"He was one of the"**: Douglas Brinkley, interview with author, October 16, 2007.

294 **"No once-wild 'party'"**: Martin Torgoff, *Can't Find My Way Home* (Simon and Schuster, 2004), p. 377.

294 **"He never liked to be alone"**: Tom Thurman, director, *Buy the Ticket, Take the Ride* (Starz Entertainment, 2006).

294 **"He loved people to read"**: Braudis interview.

295 **"It was very disturbing"**: Deborah Fuller, interview with author, November 29, 2007.

295 **"I hadn't been a"**: Ibid.

295 **"It was a godsend"**: Ibid.

296 **"There were weirdos"**: Ibid.

296 **"He liked conversations"**: Ibid.

297 **"He was, if not the"**: Jay Cowan, interview with author, July 24, 2007.

297 **"If he was on a"**: Fuller interview.

297 **"I took care of running"**: Ibid.

298 **"No one is oppressing you"**: Thompson, *Kingdom of Fear*, p. 126.

298 **"I've told Hunter he can't be out"**: Loren Jenkins, "Dr. Hunter S. Thompson and the Last Battle of Aspen," *Smart*, January–February 1990.

299 **"I'm going to send you plane tickets"**: Catherine Sabonis-Bradley, interview with author, June 13, 2006.

299 **"There was a lot of yelling"**: Ibid.

300 **"McCumber would beg and plead"**: Ibid.

301 **"I used your questions to develop"**: Ibid.

301 **"To some extent he was flattered"**: Goldstein remarks.

301 **"What it's all about"**: Martin, producer, *Biography*.

301 **"He would retreat into it"**: Sabonis-Bradley interview.

302 **"One thing about Hunter"**: Ibid.

302 **"That was so much fun"**: McCumber interview.

302 **"We were in the war room"**: Ibid.

302 **"A lot of it was dictated"**: Sabonis-Bradley interview.

302 **"Weeks would go by"**: Ibid.

304 **"I wanted to clear the house"**: Thompson, *Kingdom of Fear*, p. 136.

304 **"Who are you to Hunter"**: Ibid., p. 140.

305 **"I want you out of here"**: Ibid.

305 **"They're going to come search"**: Ibid.

305 **"It was daunting to clean"**: McCumber interview.

305 **"I don't know if that helps"**: David Matthews-Price, "DA Snags Thompson in Sex Case," *Aspen Times Daily*, February 28, 1990, p. 9.

306 **"This is a political trial"**: Thompson, *Songs of the Doomed*, pp. 336–37.

306 **"Do you think this is funny?"**: Ralph Steadman, *The Joke's Over* (New York: Harcourt, 2006), p. 279.

306 **"Please don't bitch at me"**: Ibid.

306 **"Our long twisted friendship"**: Ibid.

306 **"Not one word of thanks"**: Ibid., p. 281.

306 **"This is a *Fourth Amendment* case"**: Thompson, *Songs of the Doomed*, p. 338.

307 **"We've grown accustomed"**: Thompson, *Kingdom of Fear*, p. 267.

307 **"I have changed constantly"**: Thompson, *Songs of the Doomed*, p. 357.

308 **"I just couldn't even consider it"**: Sabonis-Bradley interview.

308 **"For a couple of years"**: Ibid.

CHAPTER 17: HOMECOMING

310 **"When they introduced me to him"**: Cheryl Frymire, interview with author, February 15, 2007.

311 **"He'd come in every day"**: Ibid.

311 **"He had a pretty tender spot"**: Ibid.

311 **"I have stolen more quotes"**: Hunter S. Thompson, *Generation of Swine* (New York: Summit Books, 1988), p. 9.

312 **"I secretly worship God"**: Hunter S. Thompson, *Kingdom of Fear* (New York: Simon and Schuster, 2003), p. 275.

312 **"I am now working on my final"**: Hunter S. Thompson, interview with author, March 1990.

313 **"Let's see what Bill Buckley thinks"**: Douglas Brinkley, interview with author, March 3, 2008.

314 **"I would have been locked into"**: Annie Nocenti and Ruth Baldwin, eds., *The High Times Reader* (New York: Nation Books, 2004), p. 66.

315 **"You wear these"**: Douglas Brinkley, interview with author, March 3, 2008.

315 **"The creepy bastard quickly sat"**: Hunter S. Thompson, *Better Than Sex* (New York: Random House, 1994), pp. 102–3.

315 **"He treated me like a roach"**: Joe Eszterhas, *American Rhapsody* (New York: Vintage Books, 2001), p. 12.

315 **"He is utterly unswervingly sincere"**: William Greider, interview with author, July 5, 2006.

316 **"He thought Bill Clinton was"**: Douglas Brinkley, remarks at the Aspen Institute, July 21, 2007.

316 **"Let's face it, Bubba"**: Thompson, *Better Than Sex*, p. 106.

317 **"a real betrayal"**: Laila Nabulsi, interview with author, October 10, 2006.

317 **"He hated all those unauthorized biographies"**: Ibid.

317 **"You have caused me a lot"**: Ralph Steadman, *The Joke's Over* (New York: Harcourt, 2006), p. 292.

318 **"It's almost embarrassing to talk":** Sara Nelson, interview with Hunter S. Thompson, *Book Report*, 1997.

318 **"It's been 12 years":** Thompson, *Better Than Sex*, p. 151.

318 **"He is the Willy Loman":** Ibid., jacket copy.

320 **"You'd better be good":** *Rolling Stone*, March 24, 2005, p. 36.

321 **"The books changed from original":** Bob Braudis, interview with author, July 19, 2007.

321 **"Hunter hated Nixon":** Brinkley interview (2008).

321 **"Nixon died! Anyone want acid?":** Brinkley remarks.

321 **"There was something peculiarly fitting":** Lawrence E. Spivak and Charles Angoff, eds., *The American Mercury Reader* (New York: Blakiston, 1944), pp. 34–36.

322 **"one of the most hideous things":** Thompson, *Better Than Sex*, p. 5.

322 **"Richard Nixon is gone now":** Ibid., pp. 239, 241, and 246.

323 **"He had a crush on an exotic":** Wayne Ewing, website remembrance.

324 **"It got to be pretty formulaic":** Greider interview.

324 **"He really worked hard":** Douglas Brinkley, interview with author, October 16, 2007.

324 **"Aspen had this reverse":** Tom Thurman, director, *Buy the Ticket, Take the Ride* (Starz Entertainment, 2006).

325 **"I set out from a young age":** *Studio for Men* (1989)

325 **"You don't live into your sixties":** Sharon Martin, producer, *Biography: Hunter S. Thompson* (Biography Channel, 2004).

325 **"We're just a very small band":** *Studio for Men* (1989).

326 **"Visiting with Virginia":** Ron Whitehead, interview with author, May 22, 2007.

328 **"Listen, if they were going to do":** Johnny Depp, "A Pair of Deviant Bookends," *Rolling Stone*, March 24, 2005, p. 49.

329 **"You are a jealous little jackass":** Hunter S. Thompson, unpublished letter, April 12, 1997.

329 **"biceps like your thighs":** Braudis interview.

329 **"My mother will be here":** David Amram, *Upbeat: Nine Lives of a Musical Cat* (Denver: Paradigm Publishers, 2007), p. 295.

330 **"Ron, you're going to have":** Whitehead interview.

330 **"It's about time we recognized":** Wayne Ewing, director, *Breakfast with Hunter* (Ewing Films, 2003).

330 **"I don't think I can do this":** Whitehead interview.

330 **"What was it like to have":** Juan Thompson, remarks at the Hunter S. Thompson tribute, Freedom Hall, Louisville, Kentucky, December 12, 1996.

331 **"a thirty-second, two-octave":** Bob Braudis, "Memo from the Sheriff," in Thompson, *Kingdom of Fear*, p. 104.

CHAPTER 18: MAN OF LETTERS

333 **"We're here tonight to do something"**: Wayne Ewing, director, *Breakfast with Hunter* (Ewing Films, 2003).

334 **"The solution to this"**: Hunter S. Thompson, unpublished letter to David Rosenthal, October 2, 1995.

334 **"I've always thought of Hunter"**: Bob Minzesheimer, "Author Hunter Thompson Dies at 67," *USA Today*, February 21, 2005.

334 **"These were the pre-Xerox days"**: Hunter S. Thompson, *The Proud Highway* (New York: Villard Books, 1997), pp. xxi–xxii.

334 **"Hunter always knew"**: Sharon Martin, producer, *Biography: Hunter S. Thompson* (Biography Channel, 2004).

334 **"At his best, he's right up there"**: Ibid.

334 **"We realized there was a genius"**: Ibid.

335 **"This is the book that launches"**: Ewing, director, *Breakfast*.

335 **"His self-esteem started"**: Douglas Brinkley, interview with author, October 16, 2007.

336 **"This is a nasty shock to me"**: Ewing, director, *Breakfast*.

336 **"If that's all that happens"**: Martin, producer, *Biography*.

337 **"Oh, God, that's where"**: Johnny Depp, "A Pair of Deviant Bookends," *Rolling Stone*, March 24, 2005, p. 49.

337 **"He looked like he was a kid"**: *The Criterion Collection: Fear and Loathing in Las Vegas* (commentary track).

337 **"The man should be sainted"**: Depp, "Pair," p. 49.

337 **"People just watched him"**: Cheryl Frymire, interview with author, February 15, 2007.

337 **"He was like the Dalai Lama"**: Tom Thurman, director, *Buy the Ticket, Take the Ride* (Starz Entertainment, 2006).

337 **"Emerson used to say"**: Martin, producer, *Biography*.

338 **"He's Mohammad and he's"**: Ibid.

338 **"With two phone calls he could"**: Bob Braudis, interview with author, July 19, 2007.

338 **"He was kind of a beacon"**: Thurman, director, *Buy the Ticket*.

338 **"No one could ever live up to"**: Ibid.

338 **"The image of the constantly"**: Braudis interview.

339 **"He always needed"**: Deborah Fuller, interview with author, November 29, 2007.

339 **"Well, fuck it, then"**: Nickole Brown, interview with author, June 5, 2007.

340 **"Even writing fiction"**: Ralph Steadman, interview with author, November 8, 2006.

340 **"Hunter, it's not your medium"**: Ewing, director, *Breakfast*.

340 **"Do you hate me"**: Thurman, director, *Buy the Ticket*.

340 **"Producing *Fear and Loathing* was"**: Laila Nabulsi, interview with author, October 10, 2006.

340 **"a horrible mess of a movie"**: Roger Ebert, "Fear and Loathing in L as Vegas," *Chicago Sun-Times*, May 22, 1998.

341 **"I never had background"**: Martin, producer, *Biography*.

341 **"He would ask what I thought"**: Anita Thompson, interview with author, February 1, 2008.

341 **"Leaving the house"**: Anita Thompson interview.

343 **"Dear Tom, You worthless"**: Hunter S. Thompson, *Fear and Loathing in America* (New York: Simon and Schuster, 2000), p. 372.

343 **"I knew Anita would be responsive"**: Frymire interview.

344 **"I think she just put her time in"**: Ibid.

344 **"Hunter had a really dark side"**: Braudis interview.

344 **"He said that sports lovers"**: Anita Thompson interview.

345 **"Hunter was a fierce libertarian"**: Douglas Brinkley, "Contentment Was Not Enough," *Rolling Stone*, March 24, 2005, p. 38.

345 **"How does *this* sound"**: Braudis interview.

345 **"Hunter privately, with his friends"**: Thurman, director, *Buy the Ticket*.

345 **"Anita was his whole life"**: Brinkley, "Contentment," p. 42.

345 **"He had a fleet of doctors"**: Braudis interview.

345 **"We tried to swim more"**: Anita Thompson interview.

346 **"He came in [the tavern] the day he got"**: Frymire interview.

346 **"Life is humming along"**: Hunter S. Thompson, note to author, April 24, 2003.

346 **"He was never loaded"**: Anita Thompson interview.

347 **"He was depressed for a long time"**: Frymire interview.

347 **"the cherry on the cake of fun"**: Thurman, director, *Buy the Ticket*.

347 **"He had a cast from his balls"**: Braudis interview.

347 **"He was talking so much about"**: Steadman interview.

348 **"The jokes disappeared"**: Brinkley, "Contentment," p. 40.

348 **"He was trapped by a mythology"**: Thurman, director, *Buy the Ticket*.

348 **"I think we've gotten closer"**: Martin, producer, *Biography*.

348 **"I have a truly wonderful life"**: Sondi Wright, letter to author, October 13, 2006.

348 **"May the right gods"**: Sondi Wright, "He Was Full Spectrum," *Rolling Stone*, May 24, 2005, p. 52.

349 **"He was a tortured tragic figure"**: Wright letter.

349 **"There was the usual hug"**: *Rolling Stone*, May 24, 2005, p. 70.

349 **"He called everybody"**: Tom Corcoran, interview with author, December 20, 2005.

349 **"He wanted to go alone"**: Anita Thompson interview.

349 **"He couldn't get up"**: William Dixon, interview with author, January 18, 2006.

350 **"My time has come to die"**: Brinkley, "Contentment," p. 40.

350 **"He didn't like being Hunter"**: Brinkley interview, 2008.

350 **"It was very difficult for him"**: Anita Thompson interview.

350 **"I went out there"**: Nabulsi interview.

351 **"You're in big trouble"**: Brinkley, "Contentment," p. 42.

EPILOGUE

353 **"Something's wrong with my dad"**: Bob Braudis, interview with author, July 19, 2007.

353 **"Is Hunter OK"**: *Rocky Mountain News*, February 21, 2005.

353 **"Hunter shot himself"**: Rick Balentine, interview with author, July 22, 2007.

353 **"Hunter sitting on his stool"**: Braudis interview.

354 **"I let the pros do their thing"**: Ibid.

354 **"Anita wanted to come in"**: Balentine interview.

354 **"He was sitting in his chair"**: *Rocky Mountain News*, February 21, 2005.

354 **"You know, property values are going"**: Braudis interview.

354 **"We need to do what we always do"**: Balentine interview.

355 **"a gesture of strength"**: *Rocky Mountain News*, February 21, 2005.

355 **"I've known for many, many years"**: Ibid.

355 **"Hunter, more than most people"**: Tom Thurman, director, *Buy the Ticket, Take the Ride* (Starz Entertainment, 2006).

355 **"Sebastian saw it on the news"**: Tom Corcoran, interview with author, December 20, 2005.

355 **"My first thought was"**: Neville Blakemore, interview with author, June 2, 2006.

355 **"The local papers had his photo"**: Porter Bibb, interview with author, July 24, 2005.

355 **"shocked, but not surprised"**: Bob Bone, website reminiscence.

355 **"I wonder how he made it so long"**: Ralph "Sonny" Barger, interview with author, February 14, 2006.

355 **"The phones there were ringing"**: Cheryl Frymire, interview with author, February 15, 2007.

356 **"I truly hope"**: Anne Willis Noonan, letter to author, October 22, 2007.

356 **"I was afraid that somehow"**: Gary Hart, interview with author, August 11, 2005.

356 **"given the medical problems"**: Russell Chatham, interview with author, July 26, 2006.

356 **"Take your phone off the hook"**: Ralph Steadman, interview with author, November 8, 2006.

357 **"He was such a big part"**: Jann Wenner, "My Brother in Arms," *Rolling Stone*, March 24, 2005, p. 33.

357 **"had he not become an alcoholic"**: Jann Wenner, interview with author, January 15, 2008.

357 **"If life is a dream"**: Ron Whitehead, interview with author, May 22, 2007.

357 **"There ain't an American Dream"**: Barger interview.

357 **"If he was searching"**: Hart interview.

357 **"He could have made"**: Steadman interview.

358 **"I'm as patriotic as anybody"**: CNBC, February 3, 2003.

358 **"comes from now finding"**: Warren Ellis, website statement.

358 **"I had no signals"**: Braudis interview.

358 **"A lot of kids want to be rebels"**: Anita Thompson, interview with author, February 1, 2008.

359 **"It's very interesting, now"**: L. Wayne Hicks, "Hunter Thompson's Life Now Open to Further Scrutiny," *Denver Business Journal*, November 3, 2006.

359 **"Something that may look"**: Douglas Brinkley, interview with author, October 16, 2007.

359 **"We're not in a hurry"**: Hicks, "Thompson's Life."

359 **"We have to think through"**: Brinkley interview.

360 **"People are going to write"**: Hicks, "Thompson's Life."

360 **"the greatest comic writer"**: Tom Wolfe, "A Gonzo in His Life and Work," *Wall Street Journal*, February 22, 2005.

360 **"All three of them"**: Tom Wolfe, interview with author, October 28, 2007.

361 **"He was just brilliant"**: Jann Wenner and Corey Seymour, *Gonzo: The Life of Hunter S. Thompson* (Boston: Little, Brown, 2007), p. 436.

361 **"Everyone there was handpicked"**: Frymire interview.

361 **"What do you think made Hunter"**: Bibb interview.

361 **"He knew that I"**: Wenner interview.

362 **"I know somewhere in his crooked mind"**: Thurman, director, *Buy the Ticket*.

364 **"No tears"**: David Amram, *Upbeat: Nine Lives of a Musical Cat* (Denver: Paradigm Publishers, 2007), p. 12.

364 **"It's like Hunter is our host"**: Ibid., p. 36.

365 **"Here's to you, Hunter:"** Corcoran interview (2005).

BIBLIOGRAPHY

I. BOOKS BY HUNTER S. THOMPSON

Hell's Angels: A Strange and Terrible Saga. New York: Random House, 1967.

Fear and Loathing in Las Vegas: A Savage Journey to the Heart of the American Dream. New York: Random House, 1972.

Fear and Loathing: On the Campaign Trail '72. San Francisco: Straight Arrow Books, 1973.

The Great Shark Hunt: Strange Tales from a Strange Time. New York: Summit Books, 1979.

The Curse of Lono. New York: Bantam Books, 1983.

Generation of Swine: Tales of Shame and Degradation in the '80s. New York: Summit Books, 1988.

Songs of the Doomed: More Notes on the Death of the American Dream. New York: Summit Books, 1990.

Screwjack. Santa Barbara, Calif.: Neville, 1991.*

Better Than Sex: Confessions of a Political Junkie. New York: Random House, 1994.

[*] denotes limited edition

The Proud Highway: The Saga of a Desperate Southern Gentleman, 1955–1967. New York: Villard Books, 1997.

Fear and Loathing in Las Vegas and Other American Stories. New York: Modern Library, 1997.

Mistah Leary, He Dead. Pasadena, Calif.: X-Ray Publishing, 1997.*

The Rum Diary: The Long Lost Novel. New York: Simon and Schuster, 1998.

Fear and Loathing in America: The Brutal Odyssey of an Outlaw Journalist, 1968–1976. New York: Simon and Schuster, 2000.

Screwjack and Other Stories. New York: Simon and Schuster, 2000.

Kingdom of Fear: Loathsome Secrets of a Star-crossed Child in the Final Days of the American Century. New York: Simon and Schuster, 2003.

Hey Rube: Blood Sport, the Bush Doctrine, and the Downward Spiral of Dumbness: Modern History from the Sports Desk. New York: Simon and Schuster, 2004.

Fire in the Nuts. Tucson, Ariz.: Sylph Publications, 2004.*

II. BOOKS

Acosta, Oscar Zeta. *The Autobiography of a Brown Buffalo.* San Francisco: Straight Arrow Books, 1972.

Amram, David. *Upbeat: Nine Lives of a Musical Cat.* Boulder, Colo.: Paradigm Publishers, 2007.

Anson, Robert Sam. *Gone Crazy and Back Again.* New York: Doubleday, 1981.

Baez, Joan. *And a Voice to Sing With.* New York: Summit Books, 1987.

Barger, Ralph "Sonny," with Keith and Kent Zimmerman. *Hell's Angel: The Life and Times of Sonny Barger and the Hell's Angels Motorcycle Club.* New York: HarperCollins, 2001.

Bernstein, Carl, and Bob Woodward. *All the President's Men.* New York: Simon and Schuster, 1973.

Brinkley, Douglas. *The Majic Bus: An American Odyssey.* New York: Harcourt Brace, 1993.

Carroll, E. Jean. *Hunter: The Strange and Savage Life of Hunter S. Thompson.* New York: Dutton, 1993.

Chance, Jean, and William McKeen, eds. *Literary Journalism: A Reader.* Belmont, Calif.: Wadsworth, 2000. Includes "Chitty and the Boohoo," adapted from Thompson's 1972 campaign coverage.

Cleverly, Michael, and Bob Braudis. *The Kitchen Readings: Untold Stories of Hunter S. Thompson.* New York: HarperCollins, 2008.

Clifford, Peggy. *To Aspen and Back: An American Journey.* New York: St. Martin's Press, 1980. Foreword by Thompson.

Conrad, Harold. *Dear Muffo: 35 Years in the Fast Lane.* New York: Stein and Day, 1982.

Corcoran, Tom. *The Mango Opera.* New York: St. Martin's Press, 1998.

———. *Bone Island Mambo.* New York: St. Martin's Press, 2001.

Crist, Steve, and Laila Nabulsi, eds. *Gonzo*. Los Angeles: Ammo Books, 2006. Features writing and photography by Thompson.

Crouse, Timothy. *The Boys on the Bus*. New York: Random House, 1973.

Dickstein, Morris. *Gates of Eden: American Culture in the Sixties*. New York: Basic Books, 1977.

Draper, Robert. *Rolling Stone: The Uncensored History*. New York: Doubleday, 1990.

Early, Gerald, ed. *The Muhammad Ali Reader*. Hopewell, N.J.: Ecco Press, 1998. Includes Thompson's Ali profile.

Fallowell, Duncan, ed. *Drug Tales*. New York: St. Martin's Press, 1979. Features a selection from *Fear and Loathing in Las Vegas*.

Fitzgerald, F. Scott. *The Great Gatsby*. New York: Charles Scribner's Sons, 1925.

Fong-Torres, Ben. *Not Fade Away: A Backstage Pass to 20 Years of Rock and Roll*. San Francisco: Miller-Freeman Books, 1999.

Gates, Gary Paul. *Air Time: The Inside Story of CBS News*. New York: Harper and Row, 1978.

Ginsberg, Allen. *Collected Poems, 1947–1980*. New York: Harper and Row, 1984.

Hale, Dennis, and Jonathan Eisen, eds. *The California Dream*. New York: Collier Books, 1968. Includes an excerpt from *Hell's Angels*.

Hart, Gary. *Right from the Start: A Chronicle of the McGovern Campaign*. New York: Quadrangle Books, 1973.

Hemingway, Ernest. *Byline*. New York: Charles Scribner's Sons, 1967.

Kerouac, Jack. *On the Road*. New York: Viking Press, 1957.

Kerrane, Kevin, and Ben Yagoda. *The Art of Fact: A Historical Anthology of Literary Journalism*. New York: Simon and Schuster, 1998. Includes Thompson's "The Scum Also Rises" from 1974.

Kurlansky, Mark. *1968: The Year That Rocked the World*. New York: Ballantine Books, 2004.

Love, Robert, ed. *The Best of Rolling Stone*. New York: Doubleday, 1993. Includes an excerpt from *Fear and Loathing in Las Vegas*.

Lytle, Mark Hamilton. *America's Uncivil Wars: The Sixties Era from Elvis to the Fall of Nixon*. New York: Oxford University Press, 2006.

Mailer, Norman. *The Fight*. Boston: Little, Brown, 1977.

Mankiewicz, Frank. *Perfectly Clear: Nixon from Whittier to Watergate*. New York: Quadrangle Books, 1973.

McKeen, William. *Hunter S. Thompson*. Boston: G. K. Hall, 1991.

McWilliams, Carey. *The Education of Carey McWilliams*. New York: Simon and Schuster, 1979.

Miller, Henry. *The Air-Conditioned Nightmare*. New York: New Directions, 1945.
———. *Tropic of Cancer*. Paris: Obelisk Press, 1934.

Miller, John. *San Francisco Stories*. San Francisco: Chronicle Books, 1990. Includes two pieces by Thompson, "Generation of Swine" and "When the Beatniks Were Social Lions."

Murphy, George, ed. *The Best of Key West's Writers, 1830–1990*. Marathon, Fla.:

Tortugas Limited Publishing, 1990. Includes Thompson's "The Gonzo Salvage Company."

National Observer editors. *The Observer's World: People, Places, and Events from the Pages of* The National Observer. Princeton, N.J.: Princeton University Press, 1965. Includes these five Thompson pieces: "End of the Beatniks," "The Extinct Hitchhiker," "Across a Frozen Desert," "The 'Gringo' and Culture Shock," and "A Footloose American in a Smuggler's Den."

Nocenti, Annie, and Ruth Baldwin, eds. *The High Times Reader*. New York: Nation Books, 2004.

Perry, Charles. *The Haight Ashbury*. New York: Random House, 1984.

———, ed. *Smokestack El-Ropo's Bedside Reader*. San Francisco: Straight Arrow Books, 1972. Two Thompson articles from the 1972 campaign first appeared in a book in this anthology.

Perry, Paul. *Fear and Loathing: The Strange and Terrible Saga of Hunter S. Thompson*. New York: Thunder's Mouth Press, 1992.

Plimpton, George. *Shadow Box*. New York: G. P. Putnam's Sons, 1977.

Pollack, Richard, ed. *Stop the Presses, I Want to Get Off*. New York: Random House, 1975.

Rolling Stone editors. *The Rolling Stone Reader*. New York: Warner Books, 1974. Includes Thompson's "Strange Rumblings in Aztlan."

Scharff, Edward. *Worldly Power: The Making of the Wall Street Journal*. New York: New American Library, 1986.

Spivak, Lawrence E., and Charles Angoff, eds. *The American Mercury Reader*. New York: Blakiston, 1944.

Steadman, Ralph. *America*. San Francisco: Straight Arrow Books, 1974. Foreword by Thompson.

———. *The Joke's Over: Bruised Memories: Gonzo, Hunter S. Thompson, and Me*. New York: Harcourt, 2006.

Taibbi, Matt. *Spanking the Donkey: Dispatches from the Dumb Season*. New York: New Press, 2005.

Thompson, Anita. *The Gonzo Way: A Celebration of Dr. Hunter S. Thompson*. Golden, Colo.: Fulcrum Publishing, 2007.

Thompson, Toby. *The 60s Report*. New York: Rawson, Wade Publishers, 1979.

Torgoff, Martin. *Can't Find My Way Home: America in the Great Stoned Age, 1945–2000*. New York: Simon and Schuster, 2004.

Torrey, Beef, and Kevin Simonson. *Conversations with Hunter S. Thompson*. Jackson, Miss.: University Press of Mississippi, 2008.

Trudeau, Garry. *Action Figure: The Life and Times of Doonesbury's Uncle Duke*. Kansas City, Mo.: Andrews-McMeel Publishing, 2001.

Weingarten, Marc. *The Gang That Wouldn't Write Straight: Wolfe, Thompson, Didion, and the New Journalism Revolution*. New York: Crown, 2005.

Wenner, Jann, and Corey Seymour. *Gonzo: The Life of Hunter S. Thompson*. Boston: Little, Brown, 2007.

White, Theodore H. *The Making of the President 1960*. New York: Atheneum, 1961.

————. *The Making of the President 1964*. New York: Atheneum, 1965.

————. *The Making of the President 1968*. New York: Atheneum, 1969.

————. *The Making of the President 1972*. New York: Atheneum, 1973.

Whitmer, Peter. *Aquarius Revisited: Seven Who Created the Sixties Counterculture That Changed America*. New York: Macmillan, 1987.

————. *When the Going Gets Weird: The Twisted Life of Hunter S. Thompson: A Very Unauthorized Biography*. New York: Hyperion, 1993.

Wilkie, Curtis. *Dixie: A Personal Odyssey through Events That Shaped the Modern South*. New York: Simon and Schuster, 2001.

Wolfe, Tom. *The Kandy-Kolored Tangerine-Flake Streamline Baby*. New York: Farrar, Straus and Giroux, 1965.

————. *The Electric Kool-Aid Acid Test*. New York: Farrar, Straus and Giroux, 1968.

————. *The New Journalism.* New York: Harper and Row, 1973. Features two selections from Thompson, the only writer with more than one piece in the anthology.

————. *The Right Stuff*. New York: Farrar, Straus and Giroux, 1979.

III. FILMS

Ewing, Wayne, director. *Breakfast with Hunter*. Ewing Films, 2003.

————, director. *When I Die*. Ewing Films, 2005.

————, director. *Free Lisl*. Ewing Films, 2007.

Finch, Nigel, director. *Fear and Loathing on the Road to Hollywood*. British Broadcasting Corporation, 1978.

Gibney, Alex, director. *Gonzo*. HDNet Films, 2008.

Gilliam, Terry, director. *Fear and Loathing in Las Vegas*. Universal Pictures, 1998.

Linson, Art, director. *Where the Buffalo Roam*. Universal Pictures, 1980.

Martin, Sharon, producer. *Biography: Hunter S. Thompson*. Biography Channel, 2004.

Thurman, Tom, director. *Buy the Ticket, Take the Ride*. Starz Entertainment, 2006.

IV. MAJOR INTERVIEWS
(LIST COMPILED BY BEEF TORREY AND KEVIN SIMONSON)

Allis, Sam. "An Evening (Gasp!) with Hunter Thompson." *Time*, January 22, 1990.

Anson, Robert Sam. "Hunter Thompson Meets Fear and Loathing Face to Face." *New Times*, December 10, 1976.

Brinkley, Douglas, Terry McDonell, and George Plimpton, "The Art of Journalism I: An Interview with Hunter S. Thompson and His Journal Notes from Vietnam." *Paris Review*, Fall 2000.

Felton, David. "Hunter Thompson Has Cashed His Check." *Rolling Stone College Papers*, 1980, no. 2.

Glassie, John. "Hunter S. Thompson." *Salon.com*, February 3, 2003.

Hahn, Matthew. "Writing on the Wall: An Interview with Hunter S. Thompson." *Atlantic Online*, August 26, 1997.

Hinkle, Warren. "Going for Gonzo." *Nation*, June 4, 1990.

Jarnow, Jesse. "Man of Action: Hunter S. Thompson Keeps Moving." *Relix*, April–May, 2003.

Kass, Jeff. "Still Gonzo after All These Years." *Denver Rocky Mountain News*, December 31, 2000, pp. 7A, 11A, 13A.

Keil, Richard. "Still Gonzo after All These Years." *American Journalism Review*, April 1, 1996.

———. "An American Original," *American Journalism Review*, April–May, 2005.

Letterman, David. *The Late Show with David Letterman*. CBS Television, November 25, 1988.

Macdonald, Marianne. "The Soft Heart within Literature's Hellraiser." *Guardian*, October 18, 1998.

Mnookin, Seth. "Fear and Writing." *Brill's Content*, January 2001.

Nelson, Sara. *Book Report*, 1997.

O'Brien, Conan. *Late Night with Conan O'Brien*, November 6, 2003.

O'Rourke, P. J. "P. J. O'Rourke Interviews Hunter S. Thompson," *Rolling Stone*, November 28, 1996. Illustrations by Ralph Steadman.

———. "Hunter S. Thompson." *Rolling Stone*, November 5–December 10, 1987.

Rentilly, J. "The Dr. Is In." *Pages*, January–February, 2003.

Rose, Charlie. *The Charlie Rose Show*. PBS, June 13, 1997.

———. *The Charlie Rose Show*. PBS, October 30, 1998.

———. *The Charlie Rose Show*. PBS, February 6, 2003.

Rosenbaum, Ron. "Hunter Thompson: The Good Doctor Tells All." *High Times*, September 1977.

Simonson, Kevin. "Exclusive Interview with Hunter S. Thompson." *SPIN*, May 1993.

———. "Fear and Loathing in Hollywood: A Strange and Terrible Saga of Guns, Drugs and Hunter S. Thompson." *Hustler*, August 1998.

Stokes, Geoffrey, and Kevin Simonson: "Gonzo's Last Stand?: The New Aspen Takes Aim at Hunter S. Thompson." *Village Voice*, May 15, 1990.

Stratton, Richard. "Hunter Thompson: The Last Outlaw." *High Times*, August 1990.

Vetter, Craig. "The Playboy Interview: Hunter Thompson." *Playboy*, November 1974.

Wertheimer, Linda, and Jacki Lyden. "Interview with Hunter S. Thompson." *All Things Considered*. NPR, August 7, 1997.

Whitmer, Peter. "Hunter Thompson: Still Crazy after All These Years." *Saturday Review*, January–February 1984.

Wilkie, Curtis. "The Doctor Is In," *Boston Globe Magazine*, February 7, 1988.

AUTHOR'S NOTE

The idea was simple: write a comprehensive and comprehensible story of Hunter S. Thompson. He lived an epic life, and it needed that sort of book. I'd written an earlier semischolarly book about him that came out in 1991, part of a series on authors and their work. I've written several books since then, but still get weekly requests for that long-out-of-print book, which is available online for hundreds of dollars.

Not only was my earlier book outdated; it was more about Thompson's work than about his life. His personality was so large that many people seemed to overlook his writing. This time, I wanted to write something that told his life story through the prism of his work.

A flurry of biographies came out after my little book. E. Jean Carroll's *Hunter* was a flight into fancy that nonetheless contained some good information and interviews. Paul Perry's *Fear and Loathing* was viewed as a betrayal by Hunter and his girlfriend Laila Nabulsi, who had invited Perry home as a friend, unaware that he would write a book about them. Like Carroll, Perry played a role, since he had briefly been Hunter's editor. Peter Whittmer's

When the Going Gets Weird was probably the most straightforward attempt to write Hunter's life story.

All of these books had merits as well as faults. No doubt my new book also has faults. I talked to as many people as would talk to me about Hunter. Some wanted to keep their memories to themselves. Others felt too much pain when they revisited time with him. Some were just tired of talking. I traveled to Louisville, San Francisco, Aspen, and Key West, trying to understand his world. But there is a part of the man that will always be a mystery to all but a few. Sitting around a table in Aspen tonight with a couple of his longtime friends, I could feel their amusement, encouragement, and sympathy as I talked about telling Hunter's story. There's so much I can never know. I appreciate the indulgence and hospitality of those friends and hope they are not disappointed with this work. Since Hunter's death, there have been several memoirs, a couple of documentaries, and a *Rolling Stone* oral history. But oral history is by its nature disjointed, and there seems to be enough disjointedness in Hunter's life. Memoirs are distorted by friendships and the fallibility of recollection.

I knew Hunter only slightly and don't believe that my great fondness for him or his work clouded my judgment. His life had enough narrative velocity to tell its own story.

The day after he died, I was asked by the newspaper in St. Petersburg, Florida, to write a what-it-all-means piece about him. When it appeared the following day, one of my colleagues said this: "I never *got it* with Hunter Thompson. I figured he was just a guy who drank a lot and took a lot of drugs. I never read anything he wrote. Now I think I get it."

So that was my mission: to take this man who became a pop culture caricature and tell the story of his life and work. I do think he was a wonderful writer. I want people to set aside his bad-craziness image and appreciate his nearly half century of writing about America. He was often his own worst enemy, creating and then watering and manuring this vivid persona that threatened to suffocate his achievements. As I say in the book, he was the favorite writer for many people who didn't read books.

When people learn of my brief acquaintance with him, they always want to know: *Was he as crazy as they say?* I take pleasure in debunking those myths. "He was very kind to me," I say. "He was nothing but a gentleman." The faces fall, so—not wanting to disappoint—I point at the letter framed on my office wall, the letter that Hunter sent me when that first book was published. "McKeen, you shit-eating freak. I warned you about writing that vicious trash about me." When my visitors read the note, their faces light up again. Myth restored.

I didn't expect perfection from Hunter Thompson. I knew of his faults before beginning this book, and in the three years I worked on it, I learned of many more. I was also disturbed not so much that he took his life but by the way he took it—with his family in his home. I can't presume to understand what he was thinking, but during the time I worked on this book, I suffered an accident, three surgeries, and a crippling injury that made it difficult to use my hands and for a while forced me into a wheelchair. I think I came to appreciate some of the frustration and pain that drove him to take that desperate step. Unlike me, he saw no light at the end of the tunnel.

—*William McKeen*

Aspen, July 18, 2007 (Hunter's seventieth birthday)

ACKNOWLEDGMENTS

There are so many people to thank that it seems most efficient to simply list them below. Two people get top billing: my editor, Amy Cherry; and my agent, Jane Dystel. Without them, nothing.

For conversation, correspondence, and commentary: David Amram, Rick Balentine, Ralph "Sonny" Barger, Ed Bastian, Steve Bennett, Carl Bernstein, Porter Bibb, Neville Blakemore, Roscoe Born, Geoff Boucher, Bob Braudis, Douglas Brinkley, DeDe Brinkman, Nickole Brown, Jon Burstein, Russell Chatham, Montgomery Chitty, Michael Cleverly, Sebastian Corcoran, Tom Corcoran, Jay Cowan, Bill Dixon, Barbara Dorsey, Wayne Ewing, Ben Fong-Torres, Jerry Footlick, Charles Fort, Cheryl Frymire, Deborah Fuller, Bill Giles, Chris Goldstein, Gerry Goldstein, Joe Gonzalez, Daniel Greene, William Greider, Margaret Harrell, Gary Hart, Troy Hooper, James Irsay, Walter Isaacson, Loren Jenkins, Walter Kaegi, Debby Kasdan, Maria Khan, John Lombardi, Michael Lydon, Don Mallard, Frank Mankiewicz, B. J. Martin, David McCumber, Laila Nabulsi, Anne Willis Noonan, Paul Pascarella, Charles Perry, Geoffrey Proud, Bob Rafelson, Chris Robinson, Catherine Sabonis-Bradley, Terry Sabonis-Heff, Paul Scanlan, Fred Schoelkopf, Paul Semonin, Bernard Shir-Cliff, Michael Solheim, Ralph

Steadman, Judy Stellings, Don Stuber, Anita Thompson, Hunter S. Thompson (interviews in 1978 and 1990), Juan Thompson, Sandy Thompson, Dick Tuck, Gerald Tyrrell, Darlene van der Hoop, John A. Walsh, Jann Wenner, Bill White, Ron Whitehead, Curtis Wilkie, Tom Wolfe, Pat Yack.

For their work: E. Jean Carroll, *Hunter* (Dutton, 1993); Michael Cleverly and Bob Braudis, *The Kitchen Readings* (HarperCollins, 2008); Wayne Ewing, *Breakfast with Hunter* (film, 2004) and *When I Die* (film, 2005); Nigel Finch, *Fear and Loathing on the Road to Hollywood* (film, 1978); Christine O. (www.gonzo .org); Paul Perry, *Fear and Loathing* (Thunder's Mouth, 1993), Jann Wenner and Corey Seymour, *Gonzo* (Little, Brown, 2007); Ralph Steadman, *The Joke's Over* (Harcourt, 2006); Craig Vetter, "The Playboy Interview with Hunter S. Thompson" (November 1974); Peter Whitmer, *When the Going Gets Weird* (Hyperion, 1993). I especially thank Douglas Brinkley, for his generosity and his editing and annotation of Hunter Thompson's correspondence. The bibliography contains a list of sources.

General advice and counsel: Harry Allen, Anna Churchill, Mike Foley, Ted Spiker.

Transcriptions and research: Andrew Bare, Marcela Bayard, Mark Berman, Tom Beshear, Ebony Bosch, Pamela Cook, Kelly Cuculianksy, Angie De Angelis, Stephanie Farr, Jesse Feldman, Suzette Jennings Foley, Lucia Howe, James Madieros, Ana Maria Malpartida, Collin McLeod, Brian Offenthaler, Patrick Reakes, Jason Sanchez, Billy Shields, Mara Sloan, Stephen Specht, Daniel Sutphin.

At W. W. Norton: Eileen Cheung, Nancy Palmquist, Otto Sonntag, Erica Stern.

For favors, mostly legal: Steve Belgard, Myra Borshoff, Danilo Cisneros, Kathryn Dennis, Isha Elkins, Megan Gales, Melissa Garcia, Christy Hamm, Amanda Maxey, Kasey Roberts, Leisa Sergeant, Victoria Solodare, Edward Toppino, Beef Torrey, Helga Williams, Mike Wilson.

Tribal council: Andrea Billups, John Marvel, Stephen F. Orlando, Jon Roosenraad.

Inspirations: Charles and Martha McKeen.

Reasons for living: Sarah, Graham, Mary, Savannah, Jack, Travis, and Charley.

Saintliness: Nicole Cisneros McKeen.

INDEX